UNN.

UNDERSTANDING
REALITY TELEVISION

'Popular factual programming' has rapidly come to occupy a place at the fore-front of contemporary television culture on an international scale. Tracing the history of Reality TV from *Candid Camera* to *The Osbournes*, *Understanding Reality Television* examines a range of programmes which claim a privileged relation to the 'real', from reality formatted game shows to 'real crime' programming and make-over TV. Contributors discuss the phenomenon of Reality TV in the context of the debates it has introduced to our social, cultural and televisual agendas, such as the construction of celebrity, fandom, surveillance, and the politics of repre-sentation.

Contributors: Daniel Biltereyst, Gray Cavender, Bradley D. Clissold, John Corner, Derek Foster, Jennifer Gillan, Craig Hight, Su Holmes, Deborah Jermyn, Misha Kavka, Gareth Palmer, Christopher Pullen, Parvati Raghuram, Rebecca L. Stephens, Estella Tincknell, Amy West.

Su Holmes is Lecturer in Film and Television at the University of Kent.

Deborah Jermyn is Senior Lecturer in Film Studies at Roehampton University. She is the co-editor, with Will Brooker, of *The Audience Studies Reader*.

UNDERSTANDING REALITY TELEVISION

Edited by Su Holmes and Deborah Jermyn

Routledge
Taylor & Francis Group

LONDON AND NEW YORK

First published 2004
by Routledge
2 Park Square, Milton Park, Abingdon, Oxon OX14 4RN

Simultaneously published in the USA and Canada
by Routledge
270 Madison Ave, New York, NY 10016

Reprinted 2005 (twice)

Routledge is an imprint of the Taylor & Francis Group

© 2004 Editorial matter and selection Su Holmes and Deborah Jermyn;
individual chapters the authors

Typeset in Perpetua by Taylor & Francis Books Ltd
Printed and bound in Great Britain by TJ International Ltd, Padstow, Cornwall

British Library Cataloguing in Publication Data
A catalogue record for this book is available from the British Library

Library of Congress Cataloging in Publication Data
A catalog record for this book has been requested

ISBN 0–415–31794–0 (hbk)
ISBN 0–415–31795–9 (pbk)

CONTENTS

CONTENTS

CONTRIBUTORS

Daniel Biltereyst is a Professor in Film, Television and Cultural Media Studies at the Department of Communication Studies, Ghent University, Belgium, where he leads the Working Group in Film and Television Studies. His main research interest is in controversial film and television within public sphere theories, and he has published widely on these issues, including articles in the *European Journal of Communication*, *Journal of Cultural Policy*, and *Media, Culture & Society*.

Gray Cavender is a Professor in the School of Justice Studies, Arizona State University, Tempe, Arizona, US. His research focuses on media and crime. With Mark Fishman, he is co-editor of *Entertaining Crime: Television Reality Programs* (Aldine de Gruyter, 1998).

Bradley D. Clissold is Assistant Professor of Modern British Literature and Film Studies at Memorial University of Newfoundland. He is currently working on a monograph entitled *Exchanging Postcards: The Cultural Impact of Postcards on Modern Literature*, which explores the influences of sent postcards on the form and content of select twentieth-century works of literature and popular culture.

John Corner is Professor in the School of Politics and Communication Studies at the University of Liverpool. His recent books include *Critical Ideas in Television Studies* (Oxford University Press, 1999) and a co-edited collection, *Media and the Re-styling of Politics* (Sage, 2003). A study of the current affairs series *World in Action* is in preparation, and with Alan Rosenthal he is preparing a second edition of the teaching anthology *New Challenges for Documentary*. He is an editor of the journal *Media, Culture and Society*.

Derek Foster is currently completing his PhD in Communication at Carleton University's school of Journalism and Mass Communication in Ottawa, Canada. His dissertation examines the media construction of squeegee kids as a social issue. His research interests and publications span urban and popular culture, broadcasting, and new information technologies. And, yes, he watches Reality TV but is still reticent about calling himself a fan.

Jennifer Gillan is an Associate Professor at Bentley College in the Boston area. Her articles have appeared in *Cinema Journal*, *American Literature* and *American Drama*, among other journals. She is the co-editor of three multicultural anthologies, *Unsettling America*, *Identity Lessons* and *Growing Up Ethnic in America* (Penguin Books), and is completing a book, *Ivory? Soap Nation*.

Craig Hight is a Lecturer with the Screen and Media Studies Department at the University of Waikato, New Zealand. With Dr Jane Roscoe, he has recently co-written a book on mock-documentary entitled *Faking It: Mock-Documentary and the Subversion of Factuality* (Manchester University Press). Craig's recent research focuses on digital media technologies, including their relationship to documentary practice, and aspects of the production, construction and reception of documentary hybrids.

Su Holmes is Senior Lecturer in Media and Cultural Studies at the Southampton Institute, UK. She has published widely on the early relations between British television and film culture in the 1950s in journals such as *Screen*, *Historical Journal of Film, Radio and Television* and *Journal of Popular British Cinema*, and is currently working on a book-length study of this topic. Her recent research also focuses more widely on Reality TV.

Deborah Jermyn is Senior Lecturer in Film Studies at the University of Surrey Roehampton, UK. She has published widely on the representation of crime in film and television, including articles in *Feminist Media Studies* and the *International Journal of Cultural Studies*, and is the co-editor of *The Audience Studies Reader* (Routledge, 2002) and *The Cinema of Kathryn Bigelow: Hollywood Transgressor* (Wallflower Press, 2003).

Misha Kavka teaches film, television and media at the University of Auckland, New Zealand. She is the co-editor, with Elisabeth Bronfen, of *Feminist Consequences: Theory for the New Century* (Columbia University Press, 2001), and has published articles on feminist and psychoanalytic theory, gothic cinema and (Reality) television in New Zealand. Her current project is a cross-cultural study of the affective basis of Reality Television programming.

Gareth Palmer is the postgraduate research tutor at the Adelphi Research Institute, University of Salford, UK. He has published widely on issues concerning governance, surveillance and television. His book *Discipline and Liberty* was published by Manchester University Press in the summer of 2003.

Christopher Pullen is Lecturer in Media Studies and Gender Identity at Bournemouth University. He is currently involved in doctoral research which considers the representation of gay identity and AIDS in confessional documentary and Reality TV.

Parvati Raghuram is Lecturer in the Department of International Studies at Nottingham Trent University. She is currently researching migration and diasporic cultures in the UK and has co-authored *Gender and International Migration in Europe*. She teaches and writes about research methods.

Rebecca L. Stephens is Assistant Professor of English at the University of Wisconsin Stevens Point, where she teaches dramatic, ethnic and young adult literature. She has written on gender, immigration and nationalism in literature and popular culture, and is currently researching censorship and the *Harry Potter* series.

Estella Tincknell is Senior Lecturer in Media and Cultural Studies at Nottingham Trent University. She has just completed co-editing a book on the film musical, and is currently researching representations of the family and familialism in contemporary culture. She is on the editorial board of *Body and Society*. Together with Richard Johnson and Deborah Chambers, she and Parvati Raghuram are the authors of *The Practice of Researching Culture* (Sage, forthcoming).

Amy West is a graduate of Christ Church College, Oxford, and the University of Auckland. She is now completing a doctoral thesis on structures of time and place in Reality Television programmes, which focuses principally on New Zealand examples of the genre.

ACKNOWLEDGEMENTS

The editors would like to thank students, friends and colleagues at the Southampton Institute, particularly Sean Redmond, David Lusted, Julian Hoxter; Kate Ahl, Rebecca Barden and Chris Cudmore at Routledge and our contributors for the enthusiasm and commitment they have brought to this collection.

Su Holmes – to Jenny Holmes for sharing an enthusiasm for Reality TV (and for *Big Brother* chats on the phone), and to my students on *Structures of Media Industries* for sharing valuable ideas, pleasures and debates about Reality TV.

Deborah Jermyn – love and gratitude to the usual suspects, especially Richard Jermyn, for always having his finger ready on the 'record' button, and Julia Jermyn, for reminding him anyway.

INTRODUCTION
Understanding Reality TV

Su Holmes and Deborah Jermyn

> As we embark upon a new century of broadcasting, it is clear that
> no genre form or type of programming has been as actively
> marketed by producers, or more enthusiastically embraced by
> viewers, than reality-based TV.
>
> (Friedman, 2002: 6)

This quote seems a pertinent way in which to open a book that seeks to 'understand
Reality TV'. It emphasises how the formats, images and conventions of Reality TV
have stitched themselves into the very fabric of television, its economic structures,
schedules and viewing cultures. Reality TV has rapidly come to occupy a place at the
forefront of contemporary television culture – a position from which it seems to
'speak' particularly clearly to the ways in which broadcasters are seeking to attract
audiences in the multichannel landscape, the ways in which television is harnessing
its aesthetic and cultural power and, as an increasingly multimedia experience, the
ways in which it resonates so extensively in the cultural sphere. This collection seeks
to respond to the complex, contested and often controversial terrain of 'popular
factual programming' (Corner, 2001b) with the broad aim of considering its
economic, aesthetic, political and cultural implications for understanding contemporary 'television' as an object of study. It is certainly the case that this terrain
continued to evolve, shift and change in the process of producing this collection,
which thus offers an investigation of the field at a particular point in time (television's rhetoric of the perpetual present of course always renders stopping the 'flow'
an impossibility). At the same time, however, this book also seeks to contribute to
the longer-term project of understanding and studying what Corner has described
as television's 'greatly expanded range of popular images of the real' (ibid.).

What's in a name? Defining 'Reality TV'

Corner's description above emerges from his suggestion that we may now live in
a 'post-documentary' culture (2001b) – an influential conception which has

1

rapidly been taken up more widely in work on Reality TV. As he explains, he does not use the term to imply that ' "documentary" is now finished, but to signal the scale of its relocation as a set of practices, forms and functions' (ibid.). Corner's argument here is based on a number of perceived shifts in the space occupied by 'factual' programming on television, particularly the 'radical dispersal' of a documentary 'look' across programme forms and schedules, and, crucially, a foregrounding of the primary impetus to deliver entertainment ('documentary as diversion'). As Corner explains, this has fostered the creation of a proliferating and much extended space for the production and consumption of 'factual' programming which problematises documentary's (already contested) generic status (see Roscoe and Hight, 2001: 7).

Within this expanded space, then, this book claims to be about 'Reality TV'. But the unavoidable question posed before we can even begin to open this terrain is: what *is* 'Reality TV'? Even the most cursory glance through the pages of the book will doubtless reveal the names of many familiar texts, but producing a particular definition of Reality TV is nevertheless complex. This is partly because of the fundamentally hybrid nature of the forms in question. Yet it is also because of the range of programming to which the term 'Reality TV' has been applied, as well as the extent to which this has shifted over time with the emergence of further permutations in 'reality-based' texts. We suggest here, however, that the issue of definition is rather more than a matter of arguing over terminology, categories and discursive 'labels'. Rather, it can equally be seen to attest to many of the central debates which have structured the discursive circulation of these contemporary programme forms. Debates over definition, we suggest, are inextricably enmeshed with the concept of generic hybridity in Reality TV, its relationship with the history and status of the documentary form and, just as crucially, issues of theoretical, critical and methodological approach involved in the study of this field.

In 1994, even Kilborn's early attempt to explore the emergence of 'Reality TV' noted that the term already had become 'something of a catch-all phrase' (1994: 423), although he nevertheless sought to offer prescriptive parameters for definition (see also O'Sullivan *et al.*, 1994: 120; Corner, 1996). According to Kilborn, Reality TV could be conceived as:

- recording 'on the wing', and frequently with the help of lightweight video equipment, of events in the lives of individuals and groups;
- the attempt to simulate such real-life events through various forms of dramatised reconstruction;
- the incorporation of this material in suitably edited form into an attractively packaged television programme which can be promoted on the strength of its reality credentials.

(Kilborn, 1994: 423)

Although the first two descriptions appear to prioritise 'real' crime or emergency services programming, the last is certainly broad enough to encompass the wide range of popular factual entertainment on our screens today. This in itself, however, points to the fact that the focus of earlier work on 'Reality TV' was primarily 'real' crime texts (particularly in the US – Nichols, 1994a; Fishman and Cavender, 1999; Bondebjerg, 2000; but also in the UK and elsewhere – Dauncey, 1996; Hill, 2000; Dovey, 2000). It is clear that we've seen the wider expansion of reality-based programming since this time. As Corner notes when surveying the period since the early 1990s, 'it was difficult to foresee how a combination of economics, scheduling practice and cultural change would bring about *such a huge expansion* of actuality-based programming' (Corner, 2001a: 687; emphasis added), and he describes a trajectory in Britain and elsewhere which moves from crime or emergency services-based texts, the docusoap trend, to what might be conceived of as a 'docu-show' or possible 'gamedoc' phase, in which factual-entertainment programming has increasingly incorporated elements of the game show (Corner, 2000: 687). Yet at the same time as this expansion has taken place the term 'Reality TV' has gained a far greater cultural currency. In 2002 Graham Barnfield commented on Kellner's (1992) use of the term ten years earlier (which at that time was in fact used in relation to the 'sensationalistic' talk show) and went on to comment that:

> It is striking that Kellner needed to use examples to explain to his readers what a reality show was. Today no such illustration would be necessary.... Nowadays the quotation marks are off. Use labels and people will instantly know what is meant.
>
> (Barnfield, 2002: 49)

However, Barnfield then goes on to acknowledge the rather 'loose usage' of the term, suggesting that 'over the last decade such a wide range of productions have been categorized as "Reality TV" that one wonders if the term is too general to be helpful' (ibid.: 49). This effectively emphasises that no such consensus ('people will instantly know what is meant') has developed, and that the increasingly familiar use of the term has paradoxically witnessed its proliferating application. One of the most significant shifts in the field between Kellner's (1992) and Barnfield's (2002) comments is the emergence of the global 'event' formats of Reality TV (such as *Big Brother*, *Popstars* and *Survivor et al.*), particularly in the period 1999–2001. It is equally possible to pinpoint that it is predominantly at this point that the term 'Reality TV' gains a wider discursive currency in areas such as the press, television trade press and TV viewing guides. A snapshot recognition of its changing definition here is suggested by the *Guardian* review of the 'mock' Reality TV film *Series 7: The Contenders* (Patterson, 2001) (discussed by

Craig Hight in this collection) and its satirical representation of the reality game show. While evidently also taking a predictably negative critical position on the form, the reviewer noted that:

> If I had been asked to define the term 'reality TV' a year ago I would have said it described footage of the Rodney King beating, or the kind of crime shows that rely on security camera footage. Apparently I've got it all wrong. What the [US] networks dub reality TV comes at us with musical cues on the soundtrack, manipulative editing…and ill-managed anger, all enacted by a cast of wannabe models, actors and game-show hosts.
>
> (Patterson, 2001: 12)

As we can see here, contrary to Barnfield's comment above, 'Reality TV' can still appear in quotation marks, which, as will be discussed, is in part a recurrent strategy intended to question the term in relation to its contested claim to 'the real'. But it equally indicates the degree to which critics are familiar, or indeed unfamiliar, with the term. As the trenchant critic of Reality TV Christopher Dunkley commented in the *Financial Times*:

> Everywhere you go within the [TV] industry you hear that something new called 'reality TV' is taking over, supposedly threatening to shove aside soap opera and sport, police dramas and lifestyle series…the message is the same: if you haven't got some great reality series for 2001, you are nobody.
>
> (Dunkley, 2001: 22)

How can it be that, explicitly separating it from existing television genres, Dunkley refers to Reality TV here as 'something new' when Kilborn had already commented back in 1994 that the term had become 'something of a catch-all phrase'? This contradiction arguably points to the wider discursive currency of the term described above, but with the increased explosion of the range of reality-based programming at this time this did not necessarily result in any 'consensus' concerning its constitutive criteria. As Friedman was still able to comment in 2002, 'the term "reality-based" is bandied about as a description for everything from video compilations to made-for-TV spectacles, newsmagazines and gameshows' (2002: 7).

Hence, clarifying issues surrounding the discursive circulation of the term 'Reality TV' may be instructive, but it does not necessarily lead us to a further understanding where issues of *definition* are concerned. In this respect, it is worth noting here that other early attempts to define Reality TV emphasised the importance of a focus on 'real life' and 'real people' as the crucial criteria, as well as the technological forms through which this subject matter was mediated (such as the video camcorder) (O'Sullivan *et al.*, 1994). Yet the more recent proliferation of Reality TV has witnessed a move away from an attempt to 'capture' 'a life lived' to the televisual arenas of formatted environments in which the more traditional observational rhetoric of documentary jostles for space with the discourses of display and performance (Corner, 2001b, 2002; Roscoe, 2001). We have also witnessed an increasing focus not simply on 'ordinary' people but also on celebrities, whether in designated formats of their own (e.g. *The Osbournes* [2002–], *The Anna Nicole Show* [2002–], *I'm a Celebrity…Get Me Out of Here!* [ITV, 2002–3, UK] – in some contexts referred to as 'Celebrity Survivor') or in celebrity versions of existing texts (such as *Celebrity Big Brother* [BBC1, 2001, C4/BBC1, 2002, UK] or *Comic Relief Does Fame Academy* [BBC1, 2003, UK]).

Ultimately, and importantly, it is perhaps only possible to suggest that what unites the range of programming conceivably described as 'Reality TV' is primarily its discursive, visual and technological *claim* to 'the real'. As Friedman suggests:

> The proliferation of reality-based programming…does not represent a fundamental shift in television programming, but the industry's reliance on 'reality' as a promotional marketing tool is unprecedented. What separates the spate of contemporary reality-based television…[is] the open and explicit sale of television programming *as a representation of reality*.
>
> (Friedman, 2002: 7; emphasis added)

It is certainly the case that the variety of programmes explored in this collection – ranging from *Candid Camera*, *Crimewatch UK*, *Big Brother*, *Survivor*, *A Wedding Story* and *The Osbournes* to *House Invaders* – may well have as many significant differences as they do commonalities, as well as different historical precedents, generic precursors, pleasures and modes of address. In fact, perhaps in itself signifying the implausibly inclusive use of the term 'Reality TV', it was also during the proliferation of formats between 1999 and 2001 that there was an attempt in critical discourse to 'pin down' different subcategories of the form – whether critics were citing terms from the TV industry or constructing descriptions of their own. At the time of the UK emergence of programmes such as *Castaway 2000* (Lion Television for BBC1, 2000–1), *Big Brother* (Endemol, C4, 2000–), *Survivor* (ITV, 2001–2) and *Shipwrecked* (RDF for C4, 2000–1), there was a struggle with terms such as 'formatted documentary' (Collins, 1999; Jeremy Mills, Managing Director at Lion Television, personal interview, 5 June 2002), 'social-experiment-cum-docusoap' (Flett, 2000), 'docusoap-cum-interactive-gameshow' (Anonymous, 2000) and

5

'Episodic Reality Soap' (ERS) (Paton, 2000). On one level this is a matter of convenience, in that critics find it easier to discuss or 'review' something when they can name it, but attempts at categorisation are also significant in speaking to debates about whether there is anything intrinsically *new* about programming associated with the 'reality' label – an issue raised by Friedman above, and one on which a range of opinions can be found (see Kilborn, 1994; Dunkley, 2002; Corner, 2001a; Hight, 2001). While Corner suggests that such programming has 'changed the way that the whole business of filming real life can be thought about, particularly for a new generation of students and programme-makers' (2001a: 352), Friedman argues that it is not necessarily 'a sudden shift in the programmatic landscape' (2002: 4). In his essay 'It's Not New and It's Not Clever', Dunkley articulates this latter position more forcefully when he contests the argument that Reality TV represents 'something quite new to television' (2002: 35) by foregrounding its relationship with previous generic forms, whether talent shows, particular game shows or documentary experiments (ibid.: 34–44). While the debate over the extent to which Reality TV is a genuinely 'innovative' form may be somewhat circuitous, the explicit (and often awkward) reaching for terminology above (which in itself largely involves references to previous hybrid texts such as the docusoap) indicates its significance for at least recombining and perhaps reinventing television's generic forms.

Equally, however, such ambiguities may reflect on the broader complexities surrounding television's relationship with genre and, concurrently, the ways in which this can be understood. John Caughie notes, for example, that while 'assumptions of genre' permeate television studies (1991: 127), these have been less theorised, interrogated and historicised than studies of film genre (see also Corner, 1999: 126). Laura Stempel-Mumford describes how 'a profound theoretical uncertainty underlies most discussions of television form: a lack of an adequate theory of television genre as a whole' (1995: 19), and relates this to the ambiguity surrounding whether the concept is in fact directly applicable to the medium. Seen as 'the primary purveyor of a postmodern sensibility', with its fluid formats and self-reflexive economy, a 'major objection to the project of genre definition is that television is resistant *as a medium* to the rigidity that such categorizations are thought to require' (ibid.: 20), while others see issues of genre as 'fundamental to television' (Caughie, 1991; cited in Stempel-Mumford, 1995: 20). While to suggest that broadcasters, critics and viewers do not think of television in terms of 'genre' is clearly overstating the case, Reality TV may well exemplify the arguments concerning the slippery and hybrid nature of television's use of the concept. While such generic intertextuality is by no means new (Neale, 1990), Reality TV is evidence of the ways in which television has increasingly combined this with a very self-reflexive and self-conscious interplay between different programme forms (Coles, 2000: 27). It is partly because of these

6

complexities and ambiguities that we have often avoided using the term 'genre' in this collection, as it remains a contested issue.

Yet one of the reasons that issues of definition, description and terminology cannot easily be solved is not simply because of hybridity (as well as the tautological problems involved in the very process of 'genre' definition) (Neale, 1990). It is also because such categorisations are also necessarily an act of discursive construction which is enmeshed with a range of other factors – not least perceptions of cultural value where popular factual programming is concerned. For example, Dunkley (2002) foregrounds Reality TV's strong relationship with the history of television's *entertainment* programming because he is intent on constructing its formal, historical, ethical and cultural *distance* from the documentary form. In this respect, there also ensued a struggle over definition and cultural value surrounding the emergence of the docusoap in the late 1990s (see Bruzzi, 2000; Coles, 2000; Dovey, 2000; Kilborn, 2000). Largely believed to be a journalistic invention intended to foreground the form's 'trivialisation' of the 'serious' project of documentary, it is fair to suggest that the term 'docusoap' almost became a 'term of abuse' (Dovey, 2000: 137). It was nevertheless rapidly adopted by the TV industry (Jeremy Mills, personal interview, 5 June 2002) but not, publicly at least, by the broadcasters themselves or, initially, as a category in the TV listings. Indicating a discursive struggle over the institutional, industrial and cultural definition of this new form, in the introductions to the programmes and in the television schedules we were invited to consume 'fly-on-the-wall documentaries'. While this may have as much to do with familiarity between industry, text and audience where 'generic' terminology is concerned (and it is certainly the case that very recently the term 'docusoap' has entered into wider use in the intertextual construction of television), it cannot be separated from conceptions of cultural value and the implicit hierarchy between documentary and soap opera which is evident here. Equally, it is interesting to note in this respect how the subsequent proliferation of reality formats referred to above (such as *Castaway 2000* and *Survivor*) have been described in different ways by public-service and commercial broadcasters. While the BBC appeared to prefer the term 'formatted documentary' (Jeremy Mills, personal interview, 5 June 2002), the commercial broadcaster ITV seemed quite happy with the concept of the 'Episodic Reality Soap' (Gray; cited in Paton, 2000) – decisions which each prioritise different generic referents in descriptions of the form.

In this respect, then, it perhaps becomes more productive to consider the variety of ways in which popular factual programming is described, and the range of institutional, economic and cultural factors which shape this. For example, Roscoe's research into *Big Brother* emphasised how the programme-makers describe the series not as a reality game show but as a 'real-life soap', primarily because of its relationship with editing and narrative construction from the perspective of production (2001: 480). Although we have questioned the ease with which Reality TV might be conceived of as a 'genre' at all, it is worth empha-sising here that this foregrounds the importance of what Neale (1990) describes as the 'intertextual relay' — that is, industrial, journalistic and marketing discourses in defining any corpus of texts. Although Neale's focus was on film, the existence of an intertextual framework is evidently also applicable to television in the consideration of the press, TV trade press and television viewing guides. Neale's emphasis on a discursive approach to genre which extends beyond the boundaries of the text itself, moreover, has implications for distinguishing between 'those studies of genres conceived as institutionalised classes of text and systems of expectation, and studies which use critically and theoretically constructed terms as the basis for discussing classes of [texts]' (ibid.: 45). This suggests, then, that if studies of genre are to remain historically grounded and linked to the contexts in which texts are produced, marketed and discussed, there are potential problems in separating academic categorisations (see Corner, 2000; Calvert, 2000; Hill, 2002) from those used by the TV industry, as well as inter-textual mediators such as critics and TV guides (Tolson, 1996). This does not in itself solve the problems and ambiguities surrounding the very definition of 'Reality TV', but rather provides a further perspective on its cultural circulation.

'Awful ordinary people': Reality TV and cultural value

The discussion concerning definitions of Reality TV has indicated the extent to which issues of cultural *value* have been on the agenda — enmeshed within the wider maelstrom of what can be described as the high-profile discursive circula-tion of the form. As Barnfield has commented: 'When, outside of university media studies departments, did entertainment programming excite such strong views?' (2002: 50). Dovey has described how such debates have tended to offer contesting perspectives on the form, variously foregrounding the regrettable dominance of economic influences ('cheap' programming = 'trash TV'), an emphasis on Reality TV as a wider 'democratisation' of television (e.g. the focus on 'ordinary' people — a position largely advanced by the programme-makers/broadcasters themselves), to concerns over the construction of 'the real' in Reality TV ('Reality TV as nightmare') (Dovey, 2000: 83). It is indeed the case that in attempts to explain the contemporary proliferation of Reality TV the influ-ence of political economy has been an important contender (Barnfield, 2002; Dauncey, 1996; Dovey, 2000; Kilborn, 1994). Summarising this position, Dovey explains that:

> The explanation…is to be found in the increased commercial pressure
> on all TV producers which follows from varying degrees of deregulation

and increased competition for audience share with new channels. This, it is argued, has driven down the costs of production throughout the early years of the 1990s, as well as increasing the necessity to produce more and more ratings-friendly programme forms.

(Dovey, 2000: 83–4)

The trajectory of Dovey's summary here makes clear how the foregrounding of economics slips easily into the terrain of cultural value where perceptions of both programming and audience are concerned. While Reality TV is certainly simply the latest example of a long history of media forms which have attracted vehement criticisms from cultural commentators (Hight, 2001: 390), these claims continue to be entrenched within discourses of 'quality' and cultural value – discourses which have become central to debates about the future of television since increased commercialisation and deregulation throughout the 1990s (Richardson and Meinhof, 1999: 117; Brunsdon, 1990). This in itself returns us to a privileging of the economic and industrial contexts of media production in explaining the explosion of reality-based texts. As Richardson and Meinhof explain, 'fears for low-quality broadcasting in the future rely upon an economic argument: that the programming of the future will be worse than that of the past because less money will be spent on it' (1999: 117). It is certainly the case that a foregrounding of political economy tends to engender a rather heavy sense of pessimism where the approaches to popular factual programming are concerned (Kilborn, 1994), and, as Dovey emphasises, this perspective is not sufficient on its own to consider the complex factors which have shaped the emergence of Reality TV, nor the ways in which its forms, aesthetics and concerns have developed (2000: 91). Debates over whether judgements concerning 'cultural value' should be on the agenda of television and cultural studies (and the ethics over whether they have been 'suspended') have a long history (see Brunsdon, 1990; McGuigan, 1992). Suffice it to say here that a key suspicion surrounding such discourses is their profoundly ideological foundations, or, as Brunsdon describes, the degree to which there are always relations of power 'at stake in notions such as quality and judgement – Quality for whom? Judgement by whom? On whose behalf?' (Brunsdon, 1990: 73); and particularly the degree to which such relations are 'shaped by legacies of social-class hierarchy' (Richardson and Meinhof, 1999: 117; see also Bourdieu, 1986). Indeed, if we consider the position – touched on by Dovey above – that Reality TV may have in some ways signalled a broader 'democratisation' of television, criticisms of why 'all these *awful ordinary* people are allowed on television' (Bazalgette, 2001: 20; emphasis added) can be seen to represent a response couched within discourses of class. From this perspective, the concept of 'trash TV' can be located as a judgement which justifies its moral and aesthetic criteria within ideological discourses. That is not to suggest that issues surrounding 'quality' and cultural value should be *absent* from the discussion, study and analysis of Reality TV – particularly when, at the level of its cultural circulation, they have been so central. Rather, it is to suggest that the factors underlying and structuring such responses should also be the focus of analysis.

Approach with caution: television, anxiety and 'the real'

These judgements concerning cultural value in Reality TV also necessarily make assumptions about its audience (Hight, 2001). In fact, the 'nervousness' surrounding its blurring of genre boundaries and manipulation of 'the real' in particular has something of a tradition in critical debates surrounding the medium (see Roscoe and Hight, 2001), and this can be related to a long history of fears both for and about the television audience which, it is implied, might be unable to engage with 'hybrid' or otherwise complex forms. Such fears are bound up again in issues of class and cultural value, and are arguably characterised by a paternalistic and conservative impulse that, within the terms of the mass-society tradition, constructs the audience as vulnerable and malleable. The reception of early 'real-crime' programming emerging in the mid-1980s provides a good illustration of such discourses. For example, writing in *The Listener* about the emergence of *Crimewatch UK* in Britain in 1984, Benjamin Wooley commented: 'The problem with reconstructions is that they are presented as being indistinguishable from real events and this confuses at least a few members of the audience' (Wooley, 1984: 10). Five years later, the same kinds of anxieties were at stake in Bob Woffinden's observation that: 'Clearly the public has a voracious appetite for true-life crime. And *Crimewatch* has enhanced entertainment value; quite simply it's better because it's real. A kind of blurring of distinctions thus occurs' (Woffinden, 1989: 10).

This 'blurring' of boundaries and the difficulty of ascribing a definition to the reconstruction form(s) was contentious long before the explosion of real-crime programming in the 1980s; the terms 'faction', 'drama-documentary' and 'reconstruction' have all involved attempts to find a truly embracing way of describing what this 'form', in these different inflections, actually does. Though there are many shades of grey encompassed within the terms 'reconstruction' and 'dramadoc', and they should not simply be conflated, its mix of 'fact' (real crimes and victims) and 'fiction' (actors playing these out) is one of the reasons that *Crimewatch* and its real-crime compatriots have been controversial around the world, as if this mixing of traits is disingenuous or unethical in some way. Indeed, until recently at least, drama-documentary has perhaps been the most controversial form in the history of British television, as the massive debates that met the work of drama-documentarists such as Peter Watkins (*The War Game*, 1966) and Ken Loach and Tony Garnett (*Cathy Come Home*, 1966) clearly suggest. *The War*

Game, for example, was initially banned by the BBC for its disingenuity, a 'docu-mentary' about a nuclear attack in Britain which it was feared would cause confusion and panic among audiences, who would take it as 'the real thing'. Yet the debates evoked by drama-documentary might be traced back further still to John Grierson's famous and rather equivocal description of documentary as '*the creative interpretation of reality*' (cited in Kerr, 1990: 77; emphasis added), high-lighting as far back as the 1930s that there have never been any easy distinctions between 'drama' and 'reality'.

Now, in the twenty-first century, discourses which admonish the breakdown of traditional generic boundaries and the manipulation of 'the real' continue to proliferate around Reality TV. In the rather apocalyptic words of Bill Nichols:

> Any firm sense of boundary which such shows attempt to uphold between fact and fiction, narrative and exposition, storytelling and reporting inevitably blurs.... Everything is up for grabs in a gigantic reshuffling of the stuff of everyday life. Everything, that is, is subject to interpretation by television as a story-telling machine.
>
> (Nichols, 1994a: 43)

It appears, then, that cultural critics and academics very often remain reluctant to relinquish evidently inadequate binaries, even while changes in television programming increasingly demand that we must. This isn't to say that the concepts of 'fact' and 'fiction' have absolutely no meaning in themselves at all any more; but rather that (as Reality TV clearly demonstrates), since these terms are always under 'reconstruction' and negotiation, our definitions of the relationship between television and realism, 'fact' and 'fiction', and 'factual' and 'entertain-ment' shows must also adapt. Yet the preoccupation with the (it is often implied somehow deceitful) capacity of television to 'blur' the boundaries continues. Thus one of the most recurrent features of the popular and critical reception of Reality TV has been comment on the ways in which it manipulates and constructs 'the real', and hence the contested nature of the term 'Reality TV' itself ('the two words are mutually exclusive' [Clark, 2002: 6]). Critics, academics, programme-makers, audiences and actual participants in Reality TV have become engaged across popular culture in discussion of the form's play with aesthetics, editing, characterisation and dramatic structures, in an entirely self-reflexive fashion. In fact, Corner identifies 'new levels of representational play and reflexivity' (2001b) as a defining feature of 'popular factual entertainment' or 'documentary as diversion'. Particularly as Reality TV formats have continued to appear, their audiences, but crucially their participants, have become increasingly familiar with and well versed in the forms and conventions of these shows – it is now routine, for example, for participants to talk explicitly about the politics of how they are being 'represented' at the level of the *text itself*. As has been noted, much work remains to be done on the ways in which Reality TV is consumed by audiences (particularly when there is little work on the reception of documentary to which it can be compared) (Hight, 2001; Corner, 2001b). Yet, at the very least, this self-reflexivity makes it difficult to concede to the popular image of the audience for Reality TV as 'unthinking voyeurs, unwitting dupes of commercialist broadcasters [and] in danger of mistaking reality-TV programmes for "reality"' (Hight, 2001: 390), given that the entire issue of '*re*-presentation' is put so self-consciously on the agenda of Reality TV by the programmes themselves. Indeed, with reference to *Big Brother*, Peter Bazalgette, Creative Director at Endemol, UK, argues that one of the reasons Reality TV 'enrages pure documentary film-makers' is because

> we expose all their tricks. We're completely up-front about it. When we want [the contestants]…to talk about their first love, you hear Big Brother say 'hey – would you talk about your first love?', but documentary filmmakers have always manipulated their material both in the ways in which they edit it, and the ways they shoot it.
>
> (Peter Bazalgette, personal interview, 14 August 2002)

Bazalgette goes on to say that the 24-hour 'live' streaming of *Big Brother* on UK digital channel E4 (a strategy also adopted in other countries) further 'democratises' the audience's relations with 'the real' in that 'it's the first time the public have been able to form a view about how a programme is edited. It's the first time they've seen the rushes' (ibid.). His comments here are clearly formulated in response to the criticisms of Reality TV's 'manipulation' of 'the real' described above, and they certainly work to obscure the ways in which – just as in the history of documentary – this *production* of 'reality' necessarily occurs (and the ways in which the audience is *not* always made aware of the effects of this). However, it does return us to the ways in which a heightened awareness of this process has circulated around the proliferation of Reality TV and the extent to which, rather than asking the increasingly tautological question 'how *real* is Reality TV?' (Cummings, 2002), we perhaps need to grasp its powerful appeal and claim to 'the real', while at the same time acknowledging the highly contested and self-conscious space in which this takes place.

'A global currency'? Reality formats as 'event TV'

While an emphasis on the primacy of political economy in Reality TV (and Reality TV as 'dumbing down') may have led to some rather simplistic conceptions of its audience, it is nevertheless the case that elements of political economy remain important in understanding the form. Key in the development, changing definitions and international visibility of Reality TV has been the circulation of what are popularly referred to as 'global formats'. One of few texts to give critical attention to the concept of format adaptation, Albert Moran's *Copycat TV: Globalisation, Programme Formats and Cultural Identity* (1998), emphasises how the economic currency of the format is by no means a phenomenon of the contemporary television landscape: its roots can be traced back to radio and the subsequent development of television as a mass medium. Yet as Moran suggests, the economic importance of the television format accelerated throughout the 1980s and 1990s (ibid.: 18), and arguably more so in subsequent years. As the industry paper *Televisual* emphasised, '[t]he well-documented success of *Millionaire*, *Survivor*, *Big Brother* et al. has already changed the business of creating and selling formats from cheap, domestic daytime fillers to international prime-time blockbusters' (Creamer, 2001b: 24). While this emphasis on 'cheap, domestic daytime fillers' downplays the pre-existing importance of the format in terms of primetime genres such as quiz shows, drama and sitcom (see Moran, 1998), it nevertheless encapsulates its increased economic importance and its particular proliferation around Reality TV (see also Brenton and Cohen, 2003). This expansion of the format market is related to a range of shifts in the economic, institutional and technological nature of the television industry in recent years.

First, the period since the 1980s has seen changes in national television systems in many parts of the world, with the impetus toward privatisation, deregulation and the emergence of new distribution technologies (see Barker, 1997; Dahlgren, 2000; Steemers, 1998; Murdock, 2000). This has seen a multiplication of channels within national borders – in many European countries invalidating the 'natural' monopoly of public-service broadcasting (PSB) and putting increased pressure on PSB to compete with the forces of marketisation. At the same time, the development of cable and satellite channels has helped to make television a more international medium demanding conceptualisation in terms of transnational and regional regulation (Barker, 1997: 29). Yet in terms of approaching the economic importance of the format, this emphasis on the rise of multichannel television (the demand for more programming) and the increasingly transnational nature of the medium (the increasing flow of television programming across national borders) would be more straightforward if we were simply dealing with the importation of programming rather than format circulation and *adaptation*.

Although multichannel television exists in most countries now, national broadcasting systems don't all have sufficiently strong production industries to create all the programming required. The format is useful here as it crucially offers the advantage of combining the adoption of an idea devised, and hence often 'proven', elsewhere with the possibility of local production, material and adaptation which has a greater chance of success with domestic audiences (Moran, 1998; Peter Bazalgette, personal interview, 14 August 2002; see also Sinclair *et*

13

al., 1996). This equally emphasises the importance of the format, not simply for channel visibility and differentiation, but also for economic predictability. As Peter Bazalgette, Creative Director of Endemol UK, expands: 'Some people call them "high concept". They make more of a mark, create more of a brand with viewers…and once established, people come back to them again and again' (Peter Bazalgette, personal interview, 14 August 2002). In short, the accelerated importance of the format is clearly also shaped by the 'risk-averse' broadcast environment – the desire to minimise risk in the face of increasing competition (Creamer, 2001a: 12). As David Lyle from FremantleMedia (the company which co-developed *Pop Idol*; see Holmes, forthcoming, 2004) explains regarding the sale of new formats, '[i]nvariably, no broadcaster wants to be the first'. He goes on to describe how a format is 'certainly easier to sell using existing [programme] tapes' (Creamer, 2001b: 24). After a format has been sold to additional territories it becomes increasingly easy to continue selling it elsewhere, and the fees often rise. As a result, format creators that exist on their own without production operations are becoming increasingly common.

The accelerated importance of the format is a product of the multichannel environment in other ways given that the increasing fragmentation of audiences accentuates the economic imperative to ensure the popularity (and economic viability) of particular programmes (Moran, 1998: 18). In this respect, Reality TV has offered the most visible examples of this economic strategy, with programmes such as *Big Brother, Survivor, Popstars* (ITV, 2001, 2002–3, UK) and *Pop Idol* (Fremantle/19TV, ITV, 2001–2, UK) discussed by the trade as having a direct relation to the 'problem' of multichannel competition and the fragmentation of audiences. As Bazalgette claims:

> How difficult it is…for any single channel to make itself heard above the noise. One answer is to commission programmes that are – in essence – major events. High concept ideas that can be stripped across a channel's schedule every day for several weeks…helping ambitious channels stand out from the crowd.
>
> (Bazalgette, 2001: 20)

In the press and trade press, such texts are popularly referred to as 'event', 'must-see' or 'watercooler TV' (in that they are perceived to generate talk around the office 'watercooler'). Indeed, in the UK, for example, *Big Brother* has given Channel 4 some of its highest audience ratings in its 21-year history (see Elliott, 2002: 3). In this respect, this particular sector of Reality programming has very clear links to the market logic described by *Television* as the move toward 'the attention economy, in which getting shown would be easy, getting watched, almost impossible' (Anonymous, 1999: 6–7). While this is somewhat overstating the case, it does accentuate the link between 'event' programming and the competitive proliferation of channel space. In this sense, these texts are an attempt to heighten and reinvigorate the importance of shared spaces of broadcasting which are under threat more broadly by the acceleration of multichannel television and 'new' delivery systems (such as pay per view) (see Murdock, 2000), particularly when the entire concept of 'channel loyalty' is said to be a thing of the past.

Notable in such quotes from industry personnel and the trade press is the repeated use of terms such as 'high concept', 'event' and 'blockbuster' – each of which has more of an economic and discursive heritage in relation to cinema than television. While television, of course, certainly has a history and status as mediator of national/international 'events' (Dayan and Katz, 1994), the concept of broadcasting is equally entrenched within a rhetoric of 'the everyday'. The terms above have primarily been associated with (Hollywood) cinema since its shift away from a mass medium in the 1950s (and particularly since the 1970s) (Schatz, 1993; Wyatt, 1994; Kramer, 1996). While television is clearly not in the same economic or cultural situation (indeed we are facing the wider expansion of the medium), it is indicative of a similar economic strategy of investing in a particular high-profile product. Indeed, some industry analysts fear that this may be at the expense of 'mid-budget programming' (Creamer, 2001a: 12), which also indicates that, contrary to the repeated emphasis on Reality TV as being stimulated by cheap economies of scale (Kilborn, 1994; Dauncey, 1996; Dovey, 2000), it is also the case that, when areas such as marketing, promotion and set construction are considered, 'a piece of "event-TV" doesn't come cheap' (Creamer, 2001a: 12). While in terms of production the cost per hour may well be less expensive than, say, primetime drama, the blanket emphasis on Reality TV as 'cheap TV' tends to conflate the 'event' shows with other areas of Reality programming (such as 'real crime', camcorder-based shows or the earlier docusoap).

While format licensing and adaptation takes place at an industrial level, it clearly also has cultural implications. The front page of the first *Format News*, for example, boldly claimed that 'formats are now the global television currency' (Schreiber, 2002: 1), and it boasts the objective of creating quiz, game and Reality shows 'for a worldwide audience' (ibid.). Here, national frontiers are envisaged as boundaries to be conquered in the 'utopian' vision of an expansive global arena. This clearly strikes a note within the context of debates surrounding the globalisation of television (and cultural life more generally) (Barker, 1997; Sinclair *et al.*, 1996). As Barker describes:

The current interest in global television stems from the rise in transnational television and the perceived threats it poses to the more bounded television services of national states. These 'threats' are described in terms of the economics of television, the regulation of television and the identities, particularly national identities, which are deemed to be in part the product of national television services.

(Barker, 1997: 27)

While equally enmeshed within further discourses concerning the interrelationships between such national television systems and (in European contexts) PSB (ibid.), this also emphasises how the concept of format circulation and adaptation – combining inflections of both international and national input – falls between the analytic cracks where debates about cultural imperialism and globalisation are concerned (Moran, 1998: 169). Furthermore, in keeping with traditional conceptions of media/cultural imperialism as dominated by Western powers, earlier interventions in the study of the political economy of Reality TV tended to emphasise the predominance of US formats (Kilborn, 1994: 429–30). Yet it is worth noting here that, as *Format News* observed, 'these days a hit international format is just as likely to have originated in the UK, Holland or even Israel, as it is in the US' (Schreiber, 2002: 2). The cultural implications of Reality TV's international circulation certainly deserve close attention, and although there is not space to consider them here, the collection seeks to contribute to an understanding of how Reality TV has been produced and consumed in different national contexts, and the ways in which this is inflected by national broadcasting systems, cultural values and ideologies.

Work in progress: approaches to Reality TV

As indicated at the start, the terms and categories used to describe reality-based programming have a broader significance which extends to issues of critical, theoretical and methodological approach. In this respect, the rise of such programming can be seen to raise new challenges for, or at least ask questions of, the *existing* analytical approaches of television and cultural studies on a number of different levels (as well as their relationship with other disciplinary fields). As such, Reality TV can be seen potentially to pose new questions for students and academics engaged in the study of television – how to 'pin down' texts which seem to raise such fundamental questions about the wider contexts of social, political and economic change in modern society, the political economy of television or the medium's contemporary address to its viewers when they may (at times) elide the grasp of conventional methodological and theoretical approaches.

In expanding on the broader cultural response to Reality TV as the ultimate example of 'dumbing down' in media culture (and its consequent assumption of a 'passive' audience), Craig Hight has emphasised how such perceptions:

typically suffer from the absence of any recognition that new theoretical tools need to be developed in order to properly understand and critique the significance of these new forms. The notion that fact–fiction hybrids such as reality-TV, docu-soaps, talk shows and reality gameshows may represent a significant and apparently permanent break from the discourses which underlie the documentary genre has been slow to arrive.

(Hight, 2001: 390)

Particularly when it comes to the *study* of Reality TV, this is a crucial point in developing a more sympathetic and indeed sophisticated approach to such texts. As already discussed, central to popular debates over Reality TV, as well as existing academic work in the field, has been a consideration of its relationship with documentary (Corner, 2001b; Dovey, 2000; Kilborn and Izod, 2000; Niichols, 1994a) – as well as a reflection on the very problematisation of the term 'documentary' that this comparison engenders. Such discussion is often intrinsically related to, but cannot necessarily be equated with or reduced to, issues of methodological *approach*.

Work on the docusoap in particular self-consciously deliberated the extent to which popular factual hybrids borrowed from, and combined, formal and aesthetic elements of existing genres – in this case documentary and soap opera (Bruzzi, 2000; Dovey, 2000; Coles, 2000). Whether implicitly or explicitly, often raised here was the extent to which existing theoretical and methodological approaches to documentary were useful in approaching the form (although the ways in which this question was posed engendered a sense of inevitability that the conclusions would be less than positive). Dovey, for example, concludes:

Trying to analyse the docu-soap within the conventional terms of documentary criticism is an unrewarding project suggesting perhaps that we should reformulate the terms of the analysis. Maybe we would make more progress if we began with the 'soap' part of the genre, to think of these new documentary series as *essentially* about entertainment and drama rather than about the world we live in. Unfortunately the fictional worlds represented in the docu-soap are not rich enough to sustain the kinds of investment and reward we are willing to make in their fully fictionalised counterparts.

(Dovey, 2000: 151–2)

While Dovey's conclusion may be seen as somewhat pessimistic (given that he offers no alternative theoretical or critical perspective on the docusoap), his self-reflexive consideration of approach here is highly valuable in opening up debate where methodology is concerned. Although a recognition of generic hybridity has been central to subsequent work on global formats (Roscoe, 2001; Tincknell and Raghuram, 2002; Hill and Palmer, 2002), the implications of this methodological approach have been less explicitly addressed as work has continued to emerge. This is all the more interesting in view of the fact that such analyses have not suggested any form of consensus as to how the programmes should be approached. In analysing *Big Brother*, for example, while Roscoe describes how, at a structural level, 'the show has a strong relationship to soap opera and it references this far more than say, observational documentary or the gameshow' (Roscoe, 2001: 480–1), Corner, although certainly acknowledging its generic hybridity, suggests that ' "documentary" is the category that seems most obvious to start with and work from...right at the heart of the series is the idea of observing what is a mode of "real" behaviour' (Corner, 2002: 256). In this respect, then, and in relation to Hight's emphasis on the need for 'new theoretical tools' (2001: 390), it seems important to foreground Reality TV as opening up a space for experimentation and exploration in this respect which we perhaps shouldn't be too eager to resolve or close down. At the same time, in rushing to emphasise what is 'new' about Reality TV, there is perhaps a cautionary note to be sounded in terms of abstracting its relationship with a range of existing critical, theoretical and methodological paradigms on a number of different levels. As a result, this collection specifically aims not simply to consider examples of historical precursors to Reality TV (see Chapters 1–3, for example); it also deliberately seeks to investigate and indeed 'test out' the implications of Reality TV for existing approaches to wider areas of critical interest, ranging from the mediation of celebrity, through the construction of fan communities, to the politics of gay representation.

Essays in this collection

Our collection opens with Bradley D. Clissold's chapter on *Candid Camera*, which situates this early American TV favourite as a key historical precedent for the Reality TV movement. First appearing on US television screens in 1948, *Candid Camera*'s overt fascination with surveillance, its adoption of unobtrusive camera technology and its desire to catch its participants 'off guard' clearly prefigure many of the characteristics which are core to numerous strands of contemporary Reality TV. Very much contextualising the programme within the period's *zeitgeist* of 'paranoia', Clissold argues that, initially at least, the programme's popularity can be attributed to the ways in which 'it successfully assuaged both simulation-anxiety – the inability to distinguish between the real and the manufactured in an age of technological reproduction – and Cold War surveillance-anxiety – the constant fear that one's actions were being secretly monitored'. He argues that by reconfiguring the invasion of privacy and the use of concealed cameras into the stuff of comic revelation the programme effectively diffused the audience's discomfort with the growing ubiquity of such intrusions during this era of US history. Through an exploration of the socio-political contexts that influenced and enabled the rise of *Candid Camera* in the late 1940s, Clissold illuminates the extent to which the programme constitutes a striking historical and aesthetic precedent to contemporary Reality TV, and indeed how the same underlying ideologies are arguably still at work in current programmes.

The question of Reality TV's indebtedness to various earlier television genres is also taken up in Chapter 2. Drawing on a range of archival material, Jennifer Gillan explores how the MTV hit *The Osbournes* engages with the traditions of the family sitcom, and the 1950s US TV 'star-sitcom' sub-genre in particular. Though MTV may have marketed the show as 'the television-family-concept-redefining reality series', Gillan suggests the programme does not so much 'redefine' the relationship between television, the family and realism as *resurrect* the very familiar formula of a 1950s televisual staple. Naturally there are some significant differences, not least, for example, in *The Osbournes'* use of 'cutting-edge digital technology' and its generic hybridity, which also employs the characteristics of soaps, talk shows and celebrity interviews. This sense of the programme not just returning to but 'improving' and updating the star-sitcom genre is essential to its 21st-century appeal. Nevertheless, by centring on 'real' public figures and setting the programme within the domain of their domestic lives, many of the pivotal scenarios, 'characters' and sentiments of *The Osbournes* clearly echo those we already know from classic series such as *I Love Lucy* (CBS, 1951–7) and *The Adventures of Ozzie and Harriet* (ABC, 1952–66). By tracing the development of what she terms the 'reality star sitcom' from these historical precursors through to the present day, Gillan contends not just that 'the 1950s star sitcoms are an embryonic form of Reality Television', but that 'Reality TV in general is not as television-"concept-redefining" as its producers would like us to believe'.

Deborah Jermyn's is the last of our chapters to look in detail at historical precedents for Reality TV (Chapter 3). Like Clissold and Gillan, she examines an earlier, established television format – in this instance, crime-appeal programming – and the ways in which contemporary Reality TV is beholden to it. Indeed, she notes that some commentators have specifically described crime-appeal programmes such as *Crimewatch UK* (BBC, 1984–) and France's *Temoin N°. 1* (TF1, 1993–6) as examples of 'Reality TV' (Kilborn, 1994; Dauncey, 1996). Certainly, many strands of the movement have been notably marked by an interest in crime stories and, as Jermyn notes, *Crimewatch UK* was a 'conspicuous precursor to the boon of real-crime programming that has constituted one of the most controversial and resilient movements in British television since the late 1980s'. She argues that many of the accusations and debates that have surrounded Reality TV in recent years – for example its alleged conflation of fact and fiction, its sensationalist claiming of 'real' stories and witness testimonies, its appeal to a mass audience to take part in a contentious television format – were put on the agenda in Britain by *Crimewatch UK* as early as 1984.

Her essay focuses on a particular aspect of crime-appeal programming that has been key to the genre's 'claim to a privileged relationship with "the real" ': its use of video technologies, notably CCTV (closed-circuit TV) and home video (which, of course, have gone on to feature heavily in numerous forms of Reality TV). She examines how the programme-makers call on these video technologies to fore-ground their claim to 'the real' in a genre where they seek continually to remind the audience that '[t]his *is* about real people!' Jermyn suggests that it was the emergence and expansion of video technologies that actually facilitated the success and growth of crime-appeal programming in the 1980s and 1990s. But while these 'new technologies' may have proved instrumental in establishing the genre, the pleasures at its core were anything but new and are ones which have been taken up again with renewed enthusiasm by Reality TV. Jermyn illustrates how Reality TV 'is only the latest articulation of a rather more enduring strain of cultural fascination around "the real", very much in evidence in real-crime stories, that has a long history both within and preceding television'; namely what she calls '*the spectacle of actuality*'. While Reality TV, then, marks 'an unquestionable shift in the make-up of contemporary television schedules…the pleasures, curiosities and structures that underlie it may not be as original or landmark as we have tended to presume'.

It is perhaps partly because of the enduring appeal of 'the spectacle of actu-ality' that Jermyn notes that television crime-appeal programming has featured in television schedules around the world. But, beyond this, the rise of Reality TV has been notably marked by the popularity and circulation of particular formats on an international scale. Daniel Biltereyst's chapter responds to this wide-scale visi-bility from a specific perspective by examining the *reception* of Reality TV in a range of European contexts (Chapter 4). Concentrating largely on the reception of the first series of *Big Brother* and *Survivor* (but primarily *Big Brother*) in countries such as France, Germany, Belgium, Italy, Spain and Portugal, Biltereyst notes how 'one is struck by how they were able to provoke such wide-scale debate, including vehement reactions and signs of public revulsion and anxiety'. In this respect, such programmes stimulated a wider debate about television's ethical and moral status, both in the contemporary cultural moment and in the context of a changing television landscape. Biltereyst explains how some scholars and journal-ists perceived this widespread public debate to have much in common with a *moral panic* – the circulation of public anxiety about key social and moral issues generated by the discursive intersection of the media, public opinion, interest groups, intellectuals, politicians, church leaders and the authorities. Indeed, in certain national contexts the controversy over the programme drove media regulators to 'concrete action' which took the form of censorship or intervening in the rules of the show itself. In this respect, the heated debate generated by the reception of these programmes took on many of the structural characteristics of a moral panic, including the presence of moral guardians, the role of experts, the centrality of the media in facilitating debate, the perception of core values under threat, and the demand for 'action, regulation, law and order'.

However, a key objective of Biltereyst's analysis is to question whether the concept of the moral panic is entirely useful in understanding the cultural reception of Reality TV. In doing so, he draws on the argument (McRobbie, 1994) that, as a critical concept developed in the 1970s, it may have outlived its usefulness in the contemporary mediascape and 'postmodern era with its abundance of (mediated) voices'. Furthermore, Reality TV has deliberately exploited controversial social or moral issues in its bid to attract an audience in the competitive television environment. In this respect, Biltereyst suggests, the *simulation* of a moral panic became an integral part of the intertextual, multimedia and 'event' status of Reality TV, and within this context, he argues, it is more appropriate to conceive of the debate generated by Reality TV as a 'media' rather than a moral panic.

The simulated moral panic which Biltereyst describes has pivoted at least partly on the distaste occasioned by the elevation of 'ordinary' people into media celebrities. Hence, Su Holmes' chapter (Chapter 5) considers the representation of 'ordinary people' in Reality TV (a theme also taken up in Chapters 8 and 10) in terms of this opportunity to emerge as a celebrity – and hence to negotiate the boundary between 'ordinary' and 'special'. Reality TV is often invoked as the epitome of all that is trivial in contemporary celebrity culture and as exemplifying the extent to which there has been a (regrettable) 'democratisation' of fame. Holmes suggests that such a perspective tends to obscure, rather than elucidate, 'what is clearly the dynamic *appeal* of the relationship between ordinary people and celebrity culture, which has occupied a central place in the rise of Reality TV'. Furthermore, focusing on the case study of *Big Brother* (UK), Holmes argues that it may be problematic to overestimate the extent to which Reality TV is exemplary of 'dramatic' shifts in cultural conceptions and understandings of fame, and a key objective of the chapter is to consider the extent to which *existing* theoretical and methodological approaches to stardom/celebrity are useful when approaching Reality TV. Although she considers the construction of the contestants' celebrity in the programme itself, Holmes is particularly interested in the role played by *intertextual* sites such as the popular press and celebrity magazines. Focusing on their intertextual 'raiding' (Klinger, 1989) of the series, she describes how the print media play a crucial role in the construction of an on/off-screen 'persona' for the contestants, functioning in 'a complex structural matrix which intervenes in the discursive construction of the programme's claim to "the real"'. Holmes argues that the decline of older ideological myths surrounding stardom/fame (such as an emphasis on special 'talent' or 'hard work') are primarily replaced by an ever more fervent negotiation of 'the real self' in celebrity discourse. This emphasis on 'really' (what is the star/celebrity *really* like?) insists on the existence of some 'inner, private, essential core' (Dyer, 1987: 14) which enables the programme to articulate discourses surrounding individualism in capitalist society – earlier identified by Dyer as a key ideological function of stardom. In engaging with discourses on self-hood, 'performance' and self-presentation, *Big Brother* may well be the exemplary text in this respect, while the dizzying array of attempts to lay claim to the 'real self' may also in part exceed the apparent coherence of these earlier models. She nevertheless concludes by suggesting that, from a semiotic and structural point of view, 'there is much that is traditional in *Big Brother*'s construction of celebrity'.

Another intriguing aspect of Reality TV has been the ways in which it manipulates and foregrounds the movement of time. The relationship between Reality TV and temporality is the subject of the next chapter, by Misha Kavka and Amy West (Chapter 6). As they note, there is a long history of work within television studies concerned with televisual temporality, and the medium's characteristic sense of 'liveness' has been conceptualised as one of its fundamental and distinguishing features. Kavka and West contend, however, that our grasp of this technological and structural feature of the medium needs to be revisited in the light of the development of Reality TV. They suggest that one of the reasons for the hostile reception of the form lies in the fact that 'Reality TV is insistently ahistorical, and as such lacks the social and material contextualisation of most documentary projects'. Rather than dismissing it on these grounds however, we need instead to adopt a different conceptualisation of time with which to understand it. Despite its 'present-ism', Reality TV pivots around counting time, replacing linear historical time with 'ever-renewable time-cycles'. Its distinctive play with temporality lies in the manner in which it 'pursues intimacy (emotional closeness) through immediacy (temporal closeness), coupling the proximity of the "here" with the urgency of the "now"', and indeed its 'social relevance…lies in its creation of intimate viewing communities'. Focusing particularly on the operation of the complex cyclical temporal parameters of *Big Brother* and *Survivor*, and the implications of these for both contestants and viewers, Kavka and West demonstrate once again that television studies' existing methodological approaches need to be revised and reconsidered in the light of the emergence of Reality TV.

Though discourses berating the emergence of Reality TV have circulated widely in the popular press, Gray Cavender's chapter is arguably the first in this collection to itself adopt a position that criticises the representational strategies of Reality TV (Chapter 7). Cavender looks specifically at *America's Most Wanted* (*AMW*) and *Survivor* to illustrate how Reality TV has recurrently manipulated the construction of communities within its various formats. He argues that while superficially these programmes may seem to adhere to or promote the value of community – be that through *AMW*'s appeal to an audience of concerned and committed citizens or *Survivor*'s construction of tribal teams – Reality TV ultimately serves to undermine and erode the notion of community. In order to function as 'entertainment', *Survivor* is as much about duplicity and competitiveness as it is about bonding and alliances; *AMW* is as much about distrust and (often racialised) exclusion from community as it is about civic union and the reinforcement of community.

For Cavender it is significant that at the very point at which the alleged attenuation of community has become a highly contentious issue in the US, Reality TV programmes have emerged to frequently deploy the concept. It is a relationship that once again constitutes evidence of the powerful ways in which television, myth and (our perception of) social disquiet are closely entwined. Cavender argues that we need to be highly critical and cautious of the programmes' particular vision of community as one which 'reinforce[s] traditional notions of individualism and competition' and depicts a world where 'life remains resolutely "them v. us"'. He concludes that the invocation of community seen in these programmes is evidence not only of the conservative impulse that informs Reality TV, but of the need for us to reconfigure our existing idealised notion of community – to one which might celebrate heterogeneity and social differentiation over a constrictive conceptualisation of 'unity'.

Albeit for different reasons and in relation to different programmes, Gareth Palmer's chapter also adopts a critical position from which to understand Reality TV (Chapter 8). He focuses on lifestyle programming – one of the most prevalent sub-genres of Reality TV and a form which now spans both the daytime and primetime schedules. Examining the proliferation of this programming in the British context, Palmer's aim is to explore the ways in which it mediates and *legitimates* particular ideological discourses on class. Although the subject of class has become increasingly 'invisible' on the agenda of media and cultural studies, Palmer questions this shift by foregrounding its crucial and central importance in the concerns and address of lifestyle television. As he suggests, the significance of lifestyle TV 'may lie in the ways in which it helps to mould and to legitimise our class membership', particularly in the context of shifting definitions of PSB. In examining the ways in which our 'citizenship is rethought as a series of choices in decor,…clothes,…and manner', Palmer explores a range of programmes focusing on home 'improvement' (*Changing Rooms*, *House Doctor*, *Property Ladder*) and fashion makeovers (*What Not to Wear*) through to the broader premise of 'self'-transformation (*Would Like to Meet*).

In doing so, he returns to Bourdieu's (1986) work on 'habitus' and 'cultural capital', which emphasised how culture, 'taste' and knowledge are a crucial means of class differentiation (rather than simply financial capital). It is from this perspective that Palmer argues that class ideologies are apparent, yet necessarily 'disguised', in lifestyle programming in that the choices which shape the makeover of the home, appearance or self are structured within discourses of petit-bourgeois tastes. In its representation of the relationship between 'experts' and 'ordinary' participants (and its consequent address to the viewer) lifestyle television legitimises the hierarchical nature of these tastes and is seen as being 'perfectly placed to service the insecurities felt by those who are uncertain of their place in a rapidly evolving social system'. Questions of class and 'taste' are seen to be further abstracted in the self-makeover programme in that its emphasis on 'flexible identities' draws on discourses of the (originally American) Personal Development Movement (PDM), in which class and background are primarily constructed as circumstances which individuals should overcome in their 'quest to selfhood'. It is through this analysis that Palmer is able to insist that '[c]lass...*is* very much on the agenda of lifestyle television, but "merely" as a question of taste'.

Like Cavender and Palmer, Rebecca L. Stephens examines how Reality TV can serve to fulfil and perpetuate dominant ideological discourses (Chapter 9). Her chapter takes the US cable channel TLC's hugely successful daytime programming as its focus, specifically the 'Life Unscripted' shows *A Wedding Story* (1995–) and *A Baby Story* (1998–). These shows, clearly targeted at women and 'rated number one in daytime cable viewing among women in the 18–34 age group', feature 'ordinary' couples' 'own' accounts of the build-up to and fulfilment of their big day, culminating in either their wedding or the birth of their child. Given their preoccupation with the 'feminine' subjects of romance and family and their evident popularity with female audiences, these programmes raise 'some serious issues for feminists'. Stephens finds that the shows' glorification of the highly conventional aspirations and institutions of marriage and motherhood are inextricably bound up in an effort to alleviate anxieties about the jeopardy of these institutions in contemporary US society, an anxiety which is evident across current debates in both popular culture and public policy. *A Wedding Story* and *A Baby Story* need to be understood within the US rhetoric of the 1990s and early 2000s which has attributed many contemporary cultural ills to the breakdown of the traditional family unit. In these programmes this tradition is unproblematically reinstated.

Rather than 'empowering' these ordinary people by giving them a platform from which to share and celebrate their personal experiences, these programmes co-opt their stories into a discourse in which the overwhelming drive is to contain and deny difference in order to embrace the apparently universal female desire for conventional marriage and motherhood. Stephens argues that in an era in which the Bush administration's revision of welfare laws has included promises to make 'marriage-related grants', TLC's programming effectively mirrors this blurring of private and public domains, where the US government is legislating to advocate and reward marriage. With its recurrent attention to and celebration of flamboyant and costly wedding ceremonies, virginal white gowns, brides being 'given away' and nurseries being decorated and shopped for by married hetero-sexual couples (always for their biological children), TLC's vision of marriage and motherhood is one which assumes affluence and compliance with dominant ideologies. With their privileging of experiential testimony, what is so powerful about these representations is that they are constructed as the object not of indi-viduals' desire, but of *mass* desire, not as mere fantasy, but as attainable fantasy; this is the 'real' experience of marriage and motherhood, and with it other lifestyles and alternatives are rendered not just marginal, but invisible.

Nevertheless, in the subsequent chapter, Christopher Pullen reflects on the potential Reality TV may offer to incorporate more expansive, even 'progressive' representational discourses around marginalised groups (Chapter 10). Specifically, his essay considers the representation of gay male identity in Reality programming, a response to what he describes as the increase in 'gay visibility across the international formats offered by Reality TV'. As Pullen observes, the 'casting' of gay participants has become something of a predictable textual strategy in Reality TV given that, as in soap opera, 'difference' provides the 'impetus for disruption on which...narrative thrive[s]' (Geraghty, 1991: 166). As this comparison suggests, genres such as the soap opera and the talk show offer important generic precursors to television's increasing interest in the representa-tion of gay identity, particularly given that they are both referenced by the hybrid generic form of Reality TV. It is from this perspective that Pullen seeks to explore the political implications of Reality TV's mediation and use of gay participants by asking: 'to what extent does the form raise new issues in the field where the construction of gay identity is concerned? How are these possibilities shaped by the particular technological, aesthetic and narrative structures of Reality TV, and what are their political implications?'

Following a trajectory which moves from the representation of the participant Pedro Zamora, who had AIDS, in *The Real World* (1994–, US) to the later exam-ples of Lee Alexander in *Eden* (2002, UK) and Brian Dowling in *Big Brother* (2001, UK), Pullen focuses on issues such as the objectification of the gay male body, the use of stereotypes and 'camp' performance, and the mediation of discourses on community, romance and marriage. While *Big Brother* and *Eden* privilege the potential for romance and partnership 'within the exclusive domain of the hetero-sexual' and use various strategies to marginalise and/or assimilate the 'problem' posed by the gay man within this terrain, *The Real World* is seen as offering a 'groundbreaking representation of non-Caucasian gay men in love' which chal-lenged cultural perceptions around AIDS and gay identity itself. Pullen's analysis indicates that Reality TV makes use of predictable and hegemonic strate-gies in its representation of gay men (particularly in the 'celebrated gay male

camp performance' of Brian Dowling, winner of the second *Big Brother* in the
UK), yet this also suggests that generalisations are problematic given that the
complexities of the field also depend upon particular programme contexts and
participants. Yet in foregrounding what he perceives as the earlier, and indeed
more progressive, example of the participant Pedro Zamora in *The Real World*,
Pullen suggests that Reality TV has subsequently failed to fulfil its political potential where the representation of gay identity is concerned. But given that the
primary impetus behind this visibility is arguably the economics of popular entertainment, the parameters in which this representation takes shape are perhaps
unlikely to change.

Beyond the press reception described by Biltereyst in Chapter 4, another
medium that has played an active role in shaping and circulating popular
discourses around Reality TV has been that of cinema. In Chapter 11 Craig Hight
examines how recent Hollywood feature films have adopted an uneasy, ambivalent and sometimes condemnatory position in their representations of Reality
TV and its audiences. Looking specifically at three films which explore documentary hybrids in their narratives – *The Truman Show* (Weir, 1998, US); *Edtv*
(Howard, 1999, US) and *Series 7: The Contenders* (Minahan, 2001, US) – Hight
demonstrates how these films constitute only the latest instance of cinema's
history of critical commentary on its 'rival' medium. As Hight notes, '[t]hese
films all incorporate critiques of the heavily commercialist institutional agenda
which frames hybrids as media products, and the various levels of exploitation,
manipulation and explicit "distortion of reality" which are seen to typify their
construction as texts'. In these ways, the films can be said to constitute 'comprehensive satires' of televisual hybrid forms. Hight goes on to examine how they
concur – in vaying degrees – with key critical discourses on Reality TV (as identified by Dovey, 2000). Thus, while they give no credence to the suggestion that
hybrid forms may 'empower' ordinary people, they explore the postmodern
theory of the 'disappearance' of reality and expose the ways in which these
forms might be said to constitute exploitative and sensationalistic 'trash TV'.
Ultimately, however, the 'satiric bite' of the films is limited by their reluctance to
move away from a conventional and conservative vision of the television audience as vacuously consuming the medium – and for 'largely avoiding the direct
suggestion that we as their audience are collectively implicated in the development of hybrids'.

As Hight notes, then, these films indicate that one of the key tensions
surrounding the cinema's critique of Reality TV has been the representation of the
TV audience as 'cultural dupes' – given that their *own* audience is very likely to be
a crossover audience composed of people who *also* watch Reality TV.
Furthermore, unlike many of the filmic representations of gullible TV audiences
described by Hight, we have seen how popular debate around Reality TV has been

notable for the way in which it has very much foregrounded an awareness of the format's manipulation of 'the real'. The question of the relationship between Reality TV and its audiences is explored further in the final two chapters in this collection. Expanding on and updating research which originally featured in the *European Journal of Cultural Studies*, Tincknell and Raghuram adopt a textual, rather than ethnographic, approach in order to explore the implications of Reality TV for current conceptualisations of the audience and 'text' in television and cultural studies (Chapter 12). Focusing on *Big Brother*, the authors suggest that in making audience participation central to the narrative and 'plot' of the programme the format 'marked a new moment of "interactive" television' and, as such, intervened in longstanding debates about the (power) relations between audience and text. Situating this within the historical trajectory of approaches to the audience in cultural studies, Tincknell and Raghuram explain how the idea of the 'active' audience has traditionally been based on the assumption that 'activity constitutes an intellectual engagement *with* a text, rather than an intervention *in* a text', and, as such, the idea of an 'interactive' text may pose new conceptual and methodological questions. This also occurs at a time when there has been increasing criticism of the conceptualisation of audience response as necessarily 'active' or 'resistant' (as well as criticism of the tendency to conflate these responses). Within this context, Tincknell and Raghuram suggest, the emergence of the interactive televisual text deserves careful consideration. An important element of their analysis considers the intertextual construction of the programme and its proliferation across a range of media sites. As in Holmes' analysis of the construction of celebrity in Chapter 5, they emphasise how this functions to multiply the semiotic meanings of the text, and in conceptualising its implications for audience engagement Tincknell and Raghuram suggest that this helped to generate different and 'contesting' discourses surrounding events in the show – hence problematising its 'preferred' meanings. In examining the importance of voting in the programme, they continue to consider the potential relationship between the 'active' audience ('negotiating or resisting the preferred meanings being offered by a text') and the *interactive* audience. The authors suggest that, although the degree of intervention on offer to the audience is limited by the range of options the text and its producers make available, the '*idea* of agency was probably central to *Big Brother*'s success'. As such, while acknowledging the programme's significance for reappraising our understanding of 'the audience' in the contemporary media landscape, they caution against the view that it radically destabilised the power relations between producers and viewers.

Finally, focusing on a more specific form of audience relationships with Reality TV, Derek Foster examines how fans engage with the US version of *Survivor* (2000–) by analysing the construction of fan communities on the Internet (Chapter 13). This focuses on two key arenas for the circulation of *Survivor* fan culture: 'fantasy pools' and 'spoiler sites'. In fantasy pools, viewers can speculate on the outcome of the game and compete with others on the web forum by earning points based on accurate predictions, while spoiler sites are bulletin boards sharing speculation with regard to how the series (and individual episodes) will end before they are broadcast. As Foster explains, '[t]hrough on-line activity, *Survivor* viewers competed with one another just as the competitors battled against each other in the weekly challenges on screen'. A key aim of Foster's piece is to explore the implications of this culture for existing critical and theoretical approaches to fandom. Central to this is a consideration of the increasingly crucial relationship which exists between the Internet and fandom – and the implications of this interaction for conceptualising the political significance of fans' relations with media culture. Drawing on the work of Jenkins (1998) and Brooker (2001), Foster emphasises the role played by the Internet in 'mainstreaming' fandom (*Survivor* is, after all, a mainstream television text aimed at the mass audience), and the increasing difficulty of making distinctions between fan culture which is 'produced' by audiences and that which is 'structured' by producers. As Foster suggests, while many sites are audience-produced (and, in the case of spoiler sites, reflect a high degree of critical distance from and ambivalence toward the series itself), they 'simultaneously work to feed fans back into the circuit of production and consumption even as they talk back'. His chapter is also particularly interested in the extremely *competitive* nature of the *Survivor* fan cultures and their apparent lack of community. In considering this, he discusses the ways in which the programme may have struck a particular chord in the US (where it was a huge success) and the ways in which its 'plot' narrativised a 'microcosm of American values' relating to self-reliance, 'hard work' and success. Foster emphasises that *Survivor* didn't offer the chance to escape 'from the mundane to the marvelous' (Jenkins, 1988: 99) (in the manner of a 'fantastic' text, for example), as by participating in pools the interpersonal networks cultivated here meant that 'fans didn't insert themselves into the fantastic, exotic locale where *Survivor* castaways were stranded. Instead, they reinforced the reality of their everyday interpersonal politics'.

Collectively, these essays cover Reality TV in its myriad forms, examining historical precedents and the international nature of its circulation and consumption, and exploring some of the key debates which Reality TV has put on the social, cultural and televisual agenda. It is our hope that at its conclusion, as readers, students, academics, cultural critics and media commentators, we will be better equipped to recognise the import and operation of this major televisual form and, as a consequence, have come rather closer to 'Understanding Reality TV'.

Su Holmes and Deborah Jermyn
May 2003

References

Anonymous (1999) 'The Other Stuff: Multichannel Marketing Conference', *Television*, June: 6–8.

Anonymous (2000) *'Big Brother –* review', *Independent*, 17 July.

Barker, Chris (1997) *Global Television: An Introduction*, Oxford: Blackwell.

Barnfield, Graham (2002) 'From Direct Cinema to Car-wreck Video: Reality TV and the Crisis of Content', in Dolan Cummings (ed.) *Reality TV: How Real is Real?*, Oxford: Hodder & Stoughton.

Bazalgette, Peter (2001) 'Big Brother and Beyond', *Television*, October: 20–3.

Bondebjerg, I. B. (2000) 'Public Discourse/Private Fascination: Hybridization in "True Life-Story" Genres', in Horace Newcomb (ed.) *Television: The Critical View* (6th edition), Oxford: Oxford University Press.

Bourdieu, Pierre (1986) *Distinction*, London: Routledge.

Brenton, Sam and Reuben Cohen (2003) *Shooting People: Adventures in Reality TV*, London: Verso.

Brooker, Will (2001) 'Living on *Dawson's Creek*: Teen Viewers, Cultural Convergence, and Television Overflow', *International Journal of Cultural Studies* 4(4): 456–72.

Brunsdon, Charlotte (1990) 'Problems with Quality', *Screen* 31(1): 67–90.

Bruzzi, Stella (2000) *New Documentary: A Critical Introduction*, London: Routledge.

Calvert, Clay (2000) *Voyeur Nation: Media, Privacy and Peering in Modern Culture*, Boulder, CO: Westview Press.

Caughie, John (1991) 'Adorno's Reproach: Repetition, Difference and Television Genre', *Screen*, 32(2), Summer: 127–53.

Clark, Bernard (2002) 'The Box of Tricks', in Dolan Cummings (ed.) *Reality TV: How Real is Real?*, Oxford: Hodder & Stoughton.

Coles, Gail (2000) 'Docusoap: Actuality and the Serial Format', Bruce Carson and Margaret Llewellyn-Jones (eds) *Frames and Fictions on Television: The Politics of Identity in Drama*, Wiltshire: Cromwell Press.

Collins, Michael (1999) 'Reality Television Boom', *Observer*, 19 December.

Corner, John (1996) *The Art of Record: A Critical Introduction to Documentary*, Manchester: Manchester University Press.

Corner, John (1999) *Critical Ideas in Television Studies*, Oxford: Oxford University Press.

Corner, John (2000) 'What Can We Say about "Documentary"?', *Media, Culture and Society* 22(5): 681–8.

Corner, John (2001a) ' "Documentary in Dispute" ', *International Journal of Cultural Studies* 4(3): 352–9.

Corner, John (2001b) 'Documentary in a Post-Documentary Culture? A Note on Forms and their Functions', available at http://www.1boro.ac.uk/research/changing.media/John%20Corner%20paper.htm (accessed 3 January 2003).

Corner, John (2002) 'Performing the Real: Documentary Diversions', *Television and New Media* 3(3): 255–69.

Creamer, Jon (2001a) 'Chain of Events', *Televisual*, September: 11–13.

Creamer, Jon (2001b) 'Intellectual Property for Sale', *Televisual*, October: 24–6.

Cummings, Dolan (ed.) (2002) *Reality TV: How Real is Real?*, Oxford: Hodder & Stoughton.

Dahlgren, Peter (2000) 'Key Trends in European Television', in Jan Wieten, Peter Dahlgren and Graham Murdock (eds) *Television Across Europe: A Comparative Introduction*, London: Sage.

Dauncey, Hugh (1996) 'French "Reality Television": More than a Matter of Taste?', *European Journal of Communication* 11(1): 83–107.

Dayan, D. and E. Katz (1994) *Media Events: The Live Broadcasting of History*, Cambridge, MA: Harvard University Press.

Dovey, Jon (2000) *Freakshow: First Person Media and Factual Television*, London: Pluto.

Dunkley, Christopher (2001) 'Reality TV', *Financial Times*, 10 January: 24.

Dunkley, Christopher (2002) 'It's Not New and It's Not Clever', in Dolan Cummings (ed.) *Reality TV: How Real is Real?*, Oxford: Hodder & Stoughton.

Dyer, Richard (1986) *Heavenly Bodies: Film Stars and Society*, London: British Film Institute.

Elliott, Katy (2002) 'Top 20 Programmes on C4 (1982–2002)', *Broadcast*, 1 November: 3.

Fishman, Mark and Gray Cavender (eds) (1997) *Entertaining Crime: Television Reality Programs*, New York: Aldine de Gruyter.

Flett, Kathryn (2000) 'Shipwrecked – Review', *Observer*, 23 January: 10.

Friedman, James (ed.) (2002) *Reality Squared: Televisual Discourse on the Real*, New Brunswick: Rutgers University Press.

Geraghty, Christine (1991) *Women and Soap Opera: A Study of Prime-time Soaps*, Cambridge: Polity.

Hight, Craig (2001) 'Debating Reality-TV', *Continuum: Journal of Media & Cultural Studies* 15(3): 389–95.

Hill, Annette (2000) 'Fearful and Safe: Audience Response to British Reality Programming', in John Izod and Richard Kilborn (eds) *From Grierson to the Docu-soap: Breaking the Boundaries*, Luton: University of Luton Press.

Hill, Annette (2002) 'Big Brother: The Real Audience', *Television and New Media* 3(3): 323–1.

Hill, Annette and Gareth Palmer (2002) 'Editorial: Big Brother', *Television and New Media* 3(3): 251–4.

Holmes, Su (forthcoming, 2004) ' "Reality Goes Pop!": Reality TV, Popular Music and Narratives of Stardom in *Pop Idol* (UK)', *Television and New Media*, 5(2) May.

Izod, John and Richard Kilborn (eds) (2000) *From Grierson to the Docu-soap: Breaking the Boundaries*, Luton: University of Luton Press.

Jenkins, Henry (1988) '*Star Trek* Rerun, Reread, Rewritten: Fan Writing as Textual Poaching', *Critical Studies in Mass Communication* 5(2): 85–107.

Jenkins, Henry (1998) 'The Poachers and the Stormtroopers: Cultural Convergence in the Digital Age', available at http://commons.somewhere.com/rre/1998/.

Kellner, Douglas (1992) 'Television, the Crisis of Democracy and the Persian Gulf War', in Marc Rabay and Bernard Dagenais (eds) *Media, Crisis and Democracy: Mass Communication and the Disruption of Social Order*, Sage: London.

Kerr, Paul (1990) ' "F for Fake?" Friction over Faction', in Andrew Goodwin and Garry Whannel (eds) *Understanding Television*, London: Routledge.

Kilborn, Richard (1994) ' "How Real Can You Get": Recent Developments in "Reality" Television', in *European Journal of Communication* 9: 421–39.

Kilborn, Richard (2000) 'The Docu-soap: A Critical Reassessment', in John Izod and Richard Kilborn (eds) *From Grierson to the Docu-soap: Breaking the Boundaries*, Luton: University of Luton Press.

Kilborn, Richard and John Izod (1997) *An Introduction to Television Documentary: Confronting Reality*, Manchester: Manchester University Press.

Klinger, Barbara (1989) 'Digressions at the Cinema: Reception and Mass Culture', *Cinema Journal* 28(4): 3–19.

Kramer, Peter (1996) 'The Lure of the Big Picture: Film, Television and Hollywood', in John Hill and Martin McLoone (eds) *Big Picture, Small Screen: The Relations Between Film and Television*, Luton: University of Luton Press.

McGuigan, Jim (1992) *Cultural Populism*, London: Routledge.

McRobbie, Angela (1994) 'The Moral Panic in the Age of the Postmodern Mass Media', in Angela McRobbie (ed.) *Postmodernism and Popular Culture*, London: Routledge.

Moran, Albert (1998) *Copycat TV: Globalisation, Programme Formats and Cultural Identity*, Luton: Luton University Press.

Murdock, Graham (2000) 'Digital Futures: European Television in the Age of Convergence', in Jan Wieten, Peter Dahlgren and Graham Murdock (eds) *Television Across Europe: A Comparative Introduction*, London: Sage.

Neale, Steve (1990) 'Questions of Genre', *Screen* 31(1): 45–66.

Nichols, Bill (1994a) *Blurred Boundaries: Questions of Meaning in Contemporary Culture*, Bloomington and Indianapolis, IN: Indiana University Press.

Nichols, Bill (1994b) *Representing Reality*, Bloomington, IN: Indiana University Press.

O'Sullivan, Tim, Brian Dutton and Philip Rayner (eds) (1994) *Studying the Media: An Introduction* (2nd edition), London: Edward Arnold.

Paton, Maureen (2000) 'Come Back Docusoap – All is Forgiven', *Times*, 28 January.

Patterson, John (2001) 'Review of *Series 7*', *Guardian*, 9 March: 12.

Richardson, Kay and Ulrike Meinhof (1999) *Worlds in Common?: Television Discourse in a Changing Europe*, London: Routledge.

Roscoe, Jane (2001) 'Big Brother Australia: Performing the "Real" Twenty-four-seven', *International Journal of Cultural Studies* 4(4): 473–88.

Roscoe, Jane and Craig Hight (2001) *Faking It: Mock-documentary and the Subversion of Factuality*, Manchester: Manchester University Press.

Scannell, Paddy (2002) 'Big Brother as Media Event', *Television and New Media* 3(3): 271–82.

Schatz, Thomas (1993) 'The New Hollywood', in Jim Collins, Hilary Radner and Ava Preacher Collins (eds) *Film Theory Goes to the Movies*, London: Routledge.

Schreiber, Dominic (2002) 'Formats – Now the Networks Are Taking Notice', *Format News*, October: 2 (supplement to *Broadcast*, 4 November 2002).

Sinclair, J., E. Jacka and S. Cunningham (1996) *New Patterns in Global Television: Peripheral Vision*, Oxford: Oxford University Press.

Steemers, Jeanette (1998) 'On the Threshold of the "Digital Age": Prospects for Public Service Broadcasting', in Jeanette Steemers (ed.) *Changing Channels: The Prospects for Television in a Digital World*, Luton: University of Luton Press.

Stempel-Mumford, Laura (1995) *Love and Ideology in the Afternoon: Soap Opera, Women and Television Genre*, Bloomington, IN: Indiana University Press.

Tincknell, Estella and Parvati Raghuram (2002) 'Big Brother: Reconfiguring the "Active" Audience of Cultural Studies?', *European Journal of Cultural Studies* 5(2): 199–215.

Tolson, Andrew (1996) *Mediations: Text and Discourse*, London: Arnold.

Woffinden, Bob (1989) 'Crime Time Viewing', *Listener* 112(3139), 9 November: 910.

Wooley, Benjamin (1984) 'An Arresting Programme', *Listener*, 112(2072), 23 August: 11.

Wyatt, Justin (1994) *High Concept: Movies and Marketing in Hollywood*, Austin, TX: University of Texas Press.

1

CANDID CAMERA AND THE ORIGINS OF REALITY TV

Contextualising a historical precedent

Bradley D. Clissold

During the years that it aired, *Candid Camera* (US, 1948–), arguably the first 'Reality TV' programme, proved itself to be one of US TV's most memorable, enduring and popular shows. Initially at least, this was arguably in part because it successfully assuaged both simulation-anxiety – the inability to distinguish between the real and the manufactured in an age of technological reproduction – and Cold War surveillance-anxiety – the constant fear that one's actions were being secretly monitored.[1] Consequently, Allen Funt's (who originally presented and developed the programme) contribution to twentieth-century culture and society goes beyond merely producing hidden-camera gags for laughs – even though this may have been *his* primary intention. His show's famous tagline, 'Smile! You're on *Candid Camera*', not only signalled the moment of comic revelation when the concealed camera was exposed; it also functioned as an ideological directive to stop worrying about being watched in the Cold War climate of surveillance (1945–91). In the shadow of the Red Menace, by converting recorded invasions of privacy into shared moments of entertainment fully endorsed (retrospectively at least) by the surveilled, Funt helped reduce his audience's surveillance-anxiety. In addition, *Candid Camera* set the industry standard for capturing individuals in unguarded moments using an unobtrusive camera, while it also helped to reinforce and perpetuate a 'poetics of the real', an aesthetic to which recent Reality TV programming is indebted.

The purpose of this chapter is to locate what I perceive to be some of the historical origins of Reality TV and to explore the socio-political contexts that influenced, and continue to influence, its development. To understand the current Reality TV craze, it is necessary, I suggest, to understand the historical and aesthetic precedent set by *Candid Camera*. The show began as *Candid Microphone* in 1948, just as classical Hollywood cinema entered its demise, at the beginning of television's household dominance and in response to Cold War fears of national security. By the time Funt changed the name to *Candid Camera* in 1949 the programme's format of surreptitiously recording ordinary people when confronted by extraordinary (staged) circumstances yielded skits whose form and content betrayed their exploitation of contemporary ideological concerns regarding surveillance and the unstable nature of reality. In what follows I trace the socio-material origins of *Candid Camera*'s production and reception, and then, through a series of close readings of representative skits taken from Candid Camera's *All-Time Funniest Moments: Parts I and II* (1993), delineate the show's embedded social and political allegiances.[2] In doing so, I want to suggest that the same underlying ideologies that informed the cultural practice of the first Reality TV programme are still at work in successor programmes.

A candid history

The early conceptualisation for *Candid Camera* began while Funt worked as a Cornell research assistant conducting psychology experiments and while he served in the armed forces during World War II. As Funt's autobiography (1994) relates, in 1934 he participated in a Cornell study of infant eating habits that involved observing and recording – through a two-way mirror – how infants responded differently when they were fed by their mothers and by nurses. A few years later, in 1941, Funt was drafted into the US Army and assigned, very appropriately, to the Signal Corps, where he recorded audio messages for GIs to send home and created radio programmes to boost the morale of enlisted men.[3] One of the programmes Funt developed was *The Gripe Booth*, a show that provided a forum for servicemen to complain about anything army-related without fear of recrimination. The problem was that as soon as soldiers entered the studio and saw the red light that indicated they were being recorded, they became self-conscious and uncommunicative. The solution, according to Funt, was to record these men secretly by disconnecting the intrusive red light: 'The conversations I obtained under these conditions were invariably more candid – a word, and a quality, I would come to value' (Funt, 1994: 26). Like his Cornell research employment, producing *The Gripe Booth* introduced Funt to the world of secret recordings at a time in modern history when security concerns had been heightened and new technologies like the two-way mirror (1903) and the portable wire recorder (1898–1900) had made surveillance more inconspicuous. More importantly for Funt, *The Gripe Booth* revealed the entertainment value of covert audio surveillance, and in 1947 *Candid Microphone* extended the practice into the postwar years as a regular radio offering.

ABC picked up the programme for the summer of 1947, and the responses to its format soon revealed the extent to which surveillance-anxiety had already saturated American society. As *Time* magazine wrote, '[w]ith this new Machiavellian inspiration, radio crosses the last threshold of privacy. The whole country seems likely to be plagued with hidden microphones' (cited in Funt, 1994: 30). The *New York Herald Tribune* saw *Candid Microphone* as a precursor to even more insidious surveilling of everyday life:

> [E]veryone may tune in on their neighbors or, at any rate, somebody's neighbors and listen to their unrehearsed, unwitting, unsponsored remarks. It's a wonderful sport, like looking through keyholes but capable of infinitely greater variety.... The possibilities are limitless: the prospect is horrifying. Wait till they get the Candid Television Camera. You won't be safe in your own bathtub.
>
> (cited in Funt, 1994: 30)

Ironically, both of these reviews managed to point a finger at Funt's programme as a source of surveillance-anxiety, rather than seeing it for what it arguably was: a cultural response to and exploitation of a social and political shift. *Candid Microphone* wasn't responsible for placing hidden microphones or cameras in suburban backyards and households; they were already there in the eyes and ears of concerned and vigilant citizens encouraged by government propaganda to report any signs of 'un-American' activity. Allen Funt claims that the US Army was 'indirectly' responsible for the creation of *Candid Camera*, but it was arguably American foreign policy after World War II that was *directly* responsible for the sustained popularity and success of the show (ibid.: 23).

The climate of Cold War politics and culture arguably made audiences ideologically receptive to reality-based hidden-camera gags. As a result, in 1948 *Candid Microphone* made the jump to television and became the first programme to be aired on the new ABC network. On 10 August 1948, the show that officially launched a new era of television broadcasting and helped to reshape the entertainment industry was also arguably a prototype for Reality TV programming. The origins of television, therefore, are historically, psychologically, materially and ideologically inseparable from the birth of Reality TV. The Cold War demand for accessible up-to-date information and in-home leisure 'escapism' informed the development of television and created a market for what would eventually become *Candid Camera*. In turn, *Candid Camera* made surveillance entertaining, less threatening and ideologically acceptable; indeed, similarly, Jermyn (in Chapter 3) argues that television crime-appeal programmes in the 1980s did much the same to popularise and de-politicise the mass expansion of CCTV (closed-circuit TV) and 'normalise' the use of CCTV footage across many television formats. Most importantly, *Candid Camera* provided cathartic release from surveillance-anxiety. In the long term, whether naturalising surveillance or providing symbolic (false) forms of resistance was constructive or not is debatable. Certainly, where there is catharsis there is also the potential for coercive neutralising of adversarial impulses (Boal,

1985; Horkheimer and Adorno, 1991). In this case, a cultural product functioned as an ideological safety valve to relieve growing tensions over increasing government surveillance of the general public. However, did *Candid Camera* actually make intrusive invasions of privacy and detailed state- and corporate-sponsored information gathering more palatable to the American populous, and even permit its unchecked expansion? Indeed, Funt's creation played as significant a role as any of the other popular culture products of the Cold War era that responded to, played off of and intensified the climate of surveillance (see Whitfield, 1996). Surveillance was a necessary evil in post-war America. Funt's brainchild may arguably have assuaged many of the accompanying tensions and, through comedy, kept reminding the public that they were being watched when they least expected.

The historical roots of *Candid Camera* reveal how the concept for the programme evolved under the influence of a constellation of post-war, century-defining cultural and historical moments that can still be broadly identified in recent incarnations of the popular television programme as well as in successor reality-based programmes. In the immediate post-war years a series of high profile British and American espionage trials (Alan Nunn May, Klaus Fuchs, Alger Hiss-Whittaker Chambers), culminating in the sensational 1953 execution of the Rosenbergs, set the dominant tone for the Cold War. Here was concrete proof of the enemy within, potentially hidden among suburban neighbourhoods and behind the closed doors of the average American family home. Over the same period of time, American paranoia escalated with a succession of world events that confirmed the imminent threat of communist infiltration: in 1949 Russia detonated its first atomic bomb and China became a communist regime; and in 1950 the Korean War began and Senator Joseph McCarthy started compiling lists of subversives and naming names. Another factor that contributed to domestic paranoia was the knowledge that Americans who quit the Communist Party for patriotic reasons in the post-war period were in effect doing exactly what the Party required of their American members who were about to engage in covert espionage activities for the USSR.

In this demonised environment, any 'strange' behaviour would potentially be interpreted as 'un-American' and therefore deemed threatening. Innuendo, unsupported by witness accounts or material evidence, was enough to generate the type of suspicion that put individuals in front of the House Committee on Un-American Activities. The seismic disruptions that occurred in American culture and society created a climate of suspicion that was registered in and perpetuated by accounts like the one found in Henry W. Bragdon and Samuel P. McCutchen's high-school textbook *History of a Free People*:

> Unquestioning party members are found everywhere. Everywhere they
> are willing to engage in spying, sabotage, and the promotion of unrest on

the orders of Moscow.... Agents of the worldwide Communist conspiracy have been active inside the United States. Some of them have been trusted officials of the State Department, regularly furnishing information to Russia. Others have passed on atomic secrets; still others have even represented the United States in the UN.

(Bragdon and McCutchen, 1954; cited in Whitfield, 1996: 33)

It was every loyal American's civic duty to observe, record and inform the government of any suspicious activities he or she witnessed. *Candid Camera* paralleled elements of this civic obligation in the format of its programme: hidden observation, recorded activities and public broadcast.

One particular incident, involving Funt's attempt to get permission to use recordings made at the gates of the White House, illustrates that *Candid Camera*'s methods of operation were not at all unlike those employed by US government agencies. It also reveals the extent to which those who surveilled were often simultaneously subjected to surveillance in a surveillance society. In the original skit Funt drives up to the guard on duty and asks to see the president. More telling than the skit itself, however, was the meeting that followed with John J. Mahoney, the head of the Secret Service, and sixteen other government officials. Funt relates that everyone in the room listened to the candid recording and not one of them even smiled. After being denied permission to air the initial recording, Funt asked if he could instead use the secret recording he had just made of the meeting: 'Listen, if you're not going to let me use that piece at the gate, can I use the recording I just made of me trying to get clearance from you? Would you like to hear that tape?' The head of the Secret Service nonchalantly responded, 'We don't need to.... We made one of our own' (Funt, 1994: 36). Acts of surveillance in the Cold War period incorporated the expectation of reciprocal observation, and this was as true in the US as it was in the USSR.

In 1961 Funt set out for Moscow with his hidden cameras and microphones to film some skits with unsuspecting Russians and thus demonstrate to American viewers that the Russians were really no different from them. Given the climate, this 'subversive mission' was an overtly political move; however, for this very reason neither the CBS network nor the Russian authorities were informed of the trip. As it turned out, similarities between Russians and Americans went beyond shared human foibles and quirky responses to strange circumstances. The Cold War had set up parallel surveillance societies in Russia and America and initiated a climate of suspicion in both. Upon checking into their Moscow hotel room, the *Candid Camera* crew discovered nine hidden microphones, and when they returned to the US with their 90,000 feet of 'tourist' film they discovered that most of the footage had been destroyed or 'fogged at ten second intervals': 'Apparently, the Russian officials, knowing full well of our activities, had attempted to destroy all the film, perhaps as it was passed through the baggage service' (ibid.: 133–44).

In the aftermath of the two world wars, the expansion of government surveillance powers that signalled the beginning of the Cold War – not unlike what we have witnessed post-9/11 – began to preoccupy the popular imagination. In 1949 George Orwell published *1984* and effectively captured the burgeoning surveillance-anxiety spreading throughout the Western world: 'Big Brother' was always watching. How much actual surveillance was taking place is impossible to measure, in part because such monitoring was hidden and secret, and needed to remain so to be effective. The nature of surveillance changed not only with the development of electronic surveillance technologies that were making it more insidious as they became more portable, discreet and accurate, but also due to the fact that average citizens had become extensions of government surveillance systems. The Cold War created a version of Jeremy Bentham's panopticon on a national, if not international, scale: the feeling that no matter where one went or what one did one was being watched, and the belief that one was under constant scrutiny – irrespective of fact – became a means of disciplining and shaping social behaviour (Bentham, 1995; Foucault, 1977).[4] In the words of two famous sociologists of the 1950s, American society was becoming a 'total institution', and as a result Americans were becoming increasingly 'other-directed' (Goffman, 1959; Riesman, 1969).[5] The figurative sense of a post-war phrase like 'flying under the radar' was erased by an ominous literalism, and the concept of Neighbourhood Watch, prior to its official institution as a community programme in the 1970s, generated feelings of paranoia and mistrust rather than comfort.

Whether or not actual surveillance ever reached the extreme levels represented culturally (in films, novels and news reports, or by conspiracy theorists) is debatable; either way *Candid Camera* still functioned as a vehicle to appease fears of being monitored. If post-war America had not in fact become a surveillance society in an absolute sense, to all intents and purposes it certainly appeared and acted like one. Looking back on the period, Funt self-consciously acknowledges the social and political context in which *Candid Microphone* first appeared:

> In those days, the late forties, the public was fascinated by the idea of recording equipment that was so small it could be hidden. Remember, this was the beginning of the Cold War and fears of the Russians spying on the U.S. were constantly on people's minds. Publicity for 'Candid Microphone' always mentioned how the microphone was hidden. I would occasionally get contacted by agents from foreign countries who wanted tips on improving their surveillance operations.
>
> (Funt, 1994: 35)

Indeed, the same recording technologies used in the entertainment industries of film and television were those used for espionage and surveillance. *Candid Camera* was the first cultural product to exploit this connection by interweaving intrusive voyeurism and amusement.

Even the friendly warning Funt offered viewers at the end of each *Candid Camera* episode could just as easily have been a press release issued by the US State Department at the onset of the Cold War: 'Don't be surprised if sometime, some-where, someplace when you least expect it, someone comes up to you and says, "Smile! You're on *Candid Camera*".' Funt's light-hearted caveat becomes threaten-ingly Kafkaesque when read in the context of post-war surveillance. Viewers are told to expect surveillance anywhere, potentially everywhere. The caveat's repeti-tion of 'some', meaning unspecified or unknown, points to the underlying Cold War fears of invisible, omnipresent, scrutinising authority ('sometime', 'some-where', 'someplace', 'someone'). Accordingly, it is not surprising to find confrontations with authority among the most successful and popular *Candid Camera* skit themes. And yet these same skits often reveal the most negative human character trait exhibited during the Cold War period: 'The worst thing I see is how easily people can be led by any kind of authority figure, or even the most minimal signs of authority' (ibid.: 223).

A classic example of such subservient acquiescence in the face of arbitrary authority (and there are multiple variants of it) is the 1965 skit where either a bill-board sign or a uniformed police officer or a construction worker with a hard hat informs motorists that the state of Delaware is closed for the day. Rather than chal-lenging the logic that a state can be closed because it is too crowded, motorists unflinchingly accept the explanation, as well as the suggestion to try New Jersey. Many *Candid Camera* set-ups illustrate the persuasive force behind the most superfi-cial signifiers of authority, such as uniforms, official-looking signs and formal tones of voice. Another popular skit that confirms the extent to which individuals in Cold War society were unquestioningly 'other-directed' involved placing in public settings (hotel lobbies, shoe stores) signs that read 'Please Walk Only on the Black Squares' or, alternatively, 'Please Walk Only on the White Squares'. In either case, the camera records individuals struggling to navigate their way across black-and-white-tile floors, stepping on the one colour and desperately trying to avoid touching the other – all of this effort in spite of the fact that there is no visibly logical reason to do so beyond the directive on the sign.

During these years of intensified national security Americans became cautious interpreters of everyday signs, and conformity soon became vested with authority. In what is perhaps one of the funniest and also one of the most disturbing *Candid Camera* skits, individual elevator passengers are seen changing direction to face in the same direction as all the other passengers. The set-up for 'Rear Facing' (1962) involves a group of elevator riders (*Candid Camera* staff) all facing unconventionally towards the back of the elevator. In some scenes, new passengers enter the elevator and immediately turn around to go along with the crowd of backward-facing riders already inside. In others, candid subjects get into the elevator first and face forward until the elevator fills up with more and more backward-facing riders. This sketch, more than any other, illustrates the power of Cold War 'other-directed' conformity. The desire not to deviate or appear deviant is epitomised when a young man with a hat enters the elevator. For no apparent reason all of the other passengers keep changing direction simultaneously, and rather than be left out the young man repeatedly turns with the group. At one point all of the men in the elevator remove their hats and the young man follows their lead. Soon after, they all put their hats back on, and so too does the candid subject. More than just exemplifying unconscious herd mentality, this skit reveals the conscious effort that Cold War individuals are forced to put into appearing 'normal' in public. Throughout this skit, the young boy checks to see if all the passengers turn, and he keeps looking side to side so as not to be left out of the next shift in direction. This entire encounter is filmed from a fixed camera set at eye level so viewers see the scene from an eyewitness's perspective. Amidst the comedy and embedded in the skit as a subtext is an ideological warning for implicated viewers to resist forms of authority that produce dehumanising conformity.

Cultural resistance to surveillance

Among Funt's list of the most common reactions individuals experience after being caught on *Candid Camera* (disbelief, anger, shock, disappointment, nonchalance), relief is perhaps the most significant in a context of Cold War anxieties (Funt, 1994: 201–2). Funt maintains that the funniest moment of any *Candid Camera* skit is the 'reveal', the instant when candid subjects are told they have just been recorded and shown the position of the hidden camera.[6] However, the accompanying close-up reaction shot of nervous laughter, relief, embarrassment, even outrage, disguises an extremely complex set of cultural anxieties. In that moment, issues of invasion of privacy, covert surveillance, social acceptance/alienation and manipulative authority all circulate – the very concerns heightened by Cold War politics, and exploited and alleviated by the *Candid Camera* format. Over the years Funt has made a concerted effort to ensure that skits are not exploitative or offensive. To redress early accusations that the concept of *Candid Camera* was sadistic and unethical (concerns which still circulate around Reality TV today), he decided only to depict individuals in situations where they were called upon to act heroically (ibid.: 54). As a result, most of the show's set-ups simultaneously exploit Cold War surveillance strategies and endorse American ideals such as sportsmanship, perseverance, ingenuity, grace and pluck – the very qualities needed to see Americans through the Cold War.

Ideologically speaking, *Candid Camera* was much more than just a reality-based show about ordinary people; it addressed the predominant anxieties of the first generation of television watchers and appeased their fears by enacting traditional American values in crudely recorded vignettes composed as short postmodern morality plays. The post-war nuclear threat, and the electronic surveillance that was developed to monitor this threat, dehumanised and alienated individuals during the Cold War period. Funt's show's celebration of positive human characteristics arguably served in some ways to counterbalance these negative social forces and rehumanise social relations.

Besides turning average Americans – those who were minding their own business (self-surveillance) and discreetly minding their neighbours' (civic duty) – into celebrated and heroic social actors, *Candid Camera* gave the surveilled an opportunity to 'answer back' to their surveillers through the 'release', a legal document granting individuals the authority to decide whether or not to allow candid recordings of themselves to be aired publicly. Without signed permission *Candid Camera* guaranteed that such recordings would be either permanently erased or destroyed. This document effectively reversed the traditional power dynamic associated with hidden surveillance. Through the release, recorded individuals were able figuratively to return the gaze of the hidden camera: the surveiller could secretly obtain audio and visual recordings, but the surveillee remained in control of how and for what purposes the recordings were used. According to the *Candid Camera* website, 99 per cent of all candid subjects enthusiastically sign the release. Ironically, the majority of outraged individuals who refuse to sign releases are those the hidden cameras catch in compromising situations: 'criminals on the lam, deserting husbands escaping alimony payments, people caught stealing or having an extramarital affair' (cited in Zimbardo, 1985: 47). Arguably, these absented, more sensational kinds of exchange later went on to become the subject matter of some of Reality TV's most contentious programmes – such as the US show *Cheaters* (1998–), which exposes unfaithful partners during the act of infidelity – and which in no small part have contributed to the popular demonisation of Reality TV as exploitative and morally bankrupt.

In order to broadcast recorded scenes, every 'victim' of *Candid Camera*'s hidden surveillance is required by law to sign a release that reads:

> I acknowledge that you have photographed me without my prior knowledge and without any preparation, coaching, or rehearsal. If this film is used, I will receive the sum of $50, in exchange for my irrevocable consent to use the silent and/or sound motion pictures in any way you see fit in perpetuity throughout the world, including use on television. I also agree that you may edit such motion pictures in any way you think

proper without obtaining any further consent from me or making any additional payment to me.

(Funt, 1994: 159)

I use the word 'victim' ironically here to signal how *Candid Camera* effectively transformed feelings of helpless victimisation into willing participation through the comic moment of revelation and the signing of the release. Although the language of the release appears to give Funt and his associates *carte blanche* in the future use of hidden recordings – and it does – each person is first given the choice to sign or not to sign. Defenceless candid 'captures' are thereby converted into 'knowledgeable agents' capable of resisting and negotiating the terms of their own surveillance (Giddens, 1981: 172). More important than the actual wording of the release is the reassertion of control that it represents for individuals. The release acknowledges the invasion of privacy and guards against its indiscriminate use without authorised permission. The release also converts invasive surveillance into a commercial commodity exchange where individuals can choose whether or not to sell their recorded surveillance for profit. Surveillance becomes a business transaction that prefigures the more pernicious late-capitalist practices of information collection and abuse characteristic of corporate 'marketing' in the age of accessible personal data.

In this respect, *Candid Camera* offered those living in constant fear of surveillance a symbolic form of cultural resistance; it also provided unintended advocacy and comfort to viewers and participants alike because it created an arena in which surveillance power dynamics were for once in favour of the average citizen. The show cleverly softened its alignment with actual surveillance practices by using a name that intentionally exudes light-heartedness through the alliterated first consonant and vowels sounds in the words 'candid' and 'camera', as well as through the syllabic balance between the two words – camera is phonetically foreshortened and pronounced with two instead of three syllables. As a result, the show's lyrical and easy-to-remember title works from both a marketing and an ideological perspective. Even the choice of the word 'candid' eases the threat associated with covert surveillance. Meaning at once 'frank, sincere, fair and impartial', as well as, when associated with the word 'camera', to take a photograph without someone's knowledge, 'candid' does not carry the pernicious undertones that synonyms like 'hidden' and 'unseen' do. Nor does it convey the same cold and threatening connotations as something like the synonymous title *Covert Surveillance Device* would have done.

Even the lyrics to the show's up-beat theme song work to alleviate surveillance-anxiety at the same time as they underscore many of the embedded concepts at work in the production of hidden camera sketches:

42

When you least expect it,
You're elected.
You're the star today.
Smile! You're on *Candid Camera.*
With a hocus-pocus,
You're in focus.
It's your lucky day.
Smile! You're on *Candid Camera.*

Rhyme scheme aside, the overarching message of this jingle is that to be under surveillance is fun ('Smile!') and fortunate ('your lucky day'). The song represents the core motifs embodied in *Candid Camera*'s mission as the first Reality TV programme, which clearly prefigure the form's textual and ideological concerns today: random democratic selection ('least expect it' and 'elected'), open and instant access to celebrity status ('You're a star today'), deceptive authority and transformation ('hocus-pocus'), and surveillance ('in focus').[7]

Consequently, one of the dangers of alleviating surveillance-anxiety through humour is that it has the potential to turn very serious issues such as invasion of privacy and national security into laughing matters. That *Candid Camera* may have put people too much at ease during the intense Cold War years is best illustrated by a hijacking incident Allen Funt experienced while flying out of Newark to Miami in 1969. In the midst of a violent skyjacking in which the airplane was rerouted, quite appropriately, to Cuba, one woman recognised Funt as a passenger and declared, 'Ladies and gentlemen, I'm pleased to tell you this is not a skyjacking. This joker is Allen Funt, and we're all on "Candid Camera"'. According to Funt,

> The plane went absolutely crazy. People began cheering and stamping their feet – with relief, really. The commotion went on for so long and was so loud that the skyjacker stuck his head out of the cabin. This only made matters worse because 150 people gave him a big round of applause.
>
> (Funt, 1994: 10)

Funt's celebrity status and the popularity of *Candid Camera* momentarily diffused a dangerous situation, but in the process made it even more life-threatening. Even after the plane landed in Cuba and Cuban soldiers, police officers and government officials stormed the plane and arrested the hijackers, passengers still thought they were part of a hidden-camera gag (ibid.: 11).

In another unsettling incident, but where the show's status saved the day this time, a teenage girl used the *Candid Camera* tagline to chase away two menacing-looking individuals who approached her in a New York City subway car in 1961.

To relieve the situation all she did was exclaim, 'Smile, boys, you're on *Candid Camera*', and the two men fled instantly. In this case the widely recognised words of the *Candid Camera* 'reveal' called forth the fear of surveillance and the two would-be assaulters ran for cover (ibid.: 100). The contexts and specific circumstances of each of these confrontations foreground the appreciable popularity of *Candid Camera* at the height of the Cold War and also exhibit the underlying surveillance-anxiety that accounted, in part, for its mass appeal. Toilet stalls around the world similarly attest to this cultural saturation. Funt estimates that 'Smile! You're on *Candid Camera*' appears in more public toilets worldwide than any other piece of graffiti (ibid.: 99). The self-conscious adjustment in behaviour that such a suggestion can create is indicative of both the show's cultural currency and the pervasive paranoia that supplies it with continued socio-cultural valences. This omnipresence in popular culture still allows convenience-store owners and public institutions where the threat of criminal activity is high to forego installing actual hidden cameras. A sign that reads 'Smile! You may be on *Candid Camera*' may be all the surveillance technology needed to curb most illegal activity (ibid.).

An instance of *Candid Camera*'s cultural pervasiveness can even be found in the 1977 James Bond film *The Spy Who Loved Me* (dir. Gilbert, 1977, US), which references the television programme in an exchange of dialogue between 007 and his Russian counterpart Major Anya Amasova (a.k.a. Triple-X). The allusion occurs as the two Cold War adversaries, temporarily working together, stealthily creep around shipping billionaire/villain Karl Stromberg's floating sea station. Once Bond discovers that eye-in-the-sky cameras are tracking their every move, he says to Triple-X, 'Don't look up, you're on *Candid Camera*'. Ian Fleming's Bond character (the protagonist of twelve best-selling novels from the 1950s and 1960s), like *Candid Camera*, is a product of Cold War popular culture – a secret agent no less. It is therefore appropriate that the screenplay should reference Funt's show in a film where two of the principal Cold War powers most deeply involved in surveillance are being threatened with nuclear attack. *The Spy Who Loved Me* formally acknowledges *Candid Camera* as a cultural benchmark in the world of surveillance, and implicitly declares that when it comes to hidden camera work 'Nobody Does It Better' than Allen Funt.

All the world's a stage

During the Cold War years, *Candid Camera* moved from network to network to network, went into syndication and movie theatres, experienced fluctuations in its ratings, was picked up and dropped and subsequently picked up again. Yet the programme never disappeared, and it is currently still in production for cable networks. However, as suggested, even before *Candid Camera* reached television, Cold War politics had already occasioned the widespread internalisation of social surveillance. Daily life had become a series of complex performances, self-scripted and self-surveilled, a desperate attempt to keep up appearances, and *Candid Camera* marketed and celebrated these performances through humorous recontextualisation. This is one of the reasons why public settings are so important for hidden-camera set-ups; they are always already sites of heightened surveillance by virtue of their publicness. The very locations *Candid Camera* selected for its skits often were already or soon would be sites of intensive surveillance, whether human or electronic. Studies of surveillance since the early 1990s give the general (and false) impression that covert monitoring has only recently expanded to include virtually every space we encounter in everyday life:

> A person can be under video surveillance at work, on the street, in a car, anywhere he or she goes. Retail stores, banks, airports, parking lots, shopping centers, and drive-up windows all have video cameras. The lenses inside cars or vans can be disguised as reflectors or mirrors or as specially made periscopes that look like air vents. People can even be under video surveillance in their homes and offices and not know it.
>
> (Shannon, 1992: 57)

This description, incidentally, references the same sites Funt and his associates regularly chose for their set-ups, and *Candid Camera* episodes from the 1950s and 1960s prove that ubiquitous surveillance was nothing new; nor was the accompanying sense of paranoia. Because each skit incorporates actual covert surveillance to generate humour, every episode provides a potential critique of existing Cold War society. Many of the most successful gags, however, also thematise acts of surveillance and incorporate into their scenes symbols and images associated with surveilling itself.

Recognising the power of public settings to alter behaviour, Funt often set up his cameras to catch candid subjects in places like restaurants, banks, hospitals, airports, parks, buses, bowling alleys, subway cars and city streets. By far the most popular setting for *Candid Camera* skits is diners — places where individuals cannot help but watch each other. The close proximity of adjacent tables and counter stools, as well as the prevalence of mirrors scattered throughout such establishments, encourages surreptitious and indirect surveillance. Because of their design, well-lit diners put intimate eating and drinking habits on display for everyone to see, and in these locales individuals often betray their internalisation of surveillance. Into these panoptical environments place something that draws people's attention, like Buster Keaton dropping his watch 'accidentally' into his soup, spoons that melt when used to stir hot coffee, ridiculously small meal portions, amplified sounds of eating and drinking, or hands that reach out from coat racks to steal food, and watch how patrons respond by trying not to respond.

The public nature of these settings makes people self-conscious about staring at others, let alone laughing at them. Candid subjects look around nonchalantly to see if anyone else has witnessed what they have, or to see if they are being watched. Most of the humour of these sketches derives from the attempts of people who are confronted with bizarre situations to act like nothing has happened. The desire not to make a scene or become part of one is as much a symptom of Cold War surveillance-anxiety as it is of polite society. Over and over again, candid subjects reveal that they would prefer to remain unnoticed rather than risk being labelled abnormal or 'un-American'.

On the other hand, 'Talking Mailbox' (1954) shows what happens when individuals do draw attention to the peculiar situations they experience. The scene begins with a man walking along a city sidewalk, and as he passes a shoebox-sized mounted mailbox the mailbox addresses him (evidently, the authority symbolised in the government mailbox is powerful enough to engage the passer-by in a conversation). The mailbox asks whether or not the candid subject has seen the mailman because it needs to be emptied. The subject goes so far as to hold open the mail slot so that the mailbox can look around. Throughout this skit the candid subject is constantly looking to see if anyone else is watching him. Finally someone walks by, and the candid subject calls the man over. He tries to show him the talking mailbox, but now the mailbox refuses to respond. As the second man quickly moves away from the candid subject he stares suspiciously over his shoulder at this seemingly delusional individual. Lurking beneath the comedy of this skit is a frighteningly uncritical acceptance of government surveillance capabilities (to place a person in a tiny mailbox) and a warning about the consequences of public deviance.

Candid Camera successfully played off public fears of surveillance as well as all the other accompanying emotional responses to Cold War tensions. In the era of 'the Bomb' individuals felt vulnerable and powerless, completely at the mercy of machines designed for destruction. Many *Candid Camera* skits pit humans against malfunctioning machines, and, while this is nothing new as a source of comedy, these scenarios take on ominous significance in the Cold War era. Skits where remote-controlled typewriters lose their cartridges when typists try to push them back, where birthday-cake assembly lines keep running and cannot be stopped, and where vending machines pull back the food they have just dispensed all seem like innocent fun. However, the ideological subtext of *Candid Camera* gags where machines cannot be controlled or shut off taps into the sense of helplessness that insinuates itself into Cold War society: a helplessness resulting from the knowledge that it only takes one mechanical malfunction to initiate nuclear holocaust.

Arguably, most skits depict subjects who either are looking at something/ someone or are themselves the object of another's gaze. However, some skits stand out as being blatantly 'surveillance-themed' (Marx, 1996: 212). The 'Magic Mirrors' skit shows women seated before mirrors trying on assorted wigs and applying make-up: a highly self-reflexive image of self-surveillance. Suddenly a *Candid Camera* crew member breaks the mirror from behind, leaving the reflective surface irreparably cracked. Shocked at this unexpected event, the women look around immediately to see if anyone is watching. Because of the camera position – an over-the-shoulder shot focused on the mirror – the skit not only produces laughter, but also works on a metacritical level as a representation of symbolic resistance. As the mirror shatters, so too does the vehicle used to frame the act of surveillance, and viewers can no longer see the reacting faces of the candid subjects. In a slightly different manner, the skit where a candid actor looks over the shoulder of unsuspecting individuals reading newspapers on park benches, in buses or in the subway creates actual opportunities to resist surveillance. Pretending not to, but at the same time making it blatantly obvious that they *are* reading over the shoulder of the candid subjects, the candid actors scrutinise what the candid subjects are reading. This skit tests just how accommodating people are willing to be when subjected to an overt form of surveillance as well as whether or not they have something to hide.

Every hidden camera skit that appeared on *Candid Camera* betrayed its ideological indebtedness to the practices of Cold War surveillance, either through its basic format or through its subject matter. Employing Cold War surveillance tactics to capture its subjects, *Candid Camera* tapped into the rich paranoia of American panopticonism. Perhaps the best example of a skit that thematically and formally exploits the codes of surveillance and yet simultaneously offers a self-referential critique of its own practices is 'Talking Automatic Photo Booth'. In this skit, a young man steps into the 'privacy' of a photo booth, and immediately an authoritative, albeit deadpan, voice materialises out of nowhere issuing directions: 'Please follow these instructions exactly. Wait for the buzzer before each picture is taken. Do not leave the booth while the lights are still working. Sit straight and look into the frame.' The candid subject strikes a series of dramatic poses as the voice prompts him: 'Pose. Next pose. Pose again.' The voice suddenly stops warning the patron to pose and some of the subsequent picture flashes catch the candid subject off guard and unposed. Soon thereafter, the booth voice announces, 'Owing to a mechanical malfunction, your pictures have been ruined. Please pose for another sequence.' The posing starts again, and then the patron says aloud, 'I hope this batch don't [*sic*] get ruined', to which the booth voice magically answers, 'So do I'. The scene ends with the booth voice saying seductively, 'If you give me a smile, I'll give you a nice surprise', and from the camera's fixed position a stream of water sprays into the patron's grinning face. The water deliberately signals that this has all been an elaborate practical joke, but not before the candid subject has been exposed both consciously and unconsciously to all the elements associated with surveillance-anxiety: invisible authority, photographic observation, posed performance and humiliating vulnerability.

The apparent thrill of 'voyeurism' offered here has often been used to describe the appeal of many contemporary forms of Reality TV (particularly, for example, at the level of press response). In this respect, it is also used to signal the perceivably 'distasteful', unethical and morally dubious pleasures of such fare. Given the highly knowing, self-reflexive and performative scenarios of contemporary Reality shows (e.g. *Big Brother*) (Corner, 2002) and the fact that conceptions of 'voyeurism' traditionally indicated a situation in which the 'voyeur' was unseen (and hence the subjects were unaware they were being observed) (Mulvey, 1975), the exact applicability of the concept here has been questioned (see, for example, Roscoe, 2001). However, in *Candid Camera* a key element of the appeal of the programme is arguably precisely the 'unseen', unacknowledged vantage point offered to the viewer (and the relations of power between viewer and subject that this may imply). Yet it is clear that *Candid Camera* – like many later Reality TV programmes – also exploits the rising anticipation of something about to happen which pivots on the unguarded, unscripted and 'intimate' experiences of other 'ordinary' people. Nevertheless, the psychology behind the continued popularity and recent explosion of Reality TV programming in the late twentieth and early twenty-first centuries, cannot be explained entirely by the voyeuristic appeal of spying/eavesdropping on other people. Nor can the materialist trappings of potential stardom wholly account for the sustained high ratings and proliferation of new Reality TV series that mark the commercial success of the phenomenon. Instead, to understand Reality TV one needs to look at the ways in which the concept of reality itself has been challenged and relativised in the age of technological reproduction.

Documenting the real

Nothing provokes existential crisis quite like the inability to distinguish the real from the non-real or the manufactured. The difficulty of establishing unqualified difference is a thematic staple of modern science fiction writers, from Philip K. Dick (1968) to William Gibson (1984). It is a mistake, however, to assume that the technologies that engender such confusion are the exclusive property of futuristic worlds. Social and cultural critics have been issuing warnings about the dehumanising potential of new technologies to blur the boundaries between the real and the artificial since the dawn of the Industrial Revolution. In the twentieth century alone the concept of realism underwent more renegotiations than in all the previous centuries of human development combined. Walter Benjamin (1985), for instance, famously labelled the twentieth century the 'age of mechanical reproduction' and lamented the subsequent loss of aura – his complexly metaphysical term for authenticity. The postmodern perspective suggests that reproducibility has quite literally spawned sameness – the very codification and modelling characteristic of Jean Baudrillard's (1983) assessment of the contemporary lifeworld as a simulacrum completely devoid of the 'real' as an antecedent. One consequence of this 'loss of aura' and the prolific development of technologies capable of reproducing the 'real', besides the creation of hyperreality, is the fetishisation of authenticity and an appreciation in the cultural currency of terms like 'truth', 'reality', 'genuine' and 'actual'. This argument suggests that the destabilisation of any concept of reality caused by new reproduction technologies has resulted in simulation-anxiety and a felt need to reassert the existence of the 'real' as an accessible domain of experience. As Jon Dovey explains, the 'disappearance of reality' debate has been offered as one of the key social, cultural (and technological) factors influencing the contemporary proliferation of Reality TV (2000: 88–91). From this point of view, 'Reality TV is the ultimate expression of the simulacrum in which the insistence upon realism is in direct proportion to the disappearance and irrelevance of any referential value' (ibid.: 83).

One of the principal ways in which Reality TV programmes attempt to create meaning is through the illusion of transparency: the attempt to capture life 'as it happens', unedited and unmediated (Barsam, 1976; Braudy and Mast, 1999; Nichols, 1991; Renov, 1993; Winston, 1995). Even though these programmes are of course highly edited and constructed works, they still give the impression of being more 'real' than the other TV programming with which they compete in the ratings. In the case of *Candid Camera*, the word 'candid' – as I have noted earlier (p. 42) – announces its commitment to objective and unqualified representation. In its attempt to capture life in unguarded moments, *Candid Camera* effectively mobilises the aesthetic codes of the documentary filmmaking tradition – the origins of which date back to and are inseparable from the emergence of cinema itself (Barnouw, 1974; Barsam, 1992; Jacobs, 1979) and which are now used extensively in a range of popular factual programming.[8]

A form of simulation-anxiety works its way into every *Candid Camera* skit, where something extraordinary occurs and candid subjects find themselves questioning the reality of the situation. In addition, two skits in particular stand out for the ways in which they overtly thematise issues of simulation-anxiety. The first represents mechanical reproduction gone haywire. In this skit a frustrated candid subject cannot turn off a duplicating machine that keeps on running, reproducing the same document over and over again. One allegorical subtext of this skit is the powerlessness of humanity when confronting the endless production of simulated sameness. By the end of the skit the original document that was being duplicated is buried somewhere beneath and made indistinguishable from all of its copies. In the second skit an invisible sheet of glass is being carried across a city pavement, i.e. sidewalk, presenting an obstacle to anyone walking. Each passer-by tries to continue on his or her way by going around the two men who are miming the effort needed to carry such a large pane of glass. As someone tries to walk around them on the pavement the workers lurch in that direction with their invisible burden and stop the person in their tracks. One woman even attempts to walk underneath the absent glass. Passers-by are fooled because they accept the codes of the real exhibited by the workers who are simulating carrying a large piece of glass. When the simulated signs of the real can bring about the same behaviour as the actual signs the boundary between simulation and reality implodes, leaving the one indistinguishable from the other. Within select skits *Candid Camera* exploits this blurring of the real, but it purposefully employs the poetics of the real in its presentation of hidden-camera gags to reassert and maintain a distinct domain of the authentic.

Because of its aesthetic commitments to authenticity, *Candid Camera* provided a bulwark against the cinematic overproduction that was starting to make its way into television production at this time. *Candid Camera* seemed more real in part because of the hidden camera – an element that even to this day greatly distinguishes types and experiences of Reality TV. In most reality programmes, like *Survivor* (2000–), *The Lofters* (2000–), *The Mole* (2001–) and *Temptation Island* (2001–), the camera remains part of the *mise-en-scène*, constantly reminding participants that they are being surveilled by millions of viewers and putting them on their strategic guard. One of the biggest criticisms of the recent Reality TV craze is that there is actually nothing 'real' about programmes such as *Survivor* where camera crews openly move around with the action and where participants directly address the camera in routine asides. In contrast, *Candid Camera* has always been about recording the 'unguarded moment' – the 'average' person responding to situations, not consciously 'performing' in them. The key difference is that the show's participants become stars for thirty seconds and are not calculating their endorsement careers before the recording even begins. Now, it would be a mistake to assume from this that *Candid Camera* represents a 'purer' form of Reality TV – although in many ways I think it does – especially when the expectation of covert surveillance so preoccupied the thoughts and patterns of behaviour of most Americans throughout the Cold War period. I would argue that the limited scope of the hidden camera, the raw production values and the historical novelty of the reality-based concept all contribute to the show's more genuine 'sense of the real', however paradoxical this last description may seem.

Today *Candid Camera* is taught in university and college psychology courses because of the unscripted insights into human behaviour and social relationships that its gags provide.[9] Allen Funt has also used copies of old skits as a form of laughter therapy for individuals suffering pain caused by illness or accident.[10] The influence of *Candid Camera*, however, extends beyond these celebrated medicinal, educational and psychological applications, and involves a much more profound contribution to society and culture, not only in America, but worldwide. *Candid*

Camera's cultural authority lies in its ability to help redefine the 'real' in an era of increased material capitalism and technological reproduction and alleviate the paranoid fears accompanying routine, covert surveillance. Broadly speaking, the history of *Candid Camera* is the history of Cold War tensions and the history of late-capitalist technologies of reproduction, because of the ways each helped to shape the show's format and create the conditions for its popular reception. A critical look at the structure and thematic subtexts of various *Candid Camera* skits reveals how they simultaneously exploit surveillance- and simulation-anxieties and serve as vehicles of symbolic resistance and psycho-social comfort. In the end, any judicious account of the meteoric rise of Reality TV as a cultural phenomenon must acknowledge the aesthetic precedent set by *Candid Camera* and consider the ways in which successor programmes share in its deep-seated ideological allegiances.

Notes

1   ABC (August 1948–December 1948), NBC (May 1949–August 1949), CBS (September 1949–September 1950), ABC (August 1951–May 1952), NBC (June 1953–August 1953), CBS (October 1960–September 1967), syndication (1974–8), CBS (May 1990–August 1990), syndication (1990–2), CBS (1996–2000), PAX (2001–).

2   All *Candid Camera* skits discussed in this essay are from Candid Camera's *All-Time Funniest Moments: Parts I and II* (1993). Variant versions of these skits appear in *The Best of* Candid Camera (1985) and *The Best of* Candid Camera:*Volume 2* (1986).

3   The Signal Corps was, and continues to be, the army branch in charge of all military communications and the electronics systems used to send and receive information. Ironically, the other infamous surveiller who also served in the Army Signal Corps during the war (before he was discharged in 1945 for being a communist), and who was later executed for passing on atomic information to the Soviets, was Julius Rosenberg.

4   See also Chapter 3, which also invokes the panopticon as a parallel to the subsequent development of CCTV.

5   David Riesman defines 'other-directed' as an internalised behaviour that is shaped by signals received from one's peers: 'What is common to all the other-directed people is that their contemporaries are the source of direction of the individual – either those known to him or those with whom he is indirectly acquainted, through friends and through the mass media' (Riesman, 1969: 34–8). Riesman also cites a *Candid Microphone* skit in his book to illustrate a point about attitudes towards recreational escapism, and he reputedly called Allen Funt the 'second-most ingenious sociologist in America' (cited in Zimbardo, 1985: 44).

6   Interestingly, this turn of phrase – 'the reveal' – has also been adopted by the strand of Reality TV known as 'makeover TV' to describe the climactic moment when the subjects or their friends and family finally get to see their new image/living room/garden, suggesting that the same spirit of (and pleasure in) revelation is at stake (see Chapter 8).

7 Little Richard's recent version (2002) of the *Candid Camera* theme song ironically includes the additional line: 'Shut up, you're on *Candid Camera*.'

8 Among these characteristic codes that I would include within what I have termed the poetics of the real and which help *Candid Camera* generate the location realism of covert surveillance for practical and aesthetics purposes are basic eye-level, straight-on camera angles; location shooting where lighting is uneven and constantly changing; lack of multiple camera positions and the absence of intentional seamless continuity editing; agitated and unsteady camera movements such as trembling pans, staccato tilts and non-fluid zooming – all made even more perceptible by periodic losses of focus; grainy, low-grade film stock; and smeared lens/blurred images (Grant and Sloniowski, 1998).

9 In 1993 Funt and Dr Philip Zimbardo, who was then head of psychology at Stanford, published a textbook and instructional video entitled *Candid Camera Classics in Introductory and Social Psychology*.

10 Officially, Funt began his non-profit Laughter Therapy programme in 1982. It involves sending tapes of *Candid Camera* skits to those in pain in an attempt to alleviate their suffering through the healing/distracting powers of laughter.

References

Barnouw, Erik (1974) *Documentary: A History of Nonfiction Film*, New York: Oxford University Press.

Barsam, Richard Meran (ed.) (1976) *Nonfiction Film Theory and Criticism*, New York: E. P. Dutton.

Barsam, Richard Meran (1992) *Nonfiction Film: A Critical History* (revised edition), Bloomington, IN: Indiana University Press.

Baudrillard, Jean (1983) *Simulations*, trans. P. Foss, P. Patton and P. Beitchman, New York: Semiotext(e).

Benjamin, Walter (1985) 'The Work of Art in the Age of Mechanical Reproduction', in Hannah Arendt (ed.) *Illuminations*, trans. Harry Zohn, New York: Schocken; first published in 1934.

Bentham, Jeremy (1995) *The Panopticon Writings*, ed. Miran Bozovic, London: Verso; first published in 1791.

Boal, Augusto (1985) *Theatre of the Oppressed*, trans. Charles A. McBride and Maria-Odilia Leal McBride, New York: Theatre Corporations Group.

Braudy, Leo and Gerald Mast (eds) (1999) *Film Theory and Criticism* (fifth edition), New York: Oxford University Press.

Candid Camera (2003) Merged Media; available at http://www.candidcamera.com/ (accessed 1 April 2003).

Corner, John (2002) 'Performing the Real: Documentary Diversions', *Television and New Media* 3(3): 255–69.

Dick, Philip K. (1968) *Do Androids Dream of Electric Sheep?*, New York: Ballantine.

Dovey, Jon (2000) *Freakshow*, London: Pluto Press.

Foucault, Michel (1977) *Discipline and Punish: The Birth of the Prison*, trans. A. M. Sheridan, New York: Pantheon.

Funt, Allen, with Philip Reed (1994) *Candidly, Allen Funt: A Million Smiles Later*, New York: Barricade.

Gibson, William (1984) *Neuromancer*, New York: Berkley.

Giddens, Anthony (1981) *A Contemporary Critique of Historical Materialism: Power, Property and the State*, vol. 1. Berkeley, CA: University of California Press.

Goffman, Erving (1959) *Asylums*, Garden City, NY: Doubleday.

Grant, Barry Keith and Jeannette Sloniowski (1998) *Documenting the Documentary: Close Readings of Documentary Film and Video*, Detroit, MI: Wayne State University Press.

Harbutt, Fraser J. (2002) *The Cold War Era*, Oxford: Blackwell.

Horkheimer, Max and Theodor W. Adorno (1991) *Dialectic of Enlightenment*, trans. John Cumming, New York: Continuum; first published in 1944.

Jacobs, Lewis (ed.) (1979) *The Documentary Tradition* (second edition), New York: Norton.

Marx, Gary T. (1996) 'Electric Eye in the Sky: Some Reflections on the New Surveillance and Popular Culture', in David Lyons and Elia Zureik (eds) *Computers, Surveillance, and Privacy*, Minneapolis: University of Minnesota Press.

Mulvey, Laura (1975) 'Visual Pleasure and Narrative Cinema', *Screen* 16(3), Autumn: 4–19.

Nichols, Bill (1991) *Representing Reality: Issues and Concepts in Documentary*, Bloomington, IN: Indiana University Press.

Renov, Michael (ed.) (1993) *Theorizing Documentary*, New York: Routledge.

Riesman, David, with Nathan Glazer and Reuel Denney (1969) *The Lonely Crowd: A Study in the Changing American Character*, New Haven, CT: Yale University Press; first published in 1950.

Roscoe, Jane (2001) 'Big Brother Australia: Performing the "Real" Twenty-four-seven', *International Journal of Cultural Studies* 4(4): 473–88.

Shannon, M. L. (1992) *Don't Bug Me: The Latest High-Tech Spy Methods*, Boulder, CO: Paladin.

Whitfield, Stephen J. (1996) *The Culture of the Cold War* (second edition), Baltimore, MD: Johns Hopkins University Press.

Winston, Brian (1995) *Claiming the Real: The Documentary Film Revisited*, London: British Film Institute.

Zimbardo, Philip G. (1985) 'Laugh Where We Must, Be Candid Where We Can', *Psychology Today* 19(6): 42–7.

Filmography

The Best of Candid Camera (video cassette) (Allen Funt Productions, Stamford, CT: Vestron, 1985).

The Best of Candid Camera: *Volume 2* (video cassette) (Allen Funt Productions, Stamford, CT: Vestron, 1986).

Candid Camera's *All-Time Funniest Moments: Parts I and II* (video cassette) (Allen Funt Productions, Firestone, 1993).

The Spy Who Loved Me (1977, US), dir. Lewis Gilbert.

2

FROM OZZIE NELSON
TO OZZY OSBOURNE[1]

The genesis and development of the
Reality (star) sitcom

Jennifer Gillan

Most commentators agree that *The Osbournes* (MTV, 2002–, US), which premiered in the United States on 5 March 2002, marks a significant milestone in the development of Reality Television. Yet there is still dissent over how to categorise the programme. It has been called a 'situation reality show', a 'reali-com' (Shales, 2002), a 'docusoap' (Robinson, 2002: 47), 'the first ever situation reality series'[2] (Peyser, 2002: 64) and, by MTV, the 'television-family-concept-redefining reality series' (Gold, 2002: back cover). This chapter adopts the term 'reality star sitcom' as it captures the new sub-genre's combination of Reality TV surveillance filming and fast-paced editing, the sitcom's focus on internal family roles, and the celebrity interview show's emphasis on the interplay between everyday social roles and star personalities and images.

Rather than address *The Osbournes* as a new hybrid form of factual entertainment TV, initial news articles characterised the show as a parody of more traditional family sitcom fare. Early descriptions of the Osbourne family – former Black Sabbath front man Ozzy Osbourne, his manager wife Sharon and their two teenage children, Kelly and Jack – emphasised its dysfunction, labelling it a 'circus' of 'sideshow freak[s]', the family that put 'the fun in dysfunctional' (Daniel, 2002: E1), and 'America's favourite dysfunctional family' (Shales, 2002). Branding the Osbournes 'the postmillennial Munsters, the gothed-up Simpsons, or the bird-flipping Cleavers' (Gilbert, 2002: E1), commentators established the dysfunctional status of the MTV family, likening it to cartoon versions of the traditional American family and contrasting it with the representative functional 1950s television family. Since its inception, *The Osbournes* has been compared to and contrasted with a wide spectrum of television programming: *The Real World* (MTV, 1992–, US), *Cribs* (MTV, 1998–, US), *Big Brother* (2000–, UK) *Father Knows Best* (CBS, NBC, 1954–60, US), *The Adventures of Ozzie and Harriet* (ABC, 1952–66, US), *The Munsters* (CBS, 1964–6,

US), *The Addams Family* (ABC, 1964–6, US), *The Simpsons* (Fox, 1989–, US), *Leave It to Beaver* (CBS, ABC, 1957–63, US), *The Beverly Hillbillies* (CBS, 1962–71, US), *The Waltons* (CBS, 1972–81, US) and *The Partridge Family* (ABC, 1970–4, US).

Too often these comparisons are made in ways that elide the differences between the shows, giving little attention in particular to the significant distinctions among the various family sitcom sub-genres. *The Osbournes* is simply contrasted to any show that represents some kind of idealisation of the family, no matter whether it's of a rural extended family, as in *The Waltons*, or of the single-parent variety, as in *The Partridge Family*. In order to understand its significance *The Osbournes* needs to be located more precisely on the continuum of television genres. MTV markets its show as an innovative form of reality programming, but the familiarity of *The Osbournes'* characters and sentiments highlights the fact that Reality TV as a whole is not as new as its producers contend. After all, even the most common Reality TV format, in which a bunch of strangers are placed in a house equipped with cameras that record whatever occurs, is a kind of technologically advanced version of a classic sitcom scenario. The same strategy of placing a variety of personality types under the same roof to produce volatility has already been effectively employed by classic sitcoms such as *All in the Family* (CBS, 1971–9, US). Even though Reality TV can claim to be less contrived than such sitcoms given that it is unscripted, its producers deliberately cast players who represent a spectrum of different personality types and thereby guarantee that the group members will interact with each other in volatile and often predictable ways. In addition, the social skill endorsed by the family sitcom – how to live together 'with tolerant mutual accommodation' (Hartley, 2001: 66) – is also at the centre of supposedly all-new Reality TV products such as MTV's *Real World*, one of *The Osbournes'* direct Reality TV antecedents.

Such antecedents are obviously significant for understanding *The Osbournes*, but an analysis of the show's less evident sitcom precursors proves more illuminating. Despite MTV's claims, *The Osbournes* is not a series that *redefines* television so much as one that *resurrects* the original early 1950s format of the American sitcom. To prove this point, in what follows I compare *The Osbournes* to the star sitcom, a sub-genre prevalent in US TV in the 1950s. The star sitcom featured star couples – such as Lucille Ball and Desi Arnaz, George Burns and Gracie Allen, Ozzie and Harriet Nelson, and Ida Lupino and Howard Duff – playing themselves in fictionalised versions of their actual lives, often in replicas of their actual houses. To establish the connection between these post-war star sitcoms and the post-millennial reality star sitcom, I draw on a range of archival data. This material includes the extensive collection of entertainment columns in local Los Angeles newspapers, publicity folders, trade journals and personal communication with news reporters, housed at the University of Southern California Cinema–Television Library (particularly in the Hal Humphrey Collection), and the collection of the early television shows themselves at University of California, Los Angeles Film and Television Archive and the Museum of Television and Radio (New York and Los Angeles).

As a result of uncovering and charting this history, I contend that the 1950s star sitcoms are an embryonic form of Reality Television and that *The Osbournes*, in turn, is a development of that form. Of course, there are obvious and significant differences in production and form between the current star sitcom and its predecessors, and those are explored in the body of this essay. Despite these differences, the appeal of MTV's reality star sitcom lies in its continuities with traditional forms, not in its groundbreaking originality. It exemplifies an effective use of the classic oxymoronic marketing strategy of the 'new and improved' – in the case of *The Osbournes*, cutting-edge digital technology combined with an updated version of classic sitcom sentiments and characters.

Monster rock Ozzy and big-band Ozzie: updating a TV classic?

The family of big bandleader Ozzie Nelson as it is depicted in *The Adventures of Ozzie and Harriet* is representative of the kind of 'normal' TV family in contrast to which MTV first marketed its odd Osbournes. The 1950s show seemed an appropriate comparative point of reference given the similarities of the sitcom dad's first name and of the show's format – a peek into the daily life of the actual family of a former star bandleader. The opposition evoked in this comparison, between the elder Ozzie's bland 'normality' and the younger Ozzy's colourful 'deviance', is obviously the gimmick at the heart of the show's initial conception and marketing.

Of course, the gimmick is not really a new one since the opposition it pivots on is similar to the premise of *The Munsters*, the 1960s sitcom in which a family of actual monsters moves into *Ozzie and Harriet*-like suburban America. One critic, implying that the Nelsons would rather have the Munsters than the Osbournes as neighbours, quips: 'This bunch makes *The Munsters* look like *Ozzie and Harriet*' (Hodges, 2002: 1). While the Nelsons, the Munsters and the Osbournes may not look alike, the shows that centre on each family offer the same implied message: this family might seem different to yours at first, but you will soon see that it is essentially 'the same'. Indeed, the Osbournes have much in common with the ghoulish families depicted in *The Munsters* and *The Addams Family*, two shows David Marc characterises as 'monster-coms' because they are shows about 'entire families of innocent monsters trying to live their deviant lives among hostile, intolerant "normal" people' (Marc, 1992: 132). The Osbournes might be 'creepy' and 'kooky', 'mysterious' and 'spooky' (the key descriptors from Vic Mizzy's

(1964) *The Addams Family* theme song), but they are also nice people we should 'learn how to love and forget how to hate' (as we are told by the lyrics of *The Osbournes* theme song, likely echoing the sentiments of the executive producer Sharon Osbourne).

Although Ozzy Osbourne's family is not composed of actual monsters, as Herman Munster's was (the union of Frankenstein monster Herman and Lily the vampire miraculously yielded Eddie the werewolf son), aesthetically and formally *The Osbournes* is a Frankensteinian creation of sorts. It is built out of parts of other TV genres – reality 'gamedocs', soap operas, 'trash', as well as therapy-based talk shows, entertainment celebrity programmes, MTV's *Cribs* celebrity house tour, and VH1-type *Behind the Music* (VH1, 1997–, US) melodramas. It is also a hybrid of several sitcom sub-genres – the magi-com, monster-com, suburban domesti-com, the 'slapstick and gag-oriented family sitcom' (Haralovich, 2003: 71), the alterna-family and anti-family sitcoms, the showbiz family or star sitcom. It is the latter category, the star sitcom, in which I am most interested, as I see *The Osbournes* as the progeny of the star sitcom and the docusoap.

The Osbournes offers us all the melodrama of a soap opera, the real-time footage of the documentary, the voyeuristic snooping of the celebrity house tour, the interaction of incompatible and competing personalities of the 'gamedoc', all combined with the themes, issues and framing of a sitcom. Given that it builds on the docusoap's combination of 'the factual/realist mode of the documentary with a privileging of the private, personal narrative values of the soap opera' (Moseley, in Brunsdon *et al.*, 2001/2: 33), *The Osbournes* may be the newest innovation in Reality TV, but its framing, its marketing, its themes and even its characters are those of the classic sitcom. While the Osbournes are actual people, they are also updates of classic sitcom types: bumbling dad, ruler-of-the-roost mother, good bad boy and perky girl. Borrowing from John Dovey's work on factual television, we can argue that there are moments in the show when we experience 'the contradictions and ambiguities' of the Osbournes' 'subjectivity' and others when 'we are offered just enough textual information about [them]...to slot the social actor into his or her role within the narrative' (Dovey, 2000: 152–3). This unstable subjectivity and fixed iconicity is a blurring of boundaries, or, as John Corner puts it, a 'play around the self observed and the self-in-performance' (Corner, 2002: 265). The combination of the classic and the cutting edge has proven a winning one for the show: the innovation hooks viewers, but the familiarity arguably keeps them. Like star sitcoms, *The Osbournes* plays with the contradictory dynamic 'stars-as-ordinary, the star-as-special' (Dyer, 1986: 49). Like a docusoap, it offers a documentary mode of representation that vacillates between observation and performance and is intended to be consumed by viewers who are both 'voyeurs and...judges' of the performance (Corner, 2002: 268).

The Reality Television viewer

Annette Hill has profiled the Reality TV viewer as 'skeptical of the more "performative" entertainment programmes about real people', but still attracted to the slippage that might occur and the possibility of even a split-second revelation of something genuine (2002: 324). As she puts it, 'audiences look for the moment of authenticity when real people are "really" themselves in an unreal environment' (ibid.). John Corner uses the term 'selving' to describe the 'central process whereby "true selves" are seen to emerge (and develop) from underneath and, indeed, through the "performed selves" projected for us' (Corner, 2002: 261). Most viewers do not watch reality shows expecting to see 'real' people living 'real' lives. They expect people who know they are being filmed to play to the cameras to some extent. Hill attributes the popularity of gamedocs like *Big Brother* to their ability to 'capitalise' on the resulting 'tension between performance and authenticity' (Hill, 2002: 324). Similarly, *The Osbournes* challenges 'viewers to look for the "moment of truth" in a highly constructed and controlled television environment' (ibid.: 324), or for what Corner calls the 'unwitting disclosure of personal core' (Corner, 2002: 261). As my invoking of Dyer's (1986) 'star-as-ordinary, star-as-special' dichotomy above suggests, this is a dynamic further complicated by the fact that Ozzy Osbourne's celebrity status, and the public's attendant fascination with his 'authentic' self, pre-existed the show.

As Ellis Cashmore explains, Reality Television viewers expect shows to be ' "realistic" in the sense that the characters and actions are tangible' and that the characters are 'liable to similar restrictions to ourselves' (1994: 70). He argues that in such shows '[c]redibility is maintained by creating characters and contexts that ring true; only the solutions are contrived' (ibid.: 113). *The Osbournes* 'rings true', I would argue, because it tackles the same familiar terrain as the classic sitcom, exploring the same issues (e.g. sibling rivalry), problems (e.g. balance of power between husband and wife), and questions (e.g. what impact will women's entrance into the public sphere have on the private sphere?). Unlike classic domesti-coms, MTV's reality sitcom does not offer ready answers to these problems. It seems 'realer' because it doesn't follow the usual televisual formula. As Tom Shales remarks,

> Television has educated the audience about television…and people, even kids, know all the formulas: the formulas for gags within sitcoms, the formulas for the 22-minute plots with the tidy endings and facile moralistic 'messages' included in some of them – usually about being yourself or being happy with yourself – whatever.
>
> (Shales, 2002)

The Osbournes is pitched to an audience of these 'TV insiders', as MTV's Dave Sirulnick explains: 'Our audience has grown up in a real media-savvy world' (cited in Cashmore, 1994: 192).

Many have also come of age with Reality TV and their viewing strategies have been adjusted to the new formats offered by shows such as *Big Brother* and *The Real World*. They understand the control 'producers have in the editing process' (Andrejevic, 2002: 261). They are 'savvy' viewers, but they still see 'perpetual surveillance' as the 'antidote to artificial interactions – to "acting"' (ibid.). They judge characters, says Mark Andrejevic, by their ability to '"be real" – to reveal their interactions and to just be themselves' (ibid.: 261). Reality TV characters are similarly continually judging themselves in this way. Ozzy and Sharon continually assert that they are just being themselves on the show.[3] They echo the belief in what Andrejevic calls '"the real in reality TV": that surveillance provides a certain guarantee of authenticity, and that this authenticity becomes a process of self-expression, self-realization, and self-validation' (ibid.: 265).

According to Paddy Scannell, viewers look for these moments of self-expression and feel that their assessments of the players in a reality show have 'a cumulative weight'. He continues:

> The more you watched the programme, the more you knew about all the inmates, their personal traits, the ways they interacted with each other. Just as in soap operas, the more you watched, the more expert you became in evaluating character and behaviour.
>
> (Scannell, 2002: 278)

I would modify Scannell's comments to read 'the more expert *you believed* you had become'. Viewers arrive at their interpretation of a moment as a 'real' one through a combination of the knowledge they believe they have acquired about the characters and the knowledge they believe they have of themselves, and, as Hill puts it, 'how they would act in a similar situation' (2002: 335). One journalist's commentary about the Osbourne family dynamics illustrates Hill's theory: 'Like my father, Ozzy can't figure out the new cable box. Jack patiently helps him, then goes back to relentlessly teasing Kelly just as my own brothers tortured me throughout my teen years' (Vejnoska, 2002: 1F). Another viewer might think of it as Kelly torturing Jack. Either way, the moment will 'ring true' to viewers. What Hill says of gamedocs in general is applicable to *The Osbournes*: 'part of the attraction in watching…is to look for a moment of authenticity in relation to selfhood…. The game is to find the "truth" in the spectacle/performance environment' (Hill, 2002: 337), a dynamic again rendered all the more acute for Ozzy's pre-existent star status. After all, *The Osbournes*, like the docusoap tradition from which this combination monster-com/reali-com was fashioned, is structured around the 'emotional realism' that characterises soaps.

From gamedoc to star sitcom

While not a gamedoc, *The Osbournes*, as the discussion above has demonstrated, certainly shares many of its strategies with that of the Reality Television subgenre. Like the designers of *Big Brother*, those of *The Osbournes* cut the raw footage they compiled in a way that would 'build momentum' and 'create involvement', to borrow the terms Scannell applies to a description of *Big Brother* (2002: 273). That the show sometimes is marked by a 'prioritisation of entertainment over social commentary' links it to the docusoap (Bruzzi, 2001: 132). As Stella Bruzzi explains, 'The term 'docusoap' itself was coined by journalists keen to dismiss this new brand of factual television, which, in their estimation, contaminated the seriousness of documentary with the frivolity of soap operas' (ibid.: 132). Unlike the docusoap's privileging of characters' personalities over their social roles, the reality sitcom emphasises both while still using the docusoap's 'fast-paced editing style, chopping together short sequences and alternating between a limited number of narrative strands per episode' (ibid.: 132; see also Bruzzi, 2000).

Despite its use of such docusoap strategies and its origins in MTV's *Cribs* and *The Real World*, *The Osbournes* has roots that stretch back to the showbiz sitcoms of the early 1950s, which themselves could be loosely categorised as the original reality sitcoms. *The Osbournes* can be categorised as a revival of the 1950s star sitcom, in which married stars 'are themselves more or less', to quote a 1957 *TV Guide* front cover (Johnson, 1957) devoted to one such show, *Mr. Adams and Eve* (CBS, 1957–8, US). Just what is added to and subtracted from their 'real lives' to create a sitcom based on the lives of star couples Ida Lupino and Howard Duff (a.k.a. Mr. Adams and his wife Eve Drake), Ozzie and Harriet Nelson, George Burns and Gracie Allen, Lucille Ball and Desi Arnaz, as well as that of Arnaz's and Nelson's fellow nightclub showman Danny Thomas, reveals much about 1950s assumptions about culture and gender, and about reality itself in the 1950s.[4] A comparison of those shows with *The Osbournes* demonstrates as many similarities as there are differences between the post-war and the post-millennial reality sitcom. Such a comparison suggests that *The Osbournes*' appeal and its high approval ratings are due as much to its commonality with foundational early television genres and scenarios as to its originality in the Reality Television arena. In the section below I will chart the history of the star sitcom in order to demonstrate what is and isn't new about *The Osbournes* and its format, themes and engagement with gender and family norms.

Sitcom antecedents and descendents

In the US TV schedules of the 1950s a common formula for sitcom success was to take a married star couple, film a fictionalised version of their real life in a set simulated to resemble their real home, and offer it to a star-obsessed public eager to see stars 'as they were' at home. These shows varied in levels of verisimilitude. *The Adventures of Ozzie and Harriet* was the most 'exact' replication of a star's life as it featured a stage-set replica of the Nelsons' actual house and cast their sons and later their wives as themselves for the duration of the show's run on ABC, from 1952 to 1966 (Best, 1952: 13; ABC Publicity Department, 1958: 20). *Make Room For Daddy*/a.k.a. *The Danny Thomas Show* (ABC, CBS, 1953–64, US) was the least exact replica. Thomas changed his name to Williams and hired actors to play his family. They helped him act out plots connected to his real experiences of domestic chaos produced during and upon his return home after absences related to the requirements of his standing gig at New York's fictional Copa Club or touring commitments that kept him away from home and on the road for longer periods of time.

The Adventures of Ozzie and Harriet never addresses Ozzie's work life. Instead it focuses on reproducing the actual home life of an actual husband and wife. It acknowledges neither that *Ozzie and Harriet* must always only be a reproduction of their real home life nor that the 'original' on which the reproduction is based is itself unstable. Instead, Ozzie claims that his family members 'reliv[e] before the camera the everyday events of their own home and neighbourhood' (Stump, 1955: 24) and because they do so they 'have an advantage over most other TV families because they are the same family in real life' (Humphrey, 1954: n.p.). Similarly, ABC's Publicity Department proclaimed that 'the on-camera characters of David and Rick [Ozzie's sons] are just extensions of their own personalities' (ABC Publicity Department, 1958: 2). In doing so, it failed to acknowledge that star personality, according to Dyer, 'was itself a construction known and expressed only through films, stories, publicity, etc.' (Dyer, 1986: 23).

While Danny Thomas's star sitcom is also marked by an underlying anxiety about 'notions of a separate self and public self presentation, performance, role-playing' (ibid.), *Make Room for Daddy* does not judge its fidelity to 'reality' by its overall 'capacity to look like…the original' (he does not cast his actual family) (Nichols, 2001: 20). Instead, it is more interested in offering, 'a *representation* of the world we already occupy' (ibid.), in providing valuable 'insight or knowledge' (ibid.: 21). Viewers categorised Thomas's representation of a bellowing, anxious father as one that 'rings true' (Castleman and Podrazik, 1989: 302), or, to borrow the phrasing of Hill's Reality TV reception theory, that conveyed the desired "moment of truth" in a highly constructed and controlled television environment' (Hill, 2002: 324).

Thomas's fictionalised re-enactments often capture some essence of the real competing demands of work and home that the young showman father/husband experiences. Of course, the kind of bad-boy behaviour we now associate with musicians, even those big-band, rat-pack types of the 1950s, is never addressed. Instead, the show's title, *Make Room for Daddy*, indicates that it is a comic take on the tension between the star's desire to be the reigning family patriarch, even though he spends a lot of time away from home, and his need to build and later maintain his status as a reigning showman. The show is mostly a showcase for Thomas's wit and comic nightclub act, and we are meant to laugh at his attempts to negotiate between his dedication to his family and to his profession. As in the case of Ozzy Osbourne, the tensions are most apparent when the children are younger. The original title, *Make Room for Daddy*, reflected the fact that the showman was away so much in the early days that when he returned his children would have to shift bedrooms to 'make room for daddy'. They called him 'Uncle Daddy' when he did come home, an expression of their confusion about their exact relationship to this stranger who caused chaos and brought excitement every time he came into their home. Such problems became less acute as the children grew up. By the show's fourth season, when the title of the show became simply *The Danny Thomas Show*, the topics changed to more general comic explorations of anxieties about gendered nuclear-family expectations and roles (Rogers & Cowan Publicity Department, 1959: 5).

In the Nelsons' reality sitcom such competing demands are never addressed. Instead, it represents showbiz and middle-class family life as 'emphatically compatible', David Marc claims.

> Ozzie Nelson's duties as a bandleader made so few demands on him that he was left virtually free twenty-four hours a day to play golf, improve the house, and otherwise cultivate himself as a source of ethical inspiration for his wife and children.
>
> (Marc, 1992: 92)

For the most part, the show plays as if the Nelsons are just an ordinary suburban family headed by a husband with some kind of job that affords him an inordinate amount of lawn-mowing and leisure time. From our extra-diegetic knowledge of the family, we know that Ozzie is a bandleader who met his wife when she becomes the girl singer for his band. Just as the show typically circumvents Ozzie's relationship to work, it also never deals with Harriet's. In real life she parlayed her success with the band into movie parts and had a promising career in film that continued after she became a wife and mother. Just a few months after David's birth, Harriet travelled to Hollywood to film a picture while Ozzie stayed in New York with the baby. Harriet's only contact with David during her time on the road was via telephone, when Ozzie would put the phone near the baby's mouth so his movie-star mother could hear his attempts at making words (Stump,

1955: 118).[5] Such tensions between the demands of career and family are never addressed in the show. Instead, Harriet appears on television to be a traditional stay-at-home mom with an ordinary past. The episode in the Nelson's actual lives nevertheless suggests a fluidity of gender roles and something unconventional about the couple, who appear to be so conventional on TV.

'Real lives' and real wives: the representation of women

The show never addresses Ozzie's and Harriet's own private thoughts about gender expectations, gendered divisions of labour and two-career families. Those tensions are, however, indirectly addressed in *I Love Lucy* (CBS, 1951–7, US) and *The George Burns and Gracie Allen Show* (CBS, 1950–8, US). In these reality star sitcoms the switch from real life to televised real life involves a power shift in which the male showman's role is enlarged to that of sole breadwinner (he is no longer a partner with his show-business wife) and the female's is reduced to economic dependant.[6] On *I Love Lucy*, for instance, Desi Arnaz played the Cuban bandleader that he was, while his wife Lucille Ball demoted herself from her real status as glamorous and talented Hollywood star to average and talentless house-wife who was nonetheless eager to break into her husband's nightclub act or at least a movie star's backyard. Gracie Allen, by contrast, often entertains minor Hollywood luminaries in her sitcom backyard. The show both calls attention to and distracts attention from the fact that Gracie and her husband George are performers on a show called *The George Burns and Gracie Allen Show*. For the most part, George is the only one who is ever shown or referred to as rehearsing or preparing for that show. This implies that Gracie just plays herself on that show and hence needs no practice. Of course, the show also undercuts that assumption and places at its centre a tension between the real and the performed. As Patricia Mellencamp puts it, 'unlike in most situation comedies it was clear that George depended on Gracie, who worked both in the series' imaginary act and the programme's narrative' (2003: 48).

Mellencamp (ibid.), Mary Beth Haralovich (2003) and Susan Douglas (1995) have all explored how these star-sitcom wives use comedy (by creating confusion in the case of Gracie Burns or by trickery in the case of Lucille Ricardo) as an indirect expression of these gender tensions. These star-sitcom wives both confirm and contradict gender norms. In this respect these star sitcoms are different from the domesti-coms that followed them. The mid-1950s and early 1960s traditional family sitcoms reflect, according to Joanne Morreale, 'the postwar economic and cultural need to restabilize the family, both by reposi-tioning women within the domestic sphere, and by reaffirming male authority' (2003: 5). As Mellencamp explains, the terrain of situation comedy altered by the 1960s:

the housewife, although still ruling the familial roost, changed from being a humorous rebel or well-dressed, wise-cracking naïve dissenter who wanted or had a paid job — from being out of control via language (Gracie) or body (Lucy) — to being a contented, if not blissfully happy, understanding homebody.

(Mellencamp, 2003: 42–3)

This was the case of the wives in 1950s shows such as *Leave It to Beaver* and 1960s shows such as *The Dick Van Dyke Show* (CBS, 1961–6, US). Sharon Osbourne's appeal stems from her ability to straddle as well as update both the humorous rebel and the happy homebody types.

Mellencamp claims that Lucy's 'discontent and ambition' are the working premise of *I Love Lucy* (ibid.: 48). Building on her theories, I contend that at the centre of *The Osbournes* is Sharon's more ambivalent combination of contentedness and ambition, of conformity to and rebellion against gender norms and expectations. Though obviously the managing partner in the family business, Sharon sometimes acts as if she is an economic dependant. Like Lucy, she expects to have to account to an angry and authoritarian husband for the money she spends. A self-diagnosed shopaholic, Sharon is not beneath Lucy Ricardo strategies of hiding new items and trying to get them in the house under her husband's radar or to pass them off as clothes she's had for a long time that he just never noticed or doesn't remember. When he does notice, Sharon just ignores Ozzy's bellowing queries, 'What did you spend my money on now?', and the viewer does as well since it is clear that she is the reason they have any money at all.[7] Although Sharon never denies her powerful role in the family, she does sometimes underplay it. She is sensitive to Ozzy's need to assert his status as breadwinner even though she grants him no actual authority over her purchasing.

The depiction of Sharon's admirable capability at juggling all the demands of wife, mother and manager make her an important site of viewer identification. Sharon seems to suggest that being a supportive wife is entirely compatible with being the family business's chief financial officer and domineering manager, even though it is the tension between these roles that is at the centre of the conflicts in this marriage, as it is in most dual-career heterosexual marriages. She is a welcome contrast to June Cleaver, who, according to Haralovich, is 'structured on the periphery of the socialization of her children, in the passive space of the home' (2003: 83).

In contrast to the 1950s wives, who television rendered 'both superfluous and subordinate' (Leibman, 1995: 202), Sharon Osbourne is at the centre of the family and makes financial and career decisions for each family member. She is often shown in the father's role — imparting her superior knowledge and acting as 'sagacious and benevolent' solver of 'family crises' (ibid.: 22). This mode was central to *Ozzie and Harriet*, a series that 'explicitly center[ed] the duties of fatherhood and Ozzie's prowess at them. Each episode ends with either Ozzie's wife or friends baring their respective souls in a declaration of how much they depend on Ozzie's wisdom, strength, and consistency of judgment' (ibid.: 34). Well aware that the central familial role is traditionally accorded to the father, Sharon makes efforts to recentre Ozzy within the family. Despite her attempts to include Ozzy, to send him to talk with the children about a problem, it is usually her advice and her wisdom that solve or at least mediate family problems.

This isn't to say that Ozzy doesn't try to impart some wisdom to his kids. The governing premise of the show is that being an insensible rock star who said yes to drugs a few times too many is compatible with being a sensible sitcom dad who counsels his children to 'say no to drugs'. How that plays out is more ambivalent. The 'Kelly's tattoo' scene I discuss below follows the show's governing pattern of representing as compatible a set of impossibly divergent traits: the maturity, benevolence and wisdom of the father figure and the immaturity, egocentrism and recklessness of the rock star. The viewer recognises that this compatibility may exist only in the 'highly constructed and controlled' (Hill, 2002: 324) environment of Reality TV, in scenes in which Ozzy offers kids 'do as I say, not as I did' advice.

Ambivalence and familial and gender norms

The tattoo discussion scene suggests how difficult it is for Ozzy to negotiate competing identities and desires. Its ambivalent message indicates that the Osbourne family is not simply the flip side of perfect cardboard 1950s families. The way Ozzy imparts his stance on education and tattoos – he encourages his children to value the former and avoid the latter, despite having had the opposite attitude in his younger years – exemplifies this contradiction. He claims to regret his youthful choices and hopes that by sharing his feelings about his past he can save his children from repeating his mistakes. But Ozzy sends an ambivalent message. He speaks of his own desire to do well in school as well as his despair at ever doing so because of what he later discovered was undiagnosed dyslexia. His story is supposed to convey his regret for coping with his frustrations by dropping out of school, a choice that led him to crime and quickly to jail. At this point in his melodramatic account the ambivalence sneaks in and Ozzy's tone changes from regret to pride as he remembers that it was in jail that he got the O–Z–Z–Y tattooed on his fingers, a tattoo that would be the first of the many that now cover his body. Not surprisingly perhaps, his children are eager to get tattoos of their own. Ozzy's parenting still surprises us though. After Kelly tells Sharon via telephone that she has had a tattoo, Sharon asks to speak to Ozzy. Nervously waiting until he hangs up the phone, Kelly asks Ozzy if Sharon is mad. Ozzy pointedly tells her, 'No, she's not mad. She's just very disappointed. She thinks you're a very stupid person.' It is an effective strategy, as it seems to deflate Kelly and make her ashamed of failing to live up to her parents' expectation that she would make better choices than they did.

The fact that this exchange centres on a tattoo is significant. Ozzy's tattoos serve as reminders that he is not an innocent victim, but a rock star who abused his own body into this state. It is also a key to the show's feeling of 'reality'. The whole exchange gives validity to Ozzy's claim that he's 'just a real guy with real feelings' (Nelson, 2002: 148). His rough image helps reinforce the show's claims to reality. In the 1950s star sitcoms the pasts of the stars playing themselves disappear and the inconsistencies of their images are smoothed out. The references to the spotted record and youthful antics of this showman/dad differentiate *The Osbournes* from the early reality star sitcoms, in which the stars never deal with the negative aspects of their celebrity or the fact that their personal lives are a matter of public record, for anyone, even the children whom they are trying to control, to know. The scenes are mostly just played for humour, though, and the more complex issue of whether Kelly feels hostile about getting advice from a man she must have seen do some fairly ill-advised and destructive things is not addressed.

Veering somewhat from the docusoap tradition of 'prioritising entertainment over social commentary' (Bruzzi, 2001: 132), the editors of *The Osbournes* often alternate between entertainment and social commentary. The end of the tattoo segment returns to the entertainment mode. The camera lingers on Ozzy's extensive tattoos and his long magenta-tinted black hair. In this moment, as in many others in the show, the seriousness of the complexity of emotions involved in the scene is diffused and the moment dissolves into spectacle. The spectacle is often verbal as well as visual given Ozzy's often comically incomprehensible utterances, produced through a combination of his broad accent and his slurred speech. Part of the humour of the show is that it could benefit from as many explanatory subtitles for Ozzy's dialogue as it needs censoring bleeps for his cursing. The show is always a combination of serious and humorous address. Ozzy's literal incomprehensibility and the need to expurgate his word choice provide a metaphoric contrast to the clearly broadcast messages about gender and familial norms in *Ozzie and Harriet*.

The Osbournes' message about familial and gender norms is as complicated and ambivalent as *Ozzie and Harriet*'s was simplistic and coherent. That complication exists alongside the spectacle of stumbling, stuttering and mumbling Ozzy puttering about the house. Certainly, there are moments when the cameras focus on Ozzy's physical movements and depict them in a way that might cause the viewer to feel twinges of pained sympathy for the man's obvious physical incapacity. Because it is so impossible to represent the complex truth of this 'body in pain' (Scarry, 1987) (not to mention the pain that his self-abuse has caused this family), it is then alleviated through the camera's playful recording of the spectacle produced by the juxtaposition of Ozzy's shuffling, aged movements with the tattoos that cover his arms and mark him as the typical young rebel.

Conclusion

The transformation of the images of shuffling Ozzy, from disconcerting to humorous, could be categorised as part of the show's sitcom mode because such moments play for endearing laughs. In contrast, the digital enhancement of the opening credit sequence and transition frames, where footage of the family is 'frozen' and made to resemble framed family photographs, is a feature of the show's docusoap mode because it highlights the show's digital effects. The typical sitcom family photo carries with it the authority of the assumption of what a typical American family should look like. In contrast, *The Osbournes'* self-reflexive use of still frames and its emphasis on their construction and manipulation embody the show's philosophy that what a real family is can never be completely contained by a still photograph.

Not a simplistic reversal of static representations, *The Osbournes* conveys an ambivalent message about the relationship between the real and the posed. This tension is reflected in the fact that the opening credit sequence and the transition sequences between segments of *The Osbournes* are a combination of real film footage and that footage then paused and transformed into what resembles a still photograph, one that is then digitally surrounded by an animated, colourful frame. The sequence is accompanied on the soundtrack by a Frank Sinatra-esque nostalgic reworking of Ozzy's song 'Crazy Train', thereby connecting the current reality sitcom with 1950s precursors on an auditory level. The right-to-left advancement of the still frames is used for the practical purpose of providing for scene transitions in a programme that might otherwise at times seem quite random and disconnected. When a picture is selected and highlighted (in a way that suggests the viewer has double-clicked on a computer icon), the camera seems to move into the picture and that segment begins to play. On a discursive level, this technique is also a visualisation of the show's ability to draw viewers in through its use of new technologies and to keep them through its covering of familiar sitcom territory in unconventional ways.

The outlandishly framed snapshots of the Osbourne family antics contrast with the traditional posed family photographs associated with classic American sitcom families. Given the show's alternation between conforming to and rebelling against traditional domesti-com gender roles, its cartoonish colourful frames can be read as displacing (yet in the process drawing attention to) anxieties about gendered and familial roles. As I have demonstrated, this same dual mode of displacement and tenuous recontainment was a central feature of the 1950s star sitcom. By positioning *The Osbournes* throughout this essay on a star-sitcom continuum and demonstrating how it resurrects the earlier star-sitcom format, I have established not only that *The Osbournes*, even with its technological innovations, builds on these earlier shows and therefore is not the first situation reality series, but also that Reality TV in general is not as television-'concept-redefining' as its producers would like us to believe (Gold, 2002: back cover).

Notes

1   For access to the 1950s sitcoms, as well as press materials and articles, I am grateful to the curators at the University of California, Los Angeles Cinema and Television Library and Archive, the Museum of Television and Radio Archives, and the University of Southern California (USC) Cinema–Television Library. I especially want to thank Ned Comstock at the USC Archive for directing me to the wonderful Hal Humphrey Collection and for sending me materials. My research trip was made possible by a grant from Bentley College, an institution that has always generously supported my research.

2   PBS claims that its 1973 *cinéma vérité* documentary series *An American Family* (PBS, 1973, US) was the first American reality show as it documented the 'real-life drama' of the Loud family of Santa Barbara, California.

3   In countless interviews, Sharon and Ozzie assert that they just are themselves on the show. See Gold (2002: 5, 7, 148) and Peyser (2002: 64), in which Ozzy is quoted as saying, 'What I'm trying to get across is the real me, the real Oz.'

4   For more discussion of such gender cultural tensions and television's role in mediating them, see Leibman (1995), Spigel (1992), Taylor (1991) and Tichi (1991).

5   This information on the Nelsons is verified in many of the documents in the Hal Humphrey Collection, USC.

6   For discussions of the subtle and not so subtle ways in which these star TV wives subverted the norms, see Douglas (1995), Haralovich (2003) and Mellencamp (2003).

7   Here Ozzy resembles the bumbling, henpecked husband hated by those columnists who preferred to champion the Jim Anderson *Father Knows Best* sagacious and benevolent father type. Rhodes claims that Anderson replaced another stock sitcom dad: the 'weak-willed, predicament-inclined clown', whose 'doltishness' is contrasted to the beauty and intelligence of his wife (1956: 125). Eddy celebrates Anderson as the new dad in town who, single-handed, brought order to the new frontier of television by overturning 'one of the more persistent clichés of television scriptwriting' in the vein of *The Life of Riley*: that of 'the mother as iron-fisted ruler of the nest, the father as a blustering chowderhead, and the children as being one sassy crack removed from juvenile delinquency' (Eddy, 1957: 29).

References

ABC Publicity Department (1958) '*Adventures of Ozzie and Harriet* Starts Seventh ABC Season Oct. 1', *ABC Trade News*, 4 September: 1–2; available in the Hal Humphrey Collection.

Andrejevic, Mark (2002) 'The Kinder, Gentler Gaze of Big Brother: Reality TV in the Era of Digital Capitalism', *New Media & Society* 4(2): 251–70.

Best, Natalie (1952) 'Ozzie Nelson Takes His Family to TV!', *TV Trade News*, September: 13; available in the Hal Humphrey Collection.

Brundson, Charlotte, Catherine Johnson, Rachel Moseley and Helen Wheatley (2001/2) 'Factual Entertainment on British Television: The Midlands TV Research Group "8–9 Project" ', *European Journal of Cultural Studies* 4(1): 29–62.

Bruzzi, Stella (2000) *New Documentary: A Critical Introduction*, London and New York: Routledge.

Bruzzi, Stella (2001) 'Docusoaps', in Glen Creeber (ed.) *The Television Genre Book*, London: British Film Institute.

Cashmore, Ellis (1994) *...And There Was Television*, New York and London: Routledge.

Castleman, Harry and Walter J. Podrazik (1989) *Harry and Wally's Favorite TV Shows*, New York: Prentice-Hall.

Corner, John (2002) 'Performing the Real: Documentary Diversions', *Television & New Media* 3(3): 255–69.

Daniel, Jeff (2002) 'Rocker Oz's Family on TV Is Throwback to the Nelsons', *St. Louis Post-Dispatch* [Internet], 28 March: E1; available at http://1180-proquest.umi.com.ezp.bentley.edu/pdqweb?Did+000000245828441&FMT=3&Deli=35970x00034EF (accessed 30 December 2002).

Douglas, Susan (1995) *Where the Girls Are: Growing Up Female With the Mass Media*, New York: Times Books.

Dovey, John (2000) *Freakshow: First Person Media and Factual Television*, London: Pluto.

Dyer, Richard (1986) *Stars*, London: British Film Institute.

Eddy, Bob (1957) 'Private Life of a Perfect Papa', *Saturday Evening Post*, 27 April: 29.

Gilbert, Matthew (2002) 'MTV's Rock 'n' Roll Family Is Back for Seconds: Will the Show Remain the Same or Will Success Alter Its Reality? "The Osbournes" Is Back, Playing For Bleeps', *Boston Globe* (third edition), 26 November: E1.

Gold, Todd, with the Obsournes (2002) *Officially Osbourne: Opening the Doors to the Land of Oz*, New York: MTV Books/Pocket Books.

Haralovich, Mary Beth (2003) 'Sitcoms and Suburbs: Positioning the Fifties Homemaker', in Joanne Morreale (ed.) (2003) *Critiquing the Sitcom: A Reader*, New York: Syracuse University Press.

Hartley, John (2001) 'Situation Comedy, Part 1', in Glen Creeber (ed.) *The Television Genre Book*, London: British Film Institute.

Hill, Annette (2002) '*Big Brother*: The Real Audience', *Television & New Media* 3(3): 323–40.

Hodges, Ann (2002) 'It Sounds Batty, but "Osbournes" Likeable', *Houston Chronicle* (2 star edition) [Internet], 5 March: 1; available at http://80-webm=c852510290af1417499da51d351d3cbbb92ed (accessed 30 December 2002).

Humphrey, Hal (1954) 'Not All Idiots, Says Oz', *Los Angeles Mirror News*, 22 December: n.p. available in the Hal Humphrey Collection.

Johnson, Robert (1957) '*Mr. Adams and Eve* Modeled After Stars Duff and Lupino: A Hollywood Married Couple Are Themselves (More or Less) on TV: Mr. Duff and Ida', *TV Guide*, 1 June: 17–19; front cover photo of Lupino and Duff and back cover with

Lupino and Duff in a *Mr. Adams and Eve* sponsor advertisement by Camel Cigarettes; available in the Hal Humphrey Collection.

Leibman, Nina C. (1995) *Living Room Lectures: The Fifties Family and Television*, Austin, TX: University of Texas Press.

Marc, David (1992) *Comic Visions: Television Comedy and American Culture*, London and New York: Routledge.

Mellencamp, Patricia (2003) 'Situation Comedy, Feminism, and Freud: Discourses of Gracie and Lucy', in Joanne Morreale (ed.) *Critiquing the Sitcom: A Reader*, New York: Syracuse University Press.

Mizzy, Vic (1964) '*The Addams Family* Theme Song' [Internet]; available at 'Blackcatter's world of TV theme song lyrics', http://classictv.about.com (accessed 6 December 2002).

Morreale, Joanne (2003) *Critiquing the Sitcom: A Reader*, New York: Syracuse University Press.

Nichols, Bill (2001) *Introduction to Documentary*, Bloomington, IN: Indiana University Press.

Peyser, Marc (2002) 'All Aboard the Crazy Train', *Newsweek*, 11 March: 64.

Rhodes, Kenneth (1956) 'Father of Two Families', *Cosmopolitan*, April: 125–7.

Robinson, John (2002) 'NME meets The Osbournes', *New Musical Express* (UK), 25 May: 22–7, 47.

Rogers & Cowan Publicity Department (1959) 'Danny Thomas Biography', Beverly Hills, CA: Rogers & Cowan; available in the Hal Humphrey Collection.

Scannell, Paddy (2002) '*Big Brother* as Television Event', *Television & New Media* 3(3): 271–82.

Scarry, Elaine (1987) *The Body in Pain: The Making and the Unmaking of the World*, New York and London: Oxford University Press.

Shales, Tom (2002) 'Essential Lessons from "The Osbournes"', *Electronic Media* [Internet], 2 December; available at http://80-web.lexis-nexis.com.ezp. bentley.edu/universe-document?—m9+e7fd4a8387a13deb2d5d5058e0609428 (accessed 30 December 2002).

Spigel, Lynn (1992) *Make Room For TV – Television and the Family in Postwar America*, Chicago: University of Chicago Press.

Stump, Al (1955) 'Meet Hollywood's Most Exciting Family', *American Magazine*, October: 24–5, 116–18; available in the Hal Humphrey Collection.

Taylor, Ella (1991) *Prime Time Families: Television Culture in Postwar America*, Berkeley, CA: University of California Press.

Tichi, Cecelia (1991) *Electronic Hearth: Creating an American Television Culture*, New York: Oxford University Press.

Vejnoska, Jill (2002) 'MTV Take on "Reality Sitcom" Has Ozzy Twist', *Atlanta Journal–Constitution*, 5 March: 1F.

Filmography

Lance Loud! A Death in an American Family (Video Verite, 2002, US), dir. Alan and Susan Raymond.

3

'THIS *IS* ABOUT REAL PEOPLE!'

Video technologies, actuality and affect in the television crime appeal

Deborah Jermyn

> [It] has an enhanced entertainment value; quite simply, it's better
> because it's real. A kind of blurring of distinctions thus occurs. One
> wonders to what extent [it] appeals to its audience on a voyeuristic or
> salacious level. It's hardly a public hanging, but is it a kind of contem-
> porary equivalent, catering to similarly unworthy sensibilities?
>
> (Woffinden, 1989: 10)

In these remarks, and in condemnatory and fearful terms that seem all too
familiar from recent media discourses, Woffinden anxiously ponders television's
latest primetime phenomenon. This alarming development on the small-screen
apparently crystallises all that is corrupt and debasing about contemporary television. It seems to demonstrate a disregard for generic distinctions, as 'fact' and
'fiction' increasingly conflate, and the targeting of the audience's lowest common
denominator, who take a shameful kind of pleasure in its sensationalistic and
exploitative narratives. But this is no denouncement of Reality TV. The year is
1989 and the 'it' in question is *Crimewatch UK* (BBC, 1984–). Prompting the
growth of crime-appeal programming in Britain – with a format where serious
unsolved crimes are reconstructed, police and victims' families interviewed,
images of suspects publicised and the public encouraged to phone in and volunteer information – by this time the series had comfortably established itself as
Britain's foremost crime-appeal programme. It is perhaps only in retrospect that
we can fully situate it as a conspicuous precursor to the boon of real-crime
programming that has constituted one of the most controversial and resilient
movements in British television since the late 1980s.

In the debates that crime-appeal programming gave rise to following the
appearance of *Crimewatch* in 1984, Woffinden was far from alone in his fears. For
example, writing in the *Guardian* in 1990, Tim Minogue observed that, with
deregulation in the offing, crime-appeal programmes like *Crimewatch, Crime*

Monthly (LWT, 1989–96) and *Crimestoppers* (ITV, 1988–95) 'could be laying the ground for a new breed of American-style shows in which the distinction between fact and fiction becomes increasingly blurred' (Minogue, 1990: 23). The same shows were still attracting condemnation some four years later, when Polly Graham noted that in this kind of 'cheap, lazy television…programme-makers realise they're on to a good thing…. No need for script-writers or imagination, it's ready-made, put in the microwave, sensational – success guaranteed' (Graham, 1994: 13). Also writing in 1994, and bemoaning the loss of 'Reithian standards', Ludovic Kennedy specifically invoked *Crimewatch* as an example of the 'ghoulish voyeurism' taking over television schedules (Kennedy, 1994: 8). What is striking about all these critiques is that any one of them could have been lifted from a recent newspaper diatribe against Reality TV. If there is any truth in such popular discourses about the breakdown of generic distinctions and audiences' increasingly salacious appetites, it would appear that the anxieties which met *Crimewatch* and real-crime programming most vociferously in the period from the mid-1980s to the mid-1990s have been not just transferred to, but borne out by, the contemporary Reality TV movement.

In this chapter I want to look more closely at how aspects of the allure of crime-appeal programming and the debates that have surrounded it prefigure many of the characteristics of Reality TV as we now understand it. There has been a growing body of academic work on real-crime programming (for example Fishman and Cavender, 1998; Leishman and Mason, 2002), but none of it has specifically sought to examine exactly how the crime-appeal format presaged many elements of the broader contemporary 'Reality TV' movement. These links demonstrate that much that is feared and condemned in Reality TV on the one hand, but also enjoyed and celebrated on the other, is only the latest articulation of a rather more enduring strain of cultural fascination around 'the real', very much evidenced in real-crime stories, that has a long history both within and preceding television. Woffinden's comparison of crime appeals to 'public hangings' in the epigraph which begins this chapter evokes a historical vision of the spectacle of crime which I will return to, and which points neatly to the nature of these links and the kind of attraction at stake here; crime appeals arguably answer to and perpetuate our pleasure in identification processes, in public punishments and in 'naming and shaming' criminals. More broadly, by examining the allure of *Crimewatch* and its compatriots we can identify how one of the enduring attractions that lies at their core is the *spectacle of actuality*, a pleasure which precedes the television crime appeal and which Reality TV explores and exploits with a renewed enthusiasm. Indeed, in a similar vein Christopher Dunkley has fiercely disputed programme-makers' claims that the structures of many of 'the best known examples' of Reality TV formats, from *Castaway 2000* to *Popstars*, represent 'new' innovations on our screens and instead points to how they are indebted to numerous televisual precedents (Dunckle, 2002: 35) (a contention taken up by Bradley Clissold and Jennifer Gillan in Chapters 1 and 2).

Examining a particular manifestation of the 'spectacle of actuality', this chapter focuses on the nature of our fascination with closed-circuit TV (CCTV) footage in the crime-appeal genre, a medium subsequently widely drawn on to become a familiar feature in the explosion of real-crime and Reality TV. This kind of technology has come to enjoy a distinctive relationship with actuality and 'the real'. As Jon Dovey notes:

> The low-grade video image has become *the* privileged form of TV 'truth telling', signifying authenticity and an indexical reproduction of the real world; indexical in the sense of presuming a direct and transparent correspondence between what is in front of the camera lens and its taped representation.
>
> (Dovey, 2000: 55)

In examining the nature of our fascination with such images, and their place within the crime-appeal format, I draw predominantly on *Crimewatch*, using a six-month sample of the programme broadcast January–June 2000, while I also refer to a lesser extent to *Britain's Most Wanted* (ITV, 1998–). Making textual analysis of *Crimewatch*, I also incorporate institutional and production-based perspectives by drawing on original interviews I have carried out with the producers of both these programmes.[1] Indeed the title of this chapter, the declaration and affirmation that *Crimewatch* '*is* about real people', directly quotes *Crimewatch* Series Producer Katie Thomson and indicates the degree to which the programme lays claim to a privileged relationship with 'the real'.

In what follows, after contextualising *Crimewatch*'s place on British television and the concomitant rise of CCTV technologies in Britain at the point at which *Crimewatch* first appeared, I examine how the spectacle and promise of CCTV material is indeed one of the fundamental allures of crime-appeal programming for its audience. Within this, I want to argue that, while the genre's adoption of CCTV in the mid-1980s may have been a celebration of the spectacular properties of 'new' technologies, the primary appeal of CCTV was/is anything but new. Rather, what it actually points to, as I indicated above, is our perennial and enduring cultural fascination with making criminals 'visible' and with seeing authentic visual records in crime stories; with actuality evidence, that is, which crucially extends to both real victims and real criminals. Finally, in seeking to understand the compelling nature of CCTV (and video footage more broadly) I also explore how one of its most potent features lies in the manner in which the medium pivots on an affective temporal conjunction. In CCTV a heightened illusion of *immediacy* converges with the *past-tense* status it holds in common with all visual records. This potency is one of its most fascinating elements, but it also highlights how much more than mere criminal apprehension and identification is at stake in the crime appeal's embracing of such footage, since it is arguably at its most affective in the genre's recollection and representation of *victims*. The crime appeal's invocation of the spectacle of actuality, then, extends as much to its victims as it does to criminals. Significantly, a similar kind of action – where the everyday and 'ordinary' people are transformed by circumstance and media attention into the 'extraordinary' – is again characteristic of many Reality TV formats.

Though it has been around for two decades now, debates around *Crimewatch* and its like have never completely subsided. They continue to rear their head intermittently, such is their contentious nature and so heavily embedded are they in the anxieties, desires and pleasures television holds for us. But in a media reception similarly marked by disquiet and unease, striking parallels to the debates about crime-appeal programming emerge in key, recurrent discourses that have circulated around Reality TV. For example, *Guardian* TV critic Gareth McLean observed in his 'Comment' column that 'the attraction of the genre is hard to explain...call it rubber-necking or empathising but everyone loves watching a tragedy being played out don't they?' (2002: 7). This account seems a pertinent and concise summary of our double-edged fascination with *Crimewatch*'s stories of loss and violence – but in fact it was written to accompany an article about ITV's *Popstars:The Rivals*. Debates about 'quality', public service, cynical and irresponsible programme-makers, commercial pressures and generic 'blurring' have all similarly characterised the opposition that has met the emergence of 'Reality TV' since the late 1990s. The parallels are more than coincidental; with its popularisation of reconstructions, its claiming of 'real' stories and testimony from real witnesses, its privileged relationship with 'actuality' via the incorporation of authentic CCTV/video/photography, its appeal to a mass audience to take a participatory role in a contentious television format and its evoking of that audience as an '(inter-)active' one which through a phone call can play a role in actually shaping the programme as it unfolds – all of which come together in a kind of hazy territory where social project and entertainment meet – *Crimewatch* was arguably a notable forerunner of numerous strands of the current Reality TV movement.

This points again both to the difficulty of ascribing a definition to 'Reality TV' and to the significance of *Crimewatch* as a precedent to it; in the UK's contemporary televisual landscape *Crimewatch* would not be among the most obvious contenders to bear this mantle, but in early work by Richard Kilborn on 'Recent Developments in "Reality" Television' (1994) he included it in his discussion. Similarly, Hugh Dauncey's discussion of 'French "Reality Television"' in 1996 referred to *Temoin N*⁰. *1* – the French equivalent of *Crimewatch UK* – as 'the doyen of French reality shows' (1996: 91), while Gray Cavender, in Chapter 7 of this volume, unequivocally situates *America's Most Wanted* as 'Reality TV'. Arguably, Kilborn's discussion rather failed to knowledge just how influential a precursor *Crimewatch* (and indeed, by extension, *Aktenzeichen XY...Ungelöst*, the German programme on which *Crimewatch* was based) was to the movement he examines. He suggests that 'the original stimulus for RP [Reality programming] came from the United States.... NBC were the first company to get in on the reality act with their *Unsolved Mysteries* (1987)', while other networks soon followed suit with police/emergency services-based reality shows such as *America's Most Wanted* on Fox (Kilborn, 1994: 426). This neglects the fact that *Crimewatch* first appeared some three years earlier, in 1984, and that, rather than *Unsolved Mysteries*, it was *Crimewatch* that provided the principal inspiration for *America's Most Wanted* (as indeed it did for *Temoin N°. 1*).

Before pursuing the issues above it would be instructive to offer some brief initial contextualisation of the place of *Crimewatch* in British television culture. While it has become one of the longest-running staples of British television schedules since its first appearance in 1984 – described by one media commentator as 'a jewel in the crown of the BBC' (Cathcart, 2001: 31) – its controversial bid to transform television audiences into police associates has nevertheless meant it has also been subject to ongoing criticism. As indicated above, throughout its tenure *Crimewatch* has intermittently featured in contentious debates about the quality and future of British television; it has stood accused of sensationalism and voyeurism; of exploiting true-crime stories in a bid to win audiences; of corrupting public-service television principles; and of blurring the boundaries between fact and fiction (Jermyn, 2004).

It is undeniably significant that the programme emerged in the mid-1980s, a period marked by a Conservative government and an 'accentuated concern with "law and order" politics' (Schlesinger and Tumber, 1995: 254) further precipitated by an apparent rise in the incidence of crime in Britain at this time. More specifically, these were the Thatcher years, an era characterised by the demise of the 'nanny state', a drive towards individual responsibility and independence and, by extension, self-policing. Hence *Crimewatch* has also been critiqued for being complicit in this ideology and for being 'in bed with' the police. But, most interestingly for the purposes of my argument here, *Crimewatch* must also be contextualised as appearing in a period which saw in the emergence of new forms of surveillance, enabled by CCTV and video technologies. Just as *Crimewatch* identified the televisual potential of such material, so too did the subsequent appearance of a whole array of Reality TV programming which has pivoted on the use of video and CCTV material (much of it not specifically concerned with crime appeals), including *999* (BBC, 1992–), *Police, Camera, Action!* (ITV, 1994–), *Crime Beat* (BBC, 1995–9), *EyeSpy* (LWT, 1995–9), *Video Diaries* (BBC, 1990–9) and *Video Nation* (BBC, 1994–2000). Indeed Dovey has described this televisual development, rather apocalyptically, as constituting the medium's 'sudden viral

Figure 3.1 Presenters Nick Ross and Fiona Bruce share centre-stage with a television monitor on the set of *Crimewatch UK*, underlining the significance of video technologies to the programme: 'one of the enduring attractions that lies at [its] core is the spectacle of actuality'. (Image courtesy of the BBC Photo Library.)

contamination by camcorder and surveillance footage' (2000: 57). The explosion of Reality TV generally since the 1990s has taken up the initiative originally pursued by the crime-appeal genre to make CCTV footage a regular component of contemporary television programming. Within this it has also repositioned (or arguably consolidated)[2] its use as an *entertainment* form, where it is increasingly less controversial and more an everyday part of the televisual landscape.

Reinventing surveillance culture

It was at the point of *Crimewatch*'s debut, from the mid-1980s, that video and surveillance technology become increasingly accessible and affordable on a wide scale, moving beyond banks and building societies into small shops and businesses and eventually, of course, to high streets, car parks and public places of every nature across the country. The first public CCTV scheme in Britain was launched in the seaside resort of Bournemouth in August 1985; just a decade later Britain had 'more public space CCTV systems than any other advanced capitalist nation' (Fyfe and Bannister, 1998: 257), and the CCTV industry is now worth more than £300m in

Britain every year (*History of Surveillance*, C4, 19 April 2001). By the early 1990s, then, the growth of this technology was such that it impacted on national everyday life – in the words of the *Guardian* crime correspondent Duncan Campbell:

> To those of you who have always wanted to be in films – congratulations, you've made it. If, in the last 24 hours, you have gone shopping, travelled to work, visited a post office, taken a train, watched a football match, put petrol in your car, visited the off-licence, or walked through a city centre, you will have played at least a small part in the one section of Britain's film industry that is experiencing astonishing growth: video surveillance.
>
> (Campbell, 1993: 2)

This shift didn't occur entirely without anxiety or opposition; campaign groups such as Liberty drew attention to issues of legislation, statutory control and personal privacy. Groups like the Surveillance Camera Players, who stage protests around CCTV sites, have emerged in the US, while in the UK Ian Toon has described how disenfranchised young people in Tamworth town centre have formed strategies of resistance to surveillance cameras, identifying and exploiting camera 'blindspots' and splitting into small groups to fragment the regulatory gaze (Toon, 2000: 155). But on the whole it appeared that the opportunities the technology offered for crime reduction and detection outweighed the concerns. Implicit in this was a sense that only those who were somehow complicit in crime would resent the introduction of CCTV; as a culture 'by and large we have bought the idea that "only the guilty have anything to fear"' from its use (Dovey, 2000: 66).

However, the arguments in favour of CCTV are by no means incontrovertible. Fyfe and Bannister claim that 'there is little consistent research evidence' to sustain claims that CCTV deters and reduces crime and suggest that the presence of cameras might even be displacing crime to other areas out of camera range (1998: 257; see also Lydall, 2003). Simon Davies, the director of Privacy International, has similarly maintained that CCTV merely relocates rather than eradicates crime. But intriguingly he further suggests that the misconception that CCTV is a deterrent against crime is one that has actually been popularised by the media and crime-appeal programmes *themselves* through their recurrent broadcasting of CCTV crime footage in crime appeals. He points to the absurdity of this:

> The reason people believe (CCTV) *affects* crime is because they keep seeing the images on TV – and bizarrely people are watching images of crime being commissioned and yet *strengthening* their belief that the technology can stop crime. It's a non-sequitur. CCTV does not cut down crime.
>
> (*History of Surveillance*, C4, 19 April 2001)

Furthermore, rather than gratifying the public with a sense of enhanced security, it may be the case that for some people surveillance systems can actually have the opposite, detrimental effect, heightening paranoia, suspicion and fear of crime by 'signposting' the possibility of crime.

Fyfe and Bannister suggest that the growth of CCTV in inner-city areas and high streets must be seen within the context of a broader economic, socio-cultural and political agenda at that time, in this instance promoting the privatisation and commodification of public space. For example, Toon contextu-alises his study of CCTV surveillance and young people in Tamworth city centre with an account of how British town centres underwent a period of economic decline during the 1980s. A growing sense of alienation from these spaces was noted as a key component in the rising fear of crime. The most visible response to this since the 1990s has been to try to revive the town centre's economic role. In the drive for urban renewal 'powerful commercial and civic interests have embraced shopping and leisure as a key economic strategy' (Toon, 2000: 148). But these are not inclusive spaces; with their low spending power, Toon found that these youths were consistently 'moved on' by police, compounding and perpetuating cultural assumptions about young people as 'troublemakers', to the extent that they have become a kind of underclass (ibid.: 149). In this way, many of the key preoccupations of the 1980s *zeitgeist* in Britain – fear of crime, law and order politics, the demise of 'community', a bid for economic renewal – come together to intersect in the heavily surveilled space of the regenerated town centre. Hence *consumerism*, rather than crime alone, appears to be a signifi-cant impetus behind the popularisation of CCTV, a notion very much borne out internationally, and in the US particularly, by the concurrent and intertwined growth of CCTV and shopping centres.

Though these technological developments are now well established, at the time of their introduction they heralded in a 'new' kind of crime discourse centred around contemporary forms of surveillance. They entailed a movement that perfectly fulfilled the needs – or, to look at it another way, actually *enabled* the development – of *Crimewatch* and its like. Not only do *Crimewatch* and *Britain's Most Wanted* draw regularly on CCTV in their appeals, but both use 'surveillance footage' as a visual referent in their title sequences, concurring with Helen Wheatley's observation that CCTV footage has become 'the trademark of real crime programming' (2001: 46). *Britain's Most Wanted*'s opening montage, for example, features genuine footage of arrests and raids as well as more abstract images of technological and surveillance devices, including fingerprints, thermal imaging, a cross-hair shifting focus and a double-helix symbol signifying DNA science. All of this is accompanied by the dramatic *Britain's Most Wanted* signature tune, adding up to a fast action-packed sequence which foregrounds detection, technology, surveillance and science in the manner of a thriller. Similarly, one of the show's recurrent icons is the use of a superimposed camera 'cross-hair' (as also seen in rifle viewfinders in fact) to 'frame' the CCTV footage shown and move into it when focusing into a close-up. Tim Miller, the Series Producer of *Britain's Most Wanted*, suggested that the aesthetic quality of the zoom in his programme's use of surveillance footage was essential to the programme's style, adding to the dramatic weight given to the CCTV footage. In his words, 'It's quite exciting. There's something about zooming in on something that is exciting in a way that just seeing it happen wouldn't be. It gives it added emphasis. And also when you zoom into something the image becomes bigger' (personal interview, 2001). Discussing these motifs further, his comments point to the real-crime and crime-appeal genres' simultaneous fascination with and contribution to contemporary surveillance culture:

> I think the idea of that sort of 'surveillance camera' was basically like you're being the criminal, you're being watched out there. I don't want to get too grand about it, but it's like a kind of metaphor for our viewers' contribution, isn't it? Like everyone out there can see it, you can see it, you're going to be caught, you're being watched, you've been warned, type of thing.
>
> (Tim Miller, personal interview, 2001)

What's interesting about his description here is its apparent blurring of criminal and public under the camera's watchful eye. This surveillance technology isn't just watching the criminals – it's watching *all* of us. So, while his description starts off imagining the surveillance imagery as vicariously placing us in the criminal's position ('like you're being the criminal'), what it also demonstrates is not only that 'everyone out there can see it', but that, equally, 'everyone out there' is 'being watched'. This echoes Wheatley's observation that 'the very presence of CCTV in people's everyday lives, drawn attention to by the real crime genre, suggests that we are not only being protected but also watched' (2001: 49).

New technologies, familiar images

Though back in 1984 this CCTV technology was (relatively speaking) 'new', its critics argued that the fascination and constraints it held were anything but. In these aspects, the structures and appeal of the medium were not so much inventive as regressive. The role and use of CCTV in contemporary society echo nothing more than Jeremy Bentham's infamous 18th-century model of 'the panopticon', the ultimate surveillance building whose enduring citation in analyses of the operation of surveillance is testimony to its powerful and discomfiting vision. The panopticon is designed with a central tower housing the supervisor at its core, surrounded by a ring of cells facing out on to the tower, whose occupants can always be seen but cannot tell whether at any time they are being watched from the tower. Foucault describes it thus:

> They are like so many cages, so many small theatres, in which each actor is alone, perfectly individualised and constantly visible. The panoptic mechanism arranges spatial unities that make it possible to see constantly and to recognise immediately.... Visibility is a trap.
>
> (Foucault, 1991: 200)

The continuities borne out here between the panopticon and CCTV seem eerily prophetic. CCTV, with its framing, focusing, zooming and panning capabilities, arranges its own 'spatial unities' – as we saw above, Tim Miller describes how the zoom restructures the action, so that the viewer's experience of it becomes different from 'just seeing it happen'. Potentially recording and/or being monitored 24 hours a day, like the panopticon, CCTV's powers of 'recognition' are also constant. Furthermore, in many instances, like the panopticon's central ever-evident tower, the vigilant CCTV camera is visible; but, like the panopticon's tower, we can never be certain when it is or isn't staffed, when it may or may not be focusing on us, and hence must act in its presence at all times as if we are being watched. Where CCTV cameras *aren't* always visible, this makes their inspection of us even more 'unverifiable' than the panopticon's. This sense of the simultaneous absence/presence of a remote but powerful sentinel is shared by both forms of surveillance, each raising questions about what we perceive to be the fundamental human right to the dignities born of privacy. Indeed, the same kinds of contentious issues about how the enactment of constant surveillance upon individuals undermines our humanity and human dignity have been at the hub of media debates about Reality TV 'game-docs' such as *Big Brother*.

In an intriguing parallel to the panopticon, there was controversy in the United States in 2000 when the first live web-broadcast from a jail went online on Crime.com, a site started by the co-founder of the US reality-crime show *Cops* (1991–). A report in the British newspaper *Metro* directly invoked the parallels between this venture and surveillance-based Reality TV shows:

> Getting jailed at the Madison Street Jail in Maricopa County, Phoenix, can make you a star – a star in a rather twisted webcam drama that turns the inside of a county jail into a worldwide *Big Brother* cum-soap opera freakshow for anyone who cares to log on.... Since July last year, the jail's four security cameras have provided live images of the men's and women's holding cells, the search area and the pre-intake area.
>
> (Anonymous, 2001: 41)

Prison reform groups were quick to point out the dubious legality of such broadcasting, where people's images were being transmitted without their consent and very often without their knowledge. Nevertheless, this curious venture underlines the enduring potency of a number of the issues raised by the panopticon: our right to privacy, whether criminal behaviour should result in the loss of such rights and our fascination with looking at criminality in its endless shapes and forms.

Foucault's work on the panopticon has been widely adopted in critiques of contemporary surveillance, where CCTV has been conceptualised as bearing out his bleak vision of a post-19th-century society managed by the spectre of discipline. But arguably television's use of CCTV represents the assimilation of aspects of the penal systems that *both* precede *and* ensue from this transitional period. To elucidate, Foucault's *Discipline and Punish* (1991) charts the shifts in the penal systems of the West over some three centuries. This transformation is most evident in the move from pre-19th-century punishment – characterised by the spectacle of public torture (like the 'public hangings' Woffinden's comparative critique of *Crimewatch* evoked in the opening epigraph) – to post-19th-century discipline, engendered through surveillance and imprisonment. Foucault describes this as a move from punishment of the body to punishment of the soul. The once huge public events that accompanied executions as massive crowds gathered at the gallows and roadsides, and the public inspection of and participation in all manner of gross tortures visited on the accused's body, now came to an end. By the end of this transitional period '[p]unishment had gradually ceased to be a spectacle. And whatever theatrical elements it still retained were now downgraded' (Foucault, 1991: 9).

I have shown above the unnerving ease with which CCTV can be seen to form a parallel with the panopticon and the notion of discipline through surveillance. But the use of CCTV in crime appeals, and later across various Reality TV formats, also seems to prolong the pre-19th-century sensibility of spectacle, of 'insatiable curiosity' (ibid.: 46) in being able to *see* the criminal. Where we can't witness their punishment we are nevertheless still fascinated by seeing *them*. The 'nice boys' robbing another youth on a train platform in Willesden in February 2000, 'the Granddad Gang' in March 2000, who rob a petrol station while one of them causes a distraction in the aisle, the April 2000 'woman on a spending spree' with a stolen credit card captured obliviously on film in a shop, all of these are examples of the many instances of CCTV footage in my sample, where, in every edition, *Crimewatch* serves up the spectacle of CCTV. Rather than the enthralled 'mob' on the street, then, we have the attentive television audience. Rather than the spectacle of gross public torture and punishment, spectacular display now focuses on seeing the performance of the crime and in identification and/or apprehension of the criminal. Public and spectacular fascination is nevertheless at the core of both scenarios, where the 'theatrical elements' Foucault spoke of persist in the extravagant narratives and confrontations seen in some CCTV footage, and where the display and inspection of the criminal *still* 'deploy[s] its pomp in public' (ibid.: 49). And, as I will go on to explore, where more apparently mundane moments are captured on CCTV – such as the woman fraudster shopping above – their repositioning within the context of real-crime stories and the fact of their actuality transform them retrospectively into spectacle.

Audiences and the appeal of actuality

However, as we've seen, despite fears about the potential abuse of CCTV cameras, their popularisation, unlike the panopticon, was swift. As the quality of (some) videos increased they became an essential staple of crime-appeal programmes, and indeed their efficacy seemed impressive: the former producer of *Crime Monthly*, Stewart Morris, claimed that an average of 80 per cent of criminals shown on video were arrested within days of the programme being aired (cited in Campbell, 1993: 2). Interestingly, though, and in apparent contradiction of Morris, in an interview *Crimewatch* Series Producer Katie Thomson commented that, although sometimes excellent quality footage is shown ('And it's so clear, you think, "We've got him"'), nevertheless the expansion of CCTV

> *hasn't* enormously increased our success rate. And we show a lot of it. But a lot of it's dreadful quality, a lot of CCTV you think, God, it's hardly worth having a camera there. It's all blurry and set in such dreadful positions.
>
> (Katie Thomson, personal interview, 2002)

Here, like Simon Davies from Privacy International, Thomson exposes the myth of CCTV as an unprecedented crime deterrent. Indeed some criminals have claimed that the poor-quality CCTV footage they witnessed on *Crimewatch* actually gave them an incentive to commit crime. Criminologist Martin Gill's interviews with 341 imprisoned 'raiders' found that they argued that watching the programme 'showed them how "easy" it was' and highlighted how 'the quality of security film was so poor suspects were difficult to identify' (Burrell, 2000: 7).

In fact this also points to a contradictory aspect of CCTV: that, while it enjoys a privileged relationship with the real, it simultaneously holds a distancing quality. The blurry images common to so much CCTV material evoke its figures as screen ghosts on occasion. CCTV footage, then, is typically both 'real' in content and un- or surreal in its rendering. As Dovey observes, '[c]ompared to, say, a 35mm slide the resolution and discernible detail from a surveillance camera [are] appalling' (2000: 66). From this we can conjecture that the concomitant reason that much CCTV footage is shown is not so much the resounding quality of the image as its popularity among audiences. This suggests again its peculiarly complex place in contemporary television's evoking of 'the real', where 'the power, significance and "truthfulness" of surveillance images have embedded themselves in the cultural body' (ibid.). Schlesinger and Tumber rightly note that *Crimewatch*'s use of videofits and video footage are 'part of a long journalistic tradition in which pictorial forms of representation have always been an audience-building technique' (1995: 259). And yet this era and its technology undeniably brought new ramifications to bear on the scopophilic pleasure of the image of the criminal. CCTV and video footage are able to transport the viewer into the 'scene of the crime', and, while it is not generally seen 'live' by the audience (O. J. Simpson's motorway police chase being a notable exception – see Bondebjerg, 1995), nevertheless it carries a sense of immediacy and privileged access which the crime appeal's other media, such as filmed reconstructions or 'videofits', cannot hope to produce.

Given all this, Thomson made a particularly thought-provoking observation in interview: that, ultimately, no crime appeal *has* to include CCTV or video footage. So, for example, in January 2000 one short *Crimewatch* appeal shows some video footage of a wanted man filmed on a boat on holiday in Torquay. He had pretended to befriend a disabled man he met there, then robbed him. The picture quality is excellent but there is no original sound; instead the footage has been overlaid with the sound of the man's voice taken from a different recording. There is absolutely no need, then, to show the moving image since it isn't even synched to the audio track. The film is all largely superfluous since the programme could make the same appeal to identify the suspect by merely showing only the clearest [still] image taken from the footage. The use of the moving image here demonstrates that more than mere identification is at stake in the crime appeal. As Thomson commented, 'That's what *Crimewatch* used to do, just show the best [still] image. But you know,…it is fair to help people be enter-tained at the same time.' It is included, then, because audiences enjoy (and indeed now expect) to see it: 'Obviously people like watching CCTV. It's the real thing, especially if it's an action piece. On CCTV it's quite exciting and again it's making this point *that it is real*' (Katie Thomson, personal interview, 2002, emphasis mine). In short, the use of CCTV conspicuously enhances the programme's claims to authenticity and underlines its sense of a privileged relationship with real crime and actuality, qualities which programme-makers evidently believe to be ratings winners.

The affective power of CCTV in the crime appeal

Tim Miller, Series Producer of *Britain's Most Wanted*, made a very similar observa-tion to Thomson's. He spoke with tangible enthusiasm about the televisual drama of CCTV footage and thus its crucial place in his programme. In his words,

> Actuality is the most dramatic thing you can have, because it's real. That's why the show's been quite successful, isn't it, really? People like watching real stuff. It's real actuality but not in real time, because you don't have to wait for the incident to unfold...you just get the punch-line of each one.
>
> (Tim Miller, personal interview, 2001)

Interestingly, what Miller points to here is a postmodern, Baudrillardan sense of CCTV as a kind of super-*enhanced* realism, as being 'more real than real'. Annette Hill's work on *Coppers*, a programme where a camera crew shadows real-life police at work, bears this out. She describes how one episode details the humdrum series of petty crimes that police work through in Southend-on-Sea. Viewers expecting thrills and drama because it's about real crime will be disappointed: 'This is real life and real life is not always exciting' (Hill, 2000: 230). Like the crime appeal and its use of CCTV, *Coppers* is about 'real' crime, but where CCTV is recurrently used as a form of spectacular display, *Coppers* is about the 'ordinariness of crime'. Another episode, for example, shows divers in the Thames discovering a body, something one might expect to be rather dramatic. But, instead, '[w]e see how long it takes...how awkward it is...and how cold everyone gets waiting for the procedure to be over' (ibid.: 231). Through its *edited* packaging on crime-appeal programmes, CCTV footage eliminates or condenses precisely this sense of 'waiting time' (akin to what Kavka and West, in Chapter 6, refer to as (Reality) TV's fear of 'dead time', namely 'time in which "nothing happens"'). Through CCTV the audience can actually experience a heightened sense of realism; they don't have to go through any superfluous narrative or, in Miller's words, 'wait for the incident to unfold'. What CCTV enables them to get is pure adrenaline, the moment of high drama, 'the punch-line'; and the pleasure it offers audiences is inextricably bound up in this.

But, crucially, the genre does not just provide these visual records and representations of *criminals*. Again, this fact underlines how the genre's fascination with looking and seeing, with privileged access to actuality evidence and with the visual records that accompany crime stories is not only, or primarily, about identifying the perpetrators of crime. For *Crimewatch* Series Producer Katie Thomson, the use of videos and photos of *victims* was again crucial to the programme's sense of realism. In a response worth quoting at length here, when I asked her why they were drawn on so heavily she commented:

> I think it's always about reminding people that this has happened to a real person, especially when you see so much crime drama, this *is* about real people... We're always trying to say these are real lives we're talking about, this isn't an interesting reconstruction, this is a real person or

family that's been destroyed. And home video helps a lot with that, because I think that has a real impact. It makes people feel this person was moving and walking and talking and enjoying a birthday party six months ago and now they're dead. And the same with their photos. I think if you had no image of the real person you'd start thinking the whole thing isn't real.

(Thomson, personal interview, 2002)

There are two other notions that Thomson alludes to here that are particularly interesting and worth further consideration. First, she immediately seeks to contextualise tragedy by placing the victim within the context of bereaved *families*. Indeed the principal way that *Crimewatch* continually positions and legitimises its victims is within their familial context(s); *Crimewatch* victims are never merely or primarily individuals, but parents, children, siblings, spouses (Jermyn, 2003). Second, she suggests that home videos, and indeed CCTV footage, of the victim are even more effective and affective in their impact on the viewer than photos; there is something potent about seeing the victim 'moving and walking and talking' which moves the audience in ways the still image cannot. This forms a parallel with the way in which, as we have seen, programme-makers believe CCTV (i.e. moving images) of criminals carry more impact than 'mug shots' or stills. There is something about seeing the criminal 'moving and walking and talking' on CCTV that makes it the more compelling medium, just as real footage of the victim seen living and breathing gives it a potency that stills do not have. So, for example, in May 2000 *Crimewatch* featured the case of Jay Abberton, murdered during an argument outside a Brighton nightclub. In a live studio interview his partner Tania Haynes painfully describes how his death has left her to bring up two children alone, as a television monitor between/behind her and the presenter Fiona Bruce carries a smiling picture of her and Jay together in happier times. She explains:

It's been devastating for my family. We were a very happy family, we were a thriving family; life was good. The bottom line is Jay went out that night to celebrate a friend's birthday, promising to take our two children for a bike ride the next day [at this point we cut to a close-up of Tania speaking] and he never came home.

(*Crimewatch*, May 2000)

As the interview goes on, we return to the image on the monitor as it cuts from the *still* photo of the couple together to what appears to be a holiday video. The footage shows Jay sitting outside in the sunshine at a table, smiling at the camera, moving and animated. In a dramatic and carefully manipulated juxtaposition, just as his partner talks about how she has tried to come to terms with his death we are confronted with a visual record of him as very much alive.

In all this we can identify how an affective conjunction is at work in the crime appeal's use of video technologies. This lies in the manner in which its *illusion of immediacy* converges with the fact of its '*this-has-been*'-*ness*. In this latter term I paraphrase Roland Barthes' description of the nature of photography, his account of how every photo is ineluctably bound up in its own past tense (1993: 77). It is a term that bears potent application to the visual medium of CCTV and video too. In fact, this conjunction, this conflictual or paradoxical meeting of present/past tenses, is arguably at its most affective in CCTV or home-video footage of the *victim*, since here its 'this-has-been'-ness is intensified by the fact of their death; we must acknowledge that the person so alive before us, 'moving and walking and talking' on our screens, will never do any of these things again. A particularly powerful instance of this is seen in April 2000 in the first-anniversary reconstruction of the murder of *Crimewatch* presenter Jill Dando.[3] Dando's cousin tells how the most traumatic aspect of dealing with the coverage of the murder was seeing the footage of Dando shopping in the high-street electrical store Dixons just minutes before she drove home and was murdered:

> The worst thing was seeing the film clip of Jill's last moments…and the fact that you do just want to be able to stop the camera and stop the action and to shout out at her and say 'Jill, don't go home!'
>
> (*Crimewatch*, April 2000)

Here, footage of a victim caught unawares by CCTV in a mundane and everyday act – the purchase of a printer cartridge – is transformed, retrospectively, into a potent and affecting spectacle. As we cut back to the studio, presenter Nick Ross comments blithely, 'Amen. If only the tape could be rewound', as if the properties of time itself were contained in or controlled by the medium – a comment which underlines my argument that CCTV holds a peculiarly potent relationship with our perceptions of the operation of temporality. The affective power of CCTV footage evoked by Dando's cousin in her appeal to the screen perfectly crystallises what I have described about the operation of the medium; how it both draws the viewer in with the illusion of immediacy (she describes wanting to address the screen as if the 'action' was live) and demands that the viewer embrace its 'this-has-been'-ness (she must accept the futility of her desire to 'stop' time, since the time of the film is past).[4]

A similar poignancy is drawn on in the appeal regarding the murder of Sara Cameron in May 2000, killed as she walked home from a night out with friends in Newcastle. During the reconstruction, which shows 'Sara' and her friends celebrating her new job with an evening spent in the city centre's bars, we are shown real CCTV footage of her entering the Metro station to catch the last train home. There is nothing of interest to see here; quite the reverse, it is even more ordinary in content than Dando's shopping expedition since the victim here is not even a celebrity. But it is retrospectively rendered compelling; there is the same sense of terrible poignancy in seeing this last captured image of the victim, knowing as we do now, and as she could not have then, that within minutes of her leaving that train she would be murdered. John Ellis has argued that it is *cinema*, not television, which is 'profoundly marked by what Roland Barthes has called the "photo effect"' (1994: 58), a quality he defines as 'the paradox that the photograph presents an absence that is present' (ibid.: 93). But in *Crimewatch* we see that, through its incorporation of CCTV, domestic video and still photography, television too can affectively co-opt 'the photo effect'. Ellis comments that the 'photo effect of present absence can produce an almost *intolerable nostalgia*' (ibid.: 58; emphasis mine), an evocative phrase which entirely mirrors the angst summoned up by *Crimewatch*'s painful reprise of the visual documenting of the now-dead – the 'present absence', in fact, of the murder victim.

An appeal to the curious

This chapter has evidenced that, whether it is in the dramatic scenes of a robbery in process or of a victim in his or her final hours unknowingly going about the mundane business of everyday life, our ongoing absorption with CCTV footage, in the crime-appeal genre and throughout real-crime and Reality TV more broadly, pivots on the spectacle of actuality. It demonstrates our enduring cultural curiosity with seeing visual evidence of real victims and real criminals in crime stories, a fascination which, Foucault demonstrates, can be traced back to a time long preceding the emergence of photographic and video technologies. Ultimately, the crime-appeal programme's reliance on and harnessing of CCTV bear out the fact that we as a culture are still drawn to the spectacular promise of crime stories, with witnessing the ordinary being trans-formed into the extraordinary, and play a large part in accounting for the fact that *Crimewatch* still holds such a visible place on British television screens some two decades after it arrived.

That debates around Reality TV have so conspicuously seemed to mimic or renew those earlier associated with the crime-appeal format is testimony to the fact that these televisual forms or movements share much common ground – and that there is much in this 'new' trend, like the 'new' technologies of CCTV and video in the 1980s, which is far from new in its attraction. The competitive environment in which television circulates ensures that it must continually develop, revive and adapt its forms and genres. Yet still, in recent years, as we have seen here, the debates and fears that accompany the arrival of 'new' televisual movements seem often to reproduce the same discourses of anxiety about the potential power (and abuse) of television.[5] Thus, misgivings about voyeuristic audiences, sensationalist narratives and the questionable use of surveillance footage were already established features within critical discourses around television in relation to crime-appeal programming when they emerged again 15 years later in relation to *Big Brother*; indeed, so too, for that matter, were anxieties about the exploitation of participants and generic slippage. Undeniably, Reality TV now constitutes an expansive and distinctive televisual movement in broadcasting history, an unquestionable shift in the make-up of contemporary television schedules; but, as this chapter has argued, the pleasures, curiosities and structures that underlie it may not be as original or landmark as we have tended to presume.

Notes

1 On 2 April 2001 I interviewed Jo Scarratt, Producer, and Tim Miller, Series Producer, of *Britain's Most Wanted* – both formerly Producers of *Crime Monthly* – at the LWT offices in London. On 22 January 2002 I interviewed Katie Thomson, Series Producer of *Crimewatch UK*, and on 19 February 2002 I interviewed Belinda Phillips, Assistant Producer of *Crimewatch UK*, both at the BBC TV offices, Wood Lane, London. I would like to thank them for so generously giving up their time to discuss these programmes with me.

2 I say *consolidated*, since, despite the worthy public-service justification for showing such footage on *Crimewatch* – i.e. criminal identification and apprehension – its use was also always simultaneously embedded in audience entertainment.

3 Jill Dando, a presenter on *Crimewatch*, was murdered on the doorstep of her home in London on 26 April 1999. For a detailed analysis of the media representation of her murder, see Jermyn (2001).

4 A similar kind of temporal friction is paralleled elsewhere in the crime appeal's format, in the way its insistent foregrounding of its *liveness* (the studio setting, phone-ins, updates and direct address) must coexist with the fact of its substantial *pre-recorded* elements (predominantly the reconstructions).

5 Indeed many of the discourses examined and arguments posited here would bear application to the emergence of the 'tabloid talk show'.

References

Anonymous (2001) 'Big Brother is Watching', *Metro*, 22 June: 41.

Barthes, Roland (1993) *Camera Lucida*, London: Vintage.

Bondebjerg, Ib (1996) 'Public Discourse/Private Fascination: Hybridization in "True-life Story" Genres', *Media, Culture and Society* 18, January: 27–45.

Burrell, Ian (2000) ' "Crimewatch"? It's Enough to Make You Go Out and Rob a Bank, Say Villains', *Independent*, 19 July.

Campbell, Duncan (1993) 'Big Brother is Here', *Guardian* (G2), 13 May: 2.

Cathcart, Brian (2001) *Jill Dando: Her Life and Murder*, London: Penguin.

Dauncey, Hugh (1996) 'French "Reality Television": More than a Matter of Taste?', *European Journal of Communication* 11(1): 83–106.

Dovey, John (2000) *Freakshow: First Person Media and Factual TV*, London: Pluto Press.

Dunkley, Christopher (2002) 'It's Not New, and It's Not Clever', *Reality TV: How Real is Real?*, London: Institute of Ideas/Hodder & Stoughton.

Ellis, John (1994) *Visible Fictions* (second edition), London and New York: Routledge.

Fishman, Mark and Gray Cavender (eds) (1998) *Entertaining Crime: Television Reality Programs*, New York: Aldine de Gruyter.

Foucault, Michel (1991) *Discipline and Punish: The Birth of the Prison*, London: Penguin.

Fyfe, Nicholas R. and Jon Bannister (1998) 'The Eyes Upon the Street – Closed-Circuit Television Surveillance and the City', in Nicholas R. Fyfe and Jon Bannister (eds) *Images of the Street: Planning, Identity and Control in Public Space*, London and New York: Routledge.

Graham, Polly (1994) 'Double Barrel: The Column that Gives Vitriol a Bad Name', *Guardian*, 19 August: 13.

Hill, Annette (2000) 'Crime and Crisis: British Reality TV in Action', in Ed Buscombe (ed.) *British Television: A Reader*, Oxford: Oxford University Press.

Jermyn, Deborah (2001) 'Death of the Girl Next Door: Celebrity, Femininity and Tragedy in the Murder of Jill Dando', *Feminist Media Studies* 1(3), November: 343–59.

Jermyn, Deborah (2003) 'Photo Stories and Family Albums: Imaging Criminals and Victims on *Crimewatch UK*', in Paul Mason (ed.) *Criminal Visions: Media Representations of Crime and Justice*, Cullompton: Willan Publishing.

Jermyn, Deborah (2004) 'Fact, Fiction and Everything in Between: Negotiating Boundaries in *Crimewatch UK*', in Jacqueline Furby and Karen Randell (eds) *Screen Method: Comparative Readings in Screen Studies*, London: Wallflower Press.

Kennedy, Ludovic (1994) 'Is TV Turning Us into Ghouls and Voyeurs?', *Daily Mail*, 23 June: 8.

Kilborn, Richard (1994) 'How Real Can You Get?: Recent Developments in "Reality" Television', *European Journal of Communications* 9: 421–39.

Leishman, Frank and Paul Mason (2002) *Policing and the Media: Facts, Fictions and Factions*, Cullompton: Willan Publishing.

Lydall, Ross (2003) 'Cameras Will Push Crime into Suburbs', *Evening Standard*, 3 February: 18.

McLean, Gareth (2002) 'No Flagging in Urge to Peep through the Keyhole', *Guardian*, 7 September: 7.

Minogue, Tim (1990) 'Putting Real Crime on Prime Time', *Guardian*, 3 September: 23.

Schlesinger, Philip and Howard Tumber (1993) 'Fighting the War against Crime: Television, Police and Audience', *British Journal of Criminology* 33(1): 19–32.

Schlesinger, Philip and Howard Tumber (1995) *Reporting Crime*, Oxford: Clarendon Press.

Toon, Ian (2000) ' "Finding a Place in the Street": CCTV Surveillance and Young People's Use of Urban Public Space', in David Bell and Azzedine Haddour (eds) *City Visions*, Essex: Prentice-Hall/Pearson Education.

Wheatley, Helen (2001) 'Real Crime Television in the 8–9 Slot – Consuming Fear', in Charlotte Brunsdon, Catherine Johnson, Rachel Moseley and Helen Wheatley, 'Factual

Entertainment on British Television', *European Journal of Cultural Studies* 4(1) February: 29–62.

Woffinden, Bob (1989) 'Crime Time Viewing', *The Listener* 112 (3139), 9 November: 9–10.

Wooley, Benjamin (1984) 'An Arresting Programme', *The Listener* 112 (2072), 23 August: 11.

4

REALITY TV, TROUBLESOME PICTURES AND PANICS[1]

Reappraising the public controversy around Reality TV in Europe

Daniel Biltereyst

> What could be so shocking in this form of entertainment called 'Loft Story'? The language, insinuations, rage and tears are real. This is what probably disturbs us most: the innocent, insistent and brutal presence of another generation and another social class.
>
> (Augé, 2002: 24; my translation)

In the 1990s the irresistible rise of reality formats attracted both audience success and heated controversy. Looking back at the reception of the first series of programmes such as *Big Brother* and *Survivor*, one is struck by how they were able to provoke such wide-scale debate, including vehement reactions and signs of public revulsion and anxiety. Both in the US and Europe, Reality TV has not only been heavily debated and, by some, seen as troublesome, controversial or scandalous; it has also grown into a social phenomenon itself. This suggests that these programmes invited criticism and whipped up debate – debates which went further than the programmes' concrete form, content or pragmatic strategies. They stimulated a wider debate about how crucial social and moral issues are treated by television, and by Reality TV in particular – what I see here as a meta-genre or a tendency in recent television production using high-reality claims and stressing everyday people's lives, actions and emotions (see also Dovey, 2000).

Critical observers tried to understand this intensive public debate on Reality TV by using labels such as 'hysteria', 'cult', 'media event' or 'media hype'. For some scholars and journalists, particularly those in the 'quality' press, the widespread public debate had much in common with what is known as a *moral panic*. The latter refers to a public anxiety about key social and moral issues, characterised by spiralling debate produced by the interaction of the media, public opinion, specific interest groups, intellectuals, politicians, church leaders and the authorities. The application of this concept was reinforced by the fact that in some countries, such as France, Germany or Portugal, the controversy and panic about some of these programmes drove media regulators to concrete action – including censorship or an intervention in the format of the text itself.

Concentrating upon the public debate about some highly controversial reality formats (mainly *Big Brother*, Endemol, 1999–) in various countries on the European continent, this chapter questions whether the concept of *moral panic* is useful in understanding Reality TV. The premise of this chapter is that Reality TV is often associated with a 'raw' exploitation of controversial social or moral issues – what may be seen as a working ethos or a pragmatic strategy for audience maximisation. Reality TV might be illustrating the situation, described by Kenneth Thompson in *Moral Panics*, of how 'certain parts of the mass media have responded to market pressures by competing with each other to present dramatic narratives and spectacles with a strong moral content' (1998: 141).

However, I will argue that the concept remains somewhat insufficient to understand Reality TV and the discursive debate which has surrounded it – especially within different national contexts. As a critical and analytical concept developed in the 1970s, the concept of a moral panic might even be outmoded in a postmodern era with its abundance of (mediated) voices. In a contemporary media context, moral panics seem to be rather simulated, only rarely resulting in social change, mainly because they are woven into a wider flow or web of news stories and media events. The fuss around Reality TV in many European countries might have had rather the characteristics of a *media panic* – referring to the historical phenomenon that the introduction of a new mass medium or a 'new' genre can cause strong public reactions, sometimes leading to a spiral of fear, threat and (in some cases) regulation or censorship. Overall, I claim that in a competitive, commercial mediascape the simulation of moral panics and the search for controversy might have become an integral part of the multimedia, interactive format of Reality TV.

Reality TV and moral panics

In examining the press coverage of controversial reality shows in the European context, it is astounding how some of these entertainment programmes were able to create, in a relatively short timespan, a true media event. This often included a public debate and a wider flow of interrelated discourses produced by different sorts of social actors. In Portugal, for instance, one of the first reality shows, *O Bar da TV* (TV Bar, SIC, 2000, Portugal), quickly became the object of intense criticism and public controversy. In *O Bar da TV*, the competitors lived in a Lisbon apartment, where they ran a bar as their only source of income. While the contestants were often shown naked, the broadcaster (SIC) at one time showed how the participants passed around a vibrator and condoms. The real fuss, however, started when SIC decided to broadcast an emotional conversation between a young female participant and her parents, who tried to convince her to leave the show. This 'private' conversation was broadcast against the will of the woman and her parents. This violation of privacy rules was seen by various groups in society to be the proverbial bridge too far. In the Portuguese media, journalists, academics, lawyers, intellectuals, church leaders and politicians attacked the programme-makers for allegedly infringing the participants' privacy. A Catholic bishop claimed that he was shocked that people 'sold their souls', while the head of the national lawyers' association described the show as the 'most vile spectacle' in the history of Portuguese television.[2] Similar voices about the debasement of quality, morality and privacy were raised in opinion pages. Finally, two ministers sent a complaint to the high authority for the media (Alta Autoridade Para a Comunicaçao Social – AACS), asking them to take appropriate measures.[3] A similar fuss was made later with the local version of *Big Brother* (TV1, 2001–, Portugal) when the competing channel, TV1, was forced to throw two contestants out after they were seen having sex. The former health minister Maria de Belem claimed that 'if a person can be jailed for exhibitionism in a town square or a municipal park, why are they permitted to do it on national television?' (EBU, 2001; Tremlett, 2001).

Similar scenarios can be found in other European countries, where controversial reality shows, and the local versions of *Big Brother* in particular, were met by protests, signs of public revulsion and denouncement by elite groups in society. Writing about the Netherlands, where *Big Brother* (Endemol for Veronica, 1999–, Netherlands) was first launched, Jaap van Ginneken tried to explain the 'waves of moral indignation' as a sign of a *moral panic* (2000: 107–8). According to van Ginneken, the sudden outbreaks of a *moral panic* illustrated a collective feeling about 'conventional values blatantly being affected' (ibid.). The first *Big Brother* series was met in the Netherlands by the rejection of clergymen, politicians and experts such as professional psychologists. The latter increased the controversy around the programme by referring to the potential psychic dangers for the participants – using as an example the earlier suicide of the first contestant who had to leave the Swedish *Expedition Robinson* in 1997 (SVT, 1997, Sweden).[4]

These and other stories about the 'dangers' of Reality TV were so powerful that they quickly became crucial reference points in the critical coverage by the European quality press, as well as in wider public debates. The *Robinson* suicide and other controversial stories grew into *media templates* (Kitzinger, 2000), meaning that they became a rhetorical shorthand for journalists, critics and readers to frame wider concerns over the legality, quality and morality of Reality TV.

Moral panics

This mixture of elements – the public outcry by representatives of key social institutions and organisations, the feeling of the transgression of moral codes, the threat to social interests, the media's role in whipping up the debate, including the use of rhetorical devices such as simplification and stigmatisation, eventually leading to concrete legal action – drove some observers to acknowledge the concept of a *moral panic* (e.g. Bondebjerg, 2002: 185; Mikos *et al.*, 2001: 200–4; Richardson and Meinhof, 1999: 126; Sampedro, 2001). Before examining whether some European societies were, even for a short period, going through a moral panic, we should go back to the theoretical underpinnings of this problematic and much-devalued concept.

In its classical sense, the term was coined by Jock Young (1971) in his analysis of the social reaction against drug-taking and by Stanley Cohen's study of teenage gangs. In his book *Folk Devils and Moral Panics* (1980), Cohen examined how society and the media responded to juvenile crime and gangs as a social and cultural phenomenon. In Cohen's definition, a moral panic could be conceptualised in the following way:

> Societies appear to be subject...to periods of moral panic. A condition, episode, person or group of persons emerges to become defined as a threat to societal values and interests; its nature is presented in a stylised and stereotypical fashion by the mass media; the moral barricades are manned by editors, bishops, politicians and other right-thinking people; socially accredited experts pronounce their diagnoses and solutions; ways of coping are evolved or (more often) resorted to; the condition then disappears, submerges or deteriorates and becomes more visible.
>
> (Cohen, 1980: 9)

The concept indicates the process through which particular groups in society – particularly areas of youth culture (e.g. rockers, mods, drug users), come to be considered a threat to core values and norms. In this gradual process of transforming these groups into deviants, the reactions of particular agents of social control (often indicated as 'moral guardians' such as clergymen, politicians and editors) can be reinforced by the authority of 'socially accredited experts' (e.g. psychologists, sociologists). In this overall process of defining deviancy, however, the media play a crucial role. By amplifying the denouncing voices of those on the 'moral barricades', the media act as catalysts in whipping up the public debate and in scapegoating particular 'folk devils'. In their rhetorical treatment of incidents and their portrayal of the deviants' behaviour, the media can use devices such as sensational and misleading headlines, melodramatic vocabulary, exaggeration, prediction (using particular events or behaviour for speculating about how consensual values and norms will be violated in the future), stereotyping, stigmatisation and so forth. Through this game of labelling and accentuating deviancy, the media are able to represent or construct certain groups in society as a threat to consensual values. According to Cohen, the media can amplify public concern and anxiety at several stages of this moral panic process – eventually leading to a spiralling debate with concrete responses and actions from powerful opinion leaders, the authorities or state institutions (e.g. police, judiciary, regulatory bodies). Finally, after a certain period a moral panic recedes or vanishes, sometimes resulting in social changes (Cohen, 1980; see also Springhall, 1998; K. Thompson, 1998).

This view of the media's role in creating public anxiety and moral panic has been explored by other scholars. From this perspective on moral panics, the media are often closely connected with conservatism: through the amplification of deviancy they actively define, (re)construct and finally underpin hegemonic values and ideologies. Mainly through the work of Hall *et al.* (1978) on mugging, the moral panics concept entered into a wider critique of the media's ideological function in constructing social 'reality'. Through moral panics, the media may even call for an increase in punitive measures and help to contribute to a 'law and order' ideology. What is interesting – and what perhaps in part functions to complicate the debate – is that the concept itself has also been used outside academia in the quality papers and the media itself.

Moral panics and the Reality TV debate

In examining the reception of controversial reality shows, it is astounding how some of the basic characteristics of the moral panic appear to be pertinent. Here I can refer to the ideas on the following:

- the presence of particular moral guardians;
- the role of experts;
- the role of the media and their techniques in whipping up the debate;
- the perception of core values being threatened;
- the call for action, regulation, law and order, and in some cases even for new forms of censorship;
- the different stages in the creation, amplification and the recession of the panic.

Writing about the fuss around the first Spanish *Big Brother* series, called *Gran Hermano* (Tele 5, 2001, Spain), critics such as Victor Sampedro talked about 'moral panics' and debates which 'are usually biased by ethical or cultural standards that are representative of elite sectors of society' (2001: 9). Attracting more than one-third of the Spanish population, *Gran Hermano* grew into a major public phenomenon. However, similar to what happened in Portugal, the programme was heavily attacked on moral grounds by many writers, intellectuals, journalists and even bishops (Garmendia, 2000: 195; Sampedro, 2001: 9). In the media they were fulminating against the exploitation of intimacy and human dignity by the programme. Ultimately they even called for concrete actions from regulators in terms of intervening in or censoring the programme.

Also in France, *Big Brother*'s local version, *Loft Story* (Endemol France for M6, 2001, France), became the televisual event of the year, inspiring leading intellectuals to introduce the words 'loft' and 'loft story' into their critical vocabulary – often as synonyms for a perceived new 'vulgarity' or barbarism. *Loft Story* and the intense media discourse which surrounded it served as a catalyst in invigorating spiralling debates on a range of social and moral issues such as the societal role of television and the media; the status of the private and public sphere; the nature of vulgarity and cultural quality; the survival of French traditional values within a global media environment; the commercialisation of intimacy, love and sex; the representation of the physical body; the 'problem' and future of youth; and so forth. The French case is interesting because it seems to include, probably more than elsewhere, the basic ingredients of the moral panic concept with moral guardians being supported by many experts (e.g. psychiatrists and psychologists supporting the idea of the programme as a 'threat') in their denunciation of how core values were perceived to be under attack. Their opinions and analyses soon appeared on the front pages of quality papers such as *Le Monde* and *Libération*, which played a significant role in circulating public reactions to *Loft Story*. The public debate even provoked street riots – only a couple of weeks after the start of the programme, protesters besieged the Paris apartment of *Loft Story*, while police forces and private guards had to use tear gas to stop activists. These images were extremely powerful and acted as a media template or a form of rhetorical shorthand in discussing and framing the programme. In these debates *Loft Story* mostly acted as a negative sounding board, used with contempt by different sorts of moral guardians and social groups. Finally, the French regulatory body intervened at several stages, forcing some modifications of the reality show's basic rules of conduct. I will return to this French case study later on, but the public controversy appeared to fuel, rather than deplete, the audience ratings for the programme (EBU, 2001; Kerviel and Psenny, 2001).

In Germany too, the *Big Brother* (Endemol for RTL2, 2000, Germany) debate had many characteristics of a moral panic (Mikos *et al.*, 2001; Müller, 2000: 177). It has rarely been the case that a television programme was able to inspire leading German intellectuals, politicians, church leaders, journalists, editors and representatives from the labour and women's movement to raise their voices – even before the show had started. The programme director of the (competing) public channel ARD denounced the programme as 'seelischer Kannibalismus' or psychic cannibalism, while the bishop of Trier attacked Endemol for its 'inhuman motifs' (Broer, 2000: 58). In the quality press, intellectuals, journalists and writers compared the programme's format and ethos with claustrophobia, concentration camps and even Nazi ideology. Leading politicians from various parties, including several minister-presidents of local states (*Länder*), joined the public denunciation and claimed that the programme should be forbidden. The German minister of domestic affairs, Otto Schily, even called for a total boycott of the programme on the basis of Article 1 of the Federal Constitution, dealing with respect for human dignity. These extreme forms of public denunciation by elite groups were supported by experts and amplified by the wide media coverage. Ultimately, this pressure drove media regulators in several regional *Länder* (notably Bavaria and Hess) to censor the programme content. This indirectly led to the modification of the programme, maintaining, for instance, that the cameras should be stopped for one hour a day. The outcry of intellectuals, politicians and other 'moral guardians' continued for a while, but soon the public anxiety receded, and then vanished at the end of the series (e.g. Broer, 2000; EBU, 2001; Mikos *et al.*, 2001; Müller, 2000).

There are certainly more cases showing a similar mixture of moral panic elements. In Greece, for instance, a leading newspaper claimed that *Big Brother* (Antenna TV, 2001, Greece) would 'bring to the surface of society the most repulsive characteristics of human nature' (ibid.). Similar to France, students and journalists organised anti-*Big Brother* rallies, while the local media regulator claimed that it would keep a close watch over obscenity and privacy rules. In Italy, too, the public debate on *Grande Fratello* (Canale 5, 2000, Italy) presented similar arguments, but again a typical national feature came along. Mainly through the public interventions of politicians, leading intellectuals and writers such as Umberto Eco, the local *Big Brother* phenomenon turned into a straight (party) political issue. Critics used the programme to uncover Berlusconi's state and media power, including its ambivalent populist ethos. The political leader Massimo D'Alema (DS, left democrats), for instance, claimed that Berlusconi allowed this kind of repulsive material on his channels, while his political discourse normally contained a conservative longing for 'high values of family, morality, solidarity and the richness of human relations' (Jozsef, 2000: 15). However, similar to what happened in other countries such as the Netherlands, Belgium (Mathijs, 2002) and most of the Nordic and Scandinavian countries, none of the responsible Italian authorities took an explicit position on the programme (EBU, 2001).

National differences and questioning moral panics

All these national stories on the reception of a controversial reality show such as *Big Brother* raise many questions – not least the issue of national specificities where reception is concerned. Before considering the critical, theoretical and methodological validity of the concept of the moral panic here, I should acknowledge significant differences in the public debate over Reality TV. Examining the press coverage in Western European countries, it is astounding how instructive the different debates on a similar Reality TV format can be – or how these debates often tell us more about the culture in which the responses emerge than about the programmes themselves. Of course, there have been important differences in the 'local' adaptations of global Reality TV formats, even within the textual parameters defined by the formats *Big Brother* or *Survivor*. In some countries, for instance, the public was able to follow the *Big Brother* participants 24 hours a day only on the Internet, while dedicated live streaming channels were set up for continuous coverage in Italy, Spain or the UK (e.g. E4). There were differences in the audience strategies, marketing devices, advertising campaigns, the basic rules of conduct, the selection of participants and so on. The *Big Brother* case is an extreme illustration of how in an increasingly transnational television landscape formats are adapted to reflect particular broadcasting regimes or socio-cultural sensibilities. (Indeed, this flexibility between a 'proven' idea and the potential for 'local' adaptation is a crucial element in the appeal of the format for the broadcasters and television industry) (see Moran, 1998).

We cannot escape the idea that the public debates on Reality TV were also highly indicative of larger national differences in terms of the status of 'moral guardians'; the position of experts, journalists or intellectuals; ongoing shifts in local television culture; as well as of strategies of distinction within the public sphere – including the fields of politics, culture and the media. It is not possible here to explore these specificities in more detail, but it is no surprise that in Italy the debate about *Grande Fratello* turned into a straight politically oriented debate, or that the one in Germany carried strong traces of a traumatic national history with references to the claustrophobic *Big Brother* house and Nazi concentration camps. Or that in Northern countries politicians were more self-restrained and restrictive in using a television programme to get a distinctive profile. Or that in the French public debate intellectuals, academics and writers were much more active in denouncing *Loft Story*: inspired by the public image of philosophers and sociologists such as Sartre or Bourdieu, there is in France a longer tradition of the 'critical intellectual' as a public/media figure, instantly reflecting upon important contemporary political, social and moral issues.

Another feature of the national differences, of course, deals with the extremity of the public anxiety and moral panic. It is remarkable how in some (often Southern European) countries controversy was particularly marked, while the same reality format caused little furore in other regions. A case in point is the USA, where the *Big Brother* and the *Survivor* formats seemed tame in comparison to other more controversial local reality shows. A major reason why these programmes were not able to whip up a moral panic relates back to earlier debates in the USA on the perceived 'excesses' of new Reality TV formats – ranging from reality crime shows (e.g. *Rescue 911* [CBS, 1989–96, US], *America's Most Wanted* [Fox, 1988–, US]) to confessional chat shows (*The Oprah Winfrey Show* [Harpo Productions for ABC, 1986–, US]). Many of the arguments found in the most extreme public debates on Reality TV in European countries such as France and Germany were already circulating several years earlier in the USA. In 1998, for instance, *The Jerry Springer Show* (Universal TV, 1991–, US) caused a wide public debate in the USA on the immorality, display and exploitation of 'deviancy' in American television (Dovey, 2000: 117).

On the European continent the Reality TV debate took quite different directions, mainly in terms of the intensity of the public anxiety or moral panic. Similarly to France, Germany, the UK and other parts of the world (see Roscoe, 2001; Tincknell and Raghuram, 2002), *Big Brother* was certainly a major success in most Northern European and Scandinavian countries, equally causing – in many instances – major media hype. However, it did not whip up such a contested discursive arena of 'moral panic' and debate. In an article on the reception of the first series of *Big Brother* in Belgium, Ernest Mathijs (2002) indicated how the original controversy quickly died out and how the initial concerns completely disappeared during the following seasons. Even during the first series Mathijs indicated several shifts in the critical reception of the programme. This was seen to move from an engaged critical debate about the 'moral' value of the programme, towards a concern with its format, rules and narrative tensions, prior to a growing lack of interest among critics and moral guardians.

In writing about the critical reception of the Danish version of the programme, Ib Bondebjerg claimed that

> the serious morning newspapers and TV-stations took a purely moral decline position calling it trash TV while the rest of the press, especially the tabloids, greedily tried to capitalize on the hot information and fuel audience interest.... The themes in the public debate in the serious press were generally very critical, although few papers went to the extreme of anticipating the decline of a whole culture.
>
> (Bondebjerg, 2002: 186)

Although it contained public denunciation and denial as part of a strategy of distinction from politicians and journalists, the Danish public debate about *Big Brother* (Endemol for TV Danmark, 2001–, Denmark) turned out to be less hysterical. In the Danish case, but also in the Netherlands (van Ginneken, 2000), the initial hysteria about the programme soon turned into a 'cult' issue – sometimes even prompting intellectuals and politicians to look at *Big Brother* and other reality shows more positively, and hence turning them into a thoughtful metaphor for changes in society and the media. Several Danish scholars, as well as well-known politicians such as Naser Khader, claimed that the programme should be considered as an instructive experiment or a school for young immigrants to learn more about Danish codes of conduct (Bondebjerg, 2002: 187). In the Netherlands several books and articles quickly appeared, which not only stressed a national pride about the export success of the Dutch format. These contesting voices also looked at the 'deeper' sense of this around-the-century programme about contemporary social and moral issues in terms of problems with human relations, intimacy and security (Beunders, 2000).

The public debate in these European contexts indicates that the moral panic atmosphere did not pass without contestation, and even questions whether we can use the concept of the 'moral panic' here. Traditional moral guardians' claims about a threat to core values in society were blatantly confronted by contesting voices from the audience, as well as from representatives of those often considered 'on the moral barricade' (e.g. politicians, opinion leaders, social scientists or experts). Another key issue in questioning moral panics deals with the status of the 'folk devils' in these public debates on Reality TV. In most countries it should be acknowledged that it remains difficult to find clear references to groups or persons which – following Cohen's (1980) definition – become defined as a threat to societal values and interests. This leads one to question the usefulness of the moral panic concept and its underlying ideas about a consensual society with clear definitions of authority, deviancy and the role of the media.

Reality TV, public discourses and the exploitation of panics

The less able the conservatives and the right are to control these changes, the more frantic their repertoire of moral panics becomes, to the extent that the panics are no longer about social control but rather about the fear of being out of control.

(McRobbie, 1994: 199)

While the moral panic concept successfully entered journalistic vocabulary as a concept of criticism and distinction, it has become the object of a growing critique and theoretical reappraisal within cultural studies and sociology. Mainly prompted by the work of Angela McRobbie (ibid.), scholars began to question the consensual view of power in society and the media's role in maintaining social control. Moral panics are generally still considered to be part of a 'powerful emotional strategy' of conservative forces (ibid.: 199), but according to McRobbie 'the model of moral panic is urgently in need of updating and revising precisely because of its success' (ibid.: 217).

A crucial point in this critique deals with some basic changes in the status of those involved in defining social deviancy and in amplifying moral panics. This includes changes in the authority of those on 'the moral barricades', and the role of media and the position of the folk devils. McRobbie argued that:

> the rectangular relationship of positions and processes which held the old model together (the sociologists on behalf of the deviant; the agencies of social control; the media; the moral guardians and experts) has been replaced by a more diverse and more fluid set of institutions, agencies and practices which sometimes interlock.
>
> (McRobbie, 1994: 211)

First, it is widely acknowledged that since the 1970s there has been a gradual undermining of the authority of some traditional agents of social control. Here we can refer to diverse groups and institutions in society (e.g. church, intellectual elites, school system, monopolistic public-service broadcasting) whose former authority in defining and safeguarding moral and social values received more competition than ever (e.g. crumbling church attendance, new forms of religion and atheism; success of commercial broadcasting and subsequent changes in the public-service ethos).

Second, this undermining of authority has gone hand in hand with an impressive growth in pressure, self-help or special-interest groups (Thompson, 1998: 11). The latter often successfully succeeded in responding to or countering stigmatising images of deviancy in relation to specific social 'problems' and moral 'issues' (e.g. the gay rights movement, ethnic minority movements). McRobbie claimed that:

> 'folk devils' have, over the last ten years, found themselves defended vociferously not so much by mainstream opposition parties…but rather by pressure groups and self-help groups which have sprung up across the country and which now play a major role in contesting what they perceive as stereotypes and popular misconceptions.
>
> (McRobbie, 1994: 213–14)

She continues that 'some "folk devils" themselves become organizers and campaigners' (ibid.). This includes not only targeted media campaigns but also the production of their own media (outlets) – certainly in this age of the Internet. According to McRobbie, this all led to a proliferation of voices in the media and in the public sphere, introducing a potentially strong contestation of the traditional moral guardians' position.

A third major shift since Cohen's conceptualisation of moral panics deals with the role of the media itself. Here, McRobbie and other scholars (Springhall,

1998; Thompson, 1998) have stressed in different ways how a more competitive commercial media environment has increased the use of stories with a moral panic angle. McRobbie claimed that moral panics have 'become the norms of journalistic practice', with even quality papers using 'exaggerated, sensational and moralistic headlines' (ibid.: 202). In a similar vein, Kenneth Thompson argued that 'certain parts of the mass media have responded to market pressures by competing with each other to present dramatic narratives and spectacles with a strong moral content' (1998: 141), thus amplifying the 'at-risk character of modern society…due to factors such as the loss of the authority of traditional elites' (ibid.).

It is clear that in this postmodern environment – with its proliferation of voices and the undermining of the positions of the authorities, moral guardians and 'folk devils' – the traditional concept of moral panic appears somewhat outmoded. Although she did not refer to Reality TV, McRobbie argues that 'the media provides a kind of non-stop floorshow upon which political issues of the day are presented, paraded and transformed, no longer into straightforward moral panics, but rather into a seamless web of narrativized news and media events' (1994: 211).

A fluid set of institutions, interests and discourses: the French case

Returning to Reality TV, it is clear that this type of television has specialised in negotiating and constructing the 'web of narrativized news and media events' that McRobbie describes. It has been important in using and exploiting stories with a moral panic angle (e.g. sexuality, human relations and violence) as essentially a working practice to attract audiences. Reality TV perfectly fits into McRobbie's and other critical scholars' view of contemporary media and their intentional production and simulation of a (possible) moral panic.

The French public debate on *Loft Story*, even in all its hysterical extremes, might be seen as a case in point.[5] The debate had already started before the programme's launch on 26 April 2001. From this beginning, various registers of public discourse were opened, including several opposing voices. On the one hand, the channel, M6, and the producer, Endemol France, used different media outlets (such as the Internet, advertising, interviews in magazines and newspapers) in order to spread a double message. This involved the image of *Loft Story* as a new type of hyper-controversial and confrontational television for the wider public, while in newspapers and magazines they used a more nuanced 'expert' discourse claiming that this *Big Brother* showed more respect for French quality, cultural and human values. On the other hand, some intellectuals and different people from the established media (such as public-service channels, quality newspapers and magazines) denounced the programme with references to foreign excesses of this type of programme.

Questions about public intervention and even censorship soon appeared in the press and on opinion pages. Only one week after the start of the programme, the French regulatory body, CSA (Conseil Supérieur de l'Audiovisuel), entered the debate. In a short directive,[6] which was widely reproduced in the press, the CSA claimed in very general terms that the channel should take care of and show respect for human dignity. In more precise terms, the body referred to the use of alcohol and tobacco, which were forbidden. In the meantime, other different players had entered the spectacle of comments and denunciation. Writers, sociologists, philosophers and other 'public' intellectuals started to give their opinion on *Loft Story*. These included very well-known public figures such as the cult writer Philippe Sollers, who looked at the programme as a prison camp and compared it with a form of new dictatorship. Politicians from various horizons also entered into the discursive arena. Left-wing politicians urged the government and the regulatory body to impose tighter regulation. The conservatives could not be left behind and whipped up the debate with statements by leading politicians such as those by the ministers for family affairs (Ségolène Royal) and of communication (Cathérine Tasca). In a vehement meeting on 9 May 2001, the CSA responded to these allegations: in a new directive the regulatory body decided to investigate the stipulations on privacy matters in the contracts between the *Loft Story* participants and Endemol. Newspapers reported considerable differences of opinion within the regulatory body, mainly between anti-*Loft* hardliners and *Loft* 'indulgents' (Roberts, 2001a). In a third and final directive, the CSA decided on 14 May 2001 to instruct Endemol to change some other basic rules of the game. It enforced two hours of privacy a day, while the procedure to eliminate candidates had to be modified in a more 'human way'.

However, for several opinion leaders, such as the former CSA president Hervé Bourges, these 'weak decisions' proved that 'nobody any more has the legitimacy to oppose this cancer of contemporary television' (Chirot, 2001: 17). Still other commentators raised questions about stricter regulation and even censorship, while the left-wing newspaper *Libération* openly demanded the replacement of the CSA members who allowed this type of 'télépoubelle' (television garbage) (Sommer, 2001: 17). In this first month of the show, several pressure groups had raised their voices, including the anti-racist movement MRAP, which asked the CSA for tighter control over racist speech in the programme. This all led to another climax in the public controversy, related to street protests around the *Loft* apartment (Chirot, 2001).

In this short timespan newspapers organised several surveys. *Le Monde*, for instance, published the results of a major audience enquiry on its front page on 4 May 2001 in an article calling *Loft Story* 'folly' (Kerviel and Psenny, 2001). In this issue the newspaper devoted several articles to the controversial programme, including both a severe denunciation by renowned psychiatrists and a well-tempered article on the wide range of audiences consuming *Loft Story*. Nearly two weeks later the results of yet another enquiry appeared in *Le Monde*, with the headline 'the French are not shocked' (Rocco, 2001). A close look at the media coverage in this 'war of commentaries' (Bauer, 2001) indicates how not only tabloid, but mainly quality papers such as *Le Monde*, *Le Figaro* or *Libération*, tried to cash in on the *Loft Story* controversy. In a mixed discourse, the programme was both the object of crude denunciation (through cartoons, opinions, external experts' analysis) and 'objective' editorial work. However, a critical analysis of the newspapers' role in stimulating this spectacle of opinions indicated that these *Loft* stories resulted in an extra 15 per cent rise in the quality newspapers' sales (Chroniques du Menteur, 2001).

A harsher register of debate, denunciation and contesting voices related to the broadcasters themselves. On several occasions, the chief executive of the prestigious German–French cultural channel Arte, Jérôme Clément, protested against what he called 'this danger for democracy' and this form of 'blatant fascism'. In a widely cited interview Clément perfectly represented what Jon Dovey (2000) called a trash TV position:

> This programme brings together all types of perversity. It is an absolute and continuous lie.... It is the first television programme which is at the centre of public debate in a very long time. Everybody, including the press, is talking about it. Politicians are driven into a corner, are pushed around, and do not want to be seen as censors because they know that the majority of young people like this programme.... It is television, which finally created Silvio Berlusconi's power. This type of absolute stupidity means an abandonment of free thought. Political power is replaced by that of the media. It is dangerous for democracy.
>
> (Vulser, 2001: 17; my translation)

The 'war of broadcasters', however, really took off when the leading commercial channel, TF1, saw its market share and advertising revenue shrinking. On 11 May 2001 the channel's chief executive, Patrick Le Lay, published his 'J'Accuse' in a crude opinion article in which he denounced the programme. Claiming that TF1 had declined the idea of broadcasting a programme such as *Big Brother* in France, Le Lay finally called upon politicians and the media regulatory body to intervene. Covering this spectacle of quarrelling broadcasters, the media also opened their pages to the M6 channel's chief executive, who reaffirmed the broadcaster's respect for basic human values and dignity (Chirot *et al.*, 2001; Garrigos and Roberts, 2001). Only one month later, when the public controversy had finally blown over, TF1 triumphantly announced that it had signed a major contract with Endemol for the production of several reality shows. Justifying its decision, the leading French channel argued that 'TF1 is in favour of the type of Reality TV which is not cut off from reality...TF1 will bring Reality TV but no trash TV' (Dutheil, 2001: 21; my translation).

As in other countries (see Mathijs, 2002), the controversy died down rather quickly. At the end of May 2001 more nuanced positions were published in the French media. These included analyses by social scientists and philosophers in which *Loft Story* was often seen rather as a metaphor for changing values in French society (Augé, 2002; Roberts, 2001b). A crucial site for competing discourses on the programme was the Internet, with a record number of chat groups and various types of *Loft*-related sites. The latter included light fan sites, humorous forums (e.g. www.poulaga.cotcot.com) and sites which denounced the programme (e.g. www.bofstory.fr), as well as more thematic or special-interest pages (for example gay sites such as www.loftscary.fr) (Kerviel and Psenny, 2001).

This French case, then, ultimately illustrates McRobbie's key arguments on the need to revise the moral panic concept. McRobbie accepted the persistence of moral panics, mainly through the media's attempt to exploit issues with a moral panic potential. As this case indicates, however, straightforward moral panics seem to be submerged in a wider, continuous web of stories, events and public discourses. In the French case we acknowledged competing discourses on different media levels – in the editorial pages of newspapers and magazines, in commentaries and opinion pages, in advertising and trailers, on the Internet, in street actions and so forth. Initially, the media played a crucial role in presenting voices which contained elite denunciations with a moral panic angle. In the first six weeks, even quality newspapers and opinion-makers were eager to whip up a spiralling moral panic debate: several provocative stories (e.g. the suicide in *Expedition Robinson*; images of violence, sex or nudity; street protests in Paris and Athens; concrete operations by media regulatory bodies in France and Germany) were issued as media templates and served to frame the lack of 'quality', legality and morality of Reality TV. However, this hysteria was countered by contesting voices in the media, by experts, on the Internet – or even within the media regulatory board itself. Six weeks after the start of the show the controversy diminished. And when the programme finally ended, on 6 July 2002, the media coverage nearly vanished.

Media panic

Here it is necessary, I think, to distinguish between a moral and a media panic. In Kirsten Drotner's definition, a media panic refers to a situation where 'the mass media are seen both as a source and a medium of public reaction' (1992: 44).

Throughout the history of modernity there have been periodic concerns about the emergence of particular new media technologies and genres. So it is a historical phenomenon where the introduction of a new popular medium (e.g. comics in the 19th century, the Internet), genre (e.g. US gangster movie in the 1930s) or thematic series (e.g. US juvenile delinquency movies in the 1950s) can cause strong public reactions, mainly among elites. This often includes a spiralling debate among elite groups characterised by denunciation, emotional language and often calls for regulation or censorship.

According to Drotner, 'media panics tackle central questions about cultural quality, personal development and social change under the rubric of enlightenment' (ibid.: 60). The denouncing discourse often contains concerns about the negative influences of these various media outlets on young people's behaviour. A media panic discourse speaks the language of ethical concerns about what young people do, the books they read, the music they listen to, the movies and TV programmes they watch, the video games they play, the Internet sites they visit and so on. However, as the history of film censorship has indicated, for instance, these concerns over the influence of troubling/troublesome pictures for children and young people often contain wider questions of cultural politics and ideology. The history of media panics (Springhall, 1998) shows that new media (genres/series) were often perceived as a threat to dominant cultural and societal values. The media panic discourse also contains references to 'various strategies of using "quality" culture as a means of a moral, and by implication social, elevation' (Drotner, 1992: 49).

It would drive one too far to compare the rise of Reality TV with other case studies in the history of the media panic phenomenon. But it seems to be fruitful to look at the hysteria around some controversial reality shows as a *media panic* (rather than simply retaining Cohen's view of moral panic being a result of the media's exploitation of sensitive moral issues). It might, in other words, be useful to consider the initial public anxieties as a result of the introduction of a controversial 'new' genre.

The media panic concept allows us to look at the public debate on Reality TV as a historical period with a start and an end, including a burst of public concern, a public demand for intervention, eventually leading to regulation or straight censorship. The range of interventions very much depends on the culture's politics and ideas about liberalism. Drotner argues here that there is a change in the media panic discourse, where in the beginning of the 20th century early panics threw up mechanisms of straight censorship and direct regulation (ibid.: 52). Gradually, it moved in the direction of more liberal policies such as 'tacit paternalistic measures' to promote 'good culture'. The case of Reality TV, and the *Big Brother* phenomenon in particular, indicates that quite different policies were followed in Europe. In most countries no interventions were made, while in others regulators went back to direct interventions. The fact that in several countries arguments about the necessity of censorship came into the public debate simply stresses the extreme nature of public reactions to the Reality TV meta-genre.

Examining the discourse generated by Reality TV as a media panic also allows us to frame the 'quality' argument clearly as a feature of cultural politics. As Drotner argues, the 'discourse of the panics is basically a discourse of power whose stakes are the right to define cultural norms and social qualifications' (ibid.: 50). From this perspective, the Reality TV debate might be seen as a public showcase for those who aspire to defend particular (elite) definitions of cultural quality against 'trash'. Referring to the French broadcasters' discursive war, it is clear that the wider Reality TV debate was often firmly rooted in a more traditional cultural critical debate on the opposition of 'quality' versus trash. In a European television context, quality culture is still often associated with a discourse on the survival of the public-service broadcasting ethos, including rhetoric about high quality, diversity, information, originality and moral/social elevation (Wieten *et al.*, 2000).

The media panic perspective finally puts the discourse about young people into a historical perspective. However, there remains a hybrid relationship with this core group of Reality TV consumers. On the one hand, the idea of a media panic includes a concept of consumers as possible victims of bad taste or vulnerable values (Hight, 2001). Hence, a media panic (as well as a moral panic) includes strong traces of paternalism, mostly directed at children and young people. On the other hand, the Reality TV phenomenon stresses the extreme distance in tastes and lifestyles between these possible victims (young people watching) and the (media) cultural guardians.

As McRobbie's (1994) argument indicates, contemporary television genres are very much aware of the entertainment and promotional value of stories with a moral and media panic angle. The case studies discussed here suggest that the programme-makers were well aware that they had to create a web of very different discourses around the programme, including attempts to whip up or simulate a panic. What was interesting in the case of *Big Brother* is that the producers in various countries explicitly teased and even *urged* for problems with moral guardians and with regulators in order to get media attention. In Belgium, for instance, months before the first series of *Big Brother* (Endemol for Kanaal 2, 2000, Belgium) a wide advertising campaign showed adverts quoting prominent politicians and well-known opinion leaders claiming that this programme was the worst ever to be shown. One big national ad quoted the former minister of justice from the conservative/Catholic party, who threatened the programme-makers and the commercial channel with a lawsuit if '*Big Brother* violated, even to a small extent, principles of human dignity' (Biltereyst, 2000). This example indicates that the programme-makers tried from the beginning to exploit the controversial moral/media panic dimension of the programme. From a cynical perspective, then, the ultimate conclusion may be that those denouncing the programme from the moral barricade or those defending elite cultural quality acted as a perfect sounding board for the industry's search for publicity.

Notes

1 I would like to thank Ib Bondebjerg. A first version of this chapter was presented during my stay at the Department of Film and Media Studies of the Copenhagen University, Denmark, in November 2002.
2 http://news.bbc.co.uk/1/hi/entertainment/tv—and—radio/1336332, 17 May 2001 (accessed 4 January 2003).
3 See, on *O Bar da TV*, the text on the AACS decision at http://www.aacs.pt/bd/Deliberacoes/20010522, as well as http://news.bbc.co.uk/1/hi/entertainment/tv—and—radio/1336332 (accessed 4 January 2003).
4 In Sweden one of the *Expedition Robinson* contestants, voted out by his fellow residents of the island, later committed suicide. This tragic event caused a wider debate on the ethics of the programme, as well as on professional issues such as the screening process and psychological guidance (e.g. De Ceulaer, 2000: 27).
5 Dauncey (1996) indicates that French television has a longer tradition of producing local formats of 'télé-réalité'.
6 CSA Communiqué n° 448, 2 May 2001. See www.ibelgique.ifrance.com/socio-media/csa448 (accessed 7 January 2003).

References

Augé, Marc (2002) 'Le Stade de l'écran', *Le Monde Diplomatique*, June: 24.

Bauer, Sebastien (2001) http://www.ornitho.org/ornitho/article29, 11 May (accessed 7 May 2003).

Ben-Yehuda, Nachman (1990) *The Politics and Morality of Deviance*, New York: University of New York Press.

Beunders, Henri (2000) *Wat je ziet ben je zelf. Big Brother: lust, leven en lijden voor de camera* [You are what you see. *Big Brother*: lust, living and suffering before the camera], Amsterdam: Prometheus.

Biltereyst, Daniel (2000) *Realiteit en fictie: Tweemaal hetzelfde*, Brussels: King Baudouin Foundation.

Bondebjerg, Ib (2002) 'The Mediation of Everyday Life. Genre, Discourse, and Spectacle in Reality TV', in Ann Jerslev (ed.) *Realism and 'Reality' in Film and Media. Northern Lights. Film and Media Studies Yearbook 2002*, Copenhagen: Museum Tusculanum Press.

Broer, Thijs (2000) 'Echte conflicten. *Big Brother* in Duitsland', *Vrij Nederland*, 18 March: 58.

Chirot, Françoise (2001) 'Le CSA demande la modification des règles du jeu "Loft Story"', *Le Monde*, 16 May: 17.

Chirot, Françoise, Guy Dutheil and Frédéric Roy (2001) 'Le Succès de "Loft Story" déclenche la guerre des chaînes', *Le Monde*, 17 May: 12.

Chroniques du Menteur (2001) http://www.menteur.com/chronik/010518, 18 May (accessed 7 January 2003).

Cohen, Stanley (1980) *Folk Devils and Moral Panics: The Creation of the Mods and Rockers* (new edition), Oxford: Martin Robertson; first published in 1972.

Dauncey, Hugh (1996) 'French Reality Television: More than a Matter of Taste?', *European Journal of Communication* 11(1): 83–106.

De Ceulaer, Joel (2000) 'Een spelletje mens-erger-je-niet', *Knack*, 30 August: 12.

Dovey, Jon (2000) *Freakshow: First Person Media and Factual Television*, London: Pluto Press.

Drotner, Kirsten (1992) 'Modernity and Media Panics', in Michael Skovmand and Kim Schroder (eds) *Media Cultures. Reappraising Transnational Media*, London: Routledge.

Dutheil, Guy (2001) 'TV1 assure son approvisionnement en émissions de télé-réalité', *Le Monde*, 12 June: 21.

EBU (2001) '*Big Brother*: an international phenomenon', *Diffusion: Quarterly Journal of the EBU* 4: 6–21.

Garmendia, Maialen (2000) '*Gran Hermano* in Spanje (I)', in Irene Costera Meier and Maarten Reesink (eds) *Reality Soap!*, Amsterdam: Boom.

Garrigos, Raffaël and Isabelle Roberts (2001) 'Loft Story: "TF1 perd ses nerfs"', *Libération*, 11 May: 25.

Goode, Erich and Nachman Ben-Yehuda (1994) *Moral Panics: The Social Construction of Deviance*, Oxford: Blackwell.

Hall, Stuart, Chas Critcher, Tony Jefferson, John Clarke and Brian Roberts (1978) *Policing the Crisis: Mugging, the State, and Law and Order*, London: Macmillan.

Hight, Craig (2001) 'Debating Reality TV', *Continuum* 15(3): 389–95.

Jozsef, Eric (2000) '"Big Brother" tourne au débat politique en Italie', *Libération*, 6 October: 15.

Kerviel, Sylvie and Daniel Psenny (2001) 'Loft Story: Enquête sur les coulisses de la première émission de télé-réalité', *Le Monde*, 4 May: 10.

Kitzinger, Jenny (2000) 'Media Templates: Patterns of Association and (Re)Construction of Meaning over Time', *Media, Culture & Society* 22(1): 61–84.

McRobbie, Angela (1994) 'The Moral Panic in the Age of the Postmodern Mass Media', in Angela McRobbie (ed.) *Postmodernism and Popular Culture*, London: Routledge.

Mathijs, Ernest (2002) '*Big Brother* and Critical Discourse: Shifts in the Reception of Big Brother Belgium', *Television and New Media* 3(3): 311–22.

Mikos, Lothar, Patricia Feise, Katja Herzog, Elizabeth Prommer and Verena Veihl (2001) *Im Auge der Kamera. Das Fernsehereignis Big Brother*, Berlin: Vistas.

Moran, Albert (1998) *Copycat Television: Program Formats and Cultural Identity*, Luton: University of Luton Press.

Müller, Eggo (2000) '*Big Brother* in Duitsland', in Irene Costera Meier and Maarten Reesink (eds) *Reality Soap!*, Amsterdam: Boom.

Richardson, Kay and Ulrike Meinhof (1999) *Worlds in Common? Television Discourse in a Changing Europe*, London, Routledge.

Roberts, Isabelle (2001a) 'Pro et anti-"Loft", la guerre fait rage jusqu'au CSA', *Libération*, 10 May: 15.

Roberts, Isabelle (2001b) 'Une Étude sociologique décrypte l'engouement des jeunes', *Libération*, 6 July: 16.

Rocco, Anne-Marie (2001) 'Qui regarde "Loft Story" et pourquoi', *Libération*, 18 May: 9.

Roscoe, Jane (2001) '"*Big Brother* Australia": Performing the "Real" Twenty-four-seven', *International Journal of Cultural Studies* 4(4): 473–88.

Sampedro, Victor (2001) *New Genres in Commercial Television and their Effect on Public Opinion*, Strasbourg: Council of Europe, 6 December.

Sommer, Martin (2001) 'Heibel om Franse televullis', *De Volkskrant*, 16 May: 17.

Springhall, John (1998) *Youth, Popular Culture and Moral Panics*, London: Macmillan.

Staiger, Janet (1995) *Bad Women: Regulating Sexuality in Early American Cinema*, Minneapolis, MN: University of Minnesota Press.

Thompson, John (2000) *Political Scandal*, Cambridge: Polity.

Thompson, Kenneth (1998) *Moral Panics*, New York and London: Routledge.

Tincknell, Estella and Parvati Raghuram (2002) '*Big Brother*: Reconfiguring the "Active" Audience of Cultural Studies?', *European Journal of Cultural Studies* 5(2): 199–215.

Tremlett, Giles (2001) 'TV Watchdog Bites after Portuguese Live Sex and Nudity', *Guardian*, 28 May: 23.

van Ginneken, Jaap (2000) 'Reality-soap en de publieke opinie', in Irene Costera Meier and Maarten Reesink (eds) *Reality Soap!*, Amsterdam: Boom.

Vulser, Nicole (2001) 'Pour Jérôme Clément, "Loft Story" annonce l'avènement d'un fascisme rampant", *Le Monde*, 15 May: 17.

Wieten, Jan, Graham Murdoch and Peter Dahlgren (eds) (2000) *Television across Europe*, London: Sage.

Young, Jock (1971) *The Drugtakers*, London: Paladin.

5

'ALL YOU'VE GOT TO WORRY ABOUT IS THE TASK, HAVING A CUP OF TEA, AND DOING A BIT OF SUNBATHING'

Approaching celebrity in *Big Brother*

Su Holmes

The development of Reality TV has made it impossible to escape the fact that we have seen an appreciable rise in the number of 'ordinary' people appearing on television. Indeed, in the intense discussion surrounding its ethical, political and cultural implications (see Cummings, 2002), Reality TV's relationship with the 'ordinary' person is used to invoke different positions in debates over the form. For example, according to its critics the relationship between Reality TV and its participants is fundamentally 'exploitative': either the programme-makers exploit their subjects through 'manipulation' and editorial control, or the participants exploit the programme in an entrepreneurial bid for media exposure. In this respect, the discourse of fame is often used as a shorthand to assert the inherent 'triviality' of Reality TV – seen as shamelessly encouraging (while also epitomising) the acceleration of a celebrity culture in which people are well known simply for their 'well-known-ness', rather than for 'greatness, worthy endeavours or talent' (Boorstin, 1963: 11). As Sam Brenton and Reuben Cohen describe, contestants find themselves 'fodder for an age-old debate about the worth and nature of modern fame' (2003: 7). One critic describes how:

> Television is now full of these walking, talking tautologies – figures merely famous for being famous – and in spite of their apparent lack of real training, talent, wisdom or humility, the medium seems only too pleased to continue feeding their craving for the camera.
>
> (McCann, 2002: 20)

Particularly during the period 2000–1, which saw a number of popular Reality game shows and global formats emerge, critics in the 'quality' press expressed a distaste for shifts in cultural conceptions of fame as part of a broader negative response to the use of factual programming as primarily entertainment – and much of the criticism of the form has centred on its perpetuation of 'fame'. In reviewing the original series of *Shipwrecked* (RDF for C4, 2000–1, UK), for example, the *Observer* was already able to advise its readers to expect '16 happy, shiny young would-be presenters...rubbing along together on an island for ten weeks', continuing its description as 'Alex Garland's *The Beach* starring the cast of [teenage soap] *Hollyoaks* in designer bikinis – not exactly the kind of serious social experiment in which to invest one's license fees' (Flett, 2000: 10).[1] In comparison, the *Guardian* pondered the shifting definitions of the term 'Reality TV', finally deciding that such programmes now incorporated 'manipulative editing, cheesecake soft porn and ill-managed anger, all enacted by a cast of wannabe models, actors and game show hosts' (Patterson, 2001: 12). Finally, in the *Financial Times* Christopher Dunkley was blunt in his insistence that 'the phrase "reality television"...is ultimately silly because...it places groups of people desperate for fame in the most contrived and artificial situations' (2001: 24). Here we can see that references to 'people desperate for fame' – that is, the 'would-be presenters' or 'wannabe models, actors and game show hosts' – are firmly set in opposition to the ideals of public-service broadcasting and perceptions of documentary's traditional claim to 'the real'. Each critic, then, displays an unease about the blurring of fictional and factual forms, and the status of factual programming as primarily entertainment, by invoking the discourses of celebrity and fame.

In contrast, others have adopted a position which conceives of the 'ordinary' person as evidence of the 'democratising' ethos of Reality TV. Described by Dovey as 'Reality TV as empowerment', this position perceives the form as a challenge to 'established paternalisms' in its bid to boldly release 'everyday voices into the public sphere' (2000: 83). Largely advanced by the broadcasters themselves (Peter Bazalgette, personal interview, 14 August 2002), this perspective downplays media 'access' in the context of fame and foregrounds the inclusion of ordinary people as evidence of a strengthened public-service agenda and participative democracy – swiftly sidelining claims of exploitation in the process. Peter Bazalgette, Creative Director of Endemol UK explains how: 'the lament today, from reality TV's critics, is why all these awful ordinary people are allowed on television. Their only distinction, apparently, is their desire to show off' (Bazalgette, 2001: 22). Referring to the winner and runner-up of the second series of the UK *Big Brother* 2001 (gay Irish air steward Brian Dowling and Welsh hairdresser Helen Adams), Bazalgette insists:

> The only way [they]...would have got on TV in the old days would have been wedged into some convenient sociological pigeonhole by the likes

of *This Week* or *World in Action*...[*Big Brother*] is an argument in favour of more diverse programming, and access to the airwaves for a more diverse spread of people.

(Bazalgette, 2001: 22)

Interesting here is the trajectory of Bazalgette's argument, in which the exhibitionist, fame-seeking rhetoric of participation (the 'desire to show off') is seen as a mistaken assumption, and then re-imagined within the context of a politicised, pluralistic framework of a 'new' public service.

Despite offering very different positions, both perspectives construct fame and celebrity as a trivial sideline in Reality TV. They are seen either as corrupting the traditionally more 'worthy' aims of factual programming or as the antithesis to the ways in which broadcasters promote the institutional and cultural value of the form. As such, neither position offers a space in which to consider what is clearly the dynamic *appeal* of the relationship between ordinary people and celebrity culture, which has occupied a central place in the rise of Reality TV. Furthermore, also obscured here are the ways in which such programming raises complex questions of methodological and theoretical approach when it comes to conceptualising fame. With this in mind, my interest here is in the extent to which existing theoretical conceptions of stardom/celebrity are useful when approaching Reality TV, which, as the quotes above suggest, has marked a significant moment in television's relations with fame, and its implications for the circulation of television culture. My interest is less in the (somewhat circuitous) debates about the 'worth' of contemporary fame as perpetuated by Reality TV, than in its ideological implications, and its broader semiotic and structural construction of a celebrity 'image'. *Big Brother* has clearly been at the forefront of this shift, and its existence in the UK context represents my focus here.

'Ordinary' people on television?

It is not, of course, new for ordinary people to appear on television. Genres as diverse as news, quiz shows and documentaries have long since relied upon the role and presence of 'real' people as opposed to media professionals and performers. The spectacle of 'real emotion' (Root, 1986: 101) or behaviour that appears 'live, uncontrolled, expressive' (Lury, 1995: 127) has also long since characterised the value and appeal of such appearances – just as it continues to do in Reality TV today (Hill, 2002). Writing in 1986, Root described the traditional genres above as offering a rather limited set of roles in which ordinary people are precisely employed to 'be ordinary' (in quiz shows, for example, displaying a nervousness and delight about appearing on television) (1986: 97), or are required to perform a 'specific task – to illustrate an expert's thesis or [to be] the

113

subjects of somebody else's show' (ibid.: 96). In fact, 'ordinary' people have more often been conceptualised as viewers (Couldry, 2000: 47). They are clearly now a much more pervasive presence on television than when Root was writing in 1986, although that is not to suggest that this has radically altered the power relations in which such appearances take place. 'Ordinary' people still remain 'the subject's of somebody else's show', albeit in different generic, technological and structural contexts than those conceived by Root. Nevertheless, the distinction in which ' "ordinary people" are not expected to be "in" the media at all, but only to appear "on" the media in certain limited circumstances' (Couldry, 2000: 46) has been blurred by Reality TV, which plays with the boundaries between on/in the media with its 'celebritisation' of the 'ordinary' person. This is clearly the case with Reality pop programmes such as *Popstars* (2001–2, UK), *Pop Idol* (19TV/Thames TV, 2001–2, UK) and *Fame Academy* (Endemol for BBC, 2002, UK) which aim to launch their winners into success on an unprecedented scale. Yet the narratives of these programmes are specifically organised around the 'search' for a star, and in their focus on a specific talent – and very self-conscious play with the discourses of stardom – they are arguably more traditional in their articulation of fame (see Holmes, forthcoming, 2004). Furthermore, their narratives necessarily invoke the existing referent of the music industry, and with their increasing emphasis on viewer interactivity, the construction of stardom here raises a more specific set of issues about the relations between the music industry, pop music and its audience – particularly as they are mediated through the figure of the star. In contrast, *Big Brother* claims no such referential context and its more autonomous arena of celebrity (in which the contestants are essentially famous for 'performing the everyday') (Roscoe, 2001) arguably poses more difficult questions for existing methodological and theoretical approaches to fame.

As many of the press comments above suggest, there is little precedent for the type of fame and celebrity in factual programming that we see in Reality TV today. This relationship is the result of a number of factors, which include the hybrid nature of Reality TV (the blurring of fictional and factual forms to produce a form primarily organised around a rhetoric of entertainment), the increasing 'personalisation' of factual programming based around character narratives and 'performance' (Dovey, 2000) and its adoption of a serial form (not forgetting, of course, the increasing cultural 'obsession' with celebrity culture more generally) (see Gamson, 1994; Rojek, 2001). Most clearly developed in the docusoap and its construction of 'real-life' stars, the importance of serialisation (and thus regular exposure) should not be underestimated.[2] Celebrity here is in part an effect of the fact that 'ordinary' people – to quote Andy Warhol's famous prediction – gain access to more than their '15 minutes of fame'. Because of their construction of entirely formatted settings, subsequent Reality texts (such as *Big Brother*, *Survivor* [2001–, UK] and the pop programmes) have moved further away from any conventional documentary base, foregrounding a space in which performance and display, rather than observation, predominate (Roscoe, 2001; Corner, 2002: 257; Hill, 2002). As a consequence, they involve overt discussion of performance, a self-reflexivity which also extends to their construction of celebrity. This is quite literally *staged* as spectacle in the format of *Big Brother*, which is to a certain extent more 'honest' and 'transparent' than the limited observational ethics of the docusoap.

Paradigms of televisual fame: a contradiction in terms?

The question remains, then, as to how to conceptualise and approach the construction of celebrity in Reality TV. Emerging from film studies and influenced by the approaches of structuralism and semiotics, earlier work on fame and stardom focused on classical Hollywood cinema (Dyer, 1998, 1986; Ellis, 1992; DeCordova, 1985), and it is testimony to the importance of these interventions that their concepts have remained remarkably flexible and useful with regard to the cinema, as well as the analysis of stardom in general. Nevertheless, the media context of stardom is now less specific (Geraghty, 2000: 184), complicating the terms used to conceptualise and categorise fame. The term 'celebrity', which, as P. David Marshall suggests, has an 'inherently ambiguous meaning' in contemporary society (1997: xii), has gained an increasing currency, and is variously used to indicate a more fleeting conception of fame (ibid.: 5; Rojek, 2001: 9), when fame rests predominantly on the private life of a person rather than their performing presence (Geraghty, 2000: 187), or simply the contemporary state of being famous in which 'meaningful' distinctions between hierarchies of importance have diminished (Gamson, 1994: 9). What this emphasises is rather the difficulties involved in categorisation, and it is worth noting here that contemporary celebrity/lifestyle magazines do not respect such discursive labels. While this of course might equally be taken to suggest precisely the disappearance of 'meaningful' distinctions in 'hierarchies' of fame, the *Big Brother* contestants are described as everything from 'celebrities', through 'stars', to 'idols' (but more frequently as 'stars').

Nevertheless, in academic analyses there often remains a perpetuation of rather restrictive categories in this respect. While early work on stardom acknowledged that the cinema was not the only site for the mediation of fame, and despite Dyer's suggestion that his analysis was 'broadly applicable' to other media such as television (1998: 3), there emerged a rather inflexible opposition drawn between the film star and the 'TV personality' (Langer, 1981; Ellis, 1992). Significantly, while this has been elaborated in subsequent work, it has not really been challenged (Tolson, 1996; Lury, 1995; Marshall, 1997). Langer (1981) and Ellis (1992) claimed that, due to the nature of television *as a medium*, there was no such thing as a television 'star'. Television's rhetoric of familiarity and intimacy, the size of the screen, the perpetual presence of its everyday flow, and its domestic context of reception all mitigated against the construction of a star, instead producing the 'personality effect'. Television's modes of address and reception were seen to engender less a sense of distance or 'aura' (in Walter Benjamin's [1973] famous conception of the term, 'aura' can be understood to be an effect of distance) than of proximity, familiarity and accessibility (Langer, 1981: 356). According to these critics, this offered an apparent contrast with the paradoxical, enigmatic construction of the film star.

While written at the time as a pioneering attempt to conceptualise the textual specificities of film and television, this dichotomy also essentialised their characteristics. It also placed only a limited emphasis on the distinctions between *different* televisual roles – presenter, newsreader, actor – (Clarke, 1987; Tolson, 1996; Lury, 1995), as well as their potential to shift and change. At the same time, however, there is a sense in which Reality TV could be seen to exemplify, and take to the extreme, the perceivably 'paradigmatic' attributes of televisual fame outlined by these earlier interventions. For example, if 'ordinariness' and familiarity are seen to structure televisual fame, Reality TV offers a literalisation of this rhetoric in its focus on 'ordinary' people who come to be seen regularly in a familiar context. In conjunction with the aesthetic and technological style of the form, the setting and context of Reality formats, while often 'extraordinary' in themselves, also play a crucial role in framing the ways in which the participants become known to us. While *Big Brother* presents us with a pseudo-domestic context, the survival-oriented formats (*Survivor*, *Eden* [RDF for C4, 2002, UK], *Shipwrecked*) engage participants in coping with depravations in 'primitive' terrain. Each offers a scenario in which contestants are often de-glamourised and 'in the raw' when filmed through the unflattering aesthetic of Reality TV, and this facilitates the programmes' claim to realism. *Big Brother's* 'simulation of the everyday' (Roscoe, 2001: 483) engages us in watching the participants cooking, eating, sleeping, washing and cleaning. We witness what they look like in the morning, when they're drunk and when they cry. Within this framework we learn such intimate details as their bad habits, favourite turn of phrase, the names of their partners, their pets and so forth. Although the media construction of stardom is precisely configured around the blurring of public and private and the illusion of intimacy (Dyer, 1998), *Big Brother* is not an intertext positioned in a contradictory dialectic with a more glamorous performance text: it is essentially the primary text. Indeed, if Reality TV depends 'for its effect on recognition – the acknowledgment that the individual on screen could be us' (Palmer, 2002: 300), this is essentially an extension of a further 'paradigmatic' aspect of televisual fame: the way in which it engenders the sense, as Langer explained, that 'both television personalities and viewers exist within a common universe of experience' (1981: 363). Seemingly anathema to the 'auratic' and ultimately 'unattainable' mediation of the star, Reality TV's particular exploitation of 'first-person' (Dovey, 2000) or 'intimate and explicitly subjective forms of knowledge' (Hight, 2001: 394) potentially fosters an equally *intimate* relationship between participant and viewer. The blurring of the distinction between audience and contestant is also shaped by the interactivity of the programme. While, as Tincknell and Raghuram suggest, 'the actual range of opportunities available to the audience to influence "the story" [of *Big Brother*] was fairly limited' (2002: 211), the viewer is nevertheless discursively constructed as occupying a position of 'power' and agency in relation to the contestants' fate. Finally, if a specificity of televisual fame is seen to be the greater blurring of on- and off-screen persona (Langer, 1981; Ellis, 1992; Lury, 1995), then what better format for the medium of television than one in which people are precisely encouraged to 'play' *themselves*?

While it is important to consider how *Big Brother*'s construction of celebrity is shaped by the specificities of the medium, adopting the theoretical and method-ological framework of these earlier conceptions of televisual fame simplifies its complexity on a number of different levels. There is a sense in existing accounts that televisual fame, based around familiarity, repetition and lack of 'aura', is almost a contradiction in terms. Yet it is surely difficult to reconcile this paradigm with the image of *Big Brother*'s staging of celebrity – the screaming crowds, the flashing camera bulbs, the waving banners – as the latest evictee-turned-celebrity leaves the house.

'The most famous non-famous people': ordinary/extraordinary

As indicated above, the concept of the ordinary/extraordinary paradox has tradi-tionally been seen to differentiate film stardom 'proper' from televisual fame (Ellis, 1992: 106). Yet it is certainly the case that the housemates are articulated through a particularly self-conscious and complex paradox of the ordinary and extraordinary. As the contestants appeared on stage in the final of the third UK *Big Brother* (2002), presenter Davina McCall asked the crowd to cheer for 'the most famous non-famous people' (26 July 2002), which precisely captures this contradictory existence. The housemates are as famous, if not more so, than many conventional celebrities, but they do not 'seem' like or behave as celebrities, at least not while in the house. A crucial element in the appeal of the programme comes from watching 'ordinary' people, which Paddy Scannell describes as 'the fundamental enigma of ordinary, everyday existence in its apparent triviality and insignificance' (2002: 280). Indeed, despite the more overt acknowledgment of celebrity and performance in *Big Brother*, this 'ordinariness' remains integral to the programme's claim to 'the real' (Couldry, 2002: 288) and, as a consequence, the extent to which celebrity is openly celebrated in the format is carefully regulated. Nevertheless, the housemates are in some sense also celebrities from the moment they *enter* the house, although the difference from the traditional temporal construction of celebrity is that this status grows simultaneously with the emergence of their 'ordinary' on-screen selves. It is important, therefore, to consider how this complex duality is played out.

While the shift toward popular factual programming has been marked by an increasing self-consciousness and self-reflexivity in processes of construction and performance (Corner, 2002), this has also accelerated *within* formats as their conventions become increasingly familiar to participants and viewers. In the second and third series of *Big Brother* (but particularly the third) contestants displayed a self-conscious awareness of the conventions of the programme, discussing which scenes would make it to the Channel 4 evening update, which clips would be shown as their 'best bits' during their eviction interview, singing the theme tune to the programme, and even imitating the voiceover to comment on their own actions. Key in displaying their oscillating position between 'ordinary' people ('like us') and their shift toward 'special' celebrity status, this self-reflexivity also extended to their conception of the celebrity status awaiting them. Series three saw a greater number of conversations about the impact fame would have on the participants' lives. P. J. Ellis in particular was apt to raise this subject, speculating (with reference to the first UK *Big Brother*) on the potential longevity of their celebrity after leaving the house, and the impact they would have if they were all 'seen out together'. It was no longer possible to suggest, as Nick Couldry does with regard to the first *Big Brother*, that, although the programme was inextricably structured around a narrative of fame, 'contestants tended not to talk about it' (2002: 289).

Yet this self-reflexivity is combined with a constant undercurrent which attests to their perception and experience of themselves as 'ordinary' people on a number of different levels. Particularly as the series progresses, the participants talk perpetually about missing their normal lives and returning to their families, homes and friends. They also discuss, as 'ordinary' people, comprehending the extremely extraordinary situation they are in. As the ultimate winner of series three, Kate Lawler, described: 'It's amazing to think the whole nation is watching *us*' (12 July 2002), a discussion later followed by her comment that she would be in awe of finally meeting the presenter of *Big Brother*, Davina McCall. Here she conceptualises herself as an 'ordinary' person temporarily touching the 'media' world (see Couldry, 2000). In the penultimate week of this series, Alex Sibley, Jonny Regan and Kate reflected more concertedly on the magnitude of the show's impact, and while Alex discussed how they no longer had faces that would simply 'blend into the crowd', Jonny interjected that they were 'all just the same people as when [they] came in – it's *out there* that's changed' (22 July 2002). This conception of being 'ordinary' people in extraordinary circumstances is reinforced by the repeated act of discussing and rehearsing their final exit from the house. This practising of celebrity – or 'celebrity in process' – both exemplifies and plays out their contradictory status at the intersection of the ordinary/extraordinary and the public/private.

As primarily developed in the work of Dyer (1998) and Ellis (1992), the concept of the ordinary/extraordinary paradox has necessarily been somewhat elusive and vague. This is partly because it is used to capture the cultural 'essence' of stardom and, as such, it is posed as a transhistorical 'myth' (Clarke, 1987; Tolson, 1996; Geraghty, 2000). While some critics use it to refer to a broad cultural fascination with stardom ('extraordinary, because the star will of course be unique…but ordinary, in that the star must be someone with whom the spectator can identify' [Clarke, 1987: 141]), others use it to refer to a more specific relationship between on- and off-screen lives, and the discursive construction of these relations in intertextual circulation. This may emphasise, for example, their 'glamorous' lifestyle yet 'ordinary' personal problems, or the combination of 'some special talent or position' with an emphasis on ordinary hobbies, desires and feelings (Ellis, 1992: 95). Either way, it is evident here that much of the 'extraordinariness' comes from the celebrity's 'talent' or lifestyle (ibid.: 105), elements difficult to reconcile with *Big Brother*. Indeed, a crucial element in the construction of the participants' 'ordinariness' can often be their ordinary or even underprivileged background, although this of course is dependent on individual cases. However, this equally has links to the conventional, *ideological* construction of stardom. The ordinary/extraordinary paradox is effectively narrativised in the success myth, which, according to Dyer, seeks to reconcile several contradictory elements, including 'ordinariness' as the hallmark of the star, an emphasis on how the system rewards 'talent and specialness', that 'lucky breaks' may happen to anyone, and that hard work and professionalism are crucial to stardom (1998: 42). The notion of the 'ordinary' person 'made good', the winner confronted with an excess of acclaim and quickly swept up into a blaze of media fame, is less innovative than it may first appear. Yet it is clear that celebrity in *Big Brother* is lacking some of the fundamental discourses of the success myth, largely the emphasis on work and traditional conceptions of talent – although the very fact that many contestants go on to work in the entertainment industry suggests that there is no radical (or least recent) disjuncture with existing conceptions of 'talent' here. Nevertheless, the decline in currency of the success myth exemplifies how we have seen an increasing challenge to the narratives and explanations of fame that were developed in the earlier part of the century (Gamson, 1994: 44). Although an emphasis on 'hard work' or an 'innate talent' (Rojek, 2001: 29) still retains its discursive currency, the visibility of the 'manufacture-of-fame narrative', as Gamson suggests, 'has become a serious contender in explaining celebrity' (1994: 44).

However, it is again worth emphasising differences between programmes here. While Reality pop series such as *Popstars* and *Pop Idol* are in many ways paradigmatic of the success myth, in that, although they certainly acknowledge elements of manufacture, they foreground the importance of 'specialness' or 'innate' talent (the stress on the elusive 'X' factor) combined with an emphasis on labour and 'hard work' (Holmes, forthcoming, 2004). In comparison, although *Big Brother* may emphasise the value of qualities such as perseverance, it does not suggest that hard work is necessary for stardom at all. Although there is an element of selling one's resources in the tasks in return for food, it is not organised around labour, but primarily an excess of *leisured* time. As contestant Helen Adams commented after appearing in the second UK series of *Big Brother*: 'all you've got to worry about is the task, having a cup of tea, doing a bit of sunbathing, and what you're going to eat for dinner.... It's fab, isn't it?',[3] while the notorious Jade Goody from the third *Big Brother* insisted: 'I don't call us celebrities – you have to *work* to be a celebrity, all we've done is been in a house.'[4] While in its elevation of a final winner *Big Brother* may still emphasise the virtues of a particular combination of 'ordinariness' and 'specialness' (winner Brian Dowling from series two, for example, was renowned for his comedic appeal), it is perhaps more honest about the fact that the acquisition of fame can simply be about being '*mediated*'. As Gamson notes, from the perspective of the celebrity system the disappearance of a 'merited claim to fame [narrative] could be disastrous' (1994: 142), but this is clearly not the case. While the increasingly fleeting nature of fame for many *Big Brother* contestants may partly be related to this logic, the success of the programme (and fascination with its participants) equally indicates that it is not fundamentally problematic in the negotiation of contemporary celebrity. Rather, with the increasing prevalence of the manufacture-of-fame discourse, the 'merited-claim-to-fame' narrative must be replaced with something else. The contestants in *Big Brother* emphasise how this is effectively represented by a more fervent negotiation of '*authenticity*' in the celebrity persona – with the dual status as both 'ordinary' person and celebrity functioning to service this logic.

'*Big Brother* exclusive!' Conceptualising intertextuality

The intertextual circulation of the programme plays a crucial role here. In terms of day-to-day life in the house, both the programme and its participants primarily conceive of celebrity in the *future* tense, and at the point at which the contestants make the transition to 'public' outside space as opposed to the pseudo-private enclosure of the house. What this signifies, however, is, rather, how the specificity of *Big Brother*'s celebrity is configured around a particular organisation of time and space. While they are in the house the programme's intertextual framework plays the central role in mediating the participants' growing celebrity status and, as such, represents a crucial site upon which to explore *Big Brother*'s implications for existing theoretical and methodological approaches to celebrity.

Commentary on *Big Brother* is produced from a range of different media sources, including the Internet (official and unofficial sites, fan discourse), the popular press, celebrity magazines, radio and of course television's own discourse on the series, which in Britain largely applies to E4/C4's companion show *Big Brother's Little Brother* (2002–) or general topical and magazine programmes. This ongoing stream of commentary contributes to the 'liveness' of the event (Tincknell and Raghuram, 2002) (see also Kavka and West on time in Reality TV in Chapter 6), while simultaneously emphasising how *Big Brother*'s 'liveness' posed a challenge for more traditional, print-based media, which had to work hard to maintain a sense of simultaneity (Hill and Palmer, 2002: 253).

Broadcast's analysis of Reality TV's relationship with the tabloids emphasised how programmes such as *Big Brother*, *Popstars* and even *Survivor* have all 'over-excited the popular press in a way that has made coverage of soaps and other TV offerings seem somewhat subdued' (Marsh, 2001: 16), foregrounding the extent to which, while such intertextual relations are not of course new to television, Reality TV has represented an acceleration of their 'synergy'. This is a relationship that is clearly attractive to both media in economic terms. While press coverage promotes the programme – the first series of *Big Brother* in the UK generated column inches or advertising in the tabloid press worth over £13 million – the focus on the programme markets papers to the 16–35-year-old bracket, a group advertisers are keen to reach, but one which has not adopted its parents' habit of buying a regular newspaper (Marsh, 2001: 16–17). But the conception of this relationship as 'simply marketing' (Peter Bazalgette, personal interview, 14 August, 2002) obscures its complex and contradictory implications for understanding the construction and reception of the programme itself.

Despite dealing with film, Barbara Klinger's (1989) work on intertextual circulation is useful here. Building on Bennett and Woollacott's conception of 'inter-textuality' as 'the social organisation of the relations between texts within specific conditions of reading' (1987: 44–5), Klinger is interested in how inter-textuality shapes strategies of reception. In considering the relationship between intertextuality and aesthetic commodification, Klinger explores how promotional materials and intermedia coverage work to construct a 'commercial life support system for a film' (1989: 5) in which the text is 'primed for digression', 'raided' for features that can be 'accentuated and extended' within its social appropriation (ibid.: 10). In order to maximise the audience, the goal is to produce 'multiple avenues' of access to the text that will make it 'resonate as extensively as possible in the social sphere' (ibid.), and this does not create a coherent reading of the text:

> The text's situation in a social, intertextual context of this sort 'opens' it to signifying activities that exceed conventions of formal resolution. The

intertextual situation of a text is then characterized by a semiotic 'spanning' from exterior sites that bear on the text with significatory pressure.

(Klinger, 1989: 7)

While clearly based on a hypothetical textual position rather than audience research, this seems to be an important possibility in approaching the circulation and reception of *Big Brother*. However, Klinger seems ultimately interested in assessing the impact of intertexts on reception (prompting 'momentary guided exits from the text') in terms of a focus on a single, primary (film) text (ibid.: 14). Yet this cannot be conceptualised as simply in relation to a television text such as *Big Brother*. As with soap opera, the medium's exploitation of serial form and liveness means that we are presented with an ongoing 'metatext' which is continually developing and changing, which in turn shapes the circulation of the intertextual framework. Nevertheless, such distinctions notwithstanding, Klinger's conception is particularly interesting here given that coverage of the star or celebrity image typically operates through a rhetoric of fragmentation and incoherence (Ellis, 1992), and it is around the contestants in *Big Brother* that this concept of 'raiding' the text operates most clearly. The concept of multiplying the semiotic base of the programme has the most significant relation with the press given that it was precisely the press which took up and recast the 'official text' in more divergent, contesting and unpredictable ways (Tincknell and Raghuram, 2002: 208–9).

In a bid to differentiate itself from the televisual text, running throughout the press and magazine coverage is the claim to offer a higher form of 'truth' on the programme, the 'reality', as it were, 'behind' the reality. While this may be conventional tabloid rhetoric, this concept of multiplying the semiotic base of the text takes on a renewed complexity in the context of Reality TV and its epistemological, discursive and visual claim to the real – which the popular press perpetually seeks to challenge and undermine. Largely prompted by the work of postmodern theorist Jean Baudrillard (1983), attempts to theorise 'the real' in Reality TV have invoked debates about 'the disappearance of reality' and 'the loss of the real', with Reality TV figured in the context of television's paradoxical attempt to recuperate its status (see Dovey, 2000: 88–91; Nichols, 1994; Robins, 1997; Fetveit, 1999). Although receiving little sustained analysis (and existing at what Dovey describes as a rather 'abstract distance' from the programmes themselves [2000: 89]), this argument predominantly operates at the level of textual aesthetics and content in Reality TV. This neglects how some of the most sustained and self-conscious attempts to articulate 'the real' around Reality TV take place at the level of its *intertextual* circulation – in the popular press and magazines.

In broad terms, there are primarily two ways in which the coverage relates to and exceeds the boundaries of the television text. First, both the popular press and celebrity magazines claim to offer the story 'behind' the events in the show, whether providing a commentary on current occurrences in the house or interviewing the latest evictee. These strategies aim to undermine the 'transparency' of *Big Brother*'s surveillance system by claiming to appeal to a voyeuristic impulse not satisfied by the programme. A typical magazine cover from *heat* (15–21 June) during the third series of *Big Brother* read: 'Jade's B'day Party: Bits TV Didn't Show', which, as seen below, is also a recurrent perspective evoked in tabloid interviews with the latest evictee. This appeal to 'voyeurism' is somewhat paradoxical for a medium more visually limited than television, and the grabbed, blurred images from the programme, while operating as a code of realism, simultaneously reveal the visual restrictions of the form. Indeed, during the second series of *Big Brother* the *Sunday Mirror*'s interview with evictee Narinder Kaur was headlined: 'Naz: At Last *I Can Tell* You What the TV Cameras Don't Show: The Racist Jibes, the Sex Drugs, the Lusting Duo' (Couzens and Lawrence, 2001: 1; emphasis mine), which in fact presents visual disclosure as verbal disclosure. The rhetoric of excess as a popular stylistic device of tabloid journalism (Fiske, 1993: 53) offers a contrast to the programme's bid to present a 'studiedly neutral' commentary of events on screen, while at the same time such coverage potentially challenges its 'preferred' meanings (Tincknell and Raghuram, 2002: 209). This intertextual framework assumes an address toward an audience that acknowledges that the programme offers a construction of 'the real'. That is not, of course, to imply that the discourse of the popular press is perceived as offering a higher form of truth. Integral to the consumption of tabloid rhetoric is potentially 'the pleasures of disbelief', or a contradictory dialectic in which we 'disbelieve the story at the same time as we believe it' (Fiske, 1993: 52). However, we still need to account for the appeal of celebrity coverage in which it is rather the *promise* of 'intimacy' or 'disclosure' that is key.

Second, and more complexly, the relations between programme and intertexts function at the level of constructing a persona for the contestants and its on/off-screen dynamic. In structural terms, the concept of stardom is essentially sustained by a relationship between the performing presence and what happens 'off stage', or the interaction between these two levels of signification (Dyer, 1998; Ellis, 1992; Geraghty, 2000: 184). Again, however, televisual and cinematic fame are seen to differ here. According to Ellis, the circulation of the film star in intertextual terms was particularly central to the incitement of spectatorial desire. The star image was seen to be not only paradoxical ('ordinary yet extraordinary') but, through the relationship between the film performance and its surrounding intertexts, also incomplete and incoherent (Ellis, 1992). From this perspective, the fragmented glimpses of the star in subsidiary circulation functioned as an 'invitation to the cinema', proposing the film as the 'synthesis of its separate fragments' (ibid.: 93). Crucially, however, given that the cinema is built upon the paradox of the 'photo-effect' of 'present-absence', this desire remains unfulfilled, perpetuating a cycle of spectatorial desire. Because of the different qualities of the medium, there was seen to be no such dynamic in the construction of the TV performer/personality which, as a consequence, has a different relationship with surrounding intertexts. Television's emphasis on liveness means that it 'presents itself as an immediate presence' (thus not engendering the photo-effect) (ibid.: 106), and, unlike the comparative 'rarity' of the film performance, the TV personality or performer is a perpetual presence in televisual flow: 'The result is a drastic reduction in distance between the circulated image and the performance. The two become very much entangled, so that the performer's image is equated with that' of the on-screen role (ibid.: 106). In fact, 'subsidiary material' can be more concerned 'with discovering if there is a personality separate from that of the television role than it is with the paradox of the ordinary-but-extraordinary' (ibid.: 107).

Since Ellis developed his argument we might reasonably suggest that the considerable increase in celebrity coverage in the popular press and magazines has evinced an appetite for disclosing the off-screen lives of all types of celebrities, thus demanding a reconceptualisation of television's intertextual frameworks in this respect. Equally, the assumption that the viewer is more likely to conceive of television personalities as 'being themselves' (in terms of a TV host, for example) assumes a rather naive view of the audience which does not sit easily with an increased awareness of celebrity manufacture and 'performance' (as well as the 'exposition' of scandals surrounding off-screen selves) (see Gamson, 1994). However, there still seems to be a wider consensus that this relationship is somehow less complex where television is concerned (Langer, 1981; Lury, 1995; Marshall, 1997). This is not the case with *Big Brother*, in which a complex dialectic between on- and off-screen persona takes on, from the perspective of this earlier work, many of the characteristics of stardom 'proper'. In doing so, it functions within a complex structural matrix which intervenes in the discursive construction of the programme's claim to 'the real'.

But what are the housemates *really* like? Mediating the ideology of 'the self'

It is certainly important for the programme to claim that, at some point, we will witness the display of 'real selves' in the house (see Ritchie, 2000: 26), and textual strategies – particularly the powerful use of the close-up – are precisely employed to this effect. This claim to display 'real selves' here shifts, but does not fully challenge, the intertextual claim to disclose the 'real person' 'behind' the 'performing' presence on screen. Although also shaped by the format of the show, which makes the contestants physically inaccessible to the media until after their eviction, rather than compete with the programme's visual claim to 'the real' the print coverage seeks to relocate and restructure the site of the 'real self' by 'raiding' the contestants' *past* selves prior to their entrance into the house. Usually focusing on past relationships (kiss 'n' tell stories in the tabloids) or excavating detailed information on the contestants' family past (often celebrity magazines), this coverage – unlike the ongoing commentary on the programme – explicitly rejects the attempt to keep pace with the 'liveness' of the series. This emphasis on the past self is paradoxically an attempt to offer the intimacy of the 'unmediated' identity. It is presented as 'authentic' precisely because it has not been subject to the manipulation of the televisual lens and the performative context this engenders.

In traditional conceptions of the duality, the on/off-screen image can exist in a complementary or contradictory relationship, or be positioned somewhere in-between (Ellis, 1992: 104; Dyer, 1998). However, in terms of *Big Brother* there is often a deliberate attempt to position this duality as conflictual, although in terms of the tabloid press, given that the stories tend to be of a particular type (sexual 'revelations'), this could be seen to create a rather homogenous, undifferentiated set of off-screen selves for the housemates which are determined exclusively by the demands of the media in which they appear. Yet in 'raiding the text' (Klinger, 1989: 10) there is necessarily the possibility for these extratextual narratives to interact in *different* ways with the on-screen selves. For example, during the first week of the third UK *Big Brother* the *Sun* published an article on Scottish contestant Lynne Moncrieff (36) which featured 'censored' nude photos revealing her identity as a 'man eater'. 'Friends' insisted that Lynne would likely be the first to enter into sexual relations in the house, insisting that 'we certainly haven't seen the real Lynne yet' (Goodwin, 2002: 10). The basis of the article, then, was precisely predicated on offering a contrast to the image of Lynne seen on screen, which at the point of the article's publication was as one of the quieter, more reserved members of the house – although this was soon to change following her unpredictable behaviour in explosive rows. As this suggests, when compared to work on stardom in classical Hollywood cinema, for example, these textual relations are necessarily somewhat changeable and fleeting as events occur and develop in the house itself, although this is precisely the way they function to multiply the semiotic base of the text. A rather more sustained and intriguing struggle between on- and off-screen persona concerned contestant Jade Goody (21). Bubbly, loud, brash, 'vulgar' and bitchy, Jade was initially notoriously unpopular with the press and was the subject of cruel verbal attacks on her weight, general physical appearance and perceived lack of education. The press took great delight in reprinting excerpts of conversations in the house which revealed her 'extraordinary' lack of intelligence (notorious mistakes included her belief that East Anglia – 'East Angular' – was near Tunisia, or that Sherlock Holmes was Mother Teresa's son), comments which swiftly laid the foundations for her status as a figure of national ridicule. While this was also an approach adopted in tamer form in celebrity magazines, they simultaneously differed from the tabloids by publishing stories from Jade's friends and family rejecting this image by foregrounding her kind nature, intelligence, past dedication at school and competent exam results (Wakeford, 2002: 32; Davies, 2002a: 6). (This in itself led to speculation not so much about her *re*presentation but about whether she was putting her 'dumb' persona on – perhaps in a bid to emulate the popularity of *Big Brother 2* contestant Helen Adams.) The past self is used here to undermine the construction of the screen self/performed self, by which it makes its greater claim to authenticity. Within this process, the audience is encouraged to be 'active' not simply by voting for (and thus evaluating) the contestants, but in relating their screen image to the contradictory matrix of 'semiotic spanning' (Klinger, 1989: 7) which circulates around them.

This is arguably paradigmatic of the ways in which, in Dyer's terms, the textual rhetoric of celebrity representation is to negotiate 'authenticity' – to make the image 'something more...more real – than an image' (Gamson, 1994: 143). Equally, it is traditionally the *intertextual* construction of the star/celebrity (particularly in terms of print media) which seeks to negotiate authenticity most forcefully – claiming to offer access to what the person is 'really' like 'behind' the image (Dyer, 1998: 61). This is significant in considering *Big Brother*'s implications for existing theoretical and methodological approaches to celebrity, as the theorisation of the relationship between the concept of the on/off-screen self is perceived to have a particular ideological significance. This primarily concerns the articulation of discourses surrounding individualism (Dyer, 1986: 18). Working from a Marxist point of view, Dyer suggests that stars articulate what 'it is to be human in society; that is, they express the particular notion we hold of the "individual"' (ibid.: 8), and they do this partly through the relationship constructed between the concept of their on/off-screen selves. P. David Marshall summarises Dyer's argument that 'the audience is obsessively and incessantly searching the star persona for the real and the authentic. We are aware that stars are appearances, "yet the whole media construction of stars encourages us to think in terms of 'really'"' (ibid.: 17). This emphasis on 'really' (what is the star *really* like?) insists on the existence of some 'inner, private, essential core' (ibid.: 14). Thus, supporting the notion of individualism upon which capitalist society depends, the construction of the relationship between the star image and the reality of the star's 'private self' mediates the concept of a 'unique' personage located 'inside consciousness', encouraging us to 'hang on to the reality of the star's private self' (ibid.: 10).

Crikey! Sharleen's ready to drop!
This week's hottest celebrity news
£1.45 27 July – 2 August 2002
heat
MAGAZINE OF THE YEAR!
Issue 178
BIG BROTHER SPECIAL ISSUE
The real Jade!
For the first time the full story of her incredible life.
Her unusual childhood
All her boyfriends
Losing her virginity!
PLUS All her best Big Brother gaffes!
Aww! Jade age 7
THE FINAL WEEK!
POSH & BECKS
The pictures that prove they are SO in love

Figure 5.1 *Heat* promises 'The Real Jade'. 'The past self is used to undermine the construction of the screen self/performed self by which it makes its greater claim to authenticity.' (With thanks to *heat* for permission to use the cover image from *heat*, 27 July–2 August, 2000.)

However, while the emphasis on what the housemates are 'really' like conforms to this paradigm, its ideological foundations now seem to be rather more 'in crisis' than Dyer's argument suggests. This is partly because what is different about Reality TV is the heightened awareness of the very *process of representation*. The strategies of the popular press which seek to undermine *Big Brother*'s claim to the real are self-conscious precisely because this is an issue put on the discursive agenda by the series itself. Although the executive producer (Ruth Wrigley) claimed in relation to the first UK *Big Brother* that 'nobody can keep up an act all the time in front of the cameras – the world was going to see them as they really were' (Ritchie, 2000: 26), what is also apparent is how this takes place in the context of an intense struggle to define 'the real' at the level of the text itself.

As indicated at the start, the concept of who is 'being themselves' or who appears to be performing for the camera is a crucial criterion in how the housemates judge and perceive one another, and equally in viewer discussion of the programme. We are precisely encouraged to debate this as part of evaluating and deciphering the events on screen. For example, Adele Roberts in series three persistently nominated fireman Jonny Regan for eviction because 'he isn't being true to himself – he's putting up a mask, being a joker. I don't think I've met the real Jonny yet' (19 June 2002). As in Dyer's discussion above, this engenders a persistent *verbal* emphasis in the programme on the value of an 'essential core' self which is authentic and 'true'. Although Dyer takes a broad historical sweep in this respect and predominantly links his argument to the rise of capitalism with the individual as its 'major moving force' (1986: 10), such discourses on the existence of an 'inner' core self can also be linked to elements of a pre-modern discourse on identity with its emphasis on a greater degree of fixity and security which is then subject to the uncertainties of modernity and postmodernity (see Kellner, 1992). In terms of its recurrence in Reality TV, this 'regressive' emphasis might then be viewed from the broader perspective of its attempt to produce the 'hyperreal' – or 'more real than real' (Baudrillard, 1983). Indeed, post-structuralist, constructivist and postmodern strands of thought have problematised 'the very notion of identity, claiming that it is a myth, an illusion' (Kellner, 1992: 143) (making a 'depth' model of the self unfashionable). *Big Brother* might equally be viewed from the perspective of identity as a shifting, superficial depthless surface, a mediatised 'theatrical play with identity' (ibid.: 174) in which the self can be produced and reproduced at will to suit the demands of its context. Acknowledging the show as a 'performance of the real' is certainly part of the media literacies it takes for granted (Roscoe, 2001: 485), yet on its own this seems to negate the powerful appeal of its *realism* and, as a consequence, the possibility of a more complex investment on the part of the audience. When approaching the possibility of an interpretive framework for such programmes, Annette Hill offers a useful conceptualisation when she suggests that they shape:

[a] particular viewing practice: audiences look for the moment of authenticity when real people are 'really' themselves in an unreal environment...[Capitalising] on the tension between performance and authenticity, [the programmes] ask contestants and viewers to look for the 'moment of truth' in a highly constructed and controlled television environment.

(Hill, 2002: 324)

Hill explains this as the appeal of looking for 'a moment of authenticity in relation to selfhood' (ibid.: 337) or 'judging the integrity of the self' (ibid.: 336). The programme, then, articulates discourses on the self, and these have further implications in conceptualising its construction of celebrity. In fact, Hill's description above is remarkably similar to Dyer's (1991) conception of a 'rhetoric of authenticity' in which the spectator may scrutinise the star's (film) performance for moments of sincerity – gestures which appear unpremeditated, uncontrolled – particularly as they are articulated through the 'revelatory' structure of the close-up. Effectively returning us to the negotiation of authenticity, this is equally resonant of the broader structure of consuming the star/celebrity image – we understand the mediated nature of the star sign, yet are nevertheless encouraged to seek out the pursuit of intimate access to their 'real' selves. It is of course paradoxical, as Dyer goes on to suggest, that these claims to work through the reality of the inner self take place in the arena of modern life most associated with 'the invasion and destruction of the inner-self and the corruptibility of public life, namely the mass media' (1986: 15). What I am suggesting is that the key link here is the extent to which *Big Brother* and the cultural construction of celebrity both play out issues surrounding the mediation of identity, which in turn speak to broader discourses concerning self-hood and individualism in modern society. Dyer makes this link with stardom clear:

If we accept for a moment the fact of uncertainty with regard to notions of a separate self and public self-presentation, performance [and] role-playing...we can I think see a connection with the star phenomenon.... The star phenomenon orchestrates the whole set of problems concerning life-as-theatre, role-playing etc., and stars do this because they are known as performers, since what is interesting about them is not the character they have constructed...but rather the business of constructing/performing/being...a 'character'.

(Dyer, 1998: 43)

The two UK series of *Celebrity Big Brother* (2001, C4/BBC1; 2002, C4) (and the example of *I'm a Celebrity...Get Me Out of Here!* [2002–3, Granada]) functioned as

129

a heightened example of this. While the appeal of watching *Celebrity Big Brother* arguably operates more traditionally in terms of celebrity coverage (presenter Davina McCall boasted in the second series of *Celebrity Big Brother* how we would get to see the celebrity housemates in all their 'ordinariness' without the trappings of stylists, agents and so forth – a recurrent feature in the intertextual coverage of celebrity) (20 November 2002), the continual discussions of whether the celebrity participants are performing their celebrity personae or revealing their 'true selves' on screen merely represent a *heightened* form of the conversations which *usually* take place in the house. In relation to Dyer's quote above, then, *Big Brother* becomes the exemplary text – in terms of both the rhetoric of the programme itself and its surrounding intertextual framework. The programme constantly articulates discourses on performing/being yourself, while at same time it is quite literally creating celebrities throughout this process. The intertextual extrapolation from the programme then plays out these issues through a more self-conscious rhetoric ('Over here! We have the *real* Jade!), and in a more condensed timeframe than is usually the case in celebrity coverage. In this sense, it could be suggested that the programme takes Dyer's model to its limit – it functions here on almost a *literal* level.

'Visibility as its own reward': the multi-spatial persona

This, of course, shifts with the changing dynamics of the game. The circulation of celebrity punctuates the different temporal cycles of *Big Brother*: the weekly eviction and the culmination of the series toward the final climax. As the weekly evictions progress, contestants are continually being released into the 'outside' media discourse and its temporal construction of celebrity – something which is literally and self-consciously showcased in the Friday night eviction coverage. As Paddy Scannell describes, 'Friday night was the moment at which the two different temporalities [of the programme] encountered each other: time-in-the-house and time-in-the-world' (2002: 274). The Friday night coverage effects a shift in the position offered to the viewer in that we are momentarily not so much offered the 'intimate' access to the 'voyeuristic' rhetoric of pseudo 'private' scenes, as invited to become witness to a live media event. As the evictee prepares to exit the house the contestants' attention is obsessively focused on the audience and the media waiting outside. The moment of exit – the outfit, the pose, the reaction to the crowd – is directed toward the on-screen audience, while at the same time the home audience is constantly invoked as witness to the event. The staging of this scene draws self-consciously on iconic images of media fame – the reaching hands of the fans, the glare of the flashing camera bulbs and even women throwing underwear at the male contestants – and is in many ways less evocative of television or even cinematic fame than of popular music. This also serves to act as the ultimate (and excessive) confirmation of their celebrity on more traditional terms. But it is crucial to ask *what* is actually being celebrated in this moment. The focal point, I would suggest, is precisely what has been absent in the circulation of the housemates' celebrity thus far: the staging of the physical encounter between the *televisual/screen self and the media*. This moment narrativises, dramatises and literalises the shift to what we might call a multi-spatial persona: one that is physically available to many media sites, spaces and discourses simultaneously. Given that both celebrity and *Big Brother* offer 'visibility as its own reward' (Gamson, 1994: 10), we effectively also see the contestants shift from one system of surveillance to another.

Until this point the contestants have 'surrendered all power over their image, allowing *Big Brother* and the media to make of them what they would' (Palmer, 2002: 303), so it is only at this stage that the participants can exercise an element of discursive control over their image. They comment on their representation in the programme and their experiences in the house, and describe events in the first person. In contrast to the 'stolen' narratives in the tabloids or the 'objective' eye of *Big Brother*, this shift to the accessing of the famous self (for the media) and the impression of discursive power (for the contestant) is explicitly marked in the press by the use of an autobiographical rhetoric which promises, for example, 'Kate's Story' (Hamilton, 2002: 2) or 'Jade's Own Story' (Marshall and Hoare, 2002: 2), again often undermining the validity of the programme's construction of 'the real' and the transparency of its surveillance gaze. Indeed, rather than the moment of exit from the house simply representing the *union* of the screen self and the media, this can again be an opportunity for the discourse on the 'real self' to be reshuffled and renegotiated, with the intertextual framework again claiming the greatest referential value in this respect. This occurs, for example, with housemates who reject their on-screen self by complaining about their representation. Equally, however, there can be a claim to a seamless continuity between on- and off-screen self – what Dyer refers to as 'bearing witness to the continuousness' of the self (1986: 11). When asked by *OK!* magazine about his new status as a 'heartthrob' and reaction to his female admirers, contestant Spencer Smith from *Big Brother 3* explained:

> I didn't go on the show for this, but I guessed things might happen because we were on telly. I'm an honest guy and I'm just me, and if people like the Spencer they have seen on TV, then that's nice.
>
> (Dyke, 2002: 6)

With the implication that he remains unchanged by his fame, Spencer draws here on his status as simply an 'ordinary' person in an extraordinary situation to authenticate what is now effectively his celebrity persona. Although configured within the specificity of *Big Brother*'s narrative trajectory or format, this clearly returns us to the negotiation of 'authenticity' and Dyer's argument that, despite the fact that we understand the celebrity image to be a sign construction, we often value those that *appear* to be 'being themselves' (1986: 8).

Equally, there is the strategy of neither fully rejecting the on-screen self nor 'bearing witness to the continuousness of the self', but rather showcasing and embracing the 'celebritised' self. In this respect it is worth noting that as the coverage of the contestants travels its cycle we see a marked shift, at a visual level, in the aesthetic and stylistic nature of their image: from the stark, unflattering closed-circuit TV (CCTV) aesthetic of the programme, the grabbed, blurred images in the press, and the amateur appearance of the family snaps in magazines, *heat* and *OK!* quickly shift to an aesthetic framework in which the contestants have been professionally styled and photographed. Jade's appearance in *heat*'s 'Look at Her Now!' 'exclusive' precisely pivoted on displaying her commodified celebrity transformation for all to see. With it fragmented into areas of 'hair', 'make-up', 'skin', 'clothes' and 'fitness', female readers are told how to 'get Jade's look' (Davies, 2002b: 71), and just in case we missed the point: 'sporting waist-length hair extensions and with her curvy figure poured into a sexy black dress, the 21-year old is *unrecognisable from the bikini-clad, "kebab-bellied" housemate*' (ibid.: 65; emphasis mine). The play with discourses of a mediated identity while *on* the show comes full circle to link up with the ultimate media self: the business of *being* a celebrity. This of course simultaneously indicates the impossibility of maintaining a conception of the 'ordinary' once it comes into contact with the 'specialness' of the media sphere (see Couldry, 2000, 2002).

Analysing *Big Brother* emphasises how questions surrounding celebrity in Reality TV demand consideration in the context of specific programme formats, while at the same time it raises issues relevant to wider analyses in the field. In assessing the programme's implications for existing methodological and theoretical approaches to media fame, it is clear that this relationship is extremely complex. While it could be seen as drawing on perceivably 'paradigmatic' attributes of televisual fame, this fails to capture the extent to which television has become one of the most exciting and contradictory arenas for the negotiation of celebrity.

Nevertheless, my semiotic and structural analysis here indicates that there is much that is traditional in *Big Brother*'s construction of celebrity. It is certainly the case that *Big Brother* effectively showcases the absence of a 'merited-claim-to-fame' narrative and applauds a world in which 'attention [is]...distributed more evenly, if in shorter increments; a world where stardom is more accessible since the inborn requirements are fewer;...a world in which anyone...can feel the glow of celebrity' (Gamson, 1994: 54). Yet rather than representing a radical shift, the disappearance of this ideological myth serves to reinflect the cultural circulation of the celebrity image in which the negotiation of authenticity (the claim to the 'real self') must be all the more fervent when faced with the discourses of manufacture, cultural emptiness and the absence of 'exceptional' talent. In fact, in terms of the ideological work of celebrity, *Big Brother* is in many ways *exemplary* as a site for playing out anxieties over identity and contemporary 'selfhood', both in terms of its focus on life lived as 'mediated' identity and in the ways in which this is taken up by the intertextual 'raiding' of the programme. At the same time, this particularly self-conscious and dizzying proliferation of attempts to lay claim to the 'real self' could be seen precisely to *exceed* the more traditional negotiation of authenticity in the celebrity image and its ideology of individualism (Dyer, 1998, 1986). The possibility of polysemic readings is of course central to the appeal of the celebrity image and to the wider success of the celebrity system (Dyer, 1998; Gamson, 1994: 144). It could be suggested that, more than ever, Reality TV's emphasis on the 'ordinary' person as the basis for contemporary celebrity 'keeps the door to success, measured as fame, always ajar; interested and determined individuals can always kick it open' (Gamson, 1994: 168). However, if *Big Brother* is a metaphor for this we should note that this 'door' is still carefully surveilled and patrolled.

Notes

1   This reference to 'license fees' is factually incorrect given that, although a public-service broadcaster, Channel 4 operates through commercial funding.
2   These were prefigured by *The Family* (1974) and *Sylvania Waters* (1993), which both involved their participants achieving a certain degree of celebrity status.
3   *Big Brother, Small World* (C4, 6 January 2002).
4   *Big Brother's Little Brother* (C4, 27 July 2002).

References

Baudrillard, Jean (1983) 'The Ecstasy of Communication', in Hal Foster (ed.) *Postmodern Culture*, London: Pluto.

Bazalgette, Peter (2001) '*Big Brother* and Beyond', *Television*, October: 20–3.

Benjamin, Walter (1973) 'The Work of Art in the Age of Mechanical Reproduction', in Hannah Arendt (ed.) *Illuminations*, London: Fontana Press; first published in 1936.

Bennett, Tony and Janet Woollacott (1987) *Bond and Beyond: The Political Career of a Popular Hero*, Basingstoke: Macmillan.

Boorstin, Daniel (1963) *The Image*, London: Penguin.

Brenton, Sam and Reuben Cohen (2003) *Shooting People: Adventures in Reality TV*, London: Verso.

Bruzzi, Stella (2000) *New Documentary: A Critical Introduction*, London: Routledge.

Clarke, Michael (1987) *Teaching Popular Television*, London: Methuen.

Corner, John (2002) 'Performing the Real: Documentary Diversions', *Television and New Media* 3(3): 255–69.

Couldry, Nick (2000) *The Place of Media Power: Pilgrims and Witnesses of the Media Age*, London, Routledge.

Couldry, Nick (2002) 'Playing for Celebrity: *Big Brother* as Ritual Event', *Television and New Media* 3(3): 283–93.

Couzens, Gerard and Lucy Lawrence (2001) 'The Big Exclusive: Naz', *Sunday Mirror*, 24 June: 4–5.

Cummings, Dolan (ed.) (2002) *Reality TV: How Real is Real?*, Oxford: Hodder & Stoughton.

Davies, Michelle (2002a) 'The *Real* Jade', *heat* 27 July–2 August: 6–8.

Davies, Michelle (2002b) 'Jade Exclusive: Look at Her Now!', *heat*, 17–23 August: 64–71.

DeCordova, Richard (1985) 'The Emergence of the Star System in America', *Wide Angle* 6(4): 4–13.

Dovey, Jon (2000) *Freakshow: First Person Media and Factual Television*, London: Pluto.

Dunkley, Christopher (2001) 'Reality TV', *Financial Times*, 10 January: 24.

Dyer, Richard (1998) *Stars*, London: British Film Institute; first published in 1979.

Dyer, Richard (1986) *Heavenly Bodies: Film Stars and Society*, London: British Film Institute.

Dyer, Richard (1991) '*A Star is Born* and the Construction of Authenticity', in Christine Gledhill (ed.) *Stardom: Industry of Desire*, London: Routledge.

Dyke, Peter (2002) 'World Exclusive: Spencer', *OK!*, 3 July: 3–6.

Ellis, John (1992) *Visible Fictions: Cinema, Television, Video* (second edition), London: Routledge.

Fetveit, Arild (1999) 'Reality TV in the Digital Era: A Paradox in Visual Culture?', *Media, Culture and Society* 21(6): 787–804.

Fiske, John (1993) 'Popularity and the Politics of Information', in Peter Dahlgren and Colin Sparks (eds) *Journalism and Popular Culture*, London: Sage.

Flett, Kathryn (2000) 'Shipwrecked', *Observer*, 23 January: 10.

Gamson, Joshua (1994) *Claims to Fame: Celebrity in Contemporary America*, Berkeley, CA: University of California Press.

Geraghty, Christine (2000) 'Re-examining Stardom: Questions of Texts, Bodies and Performance', in Christine Gledhill and Linda Williams (eds) *Reinventing Film Studies*, London: Arnold.

Goodwin, Dave (2002) 'Big Brother Exclusive: Lynne's a Big Luvva', *Sun*, 27 May: 10–11.

Hamilton, Mike (2002) 'Kate's Own Story', *Sunday Mirror*, 28 July: 2–3.

Hill, Annette (2002) '*Big Brother*: The Real Audience', *Television and New Media* 3(3): 323–41.

Hill, Annette and Gareth Palmer (2002) 'Editorial: *Big Brother*', *Television and New Media* 3(3): 251–4.

Holmes, Su (forthcoming, 2004) ' "Reality Goes Pop!": Reality TV, Popular Music and Narratives of Stardom in *Pop Idol* (UK)', *Television and New Media*, 5(2) May.

Kellner, Douglas (1992) 'Popular Culture and the Construction of Postmodern Identities', in Scott Lash and Jonathan Friedman (eds) *Modernity and Identity*, Oxford: Blackwell.

Klinger, Barbara (1989) 'Digressions at the Cinema: Reception and Mass Culture', *Cinema Journal* 28(4): 3–19.

Langer, John (1981) 'TV's Personality System', *Media, Culture and Society* 4: 351–65.

Lury, Karen (1995) 'Television Performance: Being, Acting and "Corpsing"', *New Formations* 26: 114–27.

McCann, Graham (2002) 'The Wannabe Celebrity Ego Has Landed', *Financial Times*, 22 May: 20.

Marsh, Naomi (2001) 'Tabloids in TV Romp', *Broadcast*, 20 July: 16–17.

Marshall, P. David (1997) *Celebrity and Power: Fame in Contemporary Culture*, Minnesota, MN: University of Minnesota Press.

Marshall, Sharon and Sean Hoare (2002) 'Jade's Own Story', *News of the World*, 28 July: 2–5.

Nichols, Bill (1994) *Blurred Boundaries: Questions of Meaning in Contemporary Culture*, Bloomington and Indianapolis, IN: Indiana University Press.

Palmer, Gareth (2002) '*Big Brother*: An Experiment in Governance', *Television and New Media* 3(3): 295–330.

Patterson, John (2001) 'Review of *Series 7*', *Guardian*, 9 March: 12.

Rimmer, Amanda (2002) '*Big Brother* Uncovered', *OK!*, 3 July: 52–61.

Ritchie, Jean (2000) *Big Brother: The Official Unseen Story*, Basingstoke and Oxford: Channel 4 Books.

Robins, Kevin (1997) *Into the Image*, London: Routledge.

Rojek, Chris (2001) *Celebrity*, London: Reaktion Books.

Root, Jane (1986) *Open the Box: About Television*, London: Comedia.

Roscoe, Jane (2001) '*Big Brother* Australia: Performing the "Real" Twenty-four-seven', *International Journal of Cultural Studies* 4(4): 473–88.

Scannell, Paddy (2002) '*Big Brother* as Media Event', *Television and New Media* 3(3): 271–82.

Tincknell, Estella and Parvati Raghuram (2002) '*Big Brother*: Reconfiguring the "Active" Audience of Cultural Studies?', *European Journal of Cultural Studies* 5(2): 199–215.

Tolson, Andrew (1996) *Mediations: Text and Discourse*, London: Arnold.

Wakeford, Dan (2002) 'Exclusive! "The Truth About My Jade" by Her Mum', *heat*, 20–26 July: 30–2.

6

TEMPORALITIES OF THE REAL

Conceptualising time in Reality TV

Misha Kavka and Amy West

Dates are anathema to Reality TV. As markers of historical time, dates have a distancing, objectifying effect. Instead of dates and years, Reality TV counts hours, minutes and seconds, setting participants against deadlines, insisting on time in its smallest parameters. To locate oneself in the time of history goes against the power of reality programming – and of the televisual medium itself – to create intimacy and immediacy. But what can it mean to 'create' immediacy through the medium of television, when the very technology of television mediates that which it transmits? The appeal of television has traditionally been described in terms of its capacity for live transmission, a performance of the present linked with a decontextualising of the past. We will not be the first to suggest that television presents itself as something of the moment, 'live' and lived, but this technological and structural feature of the medium needs to be revisited in light of the recent surge in the popularity of reality programming. Despite the avoidance of dates in Reality TV, it is here that time comes forward, fully present, which suggests that the appeal of Reality Television has to do with the way it fulfils the temporal potential of the medium itself.

The genre of Reality TV[1] is curiously appropriate to its medium because of the way that it manipulates time as a guarantor of both realness and social intimacy. This is not to say that the use of present-ist temporality in Reality TV makes it documentary (that is, a documentation of authentic experience). Rather, to focus on the time of Reality TV is to engage with the debate about the constructedness of the form by examining a crucial aspect of how reality programming manufactures a socially meaningful 'real'. Debates about 'the real' in reality programming (see Dovey, 2000; Fetveit, 1999) have been sensitive to the aesthetic and technological manipulations involved in producing reality effects, but have largely ignored the role of *time* in the reality project (except for Scannell, 2002). In fact, Reality TV has given time a bad name, precisely because Reality TV is insistently ahistorical, and as such lacks the social and material contextualisation of most documentary projects. In this chapter we will argue that the social relevance of

Reality TV lies in its creation of intimate viewing communities, but this is an intimacy that cannot be understood without a closer examination of the temporal (and spatial) aspects of immediacy. The aim here is to show that Reality TV pursues intimacy (emotional closeness) through immediacy (temporal closeness), coupling the proximity of the 'here' with the urgency of the 'now'. In doing so, it fulfils the promise, made by the medium of television right from the start, that viewers can traverse space in the blink of an eye.

Either as medium or institution, television has never appeared to be an appropriate vehicle for representing history, not even its own. Rather, the seamless 'flow' theorised by Raymond Williams as elemental to television has its counterpart in a necessary transience of imagery, an abundance of information that requires the disappearance of the just-seen to make way for the now-seeing (Houston, 1984). As Stephen Heath has put it, 'television produces forgetfulness, not memory, flow, not history', a result which he attributes to the 'now-thisness' of the medium itself (Heath, 1990: 279). In today's climate of media events, if there is history in television it is something hauled mercilessly into the present moment, extended into the long 'now' of a dramatic reconstruction or the painful, repetitive progress of breaking news. By contrast, as Nick Couldry points out, reality programming differs from Dayan and Katz's definition of media events because 'there [is] no antecedent event of public significance' (Couldry, 2002: 287); the event is precipitated by the presence of TV cameras, not vice versa. The same distinction could be made between reality programming and documentary, suggesting that the tools for understanding temporality in documentary are not equally serviceable for Reality TV. In this comparison, documentary is traditionally aligned with historical time, while televisual time clings to an eternal present, failing to measure the weight of the 'real' past. Given these terms, it is no surprise that television, and Reality TV in particular, have suffered critical devaluation.

In his book about the border zones of documentary film, *Blurred Boundaries*, Bill Nichols bemoans the fact that Reality TV, in its first-generation form of real-crime programming, eliminates the historical consciousness of the documentary mode. Confined to playing out a 'perpetual now', Reality TV for Nichols forecloses any possibility of action in the 'historical world', expelling audience emotion through vicarious participation: 'in the pervasive "now" of tele-reality, [s]ocial responsibility dissolves into tele-participation' (Nichols, 1994: 54).[2] The problem with Nichols' argument, however correctly he pinpoints the difference between frameworks of historical time (in documentary) and present-ism (in Reality TV), is that he uncritically applies the criteria of the former to the latter. To prioritise the time of history over the time of the present, as Nichols does, is to dismiss reality programming for its straightforward relationship to the 'now' as though the lack of historical measure were directly equivalent to a lack of cultural value. This position fails to take seriously the complex relation among the effects of immediacy, reality and intimacy brought into alignment by programmes which use 'real' people in seemingly 'real' or 'live' time. Some amount of temporal work needs to be done by successful Reality TV programmes in order to produce intimacy as an effect of immediacy. By giving precedence to what he calls the 'discourses of sobriety' (ibid.: 47) – those 'serious' discourses which add up to the practice of an enlightenment-derived civil democracy – and disparaging more everyday discourses and practices, Nichols can find little social relevance in what is most 'televisual' in the temporality of reality programmes.

Arguably, however, as the range of approaches adopted in this collection suggests, sober documentary is not a model for all factual programming to which Reality TV (poorly) aspires; rather, differences amongst kinds of factual programming have to be taken into account – differences in intent, mode and even suitability to the medium of transmission. John Corner is sensitive to such gradations in what he calls the 'postdocumentary culture of television' (Corner, 2002: 257). In this postdocumentary context he sees not the death of documentary but the rise of 'documentary as diversion' (ibid.: 261), a category marked by 'a performative, playful element', a lesser need for 'documentary credibility' and a 'broader range of cognitive and affective investments' made by viewers (ibid.: 263–5). He is, in other words, talking about reality programming as an extension of documentary, but the newer form of documentary is a mode of factual television which mobilises a different intent behind the will to display reality. In recognising this shift away from Nichols' discourses of sobriety, Corner sets the stage for a methodological understanding of the term 'postdocumentary' which takes into consideration the changing character of notions of 'the public', away from modes of citizenship and toward 'a version of "the popular", grounded in consumption' (ibid.: 265).

We would argue that television must be understood as a social technology in this basic sense of 'the popular': people watch it all the time, are affected by it, and incorporate it into the structure and reference of their daily lives. While acknowledging the critical advances made by enlightenment-derived ideas of 'the public', one must also consider that the model of a global public sphere is increasingly inadequate to people's actual lives and practices. Rather, the great amount and variety of reality programming suggests that new Reality TV audiences seek, through television consumption, a greater sense of community and even agency (and, in that sense, 'consumption' is hardly a passive activity). The intimate and involved sense of community evoked by Reality TV (examined by Chapter 7) might thus be considered a counterbalance to Nichols' more outmoded model of the 'public' based on civic participation in the historical world.

Being ahistorical does not mean that Reality TV is atemporal. The capacity of television, and reality programming in particular, to link immediacy with social intimacy is a function of time: the absence of historical time is precisely what brings things closer. Thus, Reality TV does not need to play out in real time in order to be true to its mission; rather, it reorders time, distilling it into socially recognisable units which are reiterable, and hence return as ever new, ever present. This is why Reality TV, from its early days in real-crime programming, has been about counting time in units rather than dates:[3] the second-counter of the cop surveillance camera, the countdown structure of the challenge programme, the time limit of the makeover show, the day count on *Big Brother* (Endemol, 1999–, originally Holland) and *Survivor* (Castaway Productions for CBS, 2000–, US). Reality TV creates immediacy by resuscitating the feeling of 'liveness' inherent in the medium of television.

Is it live or…?

Since the late 1970s we have witnessed a sporadic but ongoing debate about the historical, technical and metaphorical 'liveness' of television (see Heath and Skirrow, 1977; Feuer, 1983; Houston, 1984; Rath, 1989; Doane, 1990; Caldwell, 1995; Berenstein, 2002; Derrida and Stiegler, 2002; Couldry, 2002). The present-ness of television temporality is an attribute of both time and space: the seeming 'liveness' of television collapses the time of action with the time of viewing, while the domestic setting of television viewing makes the set and its continuous programming a daily, even familial, presence. Historically, industry commentators have celebrated the live transmission of 'actuality' as being the very ontology of television, for 'tele-' (*far*) 'vision' (*seeing*) allows viewers not only to see at a distance but to *be* in two places at the same time (see Berenstein, 2002). Jane Feuer, however, has drawn attention to the paradox inherent in defining television as 'live' viewing long after direct-to-air transmissions had ended in the 1950s and even sports matches had become prone to electronic manipulation (Feuer, 1983). Indeed, as John Ellis points out, the only thing that can be said any longer to be 'live' is transmission itself, the localised sending and receiving of signals through air, cables or fibres, which must occur in that instant for any image to exist on screen (Ellis, 2000: 31). Feuer's answer to the paradoxical persistence of the discourse of liveness is to argue that liveness is an (in fact *the*) ideology of television, whose function it is to overcome the fragmentation necessitated by production and programming. Though the flow posited by Raymond Williams as essential to television may be an illusion, it is an illusion that is ideologically upheld by the feeling that television comes to us live, immediate, 'direct for me' (Heath and Skirrow, 1977: 54). Even in the absence of a direct alignment between the event and its transmission, which is the case for all but the studio transmissions of Reality TV programmes, contemporary factual shows adopt the verbal and visual rhetoric of liveness, while viewers happily participate in this illusion (Ellis, 2000: 33).

And yet it is not enough to say that liveness is an illusion, a fantasy, an ideology of all television programming, for the 'live aura' of television depends not only on rhetoric but also on the temporality of transmission. Technically, the distant viewer can 'be there' only because the showing seems to happen concurrently with the viewing, which in turn seems to happen concurrently with the transmitted event. The time of transmission is a factor important enough to drive a distinction between fictional and factual programming, and even between kinds of factual programming – you may tape the news, a sports match or a Reality TV programme, but after a certain time-lapse you are unlikely to watch it. What has happened after a day or a week is that the programme has become 'old news', superseded by the next event-made-present. There is, in other words, something like a 'zone of liveness', after which the liveness effect will have expired. It is in this zone of immediacy that Reality Television functions, as much as does the news or sports – and this despite the likely delay in Reality TV between production and transmission. As any football fan knows, if you tape an important match for later viewing, then you also have to impose a news blackout, forcing yourself not to hear a result which would ruin the liveness effect of watching the game. The same point could be made just as easily for the finales of *Big Brother* and *Survivor* (which, like sports matches, are transmitted at the time of event), and even for their regular, non-live episodes. However compelling it may be, it is difficult to go back and watch last month's *Big Brother* episode even if you did not see it at the time.

What is at issue here is not only the cognitive knowledge of the result. Rather, the liveness effect is as much about belonging to an imagined community of viewers *at the moment of watching* as it is about being able to enjoy the unpredictability of proto-climactic events. The 'live aura' thus produced consists, according to Claus-Dieter Rath, in 'the collective, simultaneous perception of an event charged with symbolic value' which draws the audience into the momentary constellation of a television community (Rath, 1989: 88). It is in this sense that television as *viewing event* socialises viewers, creating a community of people who can say, 'I am among those who will have seen' (ibid.: 89), and who often talk to each other afterwards about just what they have seen (see Scannell, 2002: 276–80). You can join this community belatedly, after you have watched your own taped version, but only so long as that community still exists. Once it has reformed itself around the *next* match or Reality TV episode, then your taped version becomes worthless, for that particular community of viewers will have dispersed and reassembled itself around a different viewing event. The possibility of joining in the morning-after discussion of the media event is thus an important part of inserting oneself into the zone of liveness; whether one gossips or not, the possibility itself grounds the imagined sense of belonging to a group whose members are all watching the same thing in the same period.

This effect of community is amplified when the community of viewing coincides with an actual event, when real people occupy and reflect the same time frame as the viewers inhabit (e.g. Princess Diana's funeral). It matters more to us as viewers when the people on screen are engaged in actual, spontaneous interactions, and the fact that they are 'real' justifies our vicarious engagement. This 'spontaneous' quality is not the same as literal live transmission, which is to say that a programme may feel perfectly spontaneous even when there is no simultaneity of event and viewing (as with most reality programming). It is much more important that the emotional intensity felt by participants and viewers be coincident with the event which accounts for it. In this way, the 'electronically constituted society' of TV viewers (Rath, 1989: 89) expands to include intimacy with the TV performers precisely because the effect of liveness forecloses any preceding period in which they would have been able to practice a performance. 'Live' TV, whether taped or not, is performance which has no prequel. They are there, doing what they would do, the cameras are on, and we are watching. The actuality strengthens the effect of immediacy; immediacy strengthens the effect of social community; and the community creates a sense of intimacy with the performers. The knowledge which results is not only cognitive (about rules and results, for instance) but also an affective knowledge about the participants themselves (imaginary, perhaps, but no less powerful for that). This conjunction of immediacy, actuality and intimacy is dependent on a temporal framework which must be worked into the technical and rhetorical fabric of Reality TV programmes. It is perhaps worth noting that the word 'actual' – meaning real in English – has a temporal rather than an ontological meaning in both French and German (actuel/aktuell), where it means 'now' or 'current'. Etymologically, then, time and reality are flip sides of the same coin, which may go some way to suggesting why Reality TV makes such good use of a medium whose 'major category' is time (Doane, 1990: 222). It remains to be seen how this plays itself out.

The time of housemates

For all its present-ism, Reality Television is highly dependent on counting time. In place of linear historical time, it relies on ever-renewable time-cycles – the 24-hour clock, the three-day work schedule or the 39-day sojourn. This is a sense of time adapted to television as a present-making medium, collapsing the time of production with the time of transmission into a single order that mobilises a community of viewers. Through these cyclical temporal parameters, a several-month delay necessitated by postproduction (say, on *Survivor*) slides neatly into 'day one' of viewing, allowing programmes to traverse distance and time zones while maintaining the sense of immediacy necessary for establishing at-home intimacy between viewers and performers.

One way of distinguishing between 'linear historical time' and the 'present-ism' of Reality Television's temporal plane is to speak in terms of 'located' and 'unlocated' time. 'Located' time can be identified as that which is attached to a particular point within a historical continuum. Clock time, named days of the week and calendar dates all function in this way, locating the moment in relation to other events within a spectrum of recorded time. The alternative to this is what we term 'unlocated' time, or periods that are both finite and cyclical in ways which contravene the conventions of linear historical time. Examples of 'unlo-cated' time in Reality Television are the five minutes designated for completion of a challenge on *Fear Factor* (NBC, 2001–, US) or the 39-day sojourn determined by the *Survivor* format. As these examples suggest, 'unlocated' time borrows from the social conventions of measured time: minutes, hours, days, weeks are still the terms of reference in use (see Scannell, 2002: 272–6). However, because they are disengaged from the progression of historical time which gives them meaning, these units of measured time become no more than beads on an abacus. As such they can be moved around the board without bearing a meaningful relationship to conventional notions of historical time. This detachment is evidenced by the way in which periods of 'unlocated' time are counted backwards to zero as often as they are counted forward to a predetermined time, date or number. For instance, the participants on the garden makeover show *Ground Force* (Bazal Productions for BBC1, 1998, UK) are just as likely to say '45 minutes to go' as 'it's nearly six o'clock', making the endpoint both zero and six. Whatever the apparently arbi-trary number being aimed at there is always a predetermined endpoint, a final deadline at which the clock stops. It is this quality of finiteness, or self-deter-mined expiry, which makes 'unlocated' time paradoxically ever-renewable: the time-code graphic on *Fear Factor* is reset to '0:00:00' for each new contestant, while every series of *Survivor* starts at 'day one'. Disengaged from the linear temporal plane of 'history', units of 'unlocated' time float (backwards, forwards and around) in a temporal vacuum.

When marking time, Reality Television formats utilise the smaller units of measured time such as minutes and hours, or revolving days of the week (e.g. 2.45 a.m. on *Big Brother* or Sunday on *1900 House* [Wall to Wall for C4, 1999, UK]). The smaller the unit of time, the more easily it can be floated within a temporal frame; for instance, the screen graphic '2.45 a.m.' separates the on-screen moment from the at-home moment of viewing occurring at 8 p.m., but it does not impede the viewer's will to interpret the event as occurring earlier that same day. Thus, Reality TV programmes do not need to be live or simulcast, but only need to establish a floating-present framework that conjoins the worlds of viewing and being viewed. By contrast, the emphatic use of clock time, calendar date and year in the coverage of the World Trade Center attacks – '9:30 a.m. 11th September 2001' – anchored each moment of these dramatic events to a linear historical continuum, causing them to recede immediately into the historical past as they occurred. The use of dates in live coverage of historical events excites a sense of intimate connection between viewer and viewed precisely because it confirms that those events are occurring that same day. In such instances of public catastrophe or crisis, history comes to television, but only for the moment; the sense of intimate connection grows weaker as such televised moments rely more heavily on taped footage with the passing hours/days.

The two Reality Television formats which have become paradigms for the second-generation face of the genre – *Big Brother*[4] and *Survivor* – are both instructively bound by principles of 'unlocated' or non-historical time. Though different in their setting, daily rhythms and in-house rhetoric,[5] these two formats together represent the initial and most successful variants of what we call the 'intimate strangers' genre of Reality TV. This genre, the roots of which lie in the groundbreaking programme *The Real World* (Bunim-Murray for MTV, 1992–, USA), brings together a group of strangers in an isolated environment to cohabit for a predetermined period of time, during which they must complete certain challenges and vote individuals out of the game. In both cases the counting and structuring of passing time dominate narrative development and broadcasting rhythm, and they are crucial to the feeling of intimacy created by each series. The designated period of finite habitation constitutes an 'unlocated' timeframe as participants count down (or up) to the final day. In both series, participants are forbidden to bring timepieces, measuring the day instead by the conventions of mealtimes, rituals of sleep and patterns of challenges. What makes *Big Brother* different from *Survivor*, however, is its relationship with broadcasting. Because footage is screened daily and within 24 hours of being shot, *Big Brother* comes closer than any other reality format to replicating 'liveness'. The footage from each 24-hour period is contracted into a half-hour episode which is screened each night of the week (and in Spain three times a day). The effect of liveness comes not just from the minimal time lag between production and transmission, or the 'unlocated' regularity of activities, but also from the fact that viewers are sutured into the present time of events in the *Big Brother* house, partly through constantly updated episodes, but also, crucially, through weekly episodes which are literally live – the famed 'eviction' episodes, screened twice a week in Spain, twice on Friday in Britain and once a week everywhere else. During these eviction episodes, part of the suspense arises from waiting, in real time, for the viewers' own call-in votes to be tallied, which ultimately provides the weekly answer to the question of who will be evicted.

There is, of course, a difference between liveness and real time. For the most part, Reality TV programmes do not broach the ground of real time, largely because of the producers' fear of airing 'dead time' (time in which 'nothing happens'). Dead time belongs to other media than television, whose established practice of compacting action into narrative arcs of specific duration has taught audiences to flick to the next channel if something fails to catch their attention. In place of television, it is the Internet where the potential for voyeuristic pleasure promises to overcome the threat of being bored by real time. *Big Brother*, from its very inception, has made avid use of convergence with the Internet as a way of mixing temporalities of the real: liveness as effect reigns on television, whereas Internet streaming technology is in the grip of real time (see Couldry, 2002: 286–7). Every *Big Brother* series has a partner website, where images and sound from the house are streamed from particular cameras in real time, 24 hours a day. Viewers are thus able to access both the 'produced' (televised) and 'unproduced' (Internet) versions of the programme, with television offering a certain amount of postproduction shaping and the Internet representing the technical point at which liveness and real time merge into one.[6]

There are ways, however, in which even the televised form of *Big Brother* closes the gap between liveness and real time. The live studio episodes are obviously played out in real time, with the edginess of spontaneous possibility, as well as the ritual of spectacle, counterbalancing the threat of boredom. More notable, perhaps, was the decision of Channel 4 in the UK to show the second series of *Big Brother* (2001) in real time for 18 hours a day on its digital sister station, E4, which continued with the third series in 2002. This was basically an experiment in media crossover, bringing Internet streaming to television and replacing the multiple webcams with alternating views from TV cameras. Here, again, real time and liveness merge, shuffling somewhat uncomfortably between the fascination of raw material and the threat of boredom (as in the early-morning E4 experience of watching a housemate sleep…for hours). No doubt, filling screen time was a basic concern for the new E4, but such streaming also provides a Reality TV prototype for the sort of options that increasingly confront the cable and digital broadcaster. Indeed, it may be that the near-continuous live viewing of *Big Brother* suggests alternative modes of delivery and consumption that may suit the genre of Reality TV better than traditional scheduled programming.

In the meantime, *Big Brother* episodes on free-to-air television have shown the extent to which 'live' footage can be parcelled for television within a 24-hour timeframe. Ruth Wrigley, executive producer for the first series of the UK *Big Brother*, has commented on the sheer amount of television produced by her team in an effort to keep up the pace of the 'present' demanded by liveness:

> Every Monday evening we put on a one-hour documentary; it normally takes six to eight weeks to turn round a documentary, and we were doing it in twenty-four hours. Producers were working through the night, on twenty-four-hour shifts, to do the half-hour programmes that went out on Tuesday, Wednesday and Thursday evening, and then we had

two live shows on Friday plus the omnibus.... I wanted it to look live and exciting, I wanted viewers – and the contestants who were evicted – to see the control room, to get an idea of all the behind-the-scenes work. After all, this was not meant to be a piece of polished drama. We were filming it for real, and it was a virtue of the programme that viewers understood that.

(Ruth Wrigley; quoted in Ritchie, 2000: 10–11)

What is notable in Wrigley's description of the pace of producing liveness is her awareness that liveness takes both temporal and aesthetic forms, each of which props up the effect of the other. Thus it was important not only to have producers work through the night in order to create what she calls the 'continuity' of liveness, and not only to have two live shows broadcast several hours apart on Friday, but also to couple this with the behind-the-scenes aesthetic of actuality. The view of the control room – that place behind the two-way mirrors where the logging, editing and regulating occurs – is the opposite of 'polished' (read 'fictional') drama. To display the technology of the control room means to acknowledge to the viewer that this programme is 'film[ed] for real', an effect which carries over to the daily episodes, which are taped but no less 'real'. The day-to-day house broadcasts, punctuated weekly by views of an open studio and a working control room, are key to *Big Brother*'s effective realness. Interestingly, Wrigley justifies the live aesthetic as being appropriate, even necessary, for *Big Brother*'s target audience of younger, sophisticated viewers: 'The audience we attracted understand television, they've grown up with it, they know its grammar' (quoted in Ritchie, 2000: 10). Viewers who understand television will demand the liveness effect not because they are naïve, but precisely because they know how to read it.

Mark Burnett, the executive producer and creator of *Survivor*, has said that the production task of *Big Brother* is basically impossible: 'You're shooting all that stuff and expecting to turn around a network hour and have it be on TV *tomorrow*? We take six to seven weeks to make 44 minutes of *Survivor*!' (Burnett, 2001). Clearly, the relatively huge ratings garnered by the *Big Brother* series (which spiked the fortunes of the mostly minority channels on which it aired, especially in Holland, Spain, Germany and Britain [Hill, 2002: 325]) are evidence that such a production–transmission ratio is perfectly possible, and that the realness effects make this compelling viewing. Where *Big Brother* (in its first series) failed to make a positive impact was the US, precisely the culture in which *Survivor* was such a hit. By contrast, *Survivor* was a relative ratings disappointment for the UK channel ITV (Corner, 2002: 262; Hill, 2002: 338, fn 9). The implication is that American audiences, in comparison with their European counterparts, have a lower tolerance for the threat of televised real time – a lower boredom threshold or a higher demand for dramatic shaping – while British audiences 'prefer informative, behind the scenes factual entertainment' (ibid.: 324). Though this may explain why John Ellis (2001) conceives of the UK *Survivor* as 'dead television' in contrast to *Big Brother*'s liveness, it does not mean that American audiences of Reality Television are insensible to the effects of immediacy. On the contrary, Burnett, a British producer, had such huge success with *Survivor* in the US because he figured out how to edit this unlive television into the present-ist framework of unlocated time.

Island time

True to the primitivist romanticism of *Survivor*, participants forgo conventional timepieces for the duration of their stay and rely instead on naturalistic methods of telling the time such as the progression of the sun and moon across the sky. In keeping with this shift, the production conveys the time of day to the viewer through the use of suggestive shots of dawn, high noon or sunset. These images help structure the narrative of each episode and provide a visual shorthand for such cultural clichés as 'a new day and a new beginning'. Another way in which *Survivor* participants track and structure the passing of each day is through the observance of conventional domestic routines around sleeping, eating and bathing. As a point of connection to 'home', regular mealtimes (three times a day) and conventional sleep patterns are highly valued by the show's participants and are consistently and ritualistically observed even when little or no food or rest are to be had. This patterned behaviour continues despite the fact that the social-temporal structures which necessitate the synchronisation of certain human activities (such as the workday) are largely absent from the *Survivor* schedule. As a mode of timekeeping, these routines locate participants both temporally and socially ('breakfast time' signifying both co-operative group interaction and 8 a.m.). In this way they work towards countering the temporal disorientation engendered by the 'unlocated' timeframe of the format.

The diurnal cycle is the longest measurement of time on *Survivor* equivalent to that recognised by social convention. Beyond the day, passing time is organised in terms of a three-day 'week' and, as a multiple of three, a 39-day season. The three-day cycle may be conceptualised as a week for two reasons. First, two days of activity (reward challenge, immunity challenge and tribal council) are followed by a day of rest which imitates the weekend or the Sabbath. Second, the format's particular relationship to broadcasting makes each three-day period equivalent to a seven-day week by packaging one three-day cycle as an hour-long episode to be screened weekly. This structuring encourages the programme's audience to interpret events as unfolding in 'real time' as footage appears to be shared on a week-for-week basis. Production participants and audience members alike are made very conscious of what 'day' it is within the 39-day season. Participants and presenter frequently refer to the 'number' (rather than the name) of the day and screen graphics appear regularly, punctuating each episode silently and insistently in order to delineate the three days represented. The counting (up or down) of the 39 days is balanced by the correlative counting (up or down) of the 16 participants, a narrative–numerical relationship which is emphasised in the opening title sequence: '16 Castaways – 39 Days – One Survivor'. Participants as well as days are located by their numerical position, and audiences familiar with the format can 'tell the time' of the series by the number of participants left (or, equally, by the number who *have* left). In this way, counting becomes a way of telling the time and arbitrary number sequences replace clocks and calendars.

The final episode of the original US series of *Survivor* opens with a sequence which exemplifies some of the points made here. The screen graphic 'Day Thirty-Seven' reads over an establishing shot of daybreak on the camp beach. A tracking shot shows Kelly sleeping and Richard standing, looking out to sea. The answer to the question proposed by this sequence – 'What does this new day mean for the group?' – is provided by two 'confession cam' shots of Richard and then Susan talking about time:

RICHARD: Time is kind of out of my head. I don't have a clock or a calendar or a watch or anything. But for some reason I feel really, really comfortable.... I think it has to do with just how short – how little time is left.

SUSAN: We're down to sixty hours – so, sixty hours, if you look at it that way, I can deal with it.

Articulating their experiences of passing time, Richard and Susan both speak of time as 'finishing' soon, of 'just how little time is left'. This is evidence of the extent to which both participants and audience are sutured into the temporal logic of '*Survivor*-time'. Their statements require no qualification or explanation – Susan doesn't need to say 'We're down to sixty hours *of the game*'. For this is a kind of time which *can* end, and start again, and even go backwards. In particular, Susan's interpretation of the three remaining days as 'sixty hours' encapsulates the strategy of 'present-ist' time which dominates and characterises Reality Television as a genre. Living hour to hour rather than day to day has the effect of speeding up Susan's experience of passing time because it contracts her temporal focus to the present. By living 'in the moment' of the passing hour she does not need to locate herself within the larger timespan of the day, or the three days remaining; she thereby eliminates the processes of retrospection and anticipation (these being painful for her as they elongate her perception of her incarceration on the island), processes which contravene the temporal logic of Reality Television. As suggested, Reality Television formats favour the smaller units of measured time for this reason. Focusing on the 'now' of this minute or this hour brings things closer –

temporally, socially and emotionally – intensifying the viewing experience in a way which capitalises on the medium's propensity for 'now-thisness' (Heath, 1990).

In this sequence, the theme of passing time gives way to the requisite complaint about limited food rations. Interestingly, this topic is interpreted by Rudy in terms of a number game:

RUDY: We made about two hundred pots of rice since we been here. Sometimes we ate three times a day, sometimes twice a day, sometimes once a day. I'd say I'd lost twenty-two pounds since I've been here.

In this context bowls of rice and pounds of fat are useful to Rudy as progressive number sequences which structure and mark the passing of his time on the island – as such they are ways of telling the time in an environment in which (as testified by Richard) conventional timekeepers are missed. Rudy's lament about the number of times a day the group eats (or doesn't eat) discloses a homesick yearning for the familiar structures of 'societal' time. Counting the spaces where the meals should have been, Rudy seeks to maintain the conventional temporal structures of the society he misses. Not only did these *Survivor* participants think and speak about time in this way, but the programme's producers chose to edit their comments into a sequence which introduces the final, mega-rating episode of the first series. This is because Richard, Susan and Rudy here speak the temporal protocol of the Reality Television series. The devices which construct the present-ist timeframe of reality programming are freely acknowledged, signalling an alternative temporal frame into which the Reality TV viewer is readily inducted.

Survivor challenges operate on a time base of their own. Each challenge provides for individuated 'unlocated' timeframes within the bigger picture of the 39-day season. The *Survivor* format favours challenge contests which pit partici-pants or teams against each other rather than against a clock. These contests are set up so that competitors can keep the opposition in sight, thereby using the progression of the other team as human stopwatches showing the 'Time to Beat'. In this instance it doesn't matter how long a challenge takes to complete in minutes, seconds and hours, only that it is completed first, or in the case of the 'Who can stand on the wooden post the longest' challenge, that it is completed last. A useful point of comparison is the New Zealand take on the desert island survival formula – *Treasure Island* (Touchdown Productions for TV2, April–June 2000, New Zealand). Conceived and produced several months prior to the release of Burnett's *Survivor* in the US, *Treasure Island* similarly relocates competitors on a Pacific atoll where they complete challenges in pursuit of a grand cash prize. Where *Treasure Island* differs from *Survivor* is in its construction of time during challenge sequences. The New Zealand show chooses to set its competitors challenges which take place over long time periods (most of a day) and large geographical areas (most of the island). The temporal principle of the race is the same, but as the players are out of sight of each other for most of the contest they are unable to register their progress against one another's. They can tell the time of day by looking at the sun, but within the context of the challenge this information is irrelevant and meaningless. The only kind of time that matters is the clock running against them in the form of the opposing team, and this is hidden from them. This difficulty combines with geographic obstacles, cryptic compass directions and hidden clues to create a challenge format in which participants are frequently stranded and helpless, completely lost and disoriented spatially *and* temporally. In this set-up the absence of meaningful temporal markers compounds spatial disorientation and vice versa. For a genre predicated on the elimination of conventional temporal markers, the dislocation of geographic space is fraught with possibility. But this aspect of the game reminds us also of the equivalence of time and space within the present-ist formula. As has been suggested, Reality TV couples the proximity of the 'here' with the urgency of the 'now', producing an endlessly reiterable time of 'liveness'.

Another New Zealand variation on the 'intimate strangers' model is a challenge format entitled *100 Hours* (Avalon Productions for TV2, 2002, New Zealand). Like *Survivor* and *Big Brother* this show throws a number of pre-selected contestants together to eat, sleep and compete in a closed environment. Similarly, the contestants are isolated from the world outside the production, cut off from the people, places and activities they know. However, *100 Hours* takes this isolation a step further. Sealed inside a network of disused, underground military bunkers, the participants on *100 Hours* are completely cut off from natural light, thereby isolated from the most basic of temporal references – the diurnal cycle of the sun and moon. The elimination of 'day' and 'night' as meaningful units of measured time allows this format to enact a complete displacement of conventional timeframes. Temporal and spatial disorientation is flagged as a key principle of the *100 Hours* format. Participants enter and leave the bunkers at night, a device which largely obfuscates the time of day and exacerbates the dimness of the habitat. Daylight is correctly interpreted here as a tool for both telling the time and finding your way, its absence providing for a double dose of disorientation. The voiceover of one of the episodes acknowledges this duality:

> Torches in hand, the four guys enter the tunnels. They need to get to the common room to begin their challenge. With no idea of direction, or even time, it's a tough task.

In this instance it seems nonsensical to suggest that not knowing the correct time will make it difficult to find the common room, but the assertion bespeaks the slippage between space and time in evidence here. As for the participants on

Treasure Island, the absence of temporal locators feeds into spatial disorientation, and vice versa.

In *100 Hours* there are no days – only hours, minutes and seconds. Participants do not take watches or other clocks into the *100 Hours* habitat, as these would enable them to continue operating on a 24-hour cycle. In lieu of a conventional clock the common room features a digital screen running the countdown (or count-up) from '00:00:00:00' to '100:00:00:00' (yes, nanoseconds too). Within the rhetoric of the format, players 'tell the time' by this clock, as in 'It is nearly 50 hours' or 'At 78 hours I am going to the engine room'. The narrowing of the temporal field from a day to an hour has the effect, as for *Survivor*'s Susan, of speeding up the passing of the nominated period of play and focusing attention on the hour at hand for both participants and audience. Disengaged from the ordering principle of the 24-hour day, the hour itself assumes a free-floating quality exploited by the format. The rules of this game interpret 'hours' in two ways: first, based on the alternative temporal logic of base 10, 100 hours are counted down in a linear numerical progression; second, hours are interpreted and utilised as game tokens which can be bartered, sold or tendered in a variety of ways according to the strategy of the player. This double usage makes an hour a 'counter' in both senses – a type of timekeeper and a token with a commodity value. As the latter, an hour is entirely disengaged from the linear progression of time, resisting both the march of history and the ineluctable countdown of the game show. Time has become so dislocated from a historical spectrum that its units function in another domain altogether, as a tender of exchange, leaving the participants afloat in an underground world of measured activities unconnected to any social structure.

100 Hours, not a big ratings success for its broadcaster (TV2), perhaps takes the principle of unlocated time too far. It is a show which isolates the temporal element of Reality Television, making it useful for study but less effective for viewers. In one sense, it is a reality show which has clearly understood the principle of using time units as movable counters, making that the basis of the format itself. On the other hand, as we have been arguing, Reality Television shows are most successful when they invoke a sense of immediacy in *both* of its meanings – temporal and emotional. By taking the notion of temporal immediacy to its limit, *100 Hours* also produced a sense of affective dislocation which cut the viewers off from any feeling of intimacy with the participants. The format of *100 Hours* thus reordered time at the expense of intimacy rather than in its service – and was taken off air halfway through the series by a broadcaster disappointed with it low appeal to viewers.

Conclusion

We have suggested that it is a mistake to think that the 'now' of Reality Television signifies atemporality. Rather, Reality TV steps out of history in order to bring questions of time to the fore, proffering an alternative temporal plane pre-eminently suited to the medium of television. 'Unlocated' time works because it capitalises on television's propensity for 'now-thisness', prioritising the intimacy and immediacy of the present moment over the objectivity of historical overview. Present-ist time is 'unlocated' because it steps out of the historical continuum, transgressing the laws of linear, infinite time and manifesting a kind of cyclical present which begins and ends whenever and wherever it is transmitted. This present can be read backwards as well as forwards and, in one format at least, assumes a free-floating quality as a 'counter'. We have shown that Reality TV's present-ist timeframe utilises the smallest units of time in order to focus and inten-sify the experiences of both participants and audience. The effect of 'realness' is thus predicated in part on a 'coincidence of experience' between viewers and participants through the use of social measures of time, and in part on the 'zone of liveness' which holds together a viewing community at a particular moment.

It is this singular construction of time which separates Reality TV from other forms of factual programming, for the immediacy of Reality TV's present-ist time code realises the quintessential Reality TV experience – the moment of sponta-neous emotional disclosure experienced simultaneously by programme participant and television viewer. In documentary, news programmes and current affairs shows the emotions are part of either reports or rehearsals, dislocating the time of emotion from the time of the event. By contrast, the viewers' participa-tion in 'the moment' in Reality Television is predicated on discursive and aesthetic constructions of closeness which are themselves dependent on principles of temporal closeness – immediacy, coincidence and liveness. Intimacy in Reality Television takes both a temporal and an affective form. Although some Reality TV formats may stage-manage emotional events (e.g. diminishing rations on *Survivor*, the climactic revelation on *Changing Rooms*), they do so in order to create a move-able present in which event, emotional display and audience reception coincide. The emotion of Reality Television thus has to do with a shared sense of everyday intimacy, a being-in-community which historical time does not easily register, certainly on the small screen. Rather than writing off Reality TV for its poor understanding of historical location, then, we have been arguing for a shift in perspective to accommodate the importance of the moveable 'now'. In this view, Reality Television makes use of this temporality of the real not to negate 'the public sphere', but to register a more concrete, *actuel* and immediate sense that communities have of being in the world.

Notes

1   Despite ongoing debates about which mainstream genre(s) best characterises Reality Television (see, for example, Corner, 2002), we will use the term 'genre' to name the group of programmes which themselves constitute the range of reality programming.

We accept that the hybridising of mainstream genre conventions has created a group of shows whose boundaries are difficult to determine, yet at the same time the popular use of the term 'Reality Television' indicates that it is an effective genre marker for shows which share characteristics of using and personalising non-media cast.

2   In contrast, Jermyn's chapter on British crime-appeal programmes (Chapter 3) argues that in their recurrent use of visual 'evidence' drawn from video technologies the illusion of immediacy converges with an inescapable sense of 'this-has-been-ness'.

3   Again, see Chapter 3, where Jermyn examines how the use of CCTV in crime-appeal programming enables it to undo 'real time' in order to focus on the 'punch-line'.

4   The original *Big Brother* was produced by Endemol for Dutch television in the autumn of 1999, and soon spread first to Germany and Spain (where it ran as *Gran Hermano*), and then across Europe. The US version (Endemol for CBS) began a few weeks ahead of the British version (Bazal for C4) in the summer of 2000. We will differentiate between versions only where the specificities of format or content make it necessary.

5   There is no better evidence of the deep-seated difference between *Big Brother* and *Survivor* than the conflicting responses of audiences in the US and UK to each. While *Big Brother* was a huge success in Britain (as it was across continental Europe), it was a ratings and critical flop in the US (see Ellis, 2001); the first series of *Survivor* in each country showed precisely the reverse results, breaking summer ratings records for CBS but causing ITV to reduce the screening frequency to once a week. Though this discrepancy must be read in terms of the relative ratings expectations of the channels which aired these shows (see Hill, 2002), it nonetheless points to an interesting difference in cultural taste and viability – one which has not, of course, been lost on subsequent Reality TV producers.

6   This lack of built-in delay has led web teams of the *Big Brother* series to make ample use of the audio-off switch whenever they foresee legal problems, especially with what is being said in the house. As Helen Hawken, senior producer for the first series of *Big Brother* in the UK, explains:

> Although you can get away with a lot more on the web than you can on television, we were aware that until 9 pm our website had to be regarded as family viewing. Obviously, we couldn't avoid the odd swear word, but if there was a barrage of swear words we shut off the audio feed. Our loggers were literally listening with their fingers on the button, ready to close down anything inappropriate.

(quoted in Ritchie, 2000: 17)

References

Berenstein, Rhona J. (2002) 'Acting Live: TV Performance, Intimacy, and Immediacy', in James Friedman (ed.) *Reality Squared: Televisual Discourse on the Real*, New Brunswick, NJ, and London: Rutgers University Press.

Burnett, Mark (2001) 'From *An American Family* to *Survivor*', seminar held at the Museum of Television and Radio, New York: May.

Caldwell, John Thornton (1995) *Televisuality: Style, Crisis, and Authority in American Television*, New Brunswick, NJ, and London: Rutgers University Press.

Corner, John (2002) 'Performing the Real: Documentary Diversions', *Television & New Media* 3(3): 255–70.

Couldry, Nick (2002) 'Playing for Celebrity: *Big Brother* as Ritual Event', *Television & New Media* 3(3): 283–94.

Derrida, Jacques and Bernard Stiegler (2002) *Echographies of Television*, trans. Jennifer Bajorek, Cambridge: Polity Press.

Doane, Mary Ann (1990) 'Information, Crisis, Catastrophe', in Patricia Mellencamp (ed.) *Logics of Television*, London, British Film Institute.

Dovey, Jon (2000) *Freakshow: First Person Media and Factual Television*, London: Pluto.

Ellis, John (2000) *Seeing Things: Television in the Age of Uncertainty*, London and New York: I. B. Tauris.

Ellis, John (2001) 'Mirror, Mirror', *Sight and Sound* 11(8): 8.

Fetveit, Arild (1999) 'Reality TV in the Digital Era: A Paradox in Visual Culture?', *Media, Culture and Society* 21(6): 787–804.

Feuer, Jane (1983) 'The Concept of Live Television: Ontology as Ideology', in E. Ann Kaplan (ed.) *Regarding Television: Critical Approaches – An Anthology*, Frederick, MD: University Publications of America.

Heath, Stephen (1990) 'Representing Television', in Patricia Mellencamp (ed.) *Logics of Television*, London: British Film Institute.

Heath, Stephen and Gillian Skirrow (1977) 'Television: A World in Action', *Screen* 18(2): 7–59.

Hill, Annette (2002) '*Big Brother*: The Real Audience', *Television & New Media* 3(3): 323–40.

Houston, Beverle (1984) 'Viewing Television: The Metapsychology of Endless Consumption', *Quarterly Review of Film Studies* 9(3): 183–95.

Nichols, Bill (1994) *Blurred Boundaries*, Indianapolis, IN: Indiana University Press.

Rath, Claus-Dieter (1989) 'Live Television and Its Audiences: Challenges of Media Reality', in Ellen Seiter, Hans Borchers, Gabrielle Kreutzner and Eva-Maria Warth (eds) *Remote Control: Television Audiences and Cultural Power*, New York: Routledge.

Ritchie, Jean (2000) *Big Brother: The Official Unseen Story*, London: Channel 4 Books.

Scannell, Paddy (2002) '*Big Brother* as Television Event', *Television & New Media* 3(3): 271–82.

7

IN SEARCH OF COMMUNITY ON REALITY TV[1]

America's Most Wanted and *Survivor*

Gray Cavender

Introduction

This chapter examines how Reality TV deals with the concept of community and argues that, while in many ways the programmes under consideration adhere to or seem to promote the notion of community, ultimately they serve to undermine and erode it. My interest in this topic is prompted, first, by the observation that Reality TV recurrently invokes notions of community and, second, by the outpouring of books since the 1980s that address community. This body of work typically employs an idealised definition of community that emphasises a commitment to a set of shared values, a sense of belonging to and an identification with a group or a place (see Young, 1990), before generally detailing the decline in various aspects of community in the United States and the negative implications of this shift.

In fact, commentators from de Tocqueville (*Democracy in America*, 1969) to David Riesman (*The Lonely Crowd*, 1950) have long been interested in the health of the US community. Recently, a number of commentators have expressed concern about the vitality of community. They argue that facets of social life which are essential for a viable community (e.g. reciprocity, trust and civic engagement) have waned (Purdy, 1999; Putnam, 2000). A commitment to common values, whether political or religious, has attenuated and there is a diminution in social solidarity as measured in terms of trust, volunteerism and civic or religious participation (Etzioni, 1993; Putnam, 2000). Richard Stivers (1994), for example, argues that, amid a culture of cynicism, US morality has become an anti-morality. Amitai Etzioni (1993), a former president of the American Sociological Association, decries the waning of traditional values and cites, among other indicators, high crime rates and a deterioration of private and public morality. Commentators now describe not so much a sense of community as a culture of cynicism (Stivers, 1994) or a culture of fear (Glassner, 1999).

Significantly, at the very time that there seems to be a diminution in community in the United States, at least in terms of this more traditional definition, Reality TV programmes frequently deploy the concept. This is all the more interesting given television's role as an important purveyor of myth in our society. Perhaps our notions of community are part of some nostalgic past which television mythologises. Alternatively, television, including Reality TV, may be a part of the erosion of community. There is, of course, a long history of discourses blaming social problems on the media; commentators have blamed cinema (see Allen *et al.*, 1998), comic books (see Nyberg, 1998), and music (see Gray, 1995) for social ills ranging from sexual promiscuity to delinquency. Television has had its share of critics on this theme as well. For example, in 1976 Gerbner and Gross argued that 'heavy' television viewers were more likely to see the world as an intimidating and threatening place than 'light' viewers. In a similar vein, more recently the *National Television Violence Study* (1997) concluded that US television presents violent (and occasionally graphically violent) images which are psychologically detrimental to viewers, especially children.

The attention given in these studies to the ways that television may inform our perception of the 'real world' underlines the importance of the intersection between Reality TV and notions of community. Of course, television generally is embedded in our everyday lives and in our communities. Ellis (1992) refers to the notion of television's 'community of address', by which he means that television effects an intimacy between its viewers and its representations. Reality TV often goes further, sometimes employing a mode of address in which the programme host speaks directly to viewers as if he or she knows us and gives us a participatory role, an address which may explain a part of Reality TV's appeal. It may also reflect a sense of community that focuses less on shared values or geographical place, and instead is defined by technology and audience membership, what Rath (1985) calls an 'invisible electronic network'.

In this chapter I consider how Reality TV directly or indirectly appeals to notions of community, and how the narratives within the programmes contrive to do this. I also consider how these programmes undermine notions of a viable community – that is, how characters and situations are presented which are counterproductive to community. I will analyse two US Reality TV programmes: *America's Most Wanted* (*AMW*) (Fox, 1988–), a crime-appeal programme which depicts actual crimes in dramatised re-enactments, and *Survivor* (CBS, 2000–), a contest-type programme where sixteen contestants assigned to two teams must compete in the wilderness for rewards and immunity, voting each other off until only one person remains to win the $1m prize. For the most part, I refer to *Survivor: Africa* and *Survivor: Marquesas*, both broadcast in 2002 (for references to specific episodes, the letter 'A' denotes *Africa* and the letter 'M' denotes *Marquesas*), while analysis of *AMW* draws predominantly on the 1988–9 and

1995–6 television seasons. Complete tapes from these two seasons are supplemented here with random episodes taped over the duration of its broadcast history. These two Reality TV programmes were selected because, while they differ from one another formally and thematically, each draws conspicuously upon notions of community. Equally, there are other justifications for including these programmes in this analysis. *America's Most Wanted* is the longest-running Reality TV programme in the United States and initially its high ratings contributed to the success of the then fledgling Fox Network. Similarly, *Survivor* has proved very popular in the US; *Africa* and *Marquesas* were among the top five television programmes during the 2001–2 season among the desirable teenage audience (Anonymous, 2002), and the success of the series has helped to revitalise the image of the CBS Network.

Reality TV and community

To contextualise these programmes, Reality TV programming did not simply materialise in the United States in the 1990s. Crime dramas like *Dragnet* – which was based on actual police cases – and court-type programmes like *The Verdict Is Yours* were popular television fare in the 1950s and 1960s. Earlier, in the 1940s, police procedurals, a sub-genre of crime fiction, based film and radio dramas on real cases (Cavender and Fishman, 1998). What is new is the proliferation of this type of programming and the explicit promotion of it on the basis of its 'reality' credentials. The US experience of 'real-crime' programming can particularly be traced to two programmes: *Aktenzeichen XY...Ungelöst* (*Case XY...Unsolved*) from Germany, and the British programme which it inspired, *Crimewatch UK* (Chapter 3 examines how *Crimewatch UK* prefigured much of the appeal and many characteristics of the broader contemporary Reality TV movement). *AMW*, an Americanised version of *Crimewatch UK*, aired in the United States in January 1988 (Breslin, 1990), while *Unsolved Mysteries* became a regular programme during the 1988–9 television season. *AMW* and *Unsolved Mysteries* enjoyed good ratings and other reality crime programmes, such as *Cops*, followed. Crime-related programmes eventually waned in popularity – though *AMW* and *Cops* remain on the air – but Reality TV has very much persisted.

Scholars posit a variety of understandings regarding the cultural significance of Reality TV. Neal Gabler (2001) suggests that cable and satellite have generated such an insatiable demand for television programmes that producers of more traditional TV formats are overwhelmed; the narrative well has run dry. Others note that Reality TV's hybridisation pairs two standard but appealing aspects of television, namely entertainment and voyeurism (Ellis, 1992; Dauncey, 1996; Schlesinger and Tumber, 1994; Dovey, 2000). But Reality TV features more than voyeuristic adventure; it traffics in anxieties and claims to depict them in a 'realistic' fashion. Other scholars suggest that these anxieties symbolise more deep-seated concerns: economic insecurity, terrorism and war (Dovey, 2000; Altheide, 2002). In programmes like *America's Most Wanted* these free-floating fears are sublimated into the fear of crime. These programmes, then, appeal to people who are fearful of crime and angry at criminals, while assuaging other social concerns (Schlesinger and Tumber, 1994; Cavender *et al.*, 1998; Jermyn, 2003).

This last point – the idea of programming which taps into the fear of and anger at crime (or other anxieties) – relates to the matter of community. Indeed, Reality TV discourses presume the existence of an idealised community. Real-crime programming presents the community as under attack (by crime) and appeals to the community to aid in the fight against crime (Jermyn, 2003). This comes at a time when, as indicated above, community has become a topic of academic interest, where writers have argued that traditional communities in the US have been replaced by a culture of cynicism (Stivers, 1994) or fear (Glassner, 1999).

Two commentators link this social malaise to the media, especially television. In *For Common Things* (1999), Jedediah Purdy argues that the webs of mutual reliance that are essential for a healthy community are failing in a society which extols a 'brand you' form of individualism. 'Brand you' thinking suggests that we consider ourselves to be like a product brand. Contemporary life is frantic and competitive and in this context we should take only those actions which increase the value of our 'brand'. Purdy suggests that, as a by-product of this perspective, irony and cynicism have displaced public involvement. He uses the US television sitcom *Seinfeld* as an heuristic device to demonstrate this cynical stance. To avoid appearing 'not savvy', the characters adopt a posture of ironic cynicism. So fractured is community within their milieu that in the popular final episode of the series they actually go to jail because they refuse to help a fellow citizen.

Robert Putnam grounds his widely discussed treatise *Bowling Alone: The Collapse and Revival of American Community* (2000) in a discussion of social capital. The core idea is that social networks involve mutual obligations (ibid.: 20). Putnam distinguishes two types of social capital: bonding, which is narrow, inward looking and underpins specific reciprocity among homogeneous groups; and bridging, which is broader in terms of identity and reciprocity, and consists of networks that cross diverse groups (ibid.: 22–3). He contends that, with the decline of the bridging form of social capital, trust and civic engagement have declined in the United States. He attributes these negative shifts to increased television viewing. 'Heavy television watching by young people is associated with civic ignorance, cynicism, and lessened political involvement' (ibid.: 237). Television need not be problematic, however. Putnam offers a hierarchy of pro-social programming, ranging from news and educational programmes at the top to Reality TV programmes like *America's Most Wanted* at the bottom (ibid.: 243).

Putnam's assessment of *America's Most Wanted* fits well with earlier evaluations of Reality TV. Reality TV has been compared to the tabloid newspapers of the nineteenth century, earning it the moniker 'Tabloid TV' for this reason (Rapping, 1992). Others have characterised Reality TV as 'Infotainment' or have dismissed it as 'Trash TV' (see Dovey, 2000). Despite these dismissive labels and claims that viewers are tired of Reality TV (Stanley, 2002) or that Reality TV has reached saturation point (Kilborn, 1994), new Reality TV programmes regularly appear in TV schedules and many of these are successes in terms of ratings. During a week in the US in early January 2003, for example, Reality TV programmes were the top-rated shows in fifteen of eighteen thirty-minute time slots (Carter, 2003).

My analysis is informed by Putnam's specific reference to *AMW* as the type of TV programme that is associated with a decline in community. Similarly, I draw upon Purdy's discussion of the relationships among individualism, cynicism and TV. At the same time, however, my analysis is informed by research which argues that Reality TV goes beyond television's usual 'embeddedness' and specifically includes the viewer in a televisual community (see Rath, 1985; Cavender, 1998; Jermyn, 2003). In the analysis of community in *America's Most Wanted* and *Survivor* that follows, what I uncover is a polysemic relationship wherein these programmes assume and reinforce a traditional sense of community even as their depictions negate the viability of it.

Thus my analysis is divided into two sections, 'For community' and 'Against community'. Within each division, I focus on direct invocations of notions of community, as well as those usages which are more evocative and indirect. I am also interested in the various narrative contrivances which these programmes use – that is, how their narratives contain scripted and aesthetic motifs that at different points may reinforce or challenge the ideal of community. Accordingly, my divisions each contain three subsections: direct, indirect and narrative contrivances, an organisation that reflects the conflictual messages about community that appear on these programmes.

For community

Direct invocation

Earlier I noted that, according to some commentators, a 'culture of fear' has emerged in the United States (Glassner, 1999), a cultural shift especially noticeable in terms of crime (Garland, 2001). *AMW* responds to increased fear of crime and anger at criminals and, in so doing, tries to re-establish a sense of community. The programme directly invokes a sense of community in several ways. At the broadest level, *AMW* portrays the United States as a community which has coalesced around fighting crime. The programme's full title, *America's Most Wanted: America Fights Back*,

COMMUNITY IN *AMERICA'S MOST WANTED* AND *SURVIVOR*

demonstrates this usage. Notably, this subtitle appeared before the events of September 11. One aspect of the idea of 'America fighting back against crime' appears in claims that viewer tips help in capturing criminals. Host John Walsh recurrently directly references this claim, when, for example, after recounting a capture he adds in a standard ending, 'Thanks for helping', or, in a more patriotic vein, 'Thanks America'. This usage speaks to one aspect of community: civic engagement. *AMW* encourages its audience to become involved, to 'fight back'.

AMW recurrently uses language that invokes a sense of community or a collective. Walsh often mentions a 'Task Force', which apparently consists of the police, *AMW* and the audience. Frequent invocations of the word 'we' include the viewer in this televisual community. An episode from 2001 (1 September) depicts Walsh interacting with several Atlanta police officers. There is an easy camaraderie between Walsh and the police, reinforcing the notion of the 'law enforcement community', of which the viewer is a televisual member. Indeed, Jermyn (2003) found the usage of similar patterns of language in her analysis of *Crimewatch UK*.

One of the defining motifs of community in its traditional sense is that communities typically share a set of values. Putnam (2000) notes that manifestations of these values (e.g. religious participation or civic engagement) are in decline, but this is not the case on *AMW*. *AMW*'s values are grounded in a decidedly Durkheimian sense of community in which crime violates social norms and generates condemnation from society. When crime transgresses community norms, Walsh expresses his (and the audience's) outrage at the crime and the criminal. *AMW* invokes something akin to Purdy's webs of reliance (1999), and often grounds them in religion. Walsh also regularly expresses his (and the audience's) sympathy for crime victims. In one vignette he says, 'We've been shocked and saddened to learn what happened' (16 April 1989), while in another he mentions prayer for the victim's family (26 March 1989).

To compare all this to *Survivor*, we can see that this programme too offers a number of direct references to a sense of community. Many portray the contestants as a kind of community. For example, in *Africa* host Jeff Probst describes the sixteen contestants as castaways who will be creating a 'new society' (11 October 2001). A *Marquesas* contestant reinforces this point. 'I came here to try to build a society with seven strangers. I'm here to see if eight people from different parts of the country can do this' (28 March 2002). Other contestants make similar claims about creating a 'new society' (M, 7 March 2002). *Survivor* uses language that invokes community in two obvious ways. First, the contestants are assigned to two teams which are named for indigenous tribes – that is, real communities. The teams in *Africa* are the Sambura Tribe and the Boran Tribe, while the teams in *Marquesas* are Rotu and Maraamu. The host and the contestants constantly reference these tribal names, thus giving the teams and their members a kind of working identity. The teams even wear coloured 'buffs' (headgear), which visually suggest a team identity. Second, as a series unfolds the contestants often assess how they are doing as a team. These assessments are not only about winning contests, but entail an evaluation of coming together as a team. Comments like 'this tribe is a family' (M, 20 March 2002) or 'we've found something here that's united' (M, 4 April 2002) suggest their sense of community. Probst also assesses how the contestants are doing in terms of coming together as a team (e.g. A, 18 October 2001).

Prayers and religious invocations also occur in several *Marquesas* episodes, typically before contests (e.g. 28 March 2002). At the end of each week's programme, when a contestant is expelled, the scene occurs at 'Tribal Council'. Tribal Council meetings are steeped in ritual, both verbal and visual. Fire, sombre music, slow-motion camera work and close-up shots enhance and underline the emotional power of the community. The losing contestant is voted out by the other members, in line with the principles of democracy. Each week as this happens host Jeff Probst solemnly announces, 'The tribe has spoken', and, as a sort of banishment, adds, 'You must leave the area immediately'. Thus, both programmes directly reference a sense of community. This ranges from the ideal of community as a place with shared values to team spirit and identity, and points to how notions of community are pivotal to the frameworks of numerous strands of Reality TV.

Indirect evocations

Sometimes, however, *AMW* and *Survivor* are more indirect, more evocative in conveying notions of community. Consistent with its Durkheimian sense of community, some *AMW* vignettes open upon a town or a family which seems to be in a state of equilibrium. This sense of equilibrium is conveyed by Walsh's voiceover, and by visuals and the soundtrack. For example, one vignette (27 April 1996) opens with old photographs of a young man and a young woman. Next, we see a photograph of them as a couple. Walsh's voiceover notes that they married young and the accompanying soundtrack is of orchestral music which evokes an earlier, happier time. As the music continues, Walsh, still in voiceover, informs us that they started with little money but amassed a fortune over the years. This last comment is accompanied by a more recent photograph of the older man and woman. Walsh describes them as a happy couple. These evocative introductions are all the more powerful when crime shatters the sense of communal well-being: the happy couple is murdered. *AMW* reinforces crime's destructive impact with jump-cut edits and jarring music.

AMW adopts a 'them v. us' framework of characterisation in its depiction of community. Victims, as legitimate members of the community (which includes the audience), are broadly characterised as attractive, worthwhile people. Often, a victim's ties to the community are noted, for example they are a good family member (9 March 1996) or a community volunteer who helps the less fortunate

(26 February 1989). Juxtaposed with community members are the criminals. If victims are attractive and worthwhile, criminals are 'ugly' and worthless outsiders. Walsh often describes them in negative language, for example as having 'dirty blonde hair' (26 February 1989) or 'a scraggly beard' (2 April 1989). References to tattoos or other physical stigmata complete the description of these outsiders in a manner that portrays them as unclean, both physically and morally (see Douglas, 1966). The 'them v. us' dichotomy is heightened by the nature of the crimes that are committed. Crimes usually involve serious, reprehensible acts, such as murder or child molestation. Cavender and Bond-Maupin (1993) note that the characterisations resemble urban legends in the way that their portrayals of crime and criminals symbolise the dangers of modern life (for example criminals may be drifters or even Satanists, while victims are hard-working people who are going about their business).

These characterisations reinforce Putnam's (2000) observation that communities can be both inclusive and exclusive. On *AMW* the legitimate community includes the worthwhile victims and the audience. This point is frequently reinforced as victims or family and friends reflect on how the victimisation has hurt them. Walsh often concludes the vignettes with such evocative statements as 'our heart goes out to his family' (13 January 1996) or 'we can search for his killer while his family grieves' (16 April 1989). Of course, criminals are excluded from this community; they represent a threat. A vignette ends with a criminal's capture and Walsh says, 'Thank God he's off the streets' (1 September 2001).

Survivor: Africa begins in a state of equilibrium which also evokes a sense of community. As the first episode opens (11 October 2001) we see the sixteen contestants on a truck, which first drives through the African countryside and then passes through a village. Village people, talking in small groups and going about their activities, watch the truck pass by. Soon, a group of village children gather, and, laughing, follow the truck for a time. In later episodes of *Africa* and *Marquesas*, members of tribal communities appear on the programme. These depictions locate the contestants not only in their *Survivor* teams, but in geographical areas and with the tribes who really live there.

Community also is evoked on these programmes through frequent discussions of trust, which is essential to social bonds. Because the contestants live and work in teams, trust and bonding are common topics of discussion among the members and by host Jeff Probst. A contestant in *Africa* notes that 'trust is probably one of the biggest issues of all' (18 October 2001). When there is tension among team members Probst lectures them about bonding, exhorting them to go back to their camp (after a divisive Tribal Council) and 'do some serious mending' (A, 25 October 2001).

Both programmes, then, indirectly invoke notions of community. Each in its own way opens in a state of equilibrium in which the community exists. This status is disrupted, but the programmes suggest that by pulling together threats can be overcome. At the same time, however, as I will return to below, the fragility of community is very much built into the tensions at work in *Survivor*, since an individualist ethic must co-exist with the 'team spirit' due to the inescapable drive to whittle the contestants down to one final winner. Equally, the very fact of the existence of crime-appeal programmes underlines the precariousness of 'traditional forms of supportive and secure communities'; in a kind of internal paradox, the genre's discourse and evocation of community 'appeal...to the very thing whose loss [they] decr[y]' (Jermyn, 2003: 27).

Narrative contrivances

Despite reality claims, there is a scripted quality to *AMW* and *Survivor*. Both programmes rely on television's narrative conventions (language and visuals) to tell stories which produce a desired effect. For example, the stories try to produce a sense of interconnectedness between the people depicted and the audience. On *AMW*, host Walsh and others refer to crime victims by their first names, an address which parallels the ways in which we express familiarity with members of our own community. Family and friends relate stories about the victims which reinforce this sense of 'getting to know them'. Vignettes depict *AMW*'s victims going about their lives, at work or with friends, depictions which facilitate audience identification with the crime victim or with his or her family. Through dramatisation, a victim's fear is evident in a furtive glance; a murder victim's empty chair at the table symbolises the family's loss (6 April 1996). *AMW*'s narratives also include the audience in the restoration of community values. Sometimes *AMW* presents the viewer who phoned in a tip; for example, we learn in one vignette (1 September 2001) that, after telephoning the police, a viewer hid and videotaped the criminal's capture. *AMW* interviewed the tipster and used her home video. Scholars who study other crime-appeal programmes argue that they justify their existence and 'reward' their viewers by regularly crediting viewers with captures (Jermyn, 2003).

Survivor host Probst also refers to contestants by their first names; a brief biography helps the audience to get to know them in their pre-contest lives. A standard convention of the programme features a contestant, seemingly alone, who directly addresses the camera (and us), producing an intimacy as the contestant reveals concerns or frustrations. We also see team members sleeping side by side, trying to stay warm or getting 'mail' (announcements of the next contest). When they win, we see group hugs and high fives. When they lose, we also see a team deal with its loss and the effort to shore up a dejected member. In *Africa*, her team loses a contest because Kim falls. Later, back at camp, Kim apologises and the others forgive her. She tells them, 'It was my time to basically, you know, screw up. I just wanted you all to know how bad I feel for this.' There is a medium close-up shot of Kim as she speaks, then the camera shifts to first one and then another team-mate, who listen as Kim apologises. Off camera, others mutter 'It's OK'. Kim goes on, 'And, while I appreciate the great things you're saying, you guys would feel exactly the same.' The camera shifts to a medium close-up of Tom, who reassures her 'Well, I ain't worried about it; it's only a game. And everybody has booboos. Hey, I'm proud to be on your team'. The scene ends by framing the group in an upward-looking, low-angle shot. Although unusual and somewhat voyeuristic, the shot includes Tom, Kim and other members in the frame, giving a sense of solidarity. Off camera, someone concurs with Tom's comments: 'I agree' (A, 18 October 2001).

This evocative sense of community is especially powerful at the start of each week's programme; as the team returns from a Tribal Council having just voted out a member, the dimly lit nighttime camera work gives the contestants an eerie sense of togetherness. Narrative contrivances also circulate around the notion of idealised, shared values. The drive to win means that some *Survivor* contestants are (constructed as) arrogant, manipulative and despicable people. When other members of the tribe finally see through the 'villain' and vote her or, more often, him out, the threat is reduced and community values are restored (albeit temporarily) in a melodramatic fashion.

The invoking of community around the programme also extends to the audience. At the beginning of each episode the words 'Interactive Programming' appear on the screen. Entering into a web community (as they can with *AMW*, which also has a website for viewers to chat), the audience can log onto the *Survivor* website and become even more closely involved with the contestants (see Chapter 13 for a detailed analysis of *Survivor* web forums). Furthermore, toward the end of each week's episode a voiceover notes that the contestant just ousted will appear on the local news that follows, or on a network news programme the next morning. There also are tie-ins to the local community: a contestant may live in the viewer's city or host Jeff Probst's parents do (M, 13 March 2002). These people are interviewed in the newspaper or on the local news (GoodyKoontz, 2002; Matlock, 2002), stories that connect the viewers' community to the *Survivor* community. All these features underline the extent to which the programmes contrive, through their narratives, to pull the audience into the show, into their televisual community.

Against community

Direct invocations

As we have seen, then, *AMW* and *Survivor* depict many facets of social life that seemingly are essential elements of community. But there is a tension around this since, at the same time, both programmes simultaneously undermine community, often in very direct ways. Despite a focus on the team or on bonding, ultimately there is only one winner on *Survivor* and the stakes are high: $1 million. In such a competitive situation it is no surprise that the contestants frequently act in decidedly 'non-communal' ways. They speak of bonds or loyalty to the tribe, but in moments of candour some note that they are willing to lie, or, in the words of one, 'I'm gonna do what it takes to win' (A, 25 October 2001). They form alliances – you don't vote against me and I won't vote against you – which sometimes are real and sometimes are duplicitous, manipulative interactions which some contestants acknowledge (M, 11 April 2002).

The contestants' awareness of this, and the very structure of the contest, puts them in a strange space: they must depend upon each other, yet know that they really cannot do so. As one contestant in *Africa* puts it, 'This game breeds paranoia' (18 October 2001). Similarly, a contestant in *Marquesas* admits that she has become uncharacteristically 'seductive and cunning' and adds, 'That's what the game does to you' (2 April 2002). At best, perhaps their situation resembles Putnam's (2000) more narrow reciprocity among homogeneous groups. Even here, however, reciprocity is ephemeral: alliances are undependable. Some contestants blame strategic alliances for the destruction of team loyalty. They make comments like 'We're not much of a tribe anymore, we don't have much unity' (A, 25 October 2001) or 'There are two tribes within one' (A, 1 November 2001). One contestant says, 'I don't trust any one of these people.... I'm on my own' (M, 18 April 2002). Indeed, in such a situation trust is forfeit.

AMW addresses trust in a manner that resembles the situation on *Survivor*. If *Survivor* features false alliances and duplicity, *AMW* specialises in poseurs. Many of *AMW*'s criminals masquerade as decent members of the community, but this is a disguise. Thus, a college student – a predator who only poses as a student – rapes and murders a woman he meets at a fraternity party (29 March 1996); a trusted FBI agent murders his family (28 May 1994); the seemingly pleasant neighbour is a child molester (9 March 1996). Equally bad, some criminals have secret psychological problems. These 'crazy' people murder their parents and grandparents, their spouses or their children (e.g. 26 February 1989). *AMW* details the horrific results when victims trust these poseurs. In some vignettes, victims are good citizens who are active in their community; nevertheless, they are victimised. In other vignettes, victimisation comes about as a direct result of trusting others. On *AMW* it is most often gullible women who are victimised (Cavender *et al.*, 1998). One woman, characterised as 'a trusting girl who helps outcasts', is murdered by one such outcast (26 February 1989). *AMW* notes that these victimisations occur not only in big cities, where they might be expected, but also in small towns where we might have assumed that community was more intact. Thus we can see that, conflictually, even while the programmes venerate community in some aspects, they present characters and situations that directly negate community. False alliances and misplaced trust are the order of the day on both programmes.

Indirect evocations

Both programmes indirectly question the possibility of a viable community. On *AMW*, it is not enough to be active in the community or even to live in a small town which should be the epitome of a functioning community. Nothing is as it seems and those who trust do so at their peril. A crime victim makes this point as she describes her neighbourhood: 'I used to feel safe here, but no more' (23 March 1996).

Racialised notions of good (white) and evil (black) work against the possibility of community on *AMW*. In some ways, it is not the criminals but the victims who are the issue. Notwithstanding US crime statistics, *AMW* typically depicts white victims (Cavender *et al.*, 1998). Scholars who analyse other Reality TV crime programmes conclude that the criminals portrayed are disproportionately people of colour (Kooistra *et al.*, 1998). Such presentations, when paired with similar portrayals on local television news, depict nonwhites as outsiders who threaten the 'white' community (Oliver and Armstrong, 1998; Gilliam and Iyengar, 2000), portrayals that work to reinforce racist views.

On the five *Survivor* series, the threat to community appears in the form of two character types: the contestant who is only 'playing the game' and 'the freeloader'. The contestant who is only playing the game is so 'out to win' as to be an untrustworthy team member. When made against others, this allegation serves as an exclusionary character slur. The freeloader is a different character type. Securing food and maintaining shelter are essentials of daily life on *Survivor*, so the freeloader (someone who is lazy and does not do his or her share) increases everyone's burden and weakens the tribe in contests. These contests generate rewards (such as food and water or immunity from expulsion for that week's programme), so losses (and freeloaders) hurt.

These character types sometimes inflect other aspects of membership in (and potentially exclusion from) the tribal community, in terms of the representation of 'minority groups'. For example, *Africa* and *Marquesas* each featured a contestant who was a gay man and on both series another team member questioned the contribution that could be made by a homosexual. (See Chapter 10 for an analysis of gay male identity and Reality TV.) On *Africa* the situation was more complicated. The gay man was characterised as a freeloader, but the problem was also generational: older team members worked, while younger members (who had bonded and included the gay man) slept late. On *Marquesas* the freeloader situation was racialised as one contestant, an African-American man, was viewed as lazy. It also was assumed that he had formed an alliance with an African-American woman, an alliance which was seen as potentially detrimental to his team-mates. One contestant said, 'They're African-Americans; bonds are strong in their culture' (16 May 2002), a comment which positioned them as having splintered, as being 'other' or outside of the team proper by virtue of their own (divisive) race loyalties. At another point, when one of the African-American contestants questioned some possibly racialised aspects of treatment in the tribe, other members referred to this as 'playing the race card' (16 May 2002). Occasionally, too, social class mitigates against community on *Survivor*. In an *Africa* episode, a dentist is voted out. He appeared to be a hardworking, contributing member of his team, but some team-mates said that they were tired of hearing him talk about his lifestyle, especially owning expensive cars. Another was more succinct: the dentist did not need the $1 million, and he did (25 October 2001).

Ultimately, *AMW* and *Survivor* evoke a world that is devoid of trust and other aspects of community despite the illusion of community at some levels. A contestant on *Marquesas* dismisses team unity, noting that at Tribal Council all votes are individual votes. Another *Marquesas* contestant explains it this way. 'I'm here to win a million dollars. If I have to say something to someone and do the opposite...well, that's just the way it is, the way life is' (25 April 2002). Furthermore, both programmes indirectly negate community through divisive depictions of negative character types, which in some cases reinforce stereotypes associated with race, class or sexuality.

Narrative contrivances

On both programmes, persistent elements of the way the narratives are constructed work against the possibility of a community. On *Africa*, for example, after the host describes the castaways who will be creating a new society they begin to bicker almost immediately. Some comments are offered as private asides by a contestant to the camera (and to us), while at other times we overhear two contestants whispering. In a *Marquesas* episode, a contestant's voiceover says, 'Kathy isn't trying to be one of us...she sleeps alone out by the fire', while the visual shows Kathy doing just that (7 March 2002). The producers must believe that these asides, which often suggest divisiveness and individualism, are popular and effective, since they are a characteristic motif of the programme's aesthetic, with much time devoted to them.

There is a good deal of what appears to be contrived anger on *Survivor*, anger which seems to be as contrived as the convivial hugs and high fives. Contestants are often uncivil in their interactions over issues that are blown out of proportion. Moreover, by editing the untold hours of footage the producers can locate and adopt whatever visual fits their script. On *Africa*, perhaps Ethan's look, seemingly directed at Clarence, who has eaten more than his share of cherries, actually occurred the day before and was related to another matter (11 October 2001). Ethan's look and the expressions of other team members leave no doubt that Clarence is an outcast. In case there is any doubt about such matters, the host elicits from the contestants their bad feelings about one another, or their insecurities about their own situation. In the later stages of each *Survivor* instalment the nature of the contests changes as well. Team contests are replaced by individual competitions, which offer wonderful opportunities for the programme to show contestants' dislike for each other.

Life's uncertainties are shown in a contrived manner on *Survivor*. The instalments occur in faraway places where nature is an ever-present reminder that life is uncertain. Thus the settings themselves are used to dramatise the theme of uncertainty, when contestants bicker or struggle to win a competition and the scene shifts to a close-up of a praying mantis devouring its prey (A, 18 October 2001) or a lion on the prowl for a kill (A, 20 December 2001). The producers drive home the point about life's uncertainties by sometimes ordering a swap of members, thus realigning the two teams. On *Africa* (8 November 2001) this swap was motivated by a generational feud which undermined the programme's suspense: the younger members had the upper hand and would have voted out, one by one, the older members. When a swap occurred on *Marquesas*, host Probst informed the members that 'this part of your destiny was planned long before you got to the Marquesas Islands' (20 March 2002). The swap – and, more, the swap as whim – had become a part of the drama.

AMW deals with actual crimes, so its dramatic contrivances are of a different nature. The producers apparently select crimes and criminals that tap into current 'hot topics'. During the years of the US war on drugs *AMW* often depicted drug dealers or drug-related crimes. More recently the programme shifted its focus to kidnapping, molestation and other crimes against children. Indeed, children and women disproportionately figure as victims on *AMW*. In many *AMW* vignettes, victims appear to have been randomly chosen, or, ironically, victimised by criminals who mistook them for someone else. This approach is consistent with the notion of modern danger; it also perpetuates a culture of fear.

Nothing is ever certain (or safe) for the members of the community on *AMW* or *Survivor*. Pivoting on a surveillance culture, as so many Reality TV formats do, the only assurance is of a kind of voyeurism: we are watching them. Indeed, there is an Orwellian dimension to *AMW*'s televisual community (Cavender, 1998). Except for an occasional anecdote – a humorous newspaper story about a viewer who turns in the actor who played the criminal – we hear surprisingly little about the predictable incorrect identifications wherein innocent people are reported to the Task Force, either due to mistaken identity or on purpose. Surely *AMW*'s call for a situation in which everyone watches everyone else is as destructive of community as is the poseur. Trust and reciprocity cannot exist in a situation in which everyone – a stranger, a friend or a family member – is a potential threat. The situation is reminiscent of *1984* and Orwell's Oceania, a fictional society in which no one could trust anyone.

The voyeurism of *Survivor* is no better. An episode tends to leave one exhausted, like too much family togetherness over a long holiday. Foibles are magnified, duplicity is the norm, and trust and reciprocity are hard to find. Indeed, the actual production of *Africa* and *Marquesas* exemplifies a kind of exoticism of the indigenous people characterised by a historic lack of trust and reciprocity with a racialised dimension. Earlier I noted that members of the local indigenous communities sometimes appear on episodes. These appearances give the *Survivor* teams (and the audience) a sense of place and a glimpse of the existing communities there. However, anthropologist Kathleen Riley (2002) offers a critical view of these appearances when she notes that island crafts and cultural practices were belittled as they were used essentially as props in contest 'challenges', and that tribal chants were synthesised into background music on *Survivor: Marquesas*. Their presence was manipulated to meet the needs of programme-makers to such an extent that even the landscape was digitally remastered to obscure signs of prior human occupation. Riley also describes disagreements over the amount of money promised and actually paid by the programme producers to the local government, and similar disagreements plagued *Survivor:Africa* (Lacey, 2001).

In the end, the message that these programmes convey is destructive of community. *AMW*'s world is characterised by a sense of modern danger. The *Survivor* contestants have little choice but to forge (often false) alliances and, despite protestations to the contrary, play the game. Through their narratives, *AMW* and *Survivor* present a world that is a risky place. Trust and reciprocity are replaced by surveillance and voyeurism.

Conclusion

At a time when scholars claim that community is in decline in the United States, two very different types of Reality TV programmes appeal to notions of community. *AMW* posits a community in which the audience, the programme and the police come together to fight crime. The show extols civic engagement (reporting fugitives), and tries to build bonds between the audience and crime victims and their families. These bonds are premised on shared values, which include norms of law-abiding behaviour, religion and civic engagement.

Survivor offers a sense of community by depicting contestants as teams with common goals; they must bond by necessity. The TV audience can be a part of such a community by cheering for a team or its members, by interacting online or simply by watching television. Integrating the programme more broadly into the regular format of our lives, as television characteristically does (Altheide, 2002), we see *Survivor* contestants on our local news, on national morning news shows or, months later, in newspaper updates or on talk shows hosted by other celebrity 'friends'.

And yet there is something suspect about these communities. Like many television presentations (such as crime drama, even the news), *AMW* traffics in a culture of fear that commentators suggest characterises US society (Glassner, 1999). *AMW*'s solution is almost as bad as the problem: in a society built on fear and mistrust, we should, apparently, report on each other. This solution parallels the Terrorism Information Prevention System (TIPS), proposed as a part of President George W. Bush's Department of Homeland Security. Although never implemented, as initially proposed the mission of TIPS was to collect information from citizens (postal employees, electric company employees, truck drivers and dock workers) about 'suspicious things'. Bush's proposal and *AMW*'s standard narrative generate only a *faux* community, one that obliterates trust, a prerequisite for a viable community.

On *Survivor*, if there is reciprocity at all it is at best constituted around narrow bonds of self-interest (mirroring Putnam's 'bonding', not bridging social capital). True webs of interdependence cannot really exist: the game does not permit it. Notwithstanding teams which are named for real communities, buffs and high fives, all is not well in these communities. Instead of the 'new society' that *Survivor* promises, we see lying, false alliances, whispers and edited-in looks of suspicion. These are the antithesis of a viable community.

Occasionally there are moments when a sense of community appears on these programmes. On *AMW* (6 April 1996), a mother's joy at the return of her missing child and her tearful thanks to the audience reinforce social bonds. On *Marquesas*, as a young African-American man from New York and a white Southern judge share the rewards of a contest victory, they reflect on the racial significance of their situation (25 April 2002). In another *Marquesas* example, family members appear and engage in a competition as proxies for the contestants. As a family member is eliminated, the contestant is permitted a brief reunion with the loved one. The remaining contestants watch, awaiting their turn at a reunion. As they wait, they show genuine support for one another, even for 'enemies' (25 April 2002). But such examples are rare.

It is beyond the scope of my analysis or these data to comment on Putnam's claim (2000) that television is a chief cause of the destruction of community in the United States. Certainly the notion of the reproduction of fear (Altheide, 2002) is at the heart of *AMW*'s depictions. And on *Survivor* the contestants undoubtedly exemplify Purdy's 'brand you' individualism and cynicism (1999).

My analysis does, however, offer insights into how these programmes employ the concept 'community', and what the usage means for an understanding of

Reality TV. At the outset, I noted that many commentators offer an idealised definition of community and *AMW* and *Survivor* employ this traditional definition. This usage posits the community as a coherent unity which is threatened by external and internal forces – crime from strangers or from neighbours on *AMW*, the other team or duplicitous team members on *Survivor*. Although these problems can be resolved, or at least contained, on *AMW* and *Survivor*, the larger social anxieties that they symbolise are beyond a Reality TV solution; the programmes promise entertainment and some relief from social concerns, but they only reproduce anxieties. They also reinforce traditional notions of individualism and competition.

Of course, *AMW* and *Survivor* employ a traditional notion of community. Other commentators have noted the nostalgic quality of such a definition in Reality TV programming (Jermyn, 2003), in appeals to community policing (Crawford, 1999) and in the formulation of social policy (Young, 1990). But, significantly, elsewhere Iris Marion Young (ibid.: 12–13) offers an alternative ideal of community which stresses heterogeneity, not unity. Rather than the traditional ideal of the small village, Young begins with the metaphor of city life which privileges heterogeneity over unity, and social differentiation, not exclusion. Neither *AMW* nor *Survivor* engages with this more inclusive view of community; on these programmes life remains resolutely 'them v. us'.

Note

1   I appreciate the helpful comments of Nancy Jurik and the editors of this collection, Su Holmes and Deborah Jermyn. Madelaine Adelman and David Altheide provided helpful citations.

References

Allen, Jessica, Sonia Livingstone and Robert Reiner (1998) 'True Lies: Changing Images of Crime in Postwar Cinema', *European Journal of Communications* 13: 53–75.

Altheide, David (2002) *Creating Fear: News and the Construction of Crisis*, New York: Aldine de Gruyter.

Anonymous (2002) 'The List', *Arizona Republic*, 18 June: E2.

Breslin, Jack (1990) *America's Most Wanted: How Television Catches Crooks*, New York: Harper & Row.

Carter, Bill (2003) 'Reality Shows Alter the Way TV Does Business', *New York Times*, 25 January: A1, B14.

Cavender, Gray (1998) 'The Shadow of Shadows: Television Reality Crime Programming', in Mark Fishman and Gray Cavender (eds) *Entertaining Crime: Television Reality Programs*, New York: Aldine de Gruyter.

Cavender, Gray and Lisa Bond-Maupin (1993) 'Fear and Loathing on Reality Television: An Analysis of *America's Most Wanted* and *Unsolved Mysteries*', *Sociological Inquiry* 63: 305–17.

Cavender, Gray and Mark Fishman (1998) 'Television Reality Crime Programs: Context and History', in Mark Fishman and Gray Cavender (eds) *Entertaining Crime: Television Reality Programs*, New York: Aldine de Gruyter.

Cavender, Gray, Lisa Bond-Maupin and Nancy C. Jurik (1998) 'The Construction of Gender in Reality Crime TV', *Gender & Society* 13: 643–63.

CBS (2003) '*Survivor* Ratings Tracker', 13 February (online); available at http://www.wishingwellarts.com/Survivor/ (dated 28 February 2003; accessed 4 March 2003).

Crawford, Adam (1999) *The Local Governance of Crime: Appeals to Community and Partnerships*, Oxford: Oxford University Press.

Dauncey, Hugh (1996) 'French Reality Television', *European Journal of Communication* 11: 83–106.

de Tocqueville, Alexis (1969) *Democracy in America*, New York: Anchor Books.

Douglas, Mary (1966) *Purity and Danger: An Analysis of Concepts of Pollution and Taboo*, London: Routledge & Kegan Paul.

Dovey, Jon (2000) *Freakshow: First Person Media and Factual Television*, London: Pluto Press.

Ellis, John (1992) *Visible Fictions: Cinema, Television, Video*, New York: Routledge.

Etzioni, Amitai (1993) *The Spirit of Community: Rights, Responsibilities and the Communitarian Agenda*, New York: Crown.

Fishman, Mark (1998) 'Ratings and Reality: The Persistence of the Reality Crime Genre', in Mark Fishman and Gray Cavender (eds) *Entertaining Crime: Television Reality Programs*, New York: Aldine de Gruyter.

Gabler, Neal (2001) 'When Every TV Show Is a Rerun', *New York Times*, 4 March: WK 15.

Garland, David (2001) *The Culture of Control*, New York: Oxford University Press.

Gerbner, George and Larry Gross (1976) 'Living with Television: The Violence Profile', *Journal of Communication* 26(2): 173–99.

Gilliam, Franklin and Shanto Iyengar (2000) 'Prime Suspects: The Influence of Local Television News on the Viewing Public', *American Journal of Political Science* 44: 560–73.

Glassner, Barry (1999) *The Culture of Fear: Why Americans Are Afraid of the Wrong Things*, New York: Basic Books.

GoodyKoontz, Bill (2002) 'Reality TV Not Real Life for Mesa's Survivor', *Arizona Republic,* 4 May: E1–2.

Gray, Herman (1995) 'Popular Music as a Social Problem: A Social History of Claims Against Popular Music', in Joel Best (ed.) *Images of Issues: Typifying Contemporary Social Problems*, New York: Aldine de Gruyter.

Harrington, Lee and Denise Bielby (1995) *Soap Fans: Pursuing Pleasure and Making Meaning in Everyday Life*, Philadelphia, PN: Temple University Press.

Jermyn, Deborah (2001) 'Death of the Girl Next Door: Celebrity, Femininity, and Tragedy in the Murder of Jill Dando', *Feminist Media Studies* 1(3): 343–59.

Jermyn, Deborah (2003) 'Watching *Crimewatch UK*: Investigating Crime Appeal Programming on British Television', unpublished PhD thesis, Cardiff: University of Cardiff.

Kilborn, Richard (1994) 'How Real Can You Get? Recent Developments in Reality Television', *European Journal on Communication* 9: 421–39.

Kooistra, Paul, John Mahoney and Saundra Westervelt (1998) 'The World of Crime According to Cops', in Mark Fishman and Gray Cavender (eds) *Entertaining Crime: Television Reality Programs*, New York: Aldine de Gruyter.

Lacey, Marc (2001) 'Shaba National Reserve Journal: TV Adventure Show Ignores the Real Survivors', *New York Times*, 13 August, International: A4.

Matlock, Stephanie (2002) 'Ex-Mesa Survivor Reason to Party', *Arizona Republic*, 26 September: B3.

National Television Violence Study (vol. 1) (1997) Thousand Oaks, CA: Sage Publications.

Nyberg, Amy (1998) 'Comic Books and Juvenile Delinquency: A Historical Perspective', in Frankie Bailey and Donna Hale (eds) *Popular Culture, Crime, and Justice*, Belmont: Wadsworth Publishing.

Oliver, Mary Beth and Blake Armstrong (1998) 'The Color of Crime: Perceptions of Caucasians' and African-Americans' Involvement in Crime', in Mark Fishman and Gray Cavender (eds) *Entertaining Crime: Television Reality Programming*, New York: Aldine de Gruyter.

Purdy, Jedediah (1999) *For Common Things: Irony, Trust, and Commitment in America Today*, New York: Alfred Knopf.

Putnam, Robert (2000) *Bowling Alone: The Collapse and Revival of American Community*, New York: Simon & Schuster.

Rapping, Elayne (1992) 'Tabloid TV and Social Reality', *The Progressive*, August: 35–7.

Rath, Claus D. (1985) 'The Invisible Network: Television as an Institution in Everyday Life', in Phillip Drummond and Richard Patterson (eds) *Television in Transition: Papers from the First International Television Studies Conference*, London: British Film Institute.

Riesman, David (1950) *The Lonely Crowd*, New Haven, CT: Yale University Press.

Riley, Kathleen (2002) 'Surviving "Survivor" in the Marquesas', *Anthropology News*, May: 6.

Schlesinger, Philip and Howard Tumber (1994) *Reporting Crime: The Media Politics of Criminal Justice*, Oxford: Oxford University Press.

Stanley, Alessandra (2002) 'Wearied by Reality, Television Returns to a 1980s Mind-Set', *New York Times*, 24 July: B1, 7.

Stivers, Richard (1994) *The Culture of Cynicism: American Morality in Decline*, Cambridge: Blackwell.

Young, Iris Marion (1990) *Justice and the Politics of Difference*, Princeton, NJ: Princeton University Press.

8

'THE NEW YOU'

Class and transformation in lifestyle television

Gareth Palmer

...between the overclass and the underclass is a new and growing anxious class.

(Blair, 1996: 7)

In this chapter I will argue that lifestyle programming, far from being the froth so easily dismissed by its critics, is illustrative of significant trends in the way we understand ourselves as citizens and consumers. In relation to the above epigraph, what I want to do here is discuss the ways in which discourses of class permeate these programmes. Although the entire concept of 'class' has become increasingly complicated and ambiguous – particularly within discourses which claim the 'class-less society' as an ideal – I suggest here that issues of class *are* apparent in lifestyle television, and in fact permeate its construction on a number of different levels.

Lifestyle is a sub-genre of Reality television inasmuch as it features 'real' people in real locations undergoing 'real' traumas. In fact, lifestyle television is arguably the most prevalent sub-genre of Reality TV in Britain, a fact which alone makes it worthy of debate. Within this context, the BBC has been one of the biggest providers of lifestyle television, and as a result such programming is significant in engaging with debates about the changing status and definition of public-service broadcasting (Moseley, 2000, 2001).

What I will do in the following is to consider rarely discussed class shifts within the petit-bourgeoisie of British society as they appear in lifestyle television. Although the subject of class has increasingly been marginalised on the agenda of television and cultural studies since the 1980s (and the foregrounding of areas such as gender, ethnicity and sexuality) (Turner, 1996: 219), I believe that returning to Bourdieu's work on habitus and social fields emphasises the crucial relevance of 'class' to understandings of contemporary televisual culture. I will suggest here that the concepts of both lifestyle and surveillance are part of a new discursive formation in which appearance is of paramount importance – a concern which is also central to those strands of Reality TV in its regular explorations of proper

173

behaviour in public space. It is my belief that the flexible identities shaped in lifestyle programming may also be linked to the personal development movement, principally an American invention and one that used to sit oddly with the British sense of themselves, but one which now finds a home in lifestyle programming.

Lifestyle programming in Britain both feeds into and contributes to the nation's preoccupation with style, and outlets for styling life, home and garden proliferate as never before. In the following, I discuss whether this interest in self-presentation can be connected to shifts in our understandings of ourselves as citizens and the changing role of public-service broadcasting. To answer this question I look at the ways in which our citizenship is rethought as a series of choices in decor (*House Invaders* [Bazal for BBC1, 1999–2002], *Changing Rooms* [Bazal for BBC1, 1996–]), clothes (*What Not To Wear* [BBC2, 1999–]) and manner (*Would Love to Meet* [*WLTM*, BBC2, 2001–3]). If the public sphere is now a space where we are rethought as consumers it is important to ask how we are guided to make certain choices and what ideologies – class based or otherwise – may lie behind these programmes.

Lifestyle

It is difficult to pinpoint a beginning for lifestyle television, but all of the programmes discussed below originate in the 1990s and are at least in their second series. In the case of the BBC we might cite the appointment in 1992 of David Docherty as Head of Strategic Planning as significant, for it was he who was to take charge of the daytime ratings battle. What the programmes have in common is that they are cost-effective and linked to the retail economy and, furthermore, that the form is low cost and repeatable. Each of them features 'the reveal' – a moment when the contestants get to see what transformations have been effected in their home/face/wardrobe – and transformation is clearly at the heart of lifestyle television. This is the soft side of the empowerment thesis – the now tele-wide belief that the individual need not be bound by convention and expectation and can 'be all they can be', a view previously demonstrated in sometimes brutal fashion in talk shows (Shattuc, 1997). In what follows I discuss how participants are 'empowered' (or otherwise) via house and home, fashion and the self.

The rise of popular factual programming – its bringing of the private and the personal into the public sphere – has been conceived as 'a democratization of an old public service discourse' (Bondebjerg, 1996: 29). The decline of experts and the rise of 'ordinary people' have meant that new user-friendly forms of television have risen in prominence and importance. Thus, as Rachel Moseley describes, 'public service broadcasting now extends to the care of the self, the home and the garden, addressing its audience through a combination of consumer competence and do-it-yourself [DIY] on a shoestring' (2000: 231). In tracing this significant 'privatization of the public sphere' (2001: 34), Moseley suggests that lifestyle programming represents a particularly potent arena for conceptualising contemporary shifts in the ethos of public-service broadcasting. She argues, however, that,

> [rather than evidence of a] simple shift from citizen to consumer…what these shows represent is a complex conjunction of the two, in which the personal and the private are figured as significant spaces in which citizens can, on a small local scale, learn to make changes, make a difference, improve the person for the national good.
>
> (Moseley, 2001: 34)

It is certainly also the case that lifestyle programming has increasingly structured the primetime, as well as daytime schedule. Indeed, Moseley sees lifestyle television as emblematic of 'the daytime-ization of prime-time television' (ibid.: 32), a process which has also represented a particular negotiation of discourses on gender insofar as it is bringing in its wake an emphasis on those spheres and interests traditionally gendered as 'feminine' – the domestic, the personal and the private (Moseley, 2000, 2001).

There is as yet little academic work on lifestyle television. As Nikki Strange has written in an article on cookery programmes, it is assumed that lifestyle genres 'are transparent…and do not merit closer examination' (1998: 301). As indicated above, Moseley's work (2000, 2001) on lifestyle television argues that it is not so much indicative of a 'feminisation' of the primetime schedule as suggestive of a blurring of gendered categories (2001: 33) (and potentially a consequent 'degendering' of the medium itself). Lifestyle helps to shape a new public-service discourse in which it is acceptable for both men and women to express views on light furnishings and to share traditionally 'masculine' tasks such as DIY (Moseley, 2000). Furthermore, Moseley suggests that perceptions of a shift from 'hard' to 'soft' (factual) programming, from citizen to consumer, from public to private and from quality to 'dumbed down' television, 'make use of falsely polarized categories of classification' (2001: 33) which tend to obscure, rather than elucidate, the concerns which structure the form. Lifestyle here is part of a 'democratising' movement which has bred 'a new kind of publicness and has transformed fundamentally the conditions under which most people are able to experience what is public and participate in what could today be called a public realm' (Thompson, 1990: 246).

Moseley concludes her analysis of lifestyle television by describing the temptation – for those ill at ease with the 'excess of the ordinary' such programmes produce – to 'retreat into a position of class and taste-based superiority' (2000: 314). Indeed, an explicit example of this can be found in the work of the late broadsheet critic John Diamond:

> Were I of the snobbish sort, I might point out that most of the unfinished jobs involve the sort of stripped pine and brass-plated tat that the DIY supermarkets sell cheap to the ribbon development classes: luckily *de gustibus non est*, as far as this column is concerned, *disputandem* and if people want to clutter up their lean-to conservatories with home-made tongue and groove storage modules who are we to argue.
>
> (Diamond; cited in Moseley, 2000: 303)

Reviewed in this way, lifestyle television is seen as providing light relief for broadsheet readers – structured by the assumption that 'lifestyle' is what those with nothing better to do watch in the daytime (and, of course, increasingly in primetime). There is clearly, then, a class-based critique at work here, something made evident in the sneers about the 'almost seamless diet of improvement' which is at the core of lifestyle programmes. The very idea that television could have a practical use in changing a person's lifestyle is clearly frightful to some. (It would seem, therefore, that the Domestic Goddess Nigella Lawson – who was married to John Diamond – must occupy an entirely different space in the spectrum when she passes on cookery tips.)

Habitus

Rather than engaging directly with what this expanded public sphere may mean, there is profit here in returning to Bourdieu's work on class and taste in *Distinction* (1989). In *Distinction*, Bourdieu considered the class position, social field and taste of myriad social classes in France. Rejecting the polarised categories of agency and structure, Bourdieu argued for a more complex understanding of the individual's sense of him- or herself in relation to cultural forms. He believes that the individual is not 'free' to make stylistic choices but is placed within a given set of social positions in a highly structured society. As Gripsrud explains:

> The systematic character of our 'life conducts', or lifestyles, now springs from some principles of which we are not consciously aware and which we are therefore unable to express directly. These principles only become apparent – to an external analytical eye – in our practice.
>
> (Gripsrud, 2002: 73)

The mechanism, the almost organic unacknowledged response system guiding these choices, is the 'habitus'. The rules that seem automatic are stored in the body as a set of dispositions or tendencies to act in certain ways. It is the system of dispositions that we have internalised through our background and experiences which largely shapes our lifestyles. It represents, therefore, both the elements we do not choose ourselves and those we more consciously do. The habitus guides how the individual thinks, chooses and acts. The choices we make, the moves in the game as it were, take place in social fields, each of which has rules about conduct and language in the territory. Indeed, what is felt and understood in this territory becomes the doxa, the common sense of the group.

Bourdieu made an important distinction between educational and 'cultural capital'. What he was pointing to here is the extent to which many members of the traditionally 'subordinate' classes are comparatively more affluent, and within this context economic capital loses its ability to clearly signify class boundaries. As a result, 'culture' moves in to fill the gap (Fiske, 1987: 266). The 'cultural' is crucial here, and is understood as the amount of socially recognised and therefore 'valuable' knowledge and competencies that a person has. Cultural capital, then, is seen to be possessed by people who have the powers of 'taste and discrimination', which become central in deciding upon a person's social status (hence functioning to map the hierarchies of a stratified society). 'Good taste' and discrimination may seem (and must seem) 'effortless' and 'natural', but they are in fact not easily acquired. The mystique around the tasteful is thus crucial in keeping them in positions of cultural superiority.

In *Distinction*, Bourdieu maps out the social space of lifestyle in considerable depth. It is the richer fractions of the bourgeois who look to tasteful (and highly educated) critics and intellectuals for judgements they can place their faith in. Within this scheme he maps the variant tastes of different fractions of the petit-bourgeoisie, who are in crucial ways distinct from the established bourgeoisie. The petit-bourgeoisie comprises three factions: an old declining group of tradesman and shopkeepers, an executant class of middle managers and executives who 'owe everything to education', and a new and emergent class of what we might call presentation experts. Bourdieu discovered that each of these groups had very different orientations in relation to cultural forms. Thus those in the oldest group had little cultural capital, and were particularly nervous about venturing a view on new works of art and happiest to accord high status to the legitimated opinions of others (Bourdieu, 1989: 339–71). Their conservatism is seen as a marker of their insecurity, which expresses itself in the choices they make in terms of style. In the executant class Bourdieu found 'the most developed form of the ascetic dispositions and devotion to culture associated with the ambition to pursue by further accumulation of cultural capital a rise made possible by initial small accumulation' (ibid.: 351). As Bourdieu makes clear, choosing elements of one's lifestyle is often also choosing elements of one's identity, and vice versa. Such choices say something about who we are and, especially, about who we *want* to be – as opposed to, and as different from, others. Some lifestyles appear more attractive than others because they signify or 'mean' something that is supposedly attractive or valuable. These lifestyles are the systematic products of the *habitus*.

Through the operations of taste, the habitus of each group guides what it finds attractive. Taste governs what we regard as lifestyles and the positions within our reach, as well as those we do not wish to be associated with. Lifestyle programming in all its forms operates on exactly this assumption – that all goods (clothes, kitchens and backyards) function as signs of identity – they tell others who we are (or rather who we want to be). It may thus be perfectly placed to service the insecurities felt by those who are uncertain of their place in a rapidly evolving social system. Those who lack self-assurance may put themselves in the hands of lifestyle experts (whose success is measured and reaffirmed daily) and the old established bourgeois middle class.

Lifestyle programming in its kitchen-based variants features the bearers of old middle-classness (RP [received pronunciation] accent, distinguished manner, quietly elegant or defiantly eccentric dress sense) bringing apparently effortless 'good taste' to the new and more insecure classes. We have already mentioned the late John Diamond's former wife Nigella Lawson – she of Domestic Goddess fame. In turn, at the time of writing Lawson now dates Charles Saatchi, a man at the heart of the new arts establishment – that class so secure in its choices that it can depart from the norm and nominate a series of dots as art. Indeed, it is notable that cookery programming is now one of the few places outside historical dramas where the viewers can hear classic 'born to rule' vowels from the traditional middle class.

The traditional middle class is supplemented by the work of the new petit-bourgeoisie, which

> comes into its own in all the occupations involving presentation and representation (sales, marketing, advertising, public relations, fashion, decoration and so forth).... These include the various jobs in medical and social assistance (marriage guidance, sex therapy...) and in cultural production and organisation (youth leaders, play leaders, tutors and monitors, radio and television producers and presenters, magazine journalists) which have expanded considerably in recent years.
>
> (Bourdieu, 1989: 359)

This class is in many senses more approachable than the traditional middle class. Those belonging to it can communicate at the same friendly level as the executant petit-bourgeoisie by sanctioning the wipe-clean surfaces and focal points, and the economical use of space which fit in with their busy lifestyle. Thus, through a combination of 'effortless' middle-class taste and the new experts in presentation, the insecure fractions of the petit-bourgeoisie prepare to let themselves become stylish at minimal cost with no aesthetic involvement.

Show homes and mug-trees

Readers may not be familiar with the sheer breadth of home-related programming on offer in the British context. In one week on British television (2–9 December 2002), viewers could choose from *Real Rooms* (BBC1, 2000–), *House Invaders* (Bazal for BBC1, 1999–2002), *Housecall* (BBC1, 2000–3) and *Changing Rooms. Hot Property* (World of Wonder for Channel 5, 1996–2003), *House Doctor* (Talkback Productions for Channel 5, 1998–2003) and *Property Ladder* (Talkback for C4, 2001–3) (and many others) provide the business sense necessary to succeed in today's house market. As indicated, home-centred programming is now the dominant genre of daytime television and has made significant inroads into the evening schedule. Carole Smillie's *Changing Rooms* – in which the clash of friends' style ideas is the principal drama – can garner 8 million viewers on BBC1 at 8 p.m. All the property shows listed above occupy primetime slots. It is evident that these shows are clearly cost-effective in that they are shot on location over a few days and depend on little in-depth research. However, the political economy of television would only take us so far in explaining the proliferation and popularity of this programming.

A consideration of the ways in which such tastes are formed in the long term would have to involve the central role in the Tory governments of 1979–97 (and indeed Chapter 3 similarly evokes this period of Conservative rule as instrumental to the rise of crime-appeal programming). Mrs Thatcher and her predecessors promoted the importance of homeownership and launched policies in which council-house dwellers could become owner-occupiers and thus qualify as the new petit-bourgeoisie. Unlike many of our European cousins, Britain is a nation of homeowners clutching close the belief that the home represents a sort of castle. The house is significant because it is

> a valuable means of ensuring privacy in a crowded city; a vehicle for enforcing family solidarity and conformity; a place to practice and perfect consumption skills; a major item of personal property, which, for the head of the family…stands as a concrete symbol of his status and visible sign of his success.
>
> (Selley *et al.*; cited in Silverstone, 1994: 61)

Hence, it makes sense to produce programmes aimed at the house-proud.

Home-based programming works around a series of key themes and approaches which can be seen to function as crucial signifiers with respect to the construction of 'taste' in these texts. These include a recurrent emphasis on the following:

- the zoning of space for maximum efficiency;
- the creation of focal points in each room;

179

- the central importance of colours matching, blending;
- the importance of maximising the space available;
- the absence of clutter;
- priorities given to kitchen and bathroom;
- maximisation of available resources – reclaiming abandoned cupboards and so on;
- keeping to a budget.

It is significant to note that these styling 'tips' speak to the needs of the petit-bourgeoisie as described by Bourdieu in *Distinction*. As he writes of the executant class:

> In the home this [ingenuity is illustrated] by devising 'nooks' and 'corners' (the 'kitchen-corners', 'dining areas', 'bedroom-corners' etc. recommended by the women's magazines) intended to multiply the rooms, or the 'space-saving ideas' designed to enlarge them, 'storage areas', 'movable partitions', 'bed-settees' etc., not to mention all the forms of 'imitation' and all the things that can be made to 'look like' something they are not, so many ways in which the petit bourgeois makes his home and himself 'look' bigger than they are.
>
> (Bourdieu, 1989: 321)

The homes selected for treatment in *Changing Rooms*, *House Invaders* and *Real Rooms* are of a particular type – usually modern, often semi-detached and situated on new estates. The drama here lies in the clash of styles provided either by friends or by guest stylists such as Laurence Llewelyn-Bowen or Oliver Heath. In a fixed amount of time (see Chapter 6, on temporality and Reality TV, which references the makeover show), but with plentiful labour, a space is selected for treatment and briskly transformed. It is in the 'reveal' that we see how owners respond to such styling – the use of the extreme close-up to 'capture' the 'knee-jerk reaction of the ordinary person…[as] primary public spectacle' (Moseley, 2000: 312) – and the moment when the 'unpredictable' nature of emotional response operates as a code of authenticity in affirming the programme's claim to 'the real'. In *Changing Rooms* it is almost always the case that the newly designed room is loud, gaudy and themed – and hence often very impractical. Indeed, in this respect some of the negative reactions participants express when 'surprised' by their interior transfor-mations suggest that the 'taste' propagated by the 'experts' is not unequivocally supported or articulated in a context free of contesting views. Host Carole Smillie often mediates between the participants/homeowners and the design 'experts' in a playful reflection on the disparities between 'taste' and 'discrimination' which may be at work here – raising eyebrows at the outlandish murals or floor patterns proffered by the 'experts', and hence engaging with the potential unease of the participants involved in decorating their friend/neighbour's room. While this may function to offer some viewers ideas for 'innovative' interior design, others may of course consider how modest and 'sensible' their own taste is. Indeed, designer flamboyance does not always work. Host Smillie has said that the work done on *Changing Rooms* is 'cheap and nasty but what do you expect for £500' (Gardner, 2003: 23), and it may also be worth noting that Smillie has revealed her own taste boundaries by emphasising that the designers would never be given an opportunity to work on her *own* home (ibid.).

House Doctor and *Property Ladder* take a different approach to the home. Because the focus of these programmes is 'improving' the home in order to attract a sale (and higher price), clients are taught to see the house as an opportunity for staging. Hosts Sarah Beeny of *Property Ladder* and 'real-estate guru' Ann Maurice from *House Doctor* instruct their clients not to get attached to the property but to make it as attractive as possible for others. Style here – with the recurrent insistence on 'neutral' colours and design – often means nothing more than measured yet 'tasteful' self-effacement. The underlying project is the transformation of clutter into the order that is so central to the executant petit-bourgeois habitus. The result is nothing more stylish than a show home – one in which blandness is aimed at so that the next owner-occupier can imagine impressing their 'personality' on the home. The very point is to drive out any signs of personality, which are understood as dangerously off-putting for others.

This sort of television may be popular because it addresses the British preoccupation with the home, as well as being simple, formulaic and useful. But the style on display here also measures the limits of acceptability for a class who may be 'new' to the whole idea of 'decor'. Thus the affordable, sensible and colour co-ordinated solutions offered by the new experts offer style with minimal aesthetic involvement for a newly risen class who may be uncomfortable about making 'artistic' choices.

Fashion

> I can't remember the last time I felt this good about myself.
> (*WLTM* subject, 22 February 2003)

In looking at fashion programming we come closer to seeing how the individual should ideally be styled according to the new class of experts.

In the 1980s Jeff Banks and Karyn Franklin hosted *The Clothes Show* (BBC1, 1986–96). This was a BBC production transmitted on a Sunday afternoon and carefully aimed at those who already had an interest in clothes, but it never really suggested that individuals could be fundamentally changed by wearing them.

Instead, the viewer was asked to gaze at supermodels in *haute couture* alongside items for those on more modest budgets. The mini-soap within each show was of a bride-to-be preparing for her wedding day with the help of the *Clothes Show* team.

Programmes such as *WLTM*, *What Not to Wear* and *Tell It to Me Straight* (C4, 2002–3) represent quite a change from the friendly recommendations of Jeff and Karyn. Rather than making modest suggestions, the new wave of programmes have hit upon ridicule and shame as 'amusing' methods for persuading the subject to change style according to their rules.

In *Tell It to Me Straight* a trio of friends arrive at an interior space believing that (as the voiceover explains) 'they have arrived to fill in a questionnaire about friendship'. One friend (soon to be the subject of the makeover) is led away and positioned to watch the others discussing his or her personality/lifestyle/fashion sense from an unseen vantage point behind a two-way mirror. The rest of the programme features the friend reunited with her critical others and then a shopping trip in which they style her (for £1,000) in ways they find pleasing (the friend, however, does not always agree). Although originally scheduled late afternoon, *Tell It to Me Straight* did not linger long in this slot and was ultimately positioned in the early morning daytime schedule. Hosted by Trinny Woodall and Susannah Constantine, two upper-middle-class 'gels' licensed to abuse in their quest to transform the dowdy, BBC2's *What Not To Wear* (*WNTW*) has been far more successful.

In a heated moment on one programme David Dimbleby called the co-hosts 'two of the cruellest women on television', and it is difficult to disagree with such an assessment. The targets seen to be in need of style transformation are surveyed and observed through 'secretly' filmed surveillance footage – providing the basis for the hosts' verbal abuse. Susannah will say, 'Look at the way she walks, Trinny', and in response Trinny will berate the subject: 'You've got to be braver and become more sexy.' Any amount of bullying and abuse is necessary for the individual to be improved.

After Trinny and Susannah have discarded much of the subject's wardrobe the individual has to view herself in a 360-degree mirror, something that everyone registers as a humiliating and unpleasant experience. The rationale is that this represents an opportunity to see herself as *others* do in preparation for the necessary transformation. Properly humbled, the subject is given £2,000 to spend in the high street. Even this exercise is filmed so that Trinny and Susannah can rush in and 'correct' his or her choices. The subject – whether an actress like Lesley Joseph (star of British sitcom *Birds of a Feather*) or a humble school administrator – records her responses to the process in the form of a video diary, clips of which are interspersed throughout the show.

This description has been necessary because I want to make clear the ways in which a style programme is part of a discursive formation whose drive is presentation and order. The use of this footage illustrates the prevalence of a 'surveillance' gaze in contemporary society (see also Chapter 3) and the technologies through which this is executed. Here, it is codified within a particular context of *self*-surveillance. When looking at this footage (which is presented in monochrome, in contrast to the glorious decor and Technicolor glamour of Trinny and Susannah), the individual often exclaims in horror at his or her inadequacy – 'I feel physically sick that that's how I look' was a typical response reinforced by the presenters. But, as Susan Bordo has argued:

> Between the media images of self-containment and self-mastery and the reality of constant everyday stress and anxiety about one's appearance lies the chasm that produces bodies habituated to self-monitoring and self-normalization.... Ultimately, the body (besides being evaluated for its success or failure at getting itself in order) is seen as demonstrating correct or incorrect attitudes towards the demands of normalization itself.
>
> (Bordo, 1993: 200)

To be filmed by such cameras is suddenly to share the look of the other, to objectify yourself from a vantage point in which this look is inscribed within the seemingly 'objective' gaze of surveillance footage. This surveillance, then, trades upon the notion that such footage offers a privileged relation to an aesthetic of 'the real', exemplifying the argument that the low-grade video image has become '*the* privileged form of TV "truth telling"' (Dovey, 2000: 55). The implication here is that this provides 'objective' evidence that transformation is necessary. To become the subject of the makeover show in this manner is not necessarily experienced or presented as a gratifying experience. What follows is the individual struggling and always submitting to the rules laid down by the 'gels' – 'You gotta hand over your body and wardrobe to us.'

The presenters, of course, do not feel the need to put themselves through this process because they are already 'finished'. As John Arlidge writes about Trinny and Susannah in an *Observer* profile:

> They were born posh, have lived posh, worked posh, and even met at a posh party.... They have latched on to the three obsessions of our time – fame, image and sadomasochistic reality 'telly' and united them in the ultimate makeover show. Forget homes and gardens. This is personal.
>
> (Arlidge, 2002: 23)

Trinny and Susannah already have the taste and style that the individual is seen to need. They are the signifiers of middle-classness – in manner, accent and bearing.

We may cleave to their point of view because we, the viewing audience (discretely aspirational, yet needing confirmation for our snobbery), seek a rapport with such effortlessly stylish bullies. Unlike the majority of the viewing audience, Trinny and Susannah have classic and – crucially – effortless middle-class taste. Bourdieu describes this attitude thus:

> the arrogance, the complacency, the insolence, in a word the self-assurance, the certainty of having which is grounded in the certainty of having always had, as if in immemorial gift, and which is the exact opposite of the naiveté, innocence, seriousness which betray humility.
>
> (Bourdieu, 1989: 329)

To suggest that fashion shows should not be bitchy is utterly to miss the point. Fashion without bitchery, like academia without snobbery, is inconceivable. But the levels of bitchery licensed by *WNTW* go much further than before and are able to do so because television is increasingly given license to explore our family, sex and love life (Mysoe, 2003: 17). The use of surveillance is central here, but it is more than this. Such television is possible because it is now widely agreed and understood that 'appearance is everything'. It is clear from the video diary clips that following the edicts of Trinny and Susannah can be a humiliating experience. Nevertheless the individuals/subjects endure suffering because the eventual benefits are substantial. They look better and in the process believe themselves to have become 'better or at least happier with themselves'. Rather like the home transformations, the model being proposed here is that emphasis can and should be laid on the surface, on the *look*, for that is the dominant feature. A concern with style has become fundamental to who we are. In many senses it *is* what we are. In this information age appearance becomes precious while effective symbolism becomes priceless – you are what 'you appear to be'. The pain of transformation is worth it to feel better about 'you'.

In this respect, Bocock (1998) reminds us of the work that goes into maintaining a system of distinctions. As he explains, '[s]ocial status groups use patterns of consumption as a means of establishing their rank or worth and demarcating themselves from others…all status groups use markers to differentiate themselves from others' (ibid.: 183). The style recommended by Trinny and Susannah comes highly recommended – it is the style they use themselves professionally as well-paid fashionistas, as well as being rooted in middle-class taste. The programme demonstrates the validity of their approach week after week in the transformed subjects, each of whom has been liberated into a new self, a newly confident creature decked out in the choices of the stylish Trinny and Susannah. This is the power of the norm operated by the middle class, those whose taste determines an increasing number of areas. Thus transformed, the subject can more confidently differentiate him- or herself from others. Using rules of impeccable provenance the individual can be guided towards more confident choices. What may be left of him or her once this is stripped away is open to question, but this relies on a depth model of the self which is no longer fashionable. Hence, this perspective may suggest that, thus transformed, the petit-bourgeoisie can pass as citizens in the republic of taste wearing the style of the middle class but not owning anything of themselves.

Self

Thus far we have noted how the power of the norm is carried through traditional middle-class taste, the expertise of the new stylists and the ever-present force of surveillance. All three work as mechanisms for interrogating the subject, to hold him or her up for display so that we might all see what 'needs' to be done. However, the social experiments that represent the third section of this chapter suggest that this strand of lifestyle programming advocates ways to eliminate eccentricity or any signs of difference in the need to make the individual a better-functioning member of society.

While blurring a range of different genres from the talk show, soap opera and observational documentary, programmes such as *Big Brother* (Endemol for C4, 2000–, UK) can also be conceived of as social experiment television. They give us the opportunity to see people re-envisaging or, in the fashionable phrase, 'reinventing' themselves. Here we see people considering themselves as projects, as enterprises to be invested in. The thinking behind such an approach may usefully be connected to the personal development movement.

The use of the phrase 'personal development movement' (hereafter PDM) can be deployed to cover the philosophical leanings of many writers whose work places the individual at the centre of the world. The titles alone illustrate a passionate belief in the power of the self. Thus, Stephen Covey's *The Seven Habits of Highly Effective People* (1990), Phil McGraw's *Life Strategies* (1999), Anthony Robbins' *Awaken the Giant Within* (1991) and Louise Hay's *The Power Is Within You* (amongst many others) (1992) all proselytise for the focused, self-willed individual a set of key prescriptions for the determination of the self:

- that the individual comes before society so any societal change is effected from the inside out;
- that goals are worked out and set, planned, stages marked and celebrated;
- that the individual learns and celebrates being able to take responsibility;
- that the self is at the centre of the world.

This suggests that by focusing entirely on what you are and what you can achieve you can be happy. This brute individualism finds expression all over daytime television – in talk shows, health programmes and infomercials. Beyond this the PDM is often marketed in inspirational seminars, in books, in life coaching and countless other spaces where the 'new you' can be built. Such treatments suggest that we are all the same. The perspective is perhaps most brutally summed up in Roger Crawford's *How High Can You Bounce?*: 'The quality of our lives is governed not by outward circumstances but by the choices we make' (Crawford, 1998: 8). Crawford's own inspirational story lies behind this remark, but it is the cornerstone of so much of PDM writing. Life is all about choices for empowered individuals transcending circumstances to self-validate and realise their 'true individuality'.

The rise of writing which simplifies life as merely a question of lifestyle choices fits perfectly in an enterprise culture which envisages the *self as a project*. Society, like class and background, are merely the circumstances from which the individual has risen, indeed which he or she has overcome, on the quest to selfhood. But there are some who do not share this view. Psychologist David Smail offers his own epiphany:

> For it was the utter soulless callous indifference in the Thatcher years to the welfare and security of ordinary people that finally made it obvious that what mattered to psychological well-being was not interior attributes such as responsibility, self-reliance and initiative beloved of the New Right but the provision within society of essentially material resources.
>
> (Smail, 1996: 12)

Although the question of our ability to effect changes in ourselves is far from resolved, any account which neglects the whole range of socio-political factors is partial and potentially harmful. But I suggest here that it is understandable that lifestyle television needs to live without such complications because the drama lies with the individual and his or her struggle to overcome tasteless neighbours, big hips or ill-matched floral borders. Lifestyle teaches a variant of the PDM so that we can 'be all we can be'.

WLTM began on BBC2 in 2001 and ran on Wednesdays for six weeks at 8.15 p.m. The second series ran for a further six editions in 2002. An individual is found who has been unable to date or find a partner for some time – anything from one year to eight. At the start of the programme the subject is seen through surveillance footage on a dummy date. As with the mocking taunts of Trinny and Susannah, the subject is criticised for inappropriate manner, poor dress sense and hopeless conversational gambits by three experts in fashion, body language and verbal communication (whose task it will be to 'correct' the individual in time for a date in six weeks time). The individuals' role is simply to comply in the move from 'before' to 'after' self. This necessarily involves a struggle – a struggle we see in conflicts with the lifestyle experts and in the video diary segments.

At the end of every show the individual is reformed and has a successful date (under the same surveillance that started the show), only this time the experts can take the opportunity to congratulate themselves on a job well done, while the subject can elect to switch off the hidden microphone and continue the date in private. Once again I am conscious that complaint here may seem contrary. How can anyone object to a happy ending? The programmes are infused by the same spirit of 'can-do' enthusiasm that is the hallmark of lifestyle television and the PDM. But scrooge-like I have to point out the limits of this approach by noting the resolutely petit-bourgeois profile of the candidates, the stress on heterosexuality and the emphasis on the past as, if not irrelevant, then marginal. But it's more than this. My concern is the way in which such programming speeds what Rose has called the operation of the norm:

> Public appearance, language and conduct are not now valued for what they can achieve, but are interpreted in terms of the inner personality that is manifested; closeness, warmth, and the frank expression of the inner self have become the supreme values. The psychotherapeutic is intimately linked to this obsession with personal identity, to this tyranny of intimacy in which narcissism is mobilised in social relations and the self is defined in terms of how it feels rather than what it does.
>
> (Rose, 1990: 215–16)

More work needs to be done on television's increasingly proactive role in shaping the citizenry – like the new you, it makes itself useful (Mysoe, 2003: 17). While television's influence has now extended to directly fashioning people – for their own good, of course – this is also for television's sake, to keep proving that somehow 'it', the apparatus, *works*. And what lies behind the philosophy of such television is not merely the discourses of a reconfigured notion of public service, but also the ideologies of the PDM. Lifestyle transformations offer quick emotional returns without any complicating societal narratives. In this respect, *WLTM* represents another triumph of the therapeutic. As Bourdieu explains, '[t]he fact remains that the rise of the therapeutic morality is unquestionably linked to the constitution of a corps of professionals (psychoanalysts, sexologists, counsellors…) claiming a monopoly on the legitimate definition of legitimate pedagogic or sexual competence' (1989: 369).

This argument suggests that if everything starts with the individual and all of life is seen as a series of challenges which the empowered person overcomes, then there is no need to pay attention to anything else. In all its manifestations, lifestyle is the home of the view that eradicates, by illustration, the 'end' of class. Class, upbringing, location, education are constructs to be overcome from the vantage point of the self. If class can be defined as a boundary, as knowing one's place, then lifestyle 'proves' that one can adopt a look that fools anyone. But what I am suggesting here is that class *is* apparent. The subjects/victims of *WLTM* are being taught to create a self by learning middle-classness, but it is a task that will always feel doomed to failure:

> the cultural productions of the petit bourgeois are subtly discredited because they recall their acquisition of matters in which, more than anywhere else, the important thing is to know without ever having learnt, and because the seriousness with which they are offered reveals the ethical dispositions from which they flow, which are the antithesis of the legitimate relation to culture.
>
> (Bourdieu, 1989: 330)

It is the fragility of this new identity and the uncertain way in which it is worn which provide the pathos which makes *WLTM* so moving to watch. The focused attentions of the new lifestyle experts, underscored by the redemptive powers of the PDM, speed the operation of the norm. In some ways the experts are reincarnations of the etiquette guides that were marketed to the aspirational classes of the Victorian era. But in that time class was marked, immediately apparent and socially divisive. Now class works in subtle but definite ways though the operations of taste.

What programmes such as *WLTM* do is not simply marginalise eccentricity by demonstrating that it 'doesn't work'. Rather, they appear to threaten to take away any faith the individual might have in self-expertise by encouraging a belief in the norm. As Smail argues:

> In the rawness of our experience, the chaotic jumble of our impressions, impulses and dreams, we are all eccentrics.... Fear and shame are introduced only through the process of invidious comparison set up by a mythical normality and used in particular to disqualify the experience of those whose knowledge of the world suggests that all is not well with the organisation of society.
>
> (Smail, 1996: 23)

Conclusion

As indicated above, much of the discussion around lifestyle television focuses on the changed nature of public-service broadcasting (Moseley, 2000, 2001). We now enjoy an enlarged and 'democratised' space which has been degendered and filled with an 'excess of the ordinary' (Moseley, 2000: 314). Indeed, Livingstone and Lunt suggest that 'public access to and participation in the mass media represent a challenge to expertise' (1994: 98). But in my view the 'experts' here are those newly risen fractions of the petit-bourgeoisie whose styling tips represent an affordable option for the discrete, but insecure, new petit-bourgeoisie. Class, I have suggested here, *is* very much on the agenda of lifestyle television, but 'merely' as a question of taste. Research needs to be done into those appearing on these programmes described elsewhere as 'ordinary'. Agreeing to go on television to have some aspect of one's life restyled for public consumption is not ordinary. It is because people now understand television as an active agent of transformation, from the spectacular celebrity machine of *Big Brother* to the tribulations of *WLTM*, that we need to ask what they expect from it.

Lifestyle is the inspiration for a great deal of programming because a concern with home, fashion and identity is no longer the province of a few. In meeting the needs of petit-bourgeois fractions through such programming, the BBC is providing a public service, albeit a refashioned public service under the new director-general Greg Dyke. While, as Moseley suggests, these programmes speak significantly to 'negotiations...around gender' (2001: 32), we should also not overlook the central role that class plays in this field. As I have indicated, class is coded in a variety of ways in lifestyle shows which are indicative of rarely discussed changes in British society. Furthermore, this issue of class brings us back to Reality TV. Much of the debate in and around this much-vilified form has failed to acknowledge that many of its subjects are members of that forgotten and rarely acknowledged sector once known as the working class. As the historian David Cannadine writes:

> class is best understood as being what culture does to inequality and social structure: investing the many anonymous individuals and unfathomable collectivities in society with shape and significance, by moulding our perceptions of the unequal social world we live in.
>
> (Cannadine, 2000: 188)

The significance of Reality TV, and lifestyle programming in particular, may lie in the ways in which it helps to mould and to legitimise our class membership.

References

Arlidge, John (2002) 'Just a Couple of Swells', *Observer*, 22 December 2002: 23.

Blair, T. (1996) 'My Vision for Britain', in Giles Raddice (ed.) *What Needs to Change: New Visions of Britain*, London: HarperCollins.

Bocock, Robert (1998) *Consumption*, London: Routledge.

Bondebjerg, Ib (1996) 'Public Discourse/Private Fascination: Hybridization in "True-Life" Story Genres', *Media Culture and Society* 18: 27–45.

Bordo, Susan (1993) *Unbearable Weight: Feminism, Western Culture and the Body*, Berkeley, CA: University of California Press.

Bourdieu, Pierre (1989) *Distinction*, London: Routledge.

Brunsdon, Charlotte, Catherine Johnson, Rachel Moseley and Helen Wheatley (2001) 'Factual Entertainment on British Television – the Midlands TV Research Group's '8–9 Project', *European Journal of Cultural Studies* 4(1): 29–62.

Cannadine, D. (2000) *Class in Britain*, London: Penguin.

Covey, Stephen (1990) *The Seven Habits of Highly Effective People*, London: Simon & Shuster.

Crawford, Roger (1998) *How High Can You Bounce?*, London: Vermillion.

Diamond, John (1999) 'John Diamond on Television', *Sunday Telegraph Magazine*, 15 August: 47.

Dovey, Jon (2000) *Freakshow: First Person Media and Factual Television*, London: Pluto.

Fiske, John (1987) *Television Culture*, London: Routledge.

Franck, Thomas (1999) *The Empowered Self: Law and Society in the Age of Individualism*, Oxford: Oxford University Press.

Gardner C. (2003) 'Smillie Strips Changing Rooms Bare', *Scotland on Sunday*, 19 January: 23.

Gripsrud, Jostein (2002) *Understanding Media Culture*, London: Arnold.

Hay, Louise (1992) *The Power is Within You*, Spain: Hay House.

Hellmore, E . (2003) 'Reality TV Bites as Star Calls Shots', *Observer*, 9 Feburary.

Izod, John, Richard Kilborn and Matthew Hibberd (eds) (2001) *From Grierson to the Docu-Soap*, Luton: University of Luton Press.

Livingstone, Sonia and Peter Lunt (1994) *Talk on Television: Audience Participation and Public Debate*, London: Routledge.

McGraw, Philip (1999) *Life Strategies: Stop Making Excuses*, London: Vermillion.

Moseley, Rachel (2000) 'Makeover Takeover on British Television', *Screen* 41(3): 299–314.

Moseley, Rachel (2001) ' "Real Lads Do Cook…but Some Things Are Still Hard to Talk about": The Gendering of 8–9', in Charlotte Brunsdon, Catherine Johnson, Rachel Moseley and Helen Wheatley, 'Factual Entertainment on British Television – the Midlands TV Research Group's '8–9 Project', *European Journal of Cultural Studies* 4(1): 32–9.

Mysoe, M. 'What's Your Problem?', *Radio Times*, 15–21 March: 17–19.

Robbins, Anthony (1991) *Awaken the Giant Within*, London: Simon & Shuster.

Rose, Nikolas (1990) *Governing the Soul*, London: Routledge.

Shattuc, Jane (1997) *The Talking Cure*, London: Routledge.

Silverstone, Roger (1994) *Television and Everyday Life*, London: Routledge.

Smail, David (1996) *How to Live without Psychotherapy*, London: Constable.

Strange, Nikki (1998) 'Perform, Educate, Entertain: Ingredients of the Cookery Programme Genre', in Christine Geraghty and David Lusted (eds) *The Television Studies Book*, London: Arnold.

Thompson, John (1990) *Ideology and Modern Culture: Critical Social Theory in the Era of Mass Communication*, Cambridge: Polity Press.

Turner, Graeme (1996) *British Cultural Studies: An Introduction*, London: Routledge.

9

SOCIALLY SOOTHING STORIES?

Gender, race and class in TLC's *A Wedding Story* and *A Baby Story*

Rebecca L. Stephens

Tuning into the TLC network on any weekday might make an unwary viewer double-check her video recorder under the suspicion that some stranger's wedding or, worse yet, birth video might have somehow found its way into her machine. But what that viewer has in fact stumbled upon is currently the most successful cable programming line-up on American daytime television. Billed as 'Life Unscripted' by TLC, these shows, entitled *A Wedding Story* (Banyan Productions, 1995–, US) and *A Baby Story* (Pie Town Productions, 1998–, US), feature an endless parade of brides leaning on their fathers' arms, women puffing and grimacing as another healthy baby emerges from their carefully draped bodies, and couples gazing lovingly into one another's eyes as the sun sets/the guests party/the baby coos in their arms. This is 'Reality TV' TLC-style, and in the words of the network's daytime programming head, Chuck Gingold, 'This is happy TV' (quoted in Barovick, 1999); in other words, no one is jilted at the altar and no mother screams 'I've changed my mind' in the midst of labour in this parallel universe of bliss. It is also popular TV, garnering ratings that *Sight and Sound* magazine described as 'nothing short of sensational' (Anonymous, 2002).

Formerly the Learning Channel, TLC is one of five networks operated by Discovery Communications and is a part of most basic cable packages in the United States, which means that about 60 million households subscribe to the network per year (Leichtman Research Group, 2002). When it was the Learning Channel, before 1991, 'the channel's more scintillating programmes included an Internal Revenue Service (IRS) sponsored instructional called *The Subject is Taxes* (Barovick, 1999). Discovery, however, made over the channel under its strategy of 'narrowcasting', or marketing programmes to a small niche audience, and began offering the 'lifestyle documentaries' that have led to its staggering present-day success in adding viewers: in October of 2002, 'TLC finished in tenth place [of all networks] with a 1.1 Nielsen Media Research household rating. Its 22 per cent ratings increase over the 2001 period marked the largest gain of any top-10 service that month' (Umstead, 2002). While its evening broadcasts include grittier documentaries like *Trauma – Life in the ER* and TLC's biggest hit *Trading Spaces*, derived from the (UK) BBC-produced *Changing Rooms*, its daytime programming is now chiefly devoted to the 'Life Unscripted' reality stories. This programming line-up, also marketed under the tag 'Personal TLC', began with *A Wedding Story* but has since expanded to include *A Baby Story*; *A Dating Story* (TLC, 1999–, US), where participants are set up on a blind date by a friend; *A Makeover Story* (TLC, 2000–, US), in which a pair of people receive makeovers and then surprise their friends with a new appearance at a party; and, most recently, *A Personal Story* (TLC, 2002–, US), which narrates someone overcoming a challenge, often through surgery. These shows have in fact become so popular that TLC has devoted its entire schedule for six hours each weekday (9.00 a.m.–3.00 p.m. Central Standard Time) to this programming, including back-to-back and repeat episodes of *A Baby Story* and *A Wedding Story*.

Like the daytime perennial the soap opera, and Reality TV's close cousin the talk show, these TLC shows are very clearly targeted at women, with their emphasis on romance and relationships; and they are, in fact, rated number one in daytime cable viewing among women in the 18–34 age group (Champagne, 1999). Given these demographics, the shows' glorification of marriage and motherhood raises some serious issues for feminists. These concerns derive not just from the identity of the audience, but also from the cultural context and public discourse surrounding the production and consumption of this programming. Television offers a direct and indirect forum for cultural questions, as Newcomb and Hirsch note in *Television: The Critical View*:

> Rituals and the arts offer a meta-language, a way of understanding who and what we are, how values and attitudes are adjusted, how meaning shifts.... In its role as central cultural medium, [television] presents a multiplicity of meanings rather than a monolithic dominant point of view. It often focuses on our most prevalent concerns, our deepest dilemmas.
>
> (Newcomb and Hirsh; cited in Dow, 1996: xv)

More precisely, one can ask whether the narratives offered in *A Baby Story* and *A Wedding Story* represent a response to contemporary dilemmas about gender identity and whether they answer a need for specific rituals of normalisation needed because of prevailing concerns about the status of marriage and motherhood. In this essay I argue that the TLC shows address specific social anxieties about marriage and motherhood contentious in both popular culture and in public policy debates. I will demonstrate how *A Baby Story* and *A Wedding Story* echo public policy in their method of alleviating or soothing these prevailing social uncertainties – which is, unfortunately, to ignore complexities of gender, race and class in favour of a fantasy vision of some mythic past where gender norms were absolute, the nuclear family serenely solved individual and social ills, and consumption is the ultimate normalising rite.

But why approach Reality TV through the concerns of other socio-cultural movements? Why not just accept *A Wedding Story* and *A Baby Story* as harmless entertainment, enjoyed by a sentimental and perhaps 'unsophisticated' segment of the viewing audience? Why not just accept the participants as wanting to create the ultimate wedding video by airing their big day on national television? The answers to these questions lie in the blurring of public and private realms that happens in these shows, and in the connection between television and public discourse. Despite the idea that marriage and motherhood are essentially private concerns, the history of twentieth-century state interventions into these seemingly private realms is long and invasive. From child welfare legislation in the early twentieth century that targeted 'improper' mothering as an occasion for state intervention, to the continued discord over legal abortion in the US, the state's involvement in this 'private' affair has been virtually unceasing in the last century. Likewise, marriage, though perhaps initially a private decision, becomes public by its very nature, which relies on state sanction for recognition. State policy on marriage is also indicative of public ideology in decisions about who can legally marry, both historically, in, for example, laws prohibiting interracial marriages, and currently, in debates over recognition of same-sex marriages.

It is now a commonplace that television has become the shared public sphere of an increasingly fragmented nation, an assumption that is frequently explicitly linked with spheres of public democratic discourse in the US in the form of televised presidential addresses and, especially, in forums more open to the public at large, like the electronic town halls seen under the Clinton administration. Access to the sphere of public discourse has been seen as an empowering force, bringing inclusiveness to previously marginalised groups by offering 'ordinary' people access to the airwaves and by extending the notion that personal experience – and, particularly, self-revelation or expression of that experience – is innately political. In what she calls the ' "Oprahfication" of America', Jane M. Shattuc argues that in the fragmented contemporary American culture of the late 1990s and early 2000s the talk show has become a place where previously marginalised groups can be heard in a 'new public sphere or counter public sphere', providing access to the space of public debate that has been historically linked to the ideals of a liberal democracy but traditionally denied to all but the intellectual or economic elite (Shattuc, 1997: 93). As Shattuc notes, identity politics or the personalisation of politics is furthered by the daytime talk show, these shows 'reveal a profound political change: the authority of everyday lived experience, whether in reactionary or progressive form' (ibid.: 109). Like the daytime talk show, *A Wedding Story* and *A Baby Story* are based solely on what is perceived as experiential expertise – in each show the participants are recounting the story of their wedding or their birth, and these are experiences that, even though shared (in fact, many others have been married or have given birth), are presented as unique to the couple that 'stars' in a given episode. But in bringing what might have previously been the subject of home video entertainment to the national public forum of television, the stories on TLC can no longer be seen as operating in the private realm, instead becoming part of the discourse which shapes decisions about public policy in a liberal democratic civil society. For this reason, it is necessary to place these shows in the socio-political context that surrounds them, to understand the intersections between the shows' ideas and topics and the closely related social beliefs that ultimately shape attitudes that become part of the state apparatus governing public life.

Like the reality crime shows which were spawned within the 1980s context of the US war on drugs and its promulgation of the belief that drug traffic, even by petty offenders, was a direct threat to the social fabric of the country, TLC's programmes occur within the rhetoric of the 1990s and early 2000s which attributes many cultural ills to the breakdown of traditional families. In analysing *America's Most Wanted*, Kevin Glynn notes the political contradictions that mark the uneasy relationship between this reality show and its cultural context (a position echoed in part in chapter 7):

> On the one hand, this programme contributes to the production of a generalized ethos of fear, within which the demonization, surveillance, and repression of threatening (and often non-white) 'others' becomes a fact of everyday life. It is part of the apparatus that generates a continuous hum of 'low-level' fear that permeates U.S. popular culture.
>
> (Glynn, 2000: 4)

Yet at the same time as viewers look outward at others they must also reflect on ways they themselves must conform to the cultural institutions that surround them: 'people must submit themselves to the power carried within prescriptions to think and behave in normalized and normalizing ways' (ibid.: 6). In the same way, TLC's programmes pick up on some dominant tensions between cultural fears and a collective desire to police others' choices while confronting the same choices on an individual level. Demographics indicating a trend toward later marriage and later maternity have been echoed in media headlines about increasing divorce rates and a rising incidence of infertility problems, while surveys indicate that over 70 per cent of 18–34-year-olds believe that 'motherhood [is] the most important job in the world' (Stapinski, 1999). These trends not only have created personal dilemmas for individual women, but have precipitated large-scale concerns regarding the impact of choices about the ostensibly private decisions to marry and/or bear children. Central debates about family and motherhood in US culture have made their way into public policy as federal and state governments enact legislation to encourage and entice certain segments of the population into marriage and attempt to regulate who has children and under what circumstances. With this public discourse as a backdrop, examining the fascination with watching 'real' marriages and births ritually enacted in TLC's *A Wedding Story* and *A Baby Story* can help explore the connection between these cultural factors and social anxieties played out daily on cable television in 'reality' format.

Telling tales: the programmes

Despite the teaser for 'Life Unscripted', where the visual logo is accompanied by an audio track of the wedding march interrupted by the thud of a fall, the rip of fabric and the gasp of an audience, like most 'reality' programming these 'unscripted' shows are in actuality anything *but* unplanned. *A Wedding Story* and *A Baby Story* in particular give the sensation of watching an ordinary couple's home video, but in actuality each show is carefully constructed around a precise format that culminates in a clichéd fairy-tale ending. Each episode of *A Wedding Story* begins with the couple sitting together describing how they met, and the history of their relationship is usually partnered with flashes of photographs of the couple together at various points in their lives. Overwhelmingly, little or no information is given about the individuals' careers or educational backgrounds. Frequently their jobs aren't mentioned at all, and when work is brought in, it is only if it connects to how they met or where they live; this is particularly true of the bride's work. In one segment, for example, the couple met when performing on Broadway in the musical *The Lion King*, but this is virtually the only episode I saw in a year of watching (January 2002–January 2003) where the bride's career was given more than one minute of airtime.

The next segment (after a commercial break, of course) is shot two days before the wedding and involves what one woman who appeared on the show called the 'couple activity' (Putnam, n.d.). This ranges from a predictable walk on the beach where the couple became engaged to going to a batting cage, and serves as background for the couple to discuss their relationship and their commonalities in more detail. And it is specifically the traditional gender relationships that are frequently firmly entrenched during this section: one story, for instance, depicts the marriage of Stephanie and Bassam (tx 20 December 2002); she is a white American nurse marrying a Lebanese OB/GYN and for their activity they choose to go grocery shopping at a Lebanese store, where she selects ingredients for a meal, recounting how she 'cried [herself] sick' when Bassam left temporarily to return to Lebanon. The activity ends as she tosses an item into the shopping basket, commenting, 'I've learned, I'm now an expert on grape leaves.' The segment then normally concludes with the rehearsal dinner or another gathering where the couple's friends and family gather and interviews with the family members are clipped in.

Act 3 moves to the day of the wedding, where almost invariably the bride and her wedding party get their hair and makeup done at a salon and dress in or travel to the church. Meanwhile, the groom and the male participants stereotypically joke about how few preparations they have to make in comparison to the women, then open the gift that their wife-to-be has arranged for them to receive. We flash over to the bride-to-be opening her gift and invariably making some comment about how 'giving' her prospective husband is. The segment ends with the bride leaning on her father's arm waiting to make her grand entrance.

Act 4 brings the denouement, the wedding itself, where there is too often no surprise in the recitation of the traditional Christian vows of marriage (though other religions are represented occasionally, they are buried for viewers under the sheer volume of Christian ceremonies) and the introduction of the couple as 'Mr And Mrs X', both at the conclusion of the ceremony and at their entrance into the reception. There are brief scenes from the reception and at the close of each show the couple exchange 'private' words about living happily for the rest of their lives as the trademark music swells: 'And when the spark of youth someday surren-ders/I will have your hand to see me through/The years may come and go/But there's one thing I know/Love is all there is when I'm with you' (Curtis, 2002).

Clearly there are significant correlations between the show and traditional female fantasies under socially normalised gender roles. The most obvious is in the fairy-tale ending of each episode, a visual equivalent of 'happily ever after' that is frequently marked as well by images of feminine submission. In one episode where 'Becky and Joe' (tx 7 August 2002) marry in a medieval/Renaissance-themed wedding, the close is a mock kidnapping where the groom must fight the 'bad guys' (his groomsmen) to 'reclaim' his bride; the credits close with Joe carrying Becky out of the reception slung over his shoulder. There is also a continued implicit emphasis on a male-provider model of marriage, gifts of jewellery appear again and again and close-up shots of rings are de rigueur. Little challenge is made to patriarchal traditions in the wedding ceremonies, where virtually every bride is given away by a male, usually the father; even in the case of a widow's remarriage at approximately 60 years old she was walked down the aisle on her son-in-law's arm ('John and Bertie', tx 20 December 2002). Finally, the classic myths of romance are absolutely paramount in the show; there are daily mentions of 'it was love at first sight' and the belief that the couples are 'meant to be together forever'. As mentioned previously, careers are scarcely mentioned and the brides are regularly depicted as moving to be with their new husbands, even as far as Africa in one woman's case ('Madeleine and Puso', tx 30

August 2002), and giving up their religions (the 'Stephanie and Bassam' episode featured the bride's conversion to Greek Orthodoxy), and, always, giving up their own name to take their husband's.

Of course, there is really little new in all of this. Many films in recent years have similarly reinscribed traditional female roles in regard to marriage: *My Best Friend's Wedding* (Hogan, 1997, US), *The Runaway Bride* (Marshall, 1999, US), *Father of the Bride* (Shyer, 1991, US), to name just a few. TV sitcoms have done the same, but the key difference between these depictions and that of the TLC programming arguably lies in the audience perception of *A Wedding Story*'s 'reality'. Comments from TLC viewers, especially in the younger range of the demographic group, indicate that they consistently see these shows depicting a truth that is closer to life than other popular narrative forms such as mainstream cinema: ' "These shows just give you a different outlook on the world and how it is" stated Savanah King, a college freshman' (quoted in Littlejohn, 2002). In writing about *A Baby Story*, *A Wedding Story* and *A Makeover Story* a viewer member posting to Epinions.com echoes this assessment: 'I also like the fact that these are REAL people. They are not beauty queens or selected outcasts like on MTV's "Real World".' In addition, the form of the show picks up on attitudes toward the home video that heighten the viewer's association with 'real life'. Though the show's televisuality is not characterised by the jiggling, grainy images that signify amateur video footage in other Reality TV formats and television precursors such as *America's Funniest Home Videos* (ABC, 1990–, US), the context resonates with the familiar, especially given that weddings and births were among the first domestic events regularly taped for home entertainment. This adds to the shows' sense of presenting 'real life', particularly when the line between televised and home video is further blurred by the occasional inclusion of family camcorder footage, usually coyly labelled 'Daddy Cam' or some similar variant.

Like talk shows and other reality shows, it is clear that one of the central appeals is that ordinary people are the stars. But unlike other Reality TV shows where ordinary people are placed in extraordinary situations – on the island of Palau Tiga eating bugs or on an idyllic remote location purposely populated by attractive members of the opposite sex intent on seducing the 'couples' participants – in the TLC programming ordinary people are taking part in events which mark many ordinary lives: marriage and childbearing. Richard Dyer's ideas about what it means to be a 'star' are helpful in conceptualising the appeal of the momentary stardom offered both by the TLC shows and by the moments which they 'record' for public consumption. As Dyer notes in *Heavenly Bodies*, '[w]e're fascinated by stars because they enact ways of making sense of the experience of being a person in a particular kind of social consumption (capitalism), with its particular organisation of life in public and private spheres' (1986: 17). Weddings, particularly, offer a moment in an individual's life where a 'private' experience – love –

moves into the public realm – vows of love are spoken before others and rituals like the reception celebrate the public announcement of the private emotion in a way that foregrounds consumption as the final normalising rite. Marriage and giving birth are essentially perceived as specific times when ordinary people can be the 'stars' of their lives. Rhetoric surrounding weddings and motherhood is an ample indicator of this: brides are told that 'it's your day' and women are still raised with the traditional cultural notion that motherhood is more than a private event – it's 'the most important job that a woman can do' – and even that it is patriotic, 'as American as apple pie'. Women who have been dreaming, as they're taught to do by toys like Bride Barbie, of the 'white wedding' so carefully depicted by *A Wedding Story* can see Reality TV as depicting their reality: the day on which they too can be a temporary princess, extraordinary – a star, in other words. Of course, the nature of stardom is that it does not occur in isolation; to be a star one must have an audience watching and collectively validating the experience, and one of the appeals of *A Wedding Story* for participants is that a larger TV audience amplifies the stardom achieved and thus the psychic validation of the participants' choice of marriage. For viewers the interaction and perhaps the appeal of the show are also twofold: private in that it resonates with personal experience – weddings of family and friends attended and/or memories of their own wedding days; and public in its embracing and reinscribing of familiar rituals that help sort the world into recognisable and publicly defined social categories. Like the stars of film that Dyer writes about, the participants on *A Wedding Story* therefore become 'the embodiments of social categories in which people are placed and through which they have to make sense of their lives, and indeed through which we make our lives – categories of class, gender, ethnicity, religion, sexual orientation, and so on' (1986: 18). Seeming to see personal experience in the show again connects the experience of watching it to theories about the nature of the pleasure of identification derived from watching home videos. As Jon Dovey asserts,

> The pleasures of domestic camcorder culture are all about defining our own individual family identities around a TV screen that usually pumps out bland, homogenized otherness; representations of other loves and other families that could never match the specific delights afforded by our own personalized, intimate, closed circuit production.... What is on offer here is first person rather than third person, 'us-ness' rather than otherness', me as opposed to them.
>
> (Dovey, 2000: 65)

This assertion, however, does not just serve to explain the appeal of the programming, but also alerts us to the difficulty that arises when that 'us' versus 'them' enters the public policy arena.

TLC and social/political contexts

While there is little reason to believe that TLC has an explicit agenda of promul-gating marriage for an overt political motive, it is interesting that the show corresponds to a larger governmental push to encourage marriage, specifically for certain social segments of the population. This relatively sudden and widespread reaction to a divorce rate that has actually remained fairly consistent for years is a reflection of a conservative Republican president and Congress.[1] In November 2002, discussion of revising existing US welfare laws included promises from the Bush Administration to 'make marriage-related grants through the Office of Refugee Resettlement, the Office of Child Support Enforcement and the military, and is banking on a likely $100 million in marriage funds for welfare recipients' (Lerner, 2002). The goal of such programmes is to encourage marriage under the philosophy expressed by Brigham Young Provost Bruce Hafen in a speech given before the Panel on Children's Rights and the 104th Congress, American Bar Association Annual Meeting in Chicago, Illinois:

> As an ordering principle of national policy, I am proposing that we strongly encourage marriage, discourage divorce, favor the birth of chil-dren within married families and increase in any way we can the proportion of children who grow up in two-parent families anchored in permanent, formal marriages.
>
> (Hafen, 1995)

There is little evidence, however, to support the idea that such programmes work to accomplish the goals articulated by Hafen and other political conserva-tives. A number of states have had such programmes in place for longer periods of time. In the early 1990s Wisconsin's former Governor Tommy Thompson, now the federal Health and Human Services Secretary for the Bush Administration, initiated a programme known as Bridefare which offered teen mothers on welfare an extra $80 a month in benefits if they married, but the programme prompted no significant upturn in marriages (Pollitt, 2002). Still other states offered similar programmes or tried other alternatives to encourage marriage commitment, like Louisiana's covenant marriage bill, enacted in 1997. Under this legislation, couples can essentially choose a separate set of laws to govern their marriage: they are required to participate in premarital counselling and marital counselling if they wish to divorce and the waiting period to obtain a no-fault divorce is two years, rather than the six months required under standard state law (Nock *et al.*, 1999). Not surprisingly, these moves on both federal and state levels have prompted intense debate about the advisability of having the government advo-cating and rewarding marriage. This debate takes what might previously have been individual anxiety – will *I* get married? – and places it squarely in the realm of public anxiety and discourse – *who* will get married? – and, even more extreme, how can 'they' be *made* to get married? Like the TLC programmes which blur the domains of the public and the private, such legislation not only moves the private into the public domain, it also reinscribes a collective cultural support for the husband-provider model of marriage since the operative assumption of guiding legislation targeting poor mothers to marry is clearly that a husband will move them out of poverty and public dependence into a stable socioeconomic state.

In their insistence on marriage, explicitly for the lower socioeconomic classes and particularly focusing on welfare recipients, these legislative attempts can be seen as evidence of forced emulation of middle-class values as a panacea for poverty; an answer which is, as Katha Pollitt notes, inherently flawed:

> that marriage is a cure for poverty is only true if you marry someone who isn't poor, who will share his income with you and your children, who won't divorce you later and leave you worse off than ever. The relation between poverty and marriage is virtually the opposite of what pro-marriage ideologues claim: It isn't that getting married gives feckless poor people middle-class values and stability, it's that stable middle-class people are the ones who can 'afford' to be married. However marriage functioned a half-century ago, today it is a class marker.
>
> (Pollitt, 2002)

Consumption, weddings and the state

In *White Weddings*, Chrys Ingraham describes the vast marketing complex of the wedding industry and seconds Pollitt's sense of the class-laden meaning of the wedding ceremony, especially as portrayed in the media:

> Using the power celebrities hold as the embodiment of fantasy to authorize particular social behaviours and beliefs, the visual media demonstrate where the margin of acceptability begins and ends…the consumption of tales of romance…prevents us from seeing the underlying material consequences…these images and practices allow. They promote the 'structured invisibility' of whiteness, numb us to excess, and police the boundaries of social acceptability around categories of race, class, sexuality and even beauty.
>
> (Ingraham, 1999: 128)

A Wedding Story extends the power of celebrity to police boundaries to the 'real and ordinary' people who choose to participate in the show. The consumption necessary for a 'normal' wedding becomes one of the explicit focuses of the programme. For example, virtually every bride on *A Wedding Story*, regardless of age or wedding theme, wears an elaborate white gown. Even in an episode featuring the more alternative ceremony of a couple ('Sundance and Tom', tx 7 August 2002) who say they practice a 'nature-based, life-affirming religion' and who opt to hold their ceremony in an underground cavern, the bride, Sundance, is garbed in a traditional wedding dress while she smokes herself with a 'Native-American smudge stick to get centred and calm' and 'cleansed for her new journey as a married woman'. The dress and other trappings of a traditional wedding are not only symbolic of images of feminine purity and submission; they are also representative of socioeconomic class based on the implicit expense of the consumption of wedding commodities. According to *Bride's Magazine*, weddings in the United States generated $70 million of revenue in 2001, with the average cost of a US wedding being almost $19,000 in 1999 (Anonymous, 2001: 12). These figures include the cost of flowers, engagement and wedding rings, reception and photos – all accoutrements presented as an integral part of every wedding shown on *A Wedding Story*. Given that a poverty-level income of one person in the United States was calculated at $8,590 in 2001 (US Department of Health and Human Services, 2001) and that 32.9 million people were counted as poor by the US Commerce Department's Census (US Census Bureau, 2002), these figures suggest that the cost of what *A Wedding Story* presents as a normal wedding is far beyond the financial reach of a large percentage of the population.

Though there are certainly vastly less costly routes to marriage, such as visiting a justice of the peace, these are certainly not depicted on *A Wedding Story* or in other popular culture sites where the idea of 'real' weddings are enacted as spectacle. All classes of young women are essentially taught to aspire to this type of wedding in our culture, and there is strong evidence that young women are listening to these lessons. A study by the market research firm Roper Starch Worldwide found that engaged women ages 20–29 were spending roughly $100 billion annually during the period of their engagements, and about half that figure went toward wedding costs, while the remainder was spent on goods, like electronics and home furnishings, and even on insurance for their 'new lives' (Gardyn, 2001). Obviously, a single TV show alone isn't responsible for all this spending; there must indeed be powerful cultural forces working together to make a wedding so fraught with symbolism that people are willing to justify such expenditures. Like governmental agencies and powerful conservative individuals who see the act of marriage as an answer to cultural anxieties about poverty and class cloaked as concerns about a rising divorce rate, *A Wedding Story* merely represents an answer to these anxieties, implying, like so many other fairy-tales before it, that creating the 'perfect' wedding might lead to an equally 'perfect' life ever after – and that perfection equals consumption.

Aspirational parenting and TLC

Interestingly, in the TLC programming consumption becomes one of the 'normal-ising' mechanisms of motherhood as well as marriage. *A Baby Story*'s format is virtually interchangeable with that of *A Wedding Story*: the couple review their rela-tionship, their other children, and their decision to have this child, complete a couple or family activity preparing for the birth (ranging from creating a cast of the mother's stomach to the more mundane shopping for a crib), labour begins or is induced, the baby is born, and the programme concludes with the couple holding their (always) healthy child and discussing the joy that they've experienced in the days or weeks that have elapsed since the birth. Like the formulaic presenta-tion of *A Wedding Story*, the precisely delineated narrative structure of *A Baby Story* both elides forms of difference and responds to a nexus of individual and collective anxieties. Shari Thurer describes one source of this widespread tension:

> Motherhood and ambition are still largely seen as opposing forces. More strongly expressed, a lack of ambition – or a professed lack of ambition, a sacrificial willingness to set personal ambition aside – is still the virtuous proof of good mothering. For many women, perhaps most, motherhood versus personal ambition represents the heart of the femi-nine dilemma.
>
> (Thurer, 1994: 287)

Thurer describes an emotional-tug-of-war that helps explain the trend pairing education and career and delayed childbirth that is rising in US and in many other developed nations. Over the years between 1995 and 2000, the birth rate for American women aged 45–49 grew by 25 per cent annually, while births for women aged 25–29 increased only 3.1 per cent and teen childbirths (ages 15–19) actually fell by 2.2 per cent (Much, 2002). Switzerland, Japan and the Netherlands also report that the average age for women bearing their first child was 28 in 2000, compared to 24.9 in the US (Wetzstein, 2002). This trend is firmly linked to mothers delaying having children until after completing their education and becoming established in a career and is, again, not unique to the US. Under the current patterns, for example, only about 10 per cent of Australian women under age 30 have both a university degree and a child or chil-dren (Meryment 2002). In many cases this means that women are having children after achieving a higher income level which, under raised lifestyle expectations, contributes to some interesting results for attitudes toward childrearing.

The most direct in relationship to *A Baby Story* is in patterns of consumption and the equation of consumption with better parenting. *Investor's Business Daily* reports that older mothers are willing to 'spend more on maternity clothes than younger peers, since they've had more time to amass income' (Much, 2002), and many of the events portrayed on *A Baby Story* seem to mirror and even sanction this sense that spending money is the key way to prepare oneself for parenthood. Besides the literal shopping activities – crib purchases, baby monitors and nappy bag-buying expeditions – filmed for the programme, the other sanctions of consumption employ recognisable markers of class. Quite a few of the couples on the show hire professional artists to paint murals on the walls of their baby's room or professional photographers to capture the mother's pregnancy forever on film; still another couple asks a dog behaviourist to come to their house to help prepare their two dogs for the new baby's arrival. Clearly these expenditures indicate substantial disposable income and the inclination to pay someone else to provide for perceived 'needs' beyond the basics. Other expectant mothers attend yoga class or visit reflexologists for foot massage, activities which correlate with a middle-class (or higher) level of leisure time and, in the culture of the United States' moralistic attitudes toward health, a certain sense of class privilege and entitlement to indulge in self-care in a very public way. These prenatal moves to ensure the 'right' kind of pregnancy extend beyond the period of gestation for many. As Thurer humorously describes the accessories of this trend,

> Today's baby invariably has an assortment of black-and-white toys, the all-important downward staring mobile (to stimulate baby's brain), the clear rattle with (don't laugh) a Play and Learning TM (Guide) to instruct parents in its use, lots of Raffi records. The latest boom is magazines for toddlers.
>
> (Thurer, 1994: 296)

Even the recent downturn in the US economy seems to have made little impact on the class described here, since the *New York Times* ran a story in December of 2002 on the escalation of Christmas gifts for teachers and competitive parents upping the ante with Kate Spade designer totes to ensure that the teacher took proper notice of their children (Rosman, 2002: 3). These behaviours might seem both extravagant and laughable at first glance, but Thurer rightly points out the subtext of these patterns of consumption: 'At best, these products do nothing more than shore up mom and dad's confidence. At worst, they are examples of status-seeking and narcissistic self-absorption' (1994: 296).

Because of the formula, which remains the same, day in and day out, there is a numbing sameness in the presentation which invokes a number of contentious notions: prepare for childbirth by shopping, all mothers are stoic, and all children are healthy and wanted. In positing its stories as the 'real' experience of childbirth, *A Baby Story* shuts its doors to the enormous number of single parents and ignores the profound impact that socioeconomic class has on the experience of birth and motherhood. There are far too many women who cannot afford to shop even for the basics, and the insidious nature of equating the ability to consume with the ability to 'deserve' to have children can be seen in the proposals to penalise women on welfare for having additional children or in the moves to require women on welfare to receive Norplant contraceptive implants before receiving government benefits.

Reproductive technologies and *A Baby Story*

Tapping into yet another trigger for recent public debates, *A Baby Story* also raises the twin spectre of reproductive technologies – a hot button for individual women and public policy-makers alike in the US. One facet of this issue involves ethical and personal anxieties about women's fertility. Sylvia Ann Hewlett's book *Creating a Life* (2002) has prompted a storm of controversy on the subject. The essence of Hewlett's message is that in delaying childbirth to pursue careers women are relying on an inaccurate perception that even if they are unable to conceive when they reach the point at which they choose to have children, they can turn to assistive technology to achieve motherhood. Hewlett's research indicates that 89 per cent of the women she surveyed believed this to be true, but according to her research the truth is actually that '[a]fter age 40, only 3 to 5 per cent of those who use the new assisted reproductive technologies actually succeed in having a child' (quoted in Wishart, 2002). Judging from the vociferous debates set off by Hewlett's book, fertility issues tap into deep anxieties about combining career and motherhood for many women. Hewlett's book alone is not responsible for igniting this anxiety on a broad cultural level. News stories like 'The Baby Bias' in the *New York Times Education Life Supplement* (Cohen, 2002) paint a grim picture for professional women who want to delay childbirth. Citing unsympathetic administrations who see the pursuit of tenure and babies as incompatible, this article presented studies of women professors as representative of a wave of 'high-achieving' women who are confronting high infertility rates because they have put off having children until after they're secure in their professional lives (ibid.: 25). Due to these cultural trends and possibly other factors, the American College of Obstetricians and Gynaecologists estimates that about 15 per cent of couples, or about 6.2 million women, in the United States are impacted by infertility, and predictions indicate that this number will continue to grow, to 7.7 million by 2025 (Willis, 2002; Christensen, 1998). About 45 per cent of these couples seek treatment for infertility, so reproductive assistance is a booming business and it is also one that appears regularly on *A Baby Story*. Of the 82 episodes aired in seasons two and three (1999–2001), 11 contained accounts of couples that had struggled with infertility. The summaries of the episodes on Pie Town Productions' website (http://www.pietownprods.com/shows/babystory) almost read like a fertility specialist's brochure: 'As a last resort, after many fertility treatments, Lisa and Darrin tried artificial insemination. Though

the first two attempts were heartbreaking failures, the third took and Lisa was pregnant with twins!' (episode #308, 'Baby Lee'); 'After years of trying and endless
medical tests, Roger was finally diagnosed with a condition that affected his sperm
production. Three months after an operation to correct the problem, they were
pregnant' (episode #313, 'Baby Lyon'). It's not much of a leap to suggest that these
'real' depictions of couples conquering infertility might be a welcome balm to an
audience who might well be seeking the same resolution. On a collective level,
these internal personal debates are echoed in public forums like newspapers, where
editorials question whether it is ethically correct for women past 'natural' childbearing age to avail themselves of these technologies, and many don't hesitate to
take the position that a woman's choice to conceive is erased by her age. Adding to
these ethical interrogations are the questions raised by the technologies themselves
about defining motherhood:

> The fragmenting of the female sexual and reproductive body, through
> implantation of surrogacy, or through the removal of eggs, is a breaking
> up of that object – Mom – which has been made to symbolize so much
> of the social order for so long. All this has triggered deep cultural
> anxiety.
>
> (Thurer, 1994: 295)

A Baby Story offers a response to this anxiety by reiterating twice daily the
primacy of parents, particularly mothers. Many of the episodes feature the couple
learning about how to soothe and cater to the mother while she is in labour. A
similar recurring focal point is the mother's body itself: a massage of a woman's
swollen feet is given close-up shots and depiction of the medical process of labour is
lovingly detailed. We see the nurse contorting the woman's body to administer the
epidural, and the mother is frequently surrounded by a sea of loving friends and
relatives who rub, caress or otherwise interact on a bodily level with the labouring
woman. At the time of birth, the hordes gathered in the delivery room 'watch her
(discreetly draped) nether region as if it were a wide-screen TV' (Millman, 2000).
While there are some positive components to these facets of the show – the respect
accorded to the difficulties of childbirth, the depictions of women's bodies of
various sizes, shapes and structures in sharp contrast to the constant imagery of
thin, young female bodies which otherwise pervade the media, for example – the
focus on the body also reinforces the idea of the 'real' in the diversity of bodies
presented while paradoxically spotlighting two cultural pitfalls to this modern-day
cult of motherhood. The first is a subordination of a mother's rights to the rights of her
unborn child. The reason that these women appear on the show is because of whom
they carry. This is an attitude precariously close to the subordination of women
to the foetuses they carry implied by the Bush Administration's extension of

healthcare to unborn children and to the ideology of equating reproductive health with abortion as the reinstituted Mexico City Policy, or 'gag rule', infers.[2] Second, this centrality of the pregnant body in *A Baby Story* also serves to link parenthood to biology. As yet, there have been no stories of adoption or surrogacy on *A Baby Story*, despite the show's emphasis on infertility; again and again, the stories are about heterosexual couples giving *biological* birth, regardless of the technologies that made that birth possible. The programme's insistence on heterosexuality and biology is all the more surprising when one learns that Pie Town Productions' president and vice-president, Tara Sandler and Jennifer Davidson, are same-sex partners. Commenting on the show's lack of diversity in this area, Davidson references the show's interactions with cultural tensions, saying, 'I would be really concerned, to be honest, for a lesbian or gay couple going camera with a baby…that pushes too many buttons in this country' (quoted in Champagne, 1999). While Davidson's concern may be a reflection of 'reality', the effect of this negation of difference is that the show, unfortunately, begins to parallel too closely the repressive attitudes still evident within public discourse about difference, whether it is diversity based on sexual orientation, class or race.

Constructing the happy ever after

Ultimately, the formula of these two reality shows succeeds in levelling virtually all forms of difference even though the topics of the programmes, marriage and fertility, are inextricably bound up in American society with anxieties about sexual orientation, gender, class and race. 'Welfare mothers', for instance, is still a term unfortunately and incorrectly immediately associated with African-Americans in the popular mind, and in 2002, as in the late nineteenth and early twentieth centuries, debates about immigration restriction still centre on the fertility of women of colour and perceived fears that a racial underclass will someday dominate over 'real' (sub-text, white) United States citizens. While both *A Baby Story* and *A Wedding Story* actually do a fairly good job of presenting a diversity of races and ethnic backgrounds, the particulars get melded into sameness by both the construction of the shows' formats and the persistent presentation of class-based similarities. Even when they address these differences explicitly, viewers are soothed by simplistic answers to complex cultural concerns. The inter-racial couple (*A Baby Story*, 'Charles and Shelly Clay', tx 3 January 2003) who said they planned to address racism their children might face by 'teaching their children to be accepting, as [they] were taught to be accepting' is indicative of a common attitude of essentially hoping the problem will just go away without any real intervention. What this message boils down to is a dichotomy of 'us' versus 'them' based on consumption: those who can consume like 'us' are celebrated; those who cannot must be *regulated*. It is akin to the statements of those who proclaim welfare reform in the US a success, but neglect to mention that the statistics given to account for its success ignore all those who simply dropped below the public institutions' radar when they were dropped from welfare rolls. Realistically, this lack of complexity and ambiguity may well be the true source of the appeal of both quick-fix public policy and the TLC programmes. Caryn James writes that the appeal of another current Reality TV show, *The Bachelor*, is that,

> it is actually an exercise in nostalgia. And like all nostalgia, it speaks to the longing for an idealized past. We're in an age where sexual roles are fluid, and 'The Bachelor' offers an escape from ambiguity, a temporary and knowingly false return to an era in which male and female roles were clear – stereotypical, but clear.
>
> (James, 2002: 19)

Likewise, *A Baby Story* and *A Wedding Story* are also 'exercises in nostalgia' that help to soothe creeping, pervasive social fears by offering normalising rituals that serve to erase ambiguity. Essentially, the shows' sub-textual lullaby is that if we submit to the formula, marital bliss will be ensured by locating the right dress, right husband and 'right' interpretation of gender roles; that we too can live in an Edenic world where every child is wanted and nostalgic 1950s family values (that only ever existed in our earlier TV dreams – as Chapter 2 attests) really will come true. If we watch four hours of domestic bliss each day on TLC, divorce rates, social welfare, racial tensions and poverty can drop right off our radars too.

Notes

1   According to the US National Center for Health Statistics, the divorce rate in 1970 was 3.5 per cent per 1,000 population. Between 1980 and 1985 the number reached its highest point in thirty years, hovering around 5.0, and by 1995 the number had actually dropped to 4.4, and it declined further, to 4.1, in 2000. Figures and reports available at http://www.cdc.gov/nchs/fastats/divorce.htm.

2   The highly controversial Mexico City policy prevents US money for family planning from being distributed to clinics in countries outside the US if those clinics provide abortions; however, it is known as the 'gag rule' because the ban on funding also extends to clinics which offer counseling about abortion or lobby for increased availability of abortion. The policy was originated in the 1980s under the Reagan administration, was lifted by President Clinton on his first day in office, and then reinstated by President George W. Bush as his first decision as president.

References

Adams, Jane Meredith (2002) 'Cradle vs. Career: How One Woman Ignited a Nationwide Baby Panic', *Biography*, November: 70; available at Ebscohost Academic Search Elite, http://www.ebscohost.com (accessed 4 January 2003).

Anonymous (2001) 'Keeping Track', *Christian Science Monitor*, 4 June: 12; available at Ebscohost Academic Search Elite, http://www.ebscohost.com (accessed 21 October 2002).

Anonymous (2002) 'Reality Bites', *Sight and Sound*, September: 6.

Barovick, Harriet (1999) 'Love Labor and Ratings', *Time* (Electronic), 18 October: 103; available at Ebscohost Academic Search Elite, http://www.ebscohost.com (accessed 31 May 2002).

Champagne, Christine (1999) 'Rattles and Ratings', *Advocate*, 22 June: 107; available at Ebscohost Academic Search Elite, http://www.ebscohost.com (accessed 31 May 2002).

Christensen, Damaris (1998) 'Infertility Rates Expected to Climb in Next Century', *Intelligencer Journal* (Lancaster, PA), 4 August: A6; available at Proquest Newspapers, http://www.proquest.com (accessed 5 December 2002).

Cohen, Hal (2002) 'The Baby Bias', *New York Times Education Life Supplement*, 4 August: 24–25, 30–33.

Curtis, Chris (2002) 'When Love is All There Is', *Watch the River Run*, MP3.CD; available at http://artists.mp3s.com/artists/cds/234/234494.html (accessed 3 March 2003).

Dovey, Jon (2000) *Freakshow: First Person Media and Factual Television*, London: Pluto Press.

Dow, Bonnie J. (1996) *Prime-Time Feminism*, Philadelphia, PN: University of Pennsylvania Press.

Dyer, Richard (1986) *Heavenly Bodies: Film Stars and Society*, New York: St Martin's Press.

Epinions.com (2002) 'Home>Media>TV Channels Reviews>I Love the Stories!'; available at http://www.epinions.com/tele-review-55E1-EF64970–398DBDFB-prod1 (accessed 4 January 2003).

Gardyn, Rebecca (2001) 'Here Comes the Bride's Checkbook', *American Demographics* 23(5): 12; available at Ebscohost Academic Search Elite, http://www.ebscohost.com (accessed 4 January 2003).

Glynn, Kevin (2000) *Tabloid Culture*, Durham and London: Duke University Press.

Hafen, Bruce (1995) 'Marriage and the State's Legal Posture Toward the Family', *Vital Speeches of the Day* (Electronic), 15 October: 17; available at Ebscohost Academic Search Elite, http://www.ebscohost.com (accessed 22 December 2002).

Hewlett, Sylvia Ann (2002) *Creating a Life*, New York: Hyperion.

Ingraham, Chrys (1999) *White Weddings: Romancing Heterosexuality in Popular Culture*, New York and London: Routledge.

James, Caryn (2002) 'The Bachelor and His Barbies', *New York Times*, 17 November: 19.

K.L. (2002) 'Toss the Risotto and Tie the Knot Abroad', *Kiplinger's Personal Finance*, June: 89; available at Ebscohost Academic Search Elite, http://www.ebscohost.com (accessed 21 October 2002).

Leichtman Research Group (2002) 'LRG Research Notes', August; available at http://www.leichtmanresearch.com/research/notes08—2002.html (accessed 3 January 2003).

Lerner, Sharon (2002) 'Just Say "I Do"', *Nation* (Electronic), 25 November: 22; available at Ebscohost Academic Search Elite, http://www.ebscohost.com (accessed 22 December 2002).

Littlejohn, Janice Rhoshalle (2002) 'TLC Serves Slices of Life – and Teens Bite', *Los Angeles Times*, 7 October; available at Proquest Newspapers, http://www.proquest.com (accessed 5 December 2002).

Meryment, Elizabeth (2002) 'Singles, Sex, and Babies', *Courier Mail*, 17 August; available at LexisNexis Academic, http://www.lexisnexis.com/academic/default2.asp (accessed 1 December 2002).

Milllman, Joyce (2000) 'The Addictive Spectacle of Maternal Reality', *New York Times*, 13 August: 2.25; available at Proquest Newspapers, http://www.proquest.com (accessed 5 December 2002).

Much, Marilyn (2002) 'Mothers Work, Inc., Philadelphia, Pennsylvania: Oh Baby, Business at this Retailer is Booming', *Investor's Business Daily*, 2 December; available at Lexis-Nexis Academic, http://www.lexisnexis.com/academic/default2.asp (accessed 4 January 2003).

Nock, Steven L., James D. Wright and Laura Sanchez (1999) 'America's Divorce Problem', *Society* (Electronic), 36(4): 43; available at Ebscohost Academic Search Elite, http://www.ebscohost.com (accessed 22 December 2002).

Pollitt, Katha (2002) 'Shotgun Weddings', *Nation* (Electronic), 4 February: 10; available at Ebscohost Academic Search Elite, http://www.ebscohost.com (accessed 22 December 2002).

Putnam, Caurie Anne (n.d.) 'What It's Like to Be on "A Wedding Story"', UltimateWedding.com; available at http://www.ultimatewedding.com/articles/get.php?action=getarticle&articleid=735 (accessed 22 December 2000).

Rosman, Katherine (2002) 'Mother Lode of Gifts for Teachers', *New York Times*, 15 December: 9.1, 3.

Shattuc, Jane M. (1997) *The Talking Cure: TV Talk Shows and Women*, New York and London: Routledge.

Stapinski, Helene (1999) 'Y not Love?', *American Demographics* 21(2): 62; available at Ebscohost Academic Search Elite, http://www.ebscohost.com (accessed 31 May 2002).

Thornton, Arland and Linda Young-DeMarco (2001) 'Four Decades of Trends in Attitudes toward Family Issues in the United States: The 1960s through the 1990s', *Journal of Marriage and Family* 63(4): 1,009 (29pp.); available at Ebscohost Academic Search Elite (accessed 21 October 2002).

Thurer, Shari L. (1994) *The Myths of Motherhood: How Culture Reinvents the Good Mother*, Boston, MA: Houghton Mifflin.

Umstead, R. Thomas (2002) 'TLC Trades Up to Elite Rating Space', *Reed Business Information USA*, 18 November: A10; available at LexisNexis Academic, http://www.lexisnexis.com/academic/default2.asp (accessed 1 December 2002).

US Census Bureau (2002) *United States Department of Commerce News*; available at http://www.census.gov/Press-Release/www/2002/cb02–124.html (accessed 3 January 2003).

US Department of Health and Human Services, Office of the Assistant Secretary for Planning and Evaluation (2001) *The 2001 HHS Poverty Guidelines*; available at http://aspe.hhs.gov/poverty/01poverty.htm (accessed 3 January 2003).

Wetzstein, Cheryl (2002) 'American Women Giving Birth Later', *Washington Times*, 12 December: A8; available at LexisNexis Academic, http://www.lexisnexis.com/academic/default2.asp (accessed 4 January 2003).

Willis, Melinda T. (2002) 'Improving Success: Small Advances in Infertility Treatment Contribute to Growing Success Rates', abcNEWS.com, 12 November; available at http://abcnews.com (accessed 3 January 2003).

Wishart, Katrina (2002) 'No Shades of Grey in Two-Tone World', *Times Higher Education Supplement*, 6 September: 32; available at LexisNexis Academic, http://www.lexis-nexis.com/academic/default2.asp (accessed 4 October 2002).

10

THE HOUSEHOLD, THE BASEMENT AND *THE REAL WORLD*

Gay identity in the constructed reality environment

Christopher Pullen

Introduction: from the basement to the household

In the closing scene of *The Talented Mr Ripley* (Anthony Minghella, 1999, US) Tom Ripley (played by Matt Damon) tells Peter Smith-Kingsley (his clandestine lover, who he will later murder): 'I am lost, I am going to be stuck in the basement.... I've lied about who I am, and where I am, no-one will ever find me.' Although we are led to believe that these sentiments relate primarily to his self-effacement as a murderer, it is not difficult to imagine that they are also an allusion to the impossibility of Ripley's life as a closeted homosexual. While Ripley is not purged from the text by the final curtain in an effort to restore a heterosexual equilibrium, his metaphorical consignment to the basement reminds us that the homosexual is not always welcome in the more 'social' parts of the (hetero) household drama. Although this chapter does not intend to make comparisons between television and film, it is relevant to reflect on how this film (like many other mainstream film and television texts)[1] returns homosexual identity to the basement. However, it is increasingly the case that television – most recently and visibly in the form of Reality TV – has increasingly taken this 'outsider identity' and seemingly welcomed it into the space of the living room.

The depiction of Tom Ripley may be seen as part of a tradition of representation which, with film, commenced in the early 1900s with the appearance of the male 'sissy' (Russo, 1987). Since this time, many film and television texts have placed emphasis on the difference and 'otherness' (Hall, 1997) of non-heterosexual identities.[2] For many years, diverse sexuality – if represented at all in television and film – was signified through the use of stereotypes such as effeminacy, overt masculinity and/or isolation in ways which heightened the difference of such characters (Dyer, 1984). Although the complexities of this history cannot be investigated here, it was predominantly from the 1980s onwards that film and television increasingly incorporated representations of gay identity into mainstream texts – particularly, with respect to television, in the genres of the soap opera and the talk show. Given that the hybrid form of Reality TV in many ways draws on the codes and conventions of these genres (Roscoe, 2001), it clearly capitalised on this shift, with early texts such as *The Real World* (Bunim–Murray for MTV, 1992–, US) featuring gay participants as an accepted part of the community.

Subsequently, since the screening of *The Real World*, many reality shows have included gay participants. Indeed, the appearance of four openly gay cast members in *The Salon* (Endemol, for C4, 2003, UK)[3] may be seen as less of an extraordinary event and more of a predictable strategy of 'casting' and characterisation where Reality TV is concerned. As a result, the apparently elevated appearance of (and demand for) gay people on Reality TV stimulates enquiry. While existing work on Reality TV has considered the complex issues surrounding the mediation of 'performance' and 'selfhood' (particularly in *Big Brother*) (Corner, 2002; Couldry, 2002; Roscoe, 2001; Tincknell and Raghuram, 2002; van Zoonen, 2001), little attention has been paid to the role that gay people have increasingly played within this arena. Thus the purpose of this study is to investigate the implications of the visibility of gay participants in Reality TV: to what extent does the form raise new issues in the field where the construction of gay identity is concerned? How are these possibilities shaped by the particular technological, aesthetic and narrative structures of Reality TV, and what are their political implications?

In order to explore these questions, this chapter will specifically focus on gay identity in the context of what I refer to as the 'constructed reality environment' – a format in which the participants are placed and observed – using *The Real World*, *Big Brother* (Endemol for C4, 2000–, UK) and *Eden* (RDF for C4, 2002, UK) as examples. Focusing on the specific media performances by gay participants, critical, historical and discursive perspectives will be applied to areas such as the objectification of the body, the stereotyping of 'queer' identity and camp performance, and the mediation of discourses on 'community', romance and coupling. Although the appearance of gay women also contributes meaningfully to the subject area, the case studies selected here consider gay men.

Three gay male contestants have become eventual winners of some of the most popular Reality programmes – *Survivor* (Survivor Productions for CBS, 2000–, US), *Big Brother* and *Pop Idol* (Thames TV/19TV for ITV, 2001–2, UK). Richard Hatch, a 38-year-old corporate trainer/conflict manager won the first series of *Survivor* (2000) in the US. Brian Dowling, a 23-year-old airline cabin-crew supervisor triumphed in *Big Brother 2* (2001), while Will Young, a 23-year-old politics graduate became the overall winner of *Pop Idol* in the UK. Hatch and Dowling displayed themselves as openly gay during the production of the series, while

Young announced that he was gay shortly after winning the competition[4] (and still achieved popular support in maintaining the number one slot in the pop charts). These texts not only displayed similarities in their potential to elect gay winners, but are symptomatic of an increase in gay visibility across the international formats offered by Reality TV.[5]

With an obvious commitment to include gay participants, how does Reality TV use gay cultural/social identity? It could be argued that gay participants can be selected for performing, and adhering to, recognised dramatic traits associated with stereotypical gay performance, such as 'effeminacy, sensitivity, artistic talent or sensibility, misogyny [and] isolation' (Clum, 2000: 77). This may be seen in a popular account of the success of Richard Hatch on *Survivor* (2000, US): 'With his smirking egotism, bearish build, and preference for nudity [he was] no one's idea of a gay role model, much less a network superstar. But his soap-operatic conniving [was] the best thing for CBS's ratings [for many years]' (Meers, 2002: 42). The association here between Hatch and soap opera, as well as the stereotypical dramatic ideal of the 'isolated villain', points toward the production of a 'dramatic type' (Bourne, 1996; Capsuto, 2000; Clum, 2000; Dyer, 2000; Russo, 1987) and the construction of gay identity within predictable narrative strategies.

As indicated, prior to the advent of Reality TV and its interest in gay participants, gay people and characters had made significant appearances in both talk shows and soap operas (Finch, 1999; Gamson, 1998; Geraghty, 1991). Each drawing broadly upon the personalised structures of melodrama, narrative conflict and the blurring of public and private space, these genres have both been seen as foregrounding certain limitations where the representation of gay identity is concerned. A key debate framing the wider analysis of the talk show has been the degree to which, with respect to the appearance of subordinate groups in society, the genre facilitated (and represented) a 'democratisation' of televisual space while, in this very act, simultaneously functioning to 'reinscribe moral and political hegemonies' (Dovey, 2000: 116; see also Shattuc, 1997; Gamson, 1998; Tolson, 2001). Talk shows were accused of offering the visibility of both gay identity and 'sexual non-conformists' for vicarious entertainment, including, for example, the arbitrary presentation of 'gay teens, gay cops, lesbian cops, cross-dressing hookers, transsexual call girls [and] gay and lesbian gang members' (Gamson, 1998: 5). Yet it is important to stress here that the presence of such guests could also be groundbreaking, particularly in the willingness of gay men and women to testify their resistance to social subjugation concerning the issue of AIDS and political moves against homosexual life. In the UK talk show *Kilroy* (BBC1, 1987–, UK) numerous editions featured openly gay people (BBC, 2002) including 'Gay Christians' (1987), 'Gay Parents' (1988), 'Clause 28' (1988),[6] 'Gay Fostering' (1991), 'Gay Age of Consent' (1993), not forgetting 'Homosexuality: How Do Families Cope?' (1989), in which members of the audience discussed the topic as if coming to terms with a grave illness. As this suggests, however, particularly in the 1980s and 1990s, such appearances were also clearly framed, given the nature of the genre, within the structuring narrative of a 'problem issue' – an example of how the apparently liberal and tolerant space of the talk show is 'undermined by narrative structures in which difference and deviance are positioned as the disruption or problem that needs to be solved' (Dovey, 2000: 117). At the same time, the vivid appearance of gay people in the genre of the talk show suggested that gay 'issues' were fit for public debate and of interest to the mainstream audience.

Although clearly played out within the specificity of its own textual form, soap operas' use of a 'liberal gay discourse' (Geraghty, 1991: 160) has also been described as being overly didactic ('alerting the heterosexual audience' to the problems faced by gay people) (ibid.), as well as foregrounding the problems inherent in the 'burden of representation' – in that gay characters could 'disappear' under the issues they were required to represent (ibid.; see also Finch, 1999). As Geraghty explains, the entire concept of the community so central to the genre also repeatedly renders the representation of 'difference' (particularly in terms of ethnicity and sexuality) problematic (Geraghty, 1991: 166). On one level, difference provides the impetus for narrative disruption upon which soap opera thrives, while, at the same time, 'if differences are marked too dramatically, too distinctly, the soap's prevailing ethos that everyone shares the common experience...becomes untenable' (ibid.: 166). While Reality TV draws upon the 'first-person' confessional structures of the talk show (Dovey, 2000) and elements of editing, narrativisation and 'character' drawn from soap opera (Roscoe, 2001), it is of course not identical, or reducible, to either of these generic precursors. However, the structural, discursive and ideological parameters discussed above provide a context within which to consider the construction and implications of Reality TV's representation of gay identity.

The appearance of a gay public in the context of Reality TV did not necessarily commence in 1992 with *The Real World*.[7] Rather, it was predated by some 19 years by the docusoap precursor of *An American Family* (Alan and Susan Raymond for WNET-13, 1973, US).[8] This series depicted the lives of the Loud family, and became a highly popular contemporary text. It followed the most intimate details of the family's life, including the parents' divorce proceedings and 'the New York lifestyle of their gay son, Lance' (Ruoff, 2002: xi), who, in this sense, may be considered the first gay 'reality' participant. Whilst Lance Loud did not openly discuss his homosexuality on the series as it aired, discourse was generated within the text which signalled him as homosexual. This may be seen, for example, in the sequence where his mother leaves the family home (Santa Barbara) and visits the 'outsider child' in New York. Through the use of ambiguous signification (Lance discusses his childhood and his self-identification as outside the family unit) he revealed his contentment in living in a city where he could be 'himself'. Although Lance would later openly discuss his sexuality in various media texts (Suderburg, 1997), this veiled appearance of a 'real' gay man (as peripheral outsider, yet maternally understood family member) stimulated a transfiguration of the imagined concept of the American family.

Narrative principles and form: *The Real World*, *Big Brother* and *Eden*

The producers of *The Real World* unsurprisingly cite *An American Family* as an influential text in the development of the format (Jon Murray, producer of *The Real World*, personal interview, 8 November 2002).[9] At the same time, they readily acknowledge that the original intention had been to make a soap opera, but, as costs were over budget, they decided to use real people, thereby developing a 'living soap'.[10] While *The Real World* was established as a reality soap opera and continues in this tradition, it also functioned as a precursor to later Reality texts such as *Big Brother* and *Eden*. Similarities may be seen in the formulation of diverse 'cast' members, which provides an emphasis on the difference 'between black and white, working class and [middle class,] gay and heterosexual' (Geraghty, 1991: 166) and is similar to the 'impetus for disruption on which soap narrative [also] thrive[s]' (ibid.).[11] Yet while *The Real World* may centre its diegetic construction on the pursuits of the participants, and the cameras allegedly follow them wherever they go (for example, Pedro Zamora is filmed while visiting his family in Miami), *Big Brother* and *Eden* stimulate narrative possibilities by adopting the overarching framework of the game show and encourage confrontation through containment.

It is also important to note here that, while genres such as the talk show and the soap opera figure as crucial televisual, textual and cultural precursors to Reality TV where the representation of gay identity is concerned, an acknowledgement of differences in form, aesthetics and reception should be retained. There is equally a necessary *ambiguity* here in that while Reality TV has popularly been referred to as using 'narrativisation', 'casting' and 'characters' in the manner of soap opera (Roscoe, 2001), the complexity of the actual relations between the two forms has not been fully explored. While the producers of Reality TV – as my analysis will emphasise here – clearly play a significant role in 'characterising' the participants, who do not of course get to 'represent themselves', this is nevertheless not analogous to scripted drama. Equally, Hill's (2002) ethnographic audience research into Reality TV suggests the complexity of viewers' engagement with participants, which – in negotiating particular frames surrounding 'performance' and 'authenticity' in an otherwise 'constructed' televisual environment – is necessarily different to an engagement with fictional 'characters'.

CHRISTOPHER PULLEN

The objectification of the gay body

> How can anyone respect the opinion of a man who'd put his hands
> on the body of another man?
> (Blake Carrington from *Dynasty*; quoted in Geraghty, 1991: 165)

With respect to soap opera, this quote from the *Dynasty* (Aaron Spelling for ABC, 1982–9, US) patriarch Blake Carrington articulates a heterocentric (male) discourse surrounding the male homosexuality in the household. At the same time, it draws attention to the discursive, visual and even 'imagined' site of the male homosexual body, seen potentially as an exotic 'other' or as 'a passive object of the gaze' or desire (Dyer, 1986: 117). The gay man, like the heterosexual woman (Mulvey, 1985), may be seen as subordinate to heterosexual male authority. At the same time, he may also be considered as an object of 'alien' sexual desire, posing a threat to heterosexual order by not conforming to traditional roles (male/female engagement).

Christine Geraghty considers the threat posed by 'rampant male virility' to 'domestic order' in her analysis of the patriarchal soap, citing the evidence of male power struggles in *Dynasty* and *Dallas* (CBS, 1978–91, US), in which 'patriarchal power is continually challenged, making it difficult for the male hero to hang on to what he believes is his rightful role as head of the family' (Geraghty, 1991: 63). While the Reality TV programmes here feature performances by 'real' participants and not fictional characters, and the ambivalent narrative construction may not inform the viewer who is the 'rightful' head of the family, a struggle for power may be sensed which directly relates to male insecurity, heterosexual or otherwise. Consequently, the performances of Pedro Zamora in *The Real World* San Francisco (1994, US),[12] Brian Dowling and Josh Rafter in *Big Brother 2* and Lee Alexander in *Eden* all relate to the idea of male positioning in the formation of the narrative. Through their interrelation with opposing, or contrasting, male participants (or signifiers of male identity), they negotiate their position as 'inside-outside figures' (Geraghty, 1991: 102) who struggle for 'survival' within a heterosexual-dominated community.

Of Cuban descent, Pedro Zamora was an AIDS educator who lived with the syndrome. Consequently, he may be seen to capitalise on the importance of his message: implementing his role as a performer, he productively used his body as an object of 'desire' (his natural good looks and charm) and 'disorder' (a metaphor for the tragedy of AIDS) (Sontag, 1989).[13] Evidence of this proclivity to direct social awareness (by juxtaposing good looks against the demise of health) may be seen in the objectification of his body in a very moving sequence which occurs while Pedro visits his family in Miami. He falls ill, and telephone conversations are made by Pedro as he tries to obtain medical advice:

216

(Pedro is depicted on a bed partly clothed and sweating.)

PEDRO: Basically when I breathe my chest hurts. I am just concerned that it could be pneumonia.

HEALTHCARE VOICE ON PHONE: You know, we're a kind of corporation right now. Patients have to have insurance.

PEDRO: I want X-rays, so I could know...I'll hold.... And I'll pay for it.

HEALTHCARE VOICE: One second, caller.

(Sound as if phone cut off – Pedro looks up as if in disbelief.)

PEDRO: (to camera) If I [was] dying, I would be [fucking] dead by now.

(The RealWorld, episode 13)

This scene, through creative editing and dramatic juxtaposition, explicitly comments on the lack of state medical care available to Pedro, and entreats the audience to sympathise. Following this, further visual impact is achieved given

Figure 10.1 Pedro Zamora (1972-94) AIDS activist from *The Real World* San Francisco. 'What I was always talking about, I know, was my own death....All I want is to make people think, and make them care.' (© Ken Probst/Corbis Outline.)

that we are party to his medical examination. The apparently healthy Pedro removes his shirt and turns his back on the camera. While placing his chest within the body of the X-ray machine he holds his body taut. This vividly reveals the extent of his emaciation from AIDS, while the proffering of his body as an object for examination further displays the seriousness of his medical condition. This may return us to a consideration – particularly in linking this back to the context of soap opera – of the use of gay participants within a didactic, 'issue-based' framework; the description of the scene above signifies the use of 'the real' here to foreground the gravity of the situation (and the use of images not seen in soap opera). However, Richard Dyer explains how 'a juxtaposition of beauty and decay is part of a longstanding rhetoric of queerness…[which] allows the effects of the illness gotten through sex to be read as a metaphor for that sex itself' (2002: 172). Rather than focusing on the social tragedy of AIDS, an alternative reading may suggest an emphasis on the 'unnatural' and potentially promiscuous nature of the sex that may have caused such decay, providing evidence of *The Real World*'s potential to narrativise its participants 'in acute and excessive ways' (Caldwell, 2002: 275). This highlights the way in which AIDS has a contentious relationship not only with narrative potential, but also with 'the meaning and morality of sex' (Weeks, 1995: 20).

The objectification of the gay body is similarly used in *Big Brother 2* and *Eden*, yet their particular 'performative' contexts engender a rather different set of connotations. Emphasis is placed on the form of Lee Alexander in *Eden* which links his 'potent' interest in financial gain (his self-declared reason for appearing on the programme) to the imagined site of his sexual body. Evidence of this is presented in a scene where Lee discusses the possibility of the prize money which awaits the winner of the series. This is immediately followed by a voiceover commenting on what is described as 'Lee's bare-faced cheek' which is accompanied by an image of the other male contestants, who are seated naked (and viewed from the rear) while discussing Lee. In many ways, Lee seems to avoid the discussion of his body and any sensational display – although the conversation above illustrates how the programme-makers focus on its *imagined* potency. In comparison, Brian Dowling of *Big Brother 2* deliberately places emphasis on his physical form. This is witnessed in a scene at the swimming pool which provides the opportunity not only to exhibit the site of the gay ('other') male body, but also to signal the ongoing tension between Brian and contestant Josh Rafter, who is also gay (discussed in detail below; pp. 221–3). In this sequence Brian is subject to a 'ruse' while attempting to get out of the pool, which involves Josh pulling at Brian's swimming shorts to the extent that they become elongated and unwearable. While the suggestion is that Brian is not amused by these actions (he initially protests), the camera lingers on his naked form. Brian then performs to order, and almost glorifies the incident, by swinging the swimwear above his head with dextrous rhythm.

218

Although the gay performers in *Big Brother 2* and *Eden* do not have the obvious political agenda of Pedro Zamora, and their physical form is not encoded with the context of 'disease' and suffering, the idea of the 'subversively' exotic body is nevertheless explored. This is subliminally discussed in *Eden* (Lee's imagined physical form) and vicariously exhibited in *Big Brother* (Brian's naked display).

Unlike the gay performers in *Big Brother 2* and *Eden*, *The Real World*'s Pedro Zamora is immediately signalled as a potential leader and a central site of narrative connectedness in the opening episode.[14] Evidence of this is presented through a statement from Pedro suggesting that the house is located on a street which symbolically represents the centre of Pedro's desire: 'Lombard street is the crookedest street in the USA, which I find interesting, because I pretty [well] don't much want anything straight in my life.' This thus recognises the central position that Pedro will play in the narrative, locating the house within a domain of 'non-straight' allusion. Similarly, housemate Puck is also identified in the opening episode as a possible masculine leader. He discusses his potential roommates, saying, 'None of [them] are going to be like me!', and is then seen to let a dog eat from his plate. This statement and action clearly position him in opposition to Pedro, who is often concerned with identifying his similarity to other members of the household and, because of his illness, necessarily has strict hygiene requirements. This opposition develops throughout the series as it increasingly reveals Puck's disrespect for Pedro, as well as Pedro's uneasiness in the presence of what – in relation to soap opera – Geraghty describes as the 'bastard figure' who represents 'an attempt to establish a strong male figure' in relation to other 'subordinate' groups in the text (1991: 103).

While Puck is presented in opposition to Pedro in *The Real World*, and Josh Rafter is presented in relation to Brian Dowling in *Big Brother 2* (discussed below), two males are presented in opposition to Lee Alexander in *Eden*: Chris Dean, who is seen to make comments concerning Lee's likely sexual orientation (and alleged lack of interest in the idea of marriage), and Westley Harris, who identifies Lee as an outsider who will disrupt the community. Chris and Westley may also be seen as oppositional to Lee in their display of camp behaviour/performance, suggesting that they are 'pretenders to be gay'. This illumination was partially stimulated by textual discourse from the outside world during production through the 'web hut', a jungle-like building with computer consoles for participants to read emails from the external world commenting on the series as it unfolds. In contrast to the imposed media isolation central to *Big Brother*, this potential dialogue between viewers and participants had significant implications in shaping the events, relationships and narratives in the text. The following web contribution concerns not only the gay sexuality of a forthcoming arrival (who incidentally is not elected by the public), but also established discourse on the forum concerning the potential (homo)sexuality of Westley.

[T]here's a gay guy up for [the] vote this week to join *Eden*, perhaps if he gets [in] then Wes will feel more relaxed and be himself!?!... If [Westley] is gay it's up to him if he tells [us].

(MadAdz, 2002)

The impending tension (the potential arrival of a gay man) which is foreshadowed in this quote reveals the discursive ambiguity in the dialogue deposited on the *Eden* web forum. In the case of Westley, suggestions as to his potential identity as a gay man were never answered either through his potential response in the web forum or in the show (although it was discussed by other participants) (Eve Kay, *Eden* series producer, personal interview, 10 July 2002). Similarly, the sexuality of Chris was also discussed, and related to the openly gay Lee Alexander on the web forum: 'Lee I don't care if you're gay...if you want to make friends why don't you go talk to Chris, he is secretly gay' (Sarah, 2002). Clearly such unfounded speculation may seem arbitrary, but the promulgation of this by observers to the *Eden* camp stimulated contemplation, and possibly inspired dramatic 'performance'. Evidence of this can be seen in the way in which the allegedly heterosexual Chris took on the character of 'Captain Camp' in the '*Eden* Superheroes' event – hence deliberately playing to the possibility of a 'camp' persona. Consequently, the infiltration of the web discourse into the televisual space not only potentially contributed to the audience reception of the show; it also had scope to influence narrative events in the text and the performance of 'characters' by the participants themselves. Here, however, the web discourse specifically inflected the construction and discussion of homosexuality in the text in ways which may not have occurred solely through the interpersonal interaction (and producer construction of) the contestants themselves.

Stereotypes, 'camp' and queer performance

Although Lee Alexander did not wish to represent himself as the stereotypical gay man by the use of overt camp performance, he did parody the idea in his participation in the 'Mr Eden' contest. In this event Lee appeared as a 'female' entertainer complete with make-up and a dress made of palm leaves. He addressed the audience by saying, 'I guess this place is a little too cheap for music, so I'll have to lip-synch on my own.' At the same time, he pouted in the manner of Marilyn Monroe without uttering a word. Through this display he implied that the action of imitating a woman is entirely unnatural for gay men. In a personal interview, he confirmed that this was an opportunity to 'protest' against the likely depiction of himself in stereotypical terms (Lee Alexander, personal interview, 24 July 2002). Through the use of parody, Lee engaged with ideas of stereotypical performance, but signalled these as ironic. In this way it could be suggested that he generated a queer performance in the service of deconstructing and challenging stereotypical identity structures, thereby 'repudiating views of identity as essence' (Seidman, 1993: 130).

While Lee Alexander and Pedro Zamora appeared to be aware of their identity (how they may be represented and how they should perform), Brian Dowling expressed doubts concerning this on *Big Brother*. Brian began questioning his plausibility as a 'real' gay man after the arrival of another gay man, Josh Rafter. Josh had not been selected as one of the original contestants by the producers, but was rather 'voted in' by the audience after the series commenced (the audience selected Josh over the other two potential candidates, who were both female). Josh's video introduction promised 'nocturnal naughtiness' and the promise of sexual display, although it is quite possible that he was voted in largely by a heterosexual female audience given that it was not necessarily assumed that he was gay. (Indeed, the female housemates initially also saw Josh as a potential sexual conquest until he revealed his sexuality.) Brian then personally reflected on the implications of Josh's arrival:

> I don't think that there is a problem with myself and Josh in the house. You know at the start it was weird having someone in here [who was also gay] because,...I felt I was being judged by another gay person. [I thought] if my parents [were watching], seeing him then seeing me, he would portray himself as a gay man much better than I could.
>
> (Brian Dowling, *Big Brother 2*, day 41)

Here we see Brian's expectation (shaped by the previous 'casting' of Reality TV) that he would be the only gay man in the house, while at the same time he acknowledges the 'burden' of representation associated with his identity (and already discussed in relation to soap opera). Brian's self-confessed insecurity in the presence of an older, more sexually experienced gay man is complicated by his belief that there is a cultural expectation (and hierarchy) involved in 'performing' as a gay man on television.

However, these self-reflexive insecurities may be deemed to be part of Brian's 'knowing' performance. His apparent adherence to established cultural traditions surrounding camp performance – his use of 'irony, aestheticism, theatricality and humour' (Babuscio, 1999) – reveals Brian's pre-established knowledge of performance expectations in this respect. His conformity to these expectations gained him popular support (for example, the *Mirror*, 27 July 2001, used its front page to encourage readers to vote for him to win) and enabled the start of a successful media career (he became a popular children's television presenter after winning the series). A montage of edited images and dialogue is provided by the producers in the final episode of the series (day 64), which explicitly foreground Brian's proclivity towards entertainment and camp evocation by emphasising incidents which involved costume and role-playing. The clips are edited in quick succession:

BRIAN: I am spoilt. I am arrogant. I am self absorbed. I am up my own arse....
    But now I've changed.
(Brian dressed as gypsy woman, flamenco dancing.)
(Brian sidles provocatively past a male housemate, dressed in a blonde wig, hat with false 'comedy' breasts which pull tightly at his t-shirt, revealing his stomach.)
BRIAN: (lying on the floor as if a scolded child) Who's the bitch in the kitchen? It's Josh, he's Satan's son.

(Big Brother 2, day 64)

Through this portfolio of theatrical antics, pantomime cross-dressing and child-like behaviour, Brian presents himself as a comic, if somewhat absurd, entertaining character for the audience's consumption. In this way Brian may be deemed to be fully aware that the show was 'constructed around performance' (Roscoe, 2001: 483), by actively referencing and building on many years of readily celebrated gay male camp performance seen on UK television (and potentially familiar to its audience).[15] Although Lee Alexander and Pedro Zamora may be seen as queer 'performers' (in their position as different to the mainstream audience), it is their display of resistance to stereotypes (unless used through irony) which sets them apart from Brian's performance. Although it may well be suggested that it is difficult to ascertain the concept of intention where irony is concerned, I would suggest here that Brian engages in queer/camp performance in a more unambiguous way, directly conforming to entertainment expectations, and thereby failing to challenge identity structures.

Brian's homosexual opposite, Josh Rafter, similarly performs a queer identity. However, unlike Brian, he is vicariously explored as an object of queer desire rather than as a site of family 'entertainment'. The producers arguably distance Brian from Josh, illuminating the safety of Brian and salivating at the 'otherness' of Josh. In this respect, then, they capitalise on the tension between them. This is highlighted in the edition including Josh's eviction from the house, where the programme seems to savour stereotypical ideas of materialistic gay lifestyle and gay sex. The producers here seem to work within a discursive framework of constructing an 'appropriate' (and hence 'safe') level of queer production for the pleasure of the audience (Doty, 1993). Extracts from the Josh eviction episode follow:

DAVINA MCCALL (host): Quite upset you're not wearing the £2,500 [Versace] trousers [that you wore in the house].

DAVINA: (discusses the occasion where Josh and Brian would dine together for a romantic evening)...Then there were you two in the bedroom...

(Edited sequence of romantic evening follows.)

JOSH: (proffering a bottle of wine to Brian) I'm ready to fill you up.

(Josh looks intense and drunk.)

BRIAN: Why do you look at me like that?

JOSH: I am looking at how good your skin is.

BRIAN: (ironically) Do you think it is good?

JOSH: It's fantastic! It's fantastic!...So are you going to give me a blow-job?

(Loud applause from the eviction-crowd audience.)

DAVINA: Brian found it incredibly threatening, because, I think, you are somebody he would like to be a few years on.

(*Big Brother 2*, day 50)

Davina McCall illuminates Josh's propensity to material excess, seen not only in his lavish expenditure on clothes but also in his obsession with the body and its senses. At the same time she indicates that although Brian is the 'darling of the audience' (and Josh is the 'villain') his eventual destiny may be to become like Josh 'a few years on'. This clearly introduces a further tension in the construction of the two men as it indicates that the camp and child-like behaviour of Brian (which renders him as a likeable, 'safe' gay man) is likely to ebb – with him subsequently becoming more sexually active and a possible threat to mainstream audiences' sensibility.

Without the mediation of Davina (celebrated heterosexual female) and Brian (cheery asexual camp performer), the construction of Josh within the frame of the narrative would be as an 'outsider' and 'other'. Consequently, he is only allowed to enter the equation through the dilution of Brian's 'reassuring' presence, and the promulgation of the 'safe', camp Brian is levied at the cost of subjugating Josh. In this way, the hostile audience response that Josh received as he departed the house (Brian's fans jeering and an unfavourable reception in the press) was not entirely unexpected.

Community, family and coupling

While Brian Dowling's performance involved itself with the economics of popular entertainment and Pedro Zamora's desire to educate the public displayed evidence of a struggle for recognition, Lee Alexander concerned himself with the ethics of competition. Lee won a place in *Eden* through a direct appeal to the television audience which emphasised his desire to 'play the game' and take the prize. While the audience was unaware of his sexuality before voting for him, all is revealed as he descends through the jungle to meet the established cast. Thus, tension is signalled by the arrival of a 'competitive' homosexual male about to join an apparently exclusive heterosexual coterie. His alleged intent to 'play the game' is cited as a reason for distrust:

(VOICEOVER: Lee's arrival is tearing the Eden family apart.)

WESTLEY: He is the only person that has come in and said they are coming for the money....I just hope it doesn't disrupt our little community that we have got going.

(*Eden*, day 53)

Through allusion to the idea of monetary gain, the cast consider their new guest as a disruptive influence on the security and cohesion of the 'little community'.

This creates a disparity which may be understood if we consider *Eden* as a reference to the classic coupling of man and woman (Adam and Eve) seen in the biblical account of the birth of mankind. *Eden* even paid homage to the idea of the coupling of man and woman when participants Johnny P and Kezia were the ersatz bride and groom in a ceremony which paid tribute to their relationship and the concept of marriage. All participants are seen to support the event and make enthusiastic preparations for the mock ceremony, with the implied exception of Lee:

(VOICEOVER: Everyone is excited by Eden's first wedding, except for Lee.)

(Lee depicted alone in jungle hammock, suggesting malaise.)

(VOICEOVER: For some reason the whole idea seems to have put him off.)

(The all-male mock stag night (without Lee) gets underway.)

TIMO: Let's join together [for a drinking toast], friendship, life and beautiful women.

(Later, the girls' hen party is provided with wine and cheese, the guys' stag party with beer and curry.)

CHRIS: Life is all about beer, curry and birds...

CHRIS: It's a shame Lee can't come and join us. (Sound of gas lamp as microphone strains to hear conversation.) He's probably reading or something. [Do you think the reason he is not here is because of] him being gay and not agreeing to marriage?

(*Eden*, day 76)

Through the suggestion that Lee is not interested in the marriage ceremony, the producers cite him as an outsider to the group. While the festivities are underway, heterocentric iconography is blatantly utilised to reinforce the idea of traditional, and separate, male/female identity (including the juxtaposition of gendered nourishment: female, cheese and wine; male, curry and beer). The textual meaning gravitates towards the idea that marriage is the central prerequisite for social enfranchisement, distancing Lee (as he does not wholeheartedly participate) from the centre of 'normal' social engagement.

In similar terms this occurs in *Big Brother 2*. While the depiction of Helen and Paul (the series' romance) at the 'romantic evening' coupling event is highlighted as serious (respect for each other, plans for the future and 'natural' sexual tension), the pairing of Josh and Brian is in part intended to be ironic. Their self-confessed disrespect for each other (and the evident tension produced) indicates that this is a textual device to *parody* the idea of romantic engagement, indicating the concept of homosexual desire as amusing within this context. Consequently, similarly to the wedding in *Eden*, this recognises the idea of partnership, but places this as off limits within the context of gay identity. Christine Geraghty explains how the soap opera provides 'the ritual of the wedding to overcome difficulties' within the community (1991: 89), and it consequently becomes an event to bring people together (although also often simultaneously providing the context for further narrative disruption). Although *Big Brother 2* and *Eden* trade in these ideas (Brian and Josh may be brought together to resolve issues, and the Edenites may convene to engender a sense of community after conflict and disruption), they place the potential of the coupling event within the exclusive domain of the heterosexual. Conversely, *The RealWorld* subverts this strategy and uses the idea of the wedding to focus on the only enduring romance of the series – between two men.

The Real World same-sex 'marriage' ceremony is treated sympathetically, generating the idea that it is equivalent to a heterosexual marriage. The textual placement of this juxtaposes a comparative heterosexual relationship between Puck (who was earlier voted out of the house after untenable conflict between himself and Pedro) and Toni, who are depicted attending and participating in a popular event: a soapbox rally. Sentimental speeches are made at Pedro and Sean's wedding, the partners kiss and hold hands and rings are exchanged, all of which is complemented with the usual applause and praise from the guests. The climax is a speech from a guest, Eric:

> In your love you remind us that life is about now, and love is about being there for another. I think that it is with real bravery that you open your hearts to each other and I think that it is with real hope that you promise your lives to each other, and we stand defiantly and bravely, and with real hope.
>
> (*The RealWorld*, episode 19)

Although there is a dramatic emphasis on 'bravery' and time 'as it exists in the present', the representation of Pedro and Sean is clearly elevated and celebrated. At the same time, and in contrast, the representation of the romance between Puck and Toni is only related in the most arbitrary way (casual terms, no serious commitment to life partnership). Although Munoz argues that this comparison was made by the producers as they could not 'let a queer coupling, especially one as radical as [this] stand as the show's actual romance' (1998: 190), it is apparent that the comparison between these two sites of potential love clearly elevates the homosexual above the heterosexual – indeed potentially enabling it to become the show's 'actual romance'. While *The Real World* attempts to break stereotypes surrounding gay identity and marriage, and *Big Brother 2* parodies the potential for romantic love, *Eden* – although locating its homosexual as an outsider to the idea of marriage – offers the potential for resolution.

Lee Alexander's position as someone who apparently 'fails' to integrate with the idea of marriage creates a disparity which threatens the heterosexual verisimilitude of the 'drama'. Invoking the work of Dolan (1989) and Sinfield (1990), Clum argues:

> If there is an enigma in realism, its structural shape is bent towards unravelling and expunging [disharmonious identities].... In a structure in which the homosexual is inevitably...'the outlaw-intruder who threatens the security of characters, and by inference the audience', the purging of the homosexual gives the play closure.
>
> (Clum, 2000: 78)

As this quote suggests, while the purging of the homosexual for playwrights may require the death of the 'outlaw' character to restore normality, in the case of *Eden*'s Lee closure may require a less brutal action – that of capitulation or recognition. Consequently, it may be seen that this is attempted in *Eden* through the intimation that Lee does indeed recognise, and possibly aspire to, the 'crucible' of heterosexual design (marriage). Evidence of this may be seen at the wedding reception (day 77), where the mounting tension is addressed and Lee informs the group: 'Sadly I'm not allowed to get married.... I like the idea of spending your life with one person, and being committed, and what [marriage] stands for.' This marks the climax of a series of events which relate to Lee's original veiled signification as outsider (initially portrayed as material desire, but potentially relating to his sexuality). Through this act of confession the 'outsider identity' is tentatively purged. The testament that he accepts the basic tenets of heterosexual society (to aspire to marry, even if it is with a man) thus engenders his provisional acceptance by the group.

While Lee has to earn his place within the group, Brian of *Big Brother 2* has equally to conform to certain expectations – to play an entertainment, rather than a sexual, role associated with homosexuality – to achieve popular support. At the same time, while Pedro Zamora in *The Real World* appears to be readily accepted, this only occurs as he respects certain dominant social traditions, such as the humanitarian ethos of concern for the sick, and because of his intention to follow a dedicated relationship with a partner. In this way, all the texts display a need for performers to engage and operate meaningfully within dominant/ heterosexual ideologies – structures, of course, which are also evident in the related genres of the talk show and soap opera.

Nevertheless, unlike *Big Brother 2* and *Eden*, which may seem retrograde in political/cultural terms (requiring the participants to subjectively 'fit in' and/or entertain), a progressive opportunity was provided by *The Real World* in casting Pedro Zamora:

> The scene of two men of color, both HIV positive [Pedro's partner Sean was of black American descent], in bed together as they plan what is the equivalent of a marriage is like none that was then or now imaginable on television.
>
> (Munoz, 1998: 189)

This groundbreaking representation of non-Caucasian gay men in love,[16] who at the same time had to personally confront the issue of AIDS, became a highly politi- cised image. Zamora's appearance represented 'resistance to discrimination and...a strong rejection of "victim-hood" status' (Watney, 2000: 261). As a young man and a Cuban immigrant, his contribution also addressed issues concerning the spread of disease among youths (Brownworth, 1992) and the Latino community (Diaz, 1998). Furthermore, the appearance of a contented, loving homosexual relation- ship challenged entertainment expectations by temporally displacing gay identity as a cultural 'other' and sympathetically locating it firmly in the heartland of heterosexual engagement (the domain of romantic love).

Conclusion: following *The Real World*

In the construction of the 'reflexive reality environment', producers and performers both possess ambivalent power to suggest the definition of the 'normal', the 'extraordinary', the 'entertaining' and the periphery of 'everyday' existence. While it may not be possible for Reality TV (or of course documentary) to represent 'reality' – for 'the closer one gets to the document itself the more aware one becomes of the artifice and the impossibility of a satisfactory relation- ship between the image and the real' (Bruzzi, 2000: 21) – it is nevertheless desirable to produce images which may provide positive messages for those living in the social group represented.

However, the estimation of what form 'positive' or 'realistic' images should take is necessarily subjective. In the case of Brian Dowling and *Big Brother 2* 'posi- tive imagery' may be associating gay identity with entertainment value; for Pedro

Zamora and *The Real World* it may be emphasising the nature of human relation-ships. We must accept that Reality TV produces gay identities of varying form, which may or may not match the expectations of the producers or the audience. As Charlotte Brunsdon argues when discussing the issue of the 'real' (in soap opera), the representation of the 'real world' is contentious, as 'arguing for more realistic images is always an argument for the representation of "your" version of reality' (Brunsdon, 1997: 28). Consequently, it is evident that contemporary reality texts should 'be evaluated [more] in terms of how well they express a diversity of public voices and challenge the established power to recognise the complexities of everyday life' (Livingstone and Lunt, 1994: 35), rather than the extent to which they provide us with 'realistic' or 'positive' representations.

With its 11-year history of presenting gay identities within the reality 'house-hold', *The Real World* arguably offers such diversity. The casting of Zamora in the third series was a progressive move. This suggested not only that *The Real World* producers may have a political agenda (Grubbs, 2002), but that they may also live up to their claim that 'drama [and growth] would come from diversity' (Solomon and Carter, 1997: 5). In order for contemporary Reality TV to live up to this, and to potentially challenge 'outmoded' stereotypical ideas, it is necessary for producers to follow *The Real World*'s example and recognise the 'social expecta-tions' of gay participants (which may include relationship potential and social responsibility), as much as encouraging their value as entertainers or performers.

The precedence of *The Real World* appears to have encouraged contemporary producers of Reality TV to include gay participants as regular cast members. The presence of the gay citizen as a welcome guest in the reality household is both progressive and stimulating. Despite this, we must remember that this is a rela-tively new occurrence, and its prescription is for media entertainment. The longevity of the discourse may depend on the producers' enduring interest and the potential that gay participants may provide for entertainment. The transient nature of power relations, in Foucauldian terms, tells us that 'power can flow very quickly from one point or area to another, depending on changing alliances and circumstances' (Danaher *et al.*, 2000: 71). Cultural endurance, and meaning, is fluid. As Foucault once said: 'Do not ask me who I am, and do not ask me to remain the same' (1972: 17). In the same way, for the access offered to gay participants on contemporary television, it should not be presumed that a return to residence in the basement is entirely out of the question.

Notes

1   This is not to say that there have not been progressive films in recent times, for example the adaptation of the Jonathan Harvey play *Beautiful Thing* (Hettie MacDonald, 1996, UK) depicts a teenage gay male romance as a central story and *The Broken Hearts Club: A Romantic Comedy* (Greg Berlanti, 2000, US) depicts a central cast of gay characters

who are competent at basketball. However, these are the exceptions to the rule. Similarly, while TV drama has developed its commitment to depict gay characters (Pullen, 2000) and some soap operas (discussed below) have experimented with integrating gay identities, high-profile television drama series such as *Queer as Folk* (C4, 1999–2000, UK; Showtime, 2000–, US) and the situation comedy *Will and Grace* (NBC, 1998–, US) have placed their emphasis on sexual activity and/or entertainment value.

2 It is important to note that emphasising difference has been an important aspect of Queer Cinema (Hayward, 1996: 296), and this can be productive in an arena where gay people are in control of producing the text (heightening visibility). However, as queer theorists 'have protested against the very notion of identity' (Warner, 1993: xx), this idea does not sit easily with a text produced for popular television, which necessarily needs to relate to overarching mainstream identity structures (Pullen, 2000).

3 Ricardo, Oliver, John and AJ were openly gay cast members in *The Salon*, a Reality TV series set in a London beauty spa and hairdressers (although one that was constructed entirely for the programme itself).

4 Will Young 'came out' as gay in an article titled 'I Think It's Time My Fans Knew the Truth' published by the *News of the World* on 10 March 2002.

5 Gay people have been integrated in many Reality TV texts. If we take *Survivor* and *Big Brother* alone we can cite a number of openly gay contestants besides those discussed in this text: Brandon Quinton, *Survivor Africa* (US, 2001); John Carroll, *Survivor Marquesas* (US, 2002); Zoë Lyons, *Survivor* (UK, 2000); Bill 'Bunkie' Miller, *Big Brother* (US, 2000); Anna Nolan, *Big Brother* (UK, 2000); Adele Roberts (bisexual), *Big Brother 3* (UK, 2002); Johnnie Cass, *Big Brother* (Australia, 2001).

6 Clause 28 outlawed the 'promotion' of homosexuality in British schools, it became law as part of the Local Government Act in 1988 (Howes, 1993: 124).

7 Gay participants in *The Real World* to date have been: Norman Korpi (New York, 1992), Beth Anthony (Los Angeles, 1993), Pedro Zamora (San Franciso, 1994), Dan Renzi (Miami, 1996), Genesis Moss (Boston, 1997), Ruthie Alcaide and Justin Deabler (Hawaii, 1999), Jason Daniel 'Danny' Roberts (New Orleans, 2000), Chris Beckham and Aneesa Ferreira (Chicago, 2002), Simon (Paris, 2003).

8 Craig Gilbert, producer of *An American Family*, advises us that inspiration for the series may have originated in the observational film documentary *A Married Couple* (Allan King, 1969, Canada) (Ruoff, 2002: 12).

9 MTV represents gay identity with equality. This may be seen in an advertising campaign titled 'Do You Speak MTV?' which included an advert featuring both heterosexual and homosexual couples in amorous engagement (Commercial Closet, 2003).

10 It is interesting to note that *The Living Soap* became the title of a contentious copy of *The Real World* format, which was broadcast by the BBC in 1994 in the UK.

11 Enns and Smit (1999) argue against the potential of social diversity in *The Real World*.

12 This was also broadcast in the UK, premiering on MTV in 1994 and Channel 4 in 1996.

13 Pedro Zamora sadly died from complications with AIDS on 11 November 1994 – immediately after *The Real World* was broadcast in the US.

14 This kind of textual prediction is possible in *The Real World* as the production process is lengthy, bringing together material filmed over a number of weeks (Tracy Chaplin, Producer of *The Real World*, personal interview, 2003). In comparison, *Big Brother* and *Eden* generally produce and broadcast material on a daily basis as the narratives evolve.

15 John Inman and Larry Grayson were the mainstay of British camp humour in the 1970s, known for their effeminate and theatrical humour. Later, Julian Clary and Graham Norton took on this proclivity while foregrounding acerbic dynamics and confrontational humour.

16 Similarly *The Real World* New Orleans (2000) presents 'subjectively illicit' male homosexual coupling, in presenting Danny Roberts and Paul, a member of the US military. Paul is not allowed to be identified due to military legislation and hence his identity is concealed through a blurring of his face throughout the series.

References

Anonymous (2002) 'I Think It's Time My Fans Knew the Truth', *News of the World*, 10 March.

Babuscio, Jack (1999) 'The Cinema of Camp (*AKA* Camp and Gay Sensibility)', in Fabio Cleto (ed.) *Camp: Queer Aesthetics and the Performing Subject: A Reader*, Ann Arbor, MI: University of Michigan Press.

BBC (2002) Unpublished index of *Kilroy* editions: 1987–2002, provided by Julie Snelling of the Written Archives Centre, BBC, London.

Bourne, Stephen (1996) *Brief Encounters: Lesbians and Gays in British Cinema 1930–1971*, London: Cassell.

Brownworth, Victoria A. (1992) 'America's Worst Kept Secret: AIDS Is Devastating the Nation's Teenagers, and Gay Kids Are Dying by the Thousands', *Advocate*, 24 March: 38–46.

Brunsdon, Charlotte (1997) *Screen Tastes: Soap Opera to Satellite Dishes*, London: Routledge.

Bruzzi, Stella (2000) *New Documentary: A Critical Introduction*, London: Routledge.

Burnett, Mark, with Martin Dugard (2000) *Survivor: The Official Companion Book*, New York: TV Books.

Caldwell, John (2002) 'Prime Time Fiction Theorises The Docu-Real', in James Friedman (ed.) *Reality Squared: Televisual Discourses on the Real*, New Brunswick, N.J.: Rutgers University Press.

Capsuto, Steven (2000) *Alternate Channels: The Uncensored Story of Gay and Lesbian Images on Radio and Television*, New York: Balantine Books.

Clum, John M. (2000) *Still Acting Gay*, New York: St Martin's Griffin.

Commercial Closet (2003) ' "Language of Love" Do You Speak MTV?'; available at http://www2.commercialcloset.org/cgi-bin/iowa/portrayals.html?record=474 (accessed 15 March 2003).

Corner, John (2002) 'Performing the Real: Documentary Diversion', *Television and New Media* 3(3): 255–69.

Couldry, Nick (2002) 'Playing for Celebrity: *Big Brother* as Ritual Event', *Television and New Media* 3(3): 283–93.

Danaher, Geoff, Tony Schirato and Jenn Webb (2000) *Understanding Foucault*, London: Sage.

Diaz, Rafael. M. (1998) *Latino Men and HIV: Culture, Sexuality and Risk Behaviour*, New York: Routledge.

Dolan, Jill (1989) 'Lesbian Subjectivity in Realism: Dragging at the Margins of Structure and Ideology', in Sue-Ellen Case (ed.) *Performing Feminisms: Feminist Critical Theory and Theatre*, Baltimore, MD: John Hopkins Press.

Doty, Alexander (1993) *Making Things Perfectly Queer: Interpreting Mass Culture*, Minneapolis, MN: University of Minnesota Press.

Dovey, Jon (2000) *Freakshow: First Person Television and Factual Media*, London: Pluto.

Dyer, Richard (1984) 'Stereotyping', in Richard Dyer (ed.) *Gays and Film* (revised edition), New York: Zoetrope.

Dyer, Richard (1986) *Heavenly Bodies: Film Stars and Society*, London: Routledge.

Dyer, Richard (2000) *The Matter of Images* (second edition), London: Routledge.

Dyer, Richard (2002) *The Culture of Queers*, London: Routledge.

Enns, Anthony and Christopher R. Smit (1999) 'The Corruption of Diversity in MTV's *The Real World*', *Studies in Popular Culture* 22(1): October: 15–26.

Finch, Mark (1999) 'Sex and Address in *Dynasty*', in Fabio Cleto (ed.) *Camp: Queer Aesthetics and the Performing Subject: A Reader*, Ann Arbor, MI: University of Michigan Press.

Foucault, Michel (1972) *The Archaeology of Knowledge*, New York: Pantheon Books.

Gamson, Joshua (1998) *Freaks Talk Back: Tabloid Talk Shows and Sexual Nonconformity*, Chicago: Chicago University Press.

Geraghty, Christine (1991) *Women and Soap Opera: A Study of Prime Time Soaps*, Cambridge: Polity Press.

Grubbs, Jim (2002) 'New Channels: *The Real World* as Social Movement', unpublished dissertation, University of Illinois.

Hall, Stuart (1997) 'The Spectacle of the "Other"', in Stuart Hall (ed.) *Representation: Cultural Representations and Signifying Practices*, London: Open University Press/Sage.

Hayward, Susan (1996) *Key Concepts in Cinema Studies*, London, Routledge.

Hill, Annette (2002) '*Big Brother*: The Real Audience', *Television and New Media* 3(3): 323–41.

Howes, Keith (1993) *Broadcasting It: An Encyclopaedia of Homosexuality on Film, Radio and TV in the UK 1923–1933*, London: Cassell.

Johnson, Hillary and Nancy Rommelmann (1995) *The Real RealWorld*, New York: Simon & Schuster.

Livingstone, Sonia and Peter Lunt (1994) *Talk on Television: Audience Participation and Public Debate*, London: Routledge.

MadAdz (2002) 'Wesley. *Vote the OTHER GAY man in!!!*', Channel4.com *Eden* website forum on 6 February 2002; available at http://www.channel4.com/forums/c4—forumframeset.cfm?forum=edenite—6 (accessed 12 February 2002).

Meers, Erik (2002) 'Keeping it Real', *Advocate*, 30 April: 38–46.

Morgenthaler, Eric (1991) 'Pedro's Story: Teen with AIDS Virus Tries to Teach Youths Some Lessons for Life', *Wall Street Journal*, 4 September.

Mulvey, Laura (1985) 'Visual Pleasure and Narrative Cinema', in Tony Bennett, Susan Boyd-Bowman, Colin Mercer and Jane Wollacott (eds) *Popular Television and Film*, London: Open University Press.

Munoz, Jose Esteban (1998) 'Pedro Zamora's Real World of Counterpublicity: Performing an Ethics of the Self', in Sylvia Molly and Robert McKee Irwin (eds) *Hispanisms and Homosexualities*, Durham, NC: Duke University Press.

Pullen, Christopher (2000) 'The Performance of Identity through Confession: Considering the Contemporary Identity of Gay Men and Women on Television', unpublished master's dissertation, University of Bristol.

Ritchie, Jean (2001) *Big Brother 2: The Official Unseen Story*, London, Channel 4 Books.

Roscoe, Jane (2001) 'Big Brother Australia: Performing the "Real" Twenty-four-seven', *International Journal of Cultural Studies*, 4(4): 473–88.

Ruoff, Jeffrey (2002) *An American Family: A Televised Life*, Minneapolis, MN: University of Minnesota Press.

Russo, Vito (1987) *The Celluloid Closet* (revised edition), New York: Harper & Row.

Sarah (2002) 'Lee. *So what?*', Channel4.com *Eden* website forum on 19 March 2002; available at http://www.channel4.com/forums/c4—forumframeset.cfm?forum=edenite—13 (accessed 10 April 2002).

Seidman, Steven (1993) 'Identity and Politics in a Postmodern Gay Culture', in Mark Warner (ed.) *Fear of a Queer Planet*, Minneapolis, MN: University of Minnesota Press.

Shattuc, Jane (1997) *The Talking Cure: TV Talk Shows and Women*, New York and London: Routledge.

Sinfield, Alan (1990) 'Closet Dramas: Homosexual Representation and Class in Postwar Theatre', *Genders* 9: 113–31.

Solomon, James and Alan Carter (1997) *The Real World: The Ultimate Insider's Guide*, New York: Simon & Schuster.

Sontag, Susan (1989) *AIDS and Its Metaphors*, New York: Farrar, Strauss & Giroux.

Suderberg, Erika (1997) 'Real/Young/TV Queer', in Chris Holmlund and Cynthia Fuchs (eds) *Between the Sheets, In the Streets: Queer, Lesbian, Gay Documentary*, Minneapolis, MN: University of Minnesota Press.

Summerskill, Ben (2002) 'And Your New Pop Idol is... Will', *Observer*, 10 February.

Tincknell, Estella and Parvati Raghuram (2002) '*Big Brother*: Refiguring the "Active" Audience of Cultural Studies', *European Journal of Cultural Studies*, 5(2): 199–215.

Tolson, Andrew (ed.) (2001) *Television Talk Shows: Discourse, Performance, Spectacle*, Mahwah, NJ: Lawrence Erlbaum.

van Zoonen, Liesbet (2001) 'Desire and Resistance: *Big Brother* and the Recognition of Everyday Life', *Media Culture and Society*, 23: 669–77.

Warner, Mark (1993) 'Introduction', in Mark Warner (ed.) *Fear of a Queer Planet*, Minneapolis, MN: University of Minnesota Press.

Watney, Simon (2000) *Imagine Hope: AIDS and Gay Identity*, London: Routledge.

Weeks, Jeffrey (1995) *Invented Moralities*, New York: Columbia University Press.

11

'IT ISN'T ALWAYS SHAKESPEARE, BUT IT'S GENUINE'

Cinema's commentary on documentary hybrids

Craig Hight

Recent critical debates over the social, political and cultural significance of documentary hybrid forms[1] such as Reality TV, docu-soaps and reality game shows have been characterised by quite marked divisions. One end of this critical spectrum has tended to decry the 'perversion' (Nichols, 1994: 51) of documentary's agenda which such texts appear to entail, with commentators expressing various levels of alarm at the abandonment of well-established ethical and aesthetic standards of documentary production. Here, documentary is seen to have fallen from its privileged social-political position to become simply another entertainment genre. On the opposite pole of these debates is a recognition of the elitist assumptions which are often bound up with critical commentary, and a consequent tendency to acknowledge the significance of documentary hybrids as cultural texts in part precisely because of their popularity.

Underlying these divisions is a fundamental disagreement over the proper relationship between notions of the 'public' and popular cultural forms; with the manner in which documentary *should* be engaging with social and political practice. In Corner's words, 'a degree of ambivalence is often a defining feature of academic commentary [on hybrids], as the diverse commercial and socio-cultural dimensions of the "popular" seem to resist neat separation' (2002: 267). This critical ambivalence is partly derived from an absence within documentary theory of a detailed understanding of the nature of viewer engagement with hybrid forms (Blumler, 1999; Dovey, 2000; Corner, 2001; Roscoe and Hight, 2001) – itself a continuation of the neglect of audience understandings within research into the documentary genre as a whole. To a large extent, commentators' arguments over hybrids have consequently been forced to rely on their *speculations* on how viewers interpret and respond to such forms.

Cinematic representations of hybrids offer a distinctive contribution to these debates. In part, cinema collectively offers one site in which debates concerning television are popularised, with individual texts drawing upon and visualising arguments concerning hybrids. This chapter looks at the manner in which such discourses are played out in three key cinematic texts offering commentaries on documentary hybrids: *The Truman Show* (Peter Weir, 1998, US), *EDtv* (Ron Howard, 1999, US) and *Series 7:The Contenders* (Daniel Minahan, 2001, US).These three are by no means the only recent films which represent debates over documentary hybrids, but collectively they do suggest something of the range and complexity of recent cinematic discourse on the social and cultural significance of such forms. These films all incorporate critiques of the heavily commercialist institutional agenda which frames hybrids as media products, and the various levels of exploitation, manipulation and explicit 'distortion of reality' which are seen to typify their construction as texts. However, in various ways these three films also express a recognition of the cultural significance of hybrid forms, and it is the form of that recognition that suggests the significance of these films' contribution to debates over hybrids and more generally television itself. This chapter argues, in particular, that cinematic texts offering commentary on hybrid forms can be seen as a key site where tensions between competing constructions of hybrid audiences are played out.

While cinematic texts have been willing to deconstruct the agenda and form of television formats, because of their own need to secure large general audiences they also tend to avoid promoting more in-depth critiques of the nature and role of media *as a whole* within contemporary society. In other words, cinematic texts which offer commentaries on documentary hybrids have tended to reflect their own particular ambivalence toward these television forms. This is an ambivalence which, while derived from a different agenda, is centred on the same uneasiness and confusion over the precise nature of hybrids' appeal to their *audiences* which characterises critical and theoretical debates.

Cinematic commentary on television

Before considering these three films in detail, it is useful to position their specific commentaries in relation to the long tradition within cinema of critical examinations of television – examining television as an institution, as a distinct medium and as an increasingly significant feature of everyday social practices. There is a small body of existing work on cinematic representations of television; for example Barr, 1986; Anderson, 1991; Stokes, 1999. This work has examined how cinema has regularly developed representations of its 'rival', partly as a means of differentiating its own status from other media, and more typically as a means of reinforcing popular notions of itself as an art form in contrast to the 'low culture' of television.[2] It is extremely difficult to summarise all of the various aspects of this wider cinematic discourse on television, and for the purposes of this chapter the discussion below looks to suggest only some of its outlines. I have also chosen to focus only on films from the early 1990s up to 2002, those that begin to offer more distinctive arguments over the nature of television's position within the contemporary, electronically mediated society. The discussions below are intended only to suggest the broadest tendencies of cinematic discourse on television, and in such a way that suggests specific linkages with the emerging discourse on documentary hybrids that are represented in films such as *The Truman Show*, *EDtv* and *Series 7*.

First, it needs to be recognised that in the broadest terms cinema's representation of television has tended to be a negative one, although there still exists a spectrum of critique. In specific terms, mainstream American cinema has tended to target television for its specific institutional practices, the form and nature of its address to audiences, and to reinforce a simplistic and negative effects model of television's social and cultural impact. A key reference point for both the full range of cinematic commentaries on television broadcasting and especially the more recent crop of films which deal specifically with documentary hybrids (such as *The Truman Show*, *EDtv* and *Series 7*) is Sidney Lumet's *Network* (1976, US).

In *Network*, Howard Beale (Peter Finch) plays a network news presenter at UBS–TV, a fictional network struggling to survive against the real ABC, NBC and CBS. When Beale is told he will be fired in two weeks, he announces that he will kill himself on live television. Capitalising on Beale's sensational announcement, the network's executives transform their flagship nightly news programme into a combination of variety show and evangelical broadcast. Beale, promoted as the 'Mad Prophet of the Airwaves' becomes a cultural phenomenon with his live proclamations against the social, political and economic role played by television in America. *Network* articulates a comprehensive critique of the political economy of television, providing a perspective on the development of factual television programming which anticipates a core part of the critiques that later films would make of documentary hybrids.

A key thematic problem which *Network* represents is the same one which appears throughout cinematic discourse on television (and most markedly in representations of documentary hybrids): how to critique television as a medium without directly attacking viewers who are likely to also form the audience for the film itself. This dilemma perhaps underlies any critique of popular forms which is itself aimed at a wide audience, but, as mentioned above, it also explains the often marked ambivalence which cinematic texts exhibit towards television (including hybrid forms). *Network*, however, goes further than most other subsequent cinematic critiques, as Beale admonishes both a rapt studio audience and his millions of viewers:

> You people sit there day after day, night after night, all ages, colours, creeds. We're all you know. You're beginning to believe the illusions

we're spinning here. You're beginning to think that the tube is reality and that your own lives are unreal. You do whatever the tube tells you. You dress like the tube, you eat like the tube, you raise your children like the tube, you even think like the tube. This is madness, you maniacs!

(Howard Beale, in *Network*)

To an ultimately limited extent, the film challenges its viewers to recognise themselves in the television audiences portrayed in the film. It constructs the (American) television audience as having both an unhealthy fascination with the scandalous and the shocking, and a short attention span. The film does not pretend to offer a solution for its own pessimistic perspective on the television wasteland that it constructs, and the film ends with Beale's on-air death, engineered by television executives, which becomes just another sensational, and meaningless, image within television metadiscourse. In this way the film also presages a recurrent and emotive line of critique circulating around Reality TV which fears its quest for ratings will continue to reconfigure the boundaries of television to such a degree that ultimately no experience or event will be off limits to the camera.

The various strains of *Network*'s critique of television have been taken up, in much milder form, in subsequent films. Few of these films attempt anything near the depth of social and political critique (however ultimately limited) that this film achieved. For the purposes of this discussion they can easily be seen to fall generally into those that deal with aspects of the institutional practices of television, those that examine the form of the medium itself, and those that explore its social and political impact within modern America through a commentary on television viewers.

There are any number of films which attempt an indictment of the political economy of television, critiquing for example the commercialist agenda behind the game show scandals of the late 1950s (*Quiz Show*, Robert Redford, 1994, US), the appropriation and exploitation of young talent (*Wayne's World*, Penelope Spheeris, 1992, US; and *Reality Bites*, Ben Stiller, 1994, US) or the marginalisation of African-Americans (*Bamboozled*, Spike Lee, 2000, US). There are also films which have focused more specifically on representing the nature of factual television production, and these offer perspectives which are more directly linked to recent film commentaries on documentary hybrids. *Broadcast News* (James L. Brooks, 1987, US), for example, adopts the broad themes of *Network* but is considerably more muted in tone, and consequently in its satiric potential. Essentially a romantic comedy set within the production offices of a local network news production office, many of the film's more pointed barbs are aimed at the increasingly commercial environment in which its characters must operate. *Bob Roberts* (Tim Robbins, 1992, US) uses the mock-documentary form to develop a satiric examination of media practices and their role within the American political system. The film constructs American news media as corrupt, sanitised, trivialised and sensationalist in their coverage of political campaigns, and incapable of dealing with the degree of sophistication and subtlety exhibited by modern political candidates. A more common personification of television's news approach is found in *Die Hard* (John McTiernan, 1988, US), which offers a characterisation of the tabloid television reporter clearly drawing upon familiar stereotypes. Played here by William Atherton, he is amoral, exploitative, unliked by colleagues, and will use whatever methods he can to get a 'scoop'. A more complex portrayal is found in the recent *No Man's Land* (Danis Tanovic, 2001, Bosnia-Herzegovina), which has Katrin Cartlidge as a reporter who, pushed by distant producers to get visual material of the United Nations peacekeeping mission in the former Yugoslavia, becomes a largely ignorant pawn in a game of multinational politics.

For the purposes of this discussion, the most interesting range of cinematic commentaries on television are those which develop pointed critiques of aspects of the relationship between the medium and its audience. As suggested above, many critical discourses on documentary hybrids draw on narrow understandings of their relationships with their audience, and cinematic commentaries on television operate within a similar well-established tradition of the dismissal of viewers. Collectively, these films develop simplistic constructions of television viewers, articulating especially the assumptions behind an effects model of spectatorship. The themes which are most commonly explored here are the medium's appeal to the passive and simple-minded (*Being There*, Hal Ashby, 1979, US); the distorting nature of a television-induced fame (*The King of Comedy*, Martin Scorsese, 1983, US; and *To Die For*, Gus van Sant, 1995, US); the 'dangerous' effects of exposure to television (*The Cable Guy*, Ben Stiller, 1996, US); and the stereotypical concept of an 'addiction' to television (*Videodrome*, David Cronenberg, 1983, US/Canada). These dysfunctional characters are constructed as having more extreme versions of the characteristics that most mainstream television viewers are assumed to share – we are meant to recognise something of ourselves in their motivations, but also to be able to laugh at the extremity of their actions.

In *The King of Comedy*, Robert De Niro is Robert Pupkin, a wannabe comedian on a single-minded quest for television fame, who kidnaps Jerry Langford (Jerry Lewis) in order to feature on his talk show. Prefiguring the more recent and expansive rise of a 'celebrity culture' that Reality TV is very much bound up in, television is implicated as both the inspiration for his extreme behaviour and an obvious benefactor, as Pupkin eventually emerges as a television star, despite his lack of talent. *To Die For* presents the story of Suzanne Maretto (Nicole Kidman), a weather girl for a small local television station who manipulates two local teenagers into killing her husband when he looks to stifle her considerable ambitions. Maretto's bizarre mantra is that 'you're not anybody in American unless you're on TV'. She mouths platitudes about the significance of television as an instigator of a global community, statements which simply mask an extreme form of narcissism that is reinforced and fed by media exposure. Home-movie footage of Maretto as a young girl shows her immediate fascination, and the beginnings of her obsession, when she recognises herself on a television screen. Like Pupkin, her character is partly constructed as merely an extreme manifestation of the assumed desire of many television viewers to have their lives legitimated through an appearance on the medium.

All of the tendencies toward critical representation of aspects of the personnel, practices and audiences of television which are (briefly) outlined above return with a vengeance within films that contribute to a cinematic discourse on documentary hybrids. Outside the three texts which are the specific focus of this chapter, there is a range of films with commentaries all suggesting a denigratory perception of documentary hybrids. An interesting instance is *Real Life* (Albert Brooks, 1979, US), which draws its inspiration especially from prototypical docu-soap *An American Family* (PBS, 1973, US) to savage what it perceives to be the exploitative and superficial agenda behind such early versions of hybrid formats. Here, Albert Brooks plays a director who looks to explore the lives of a typical American family for an entire year, but cannot resist manipulating their reality to make for a more compelling film.

The more recent *Natural Born Killers* (Oliver Stone, 1994, US), *15 Minutes* (John Herzfeld, 2001, US) and *Showtime* (Tom Dey, 2002, US) all present constructions of tabloid television programming that are projections of existing tendencies within particularly American mainstream television. Both *Natural Born Killers* and *15 Minutes* make familiar, although ultimately simplistic, arguments about the manner in which television shapes the reality of sensational crimes. One of *Natural Born Killer*'s secondary characters is Wayne Gale (Robert Downey Jr), the host of *American Maniacs*, a tabloid series on serial killers which deliberately generates such figures as media phenomena, then exploits their notoriety. And *15 Minutes* features a show called *Top Story*, hosted by Robert Hawkins (Kelsey Grammer) and obviously derived from tabloid news programmes such as *Hard Copy* (1989–, US), as one of a series of hybrid programmes which provide direct inspiration for the killing spree of recent Eastern European immigrants Oleg (Oleg Taktarov) and Emil (Karel Roden). Hawkins personifies the unethical and amoral perspective of tabloid journalism and continues the tradition of negative portrayal of television journalists featured in films such as *Die Hard*. The most comprehensive satires constructed specifically in response to hybrid forms, however, are *The Truman Show*, *EDtv* and *Series 7: The Contenders*. The key to their perspectives is that they offer constructions of hybrid forms which take existing premises of hybrid programming and extrapolate them to apparently logical (but patently absurd) ends.

The Truman Show, *EDtv* and *Series 7:*
The Contenders as satire

The Truman Show is the most explicit of these three films in its engagement with social and cultural debates surrounding the significance of hybrid forms, using particularly the cathartic journey of its main character to articulate concerns about the implications of his global television celebrity. The 'Truman Show' of the title is the ultimate docu-soap, with Truman Burbank (Jim Carrey) the only person who remains unaware of his starring role. He is the target of 5,000 cameras, operating 24 hours a day to record every single moment of his life within an enormous studio set. The film opens with a mock-documentary sequence constructed as a news story on the Truman phenomenon, and here the programme's creator, Christof (Ed Harris) offers a pat explanation for the popularity of the show:

> We've become bored with watching actors give us phony emotions. We've tired of pyrotechnics and special effects. While the world he inhabits is, in some respects, counterfeit, there's nothing fake about Truman himself. No scripts. No cue cards. It isn't always Shakespeare, but it's genuine. It's a life.

> (Christof, in *The Truman Show*)

This nicely expresses both any hybrid's rhetorical lip-service to documentary's assumed status as a 'window on reality' and also the level of construction which is central to any form of docu-soap. The actor who plays Truman's best friend 'Marlon' (Louis Coltrane) then insists: 'It's all true, it's all real. Nothing here is fake. Nothing you see on this show is fake. It's merely controlled.'

The Truman Show is largely set within the studio set of Seahaven Island, with its carefully scripted, stifling and sterile conformity, and director Peter Weir calls upon a sparse style to match, emphasising the artificiality of the perfectly clean suburbs and choreographed nature of Truman's encounters with the community's fake residents. This style is combined with frequent unusual point-of-view shots which suggest the variety of hidden cameras that continually monitor Truman's life (hidden within his car stereo, pencil sharpener, his neighbour's bin, and so on). And the film demonstrates a wider fascination with the technology behind this experiment in human existence. The introduction to an interview with the programme's creator offers the following summary of its premise:

> 1.7 billion were there for his birth. Two hundred and twenty countries tuned in for his first step. The world stood still for that stolen kiss, and as he grew so did the technology. An entire human life recorded on an intricate network of hidden cameras, and broadcast live and unedited, 24 hours a day, 7 days a week to an audience around the globe.

> Coming to you now from Seahaven Island, enclosed in the largest studio ever constructed, and along with the Great Wall of China, one of only two man-made structures visible from space, now in its 30th great year – it's *The Truman Show*.
>
> (Presenter, in *The Truman Show*)

In contrast to the bright sterility of Seahaven Island, the darkened booth where Christof and his production team manipulate Truman's life resembles the sophisti-cated environment of a NASA (National Aeronautics and Space Administration) mission control room, with banks of instruments and the image of Truman domi-nating the multiple screens that line the walls.

The focus of *EDtv* is more on documentary hybrids' inversion of the public and the private, driven by the commercialist agenda of primetime television. Unlike the (implausibly) uncomprehending Truman, 31-year-old video-store clerk Ed Pekurny (Mathew McConaughey) is a willing participant in a perpetual docu-soap, and must confront the explosion of his private life into the public sphere. *EDtv*'s premise is the most credible of the three films discussed here, and as a consequence does not offer the same satiric impact as the other two.

EDtv's opening sequence suggests the television metadiscourse which hybrids operate within. A dramatic male voiceover quickly lists where the network has taken viewers (from the 'edge of the world' to the 'edge of your seat', from the 'streets of LA' to the 'plains of the Serengeti', from 'inner space' to 'outer space'), accompanied by a slick montage of visually spectacular shots representing highlights from fictional (but recognisable) hybrid forms. The narrator then intro-duces a new format which he insists will take viewers where they have never been before ('no action, no script, no editing, all day all night, all time 'True TV'!'). A cut then reveals that this is part of an audio-visual presentation at a press confer-ence announcing the new programme, where its producer Cynthia Topping (Ellen DeGeneres) insists that her production will be much more realistic than formats such as MTV's *The Real World* (1992–, US), because there will be no manipulation (no editing) on the part of her production team. This intercutting between a simulation of television's address and the action behind the screen is continued throughout *EDtv*. The handheld footage captured by the film crew continually following Ed is combined with other roving cameras which generate a sense of bustling action by moving quickly through scenes and chasing Ed and the crew through corridors and down streets.

The third of these films, *Series 7: The Contenders*, acknowledges the more recent emergence of reality game shows such as *Big Brother* (Endemol, 1999–, Netherlands) and *Survivor* (CBS, 2000–, US). It develops a satire of reality game shows by extending a central premise of this particular hybrid form to its logical conclusion. An early voiceover outlines the premise of the film's game show format: 'Six strangers, brought together by the luck of the draw, in a game without rules, where the only prize is the only prize that counts – your life.' Instead of cameras capturing volunteer players in a series of contests to determine an eventual winner, here drafted contestants must literally eliminate each other from competition until there is only one survivor left. Like *Bob Roberts* and *Man Bites Dog*, the film is a mock-documentary and its success as a satire likewise stems from its convincing, if exaggerated, pastiche of the conventions of a hybrid.

Series 7 is constructed as an extended version of the tone and style that is simulated in just the opening sequence of *EDtv*. The opening voiceover insists that 'Everything you are about to see is real. Real people in real danger, in a fight for their lives'. The opening credits feature its players running, chased by the camera, and superimposed on a graphic of a rifle sight's crosshairs. This signature reappears at regular points, as the film's narrative structure also conforms to hybrid conventions – it is broken into segments, with regular breaks where advertisements would be, each ending with a teaser for the next section of narrative, and frequent reviews of the action that has just been seen. There is the same fast-paced editing style and archetypal dramatic voiceover narration (from both male and female announcers) that characterises reality game shows. Each of the contestants appears to be accompanied by a film crew that occasionally appears in frame or can be heard responding off camera to contestants' questions and demands. At key points in the film, *Series 7* also directly copies the established formats of early reality television formats such as *America's Most Wanted* (1988–, US) and *Cops* (1989–, US) (with the film here implicitly incorporating a sense of the development of hybrid forms themselves).[3]

As is typical of reality game shows, each contestant is economically introduced with a montage overlaid with dramatic music and a voiceover providing a pat summary of their circumstances – effectively defining them in the simplistic terms of television characterisation. These introductions are also an obvious parody of the *Cops* formulaic style. In an ambush-style encounter, with cameras in tow, all new contestants receive a visit from a representative of the programme, dressed in black and wearing a balaclava, who hands them a gun and welcomes them to the contest. Instead of the cameras following in the wake of a SWAT (Special Weapons and Tactics) team that has come to apprehend an apparent criminal, and filming their wild attempts to elude arrest (as in *Cops*), here handheld footage quickly moves into a close-up, then freeze-frame, to capture the shock and confusion of these contestants. These are all people who are more likely to be *Cops*' viewers than its weekly targets – not least because of their ethnicity.[4] The only confident first appearance by a contestant is that of the 'reigning champion', and dominant character, Dawn (Brooke Smith), an eighth-month pregnant, solo mother returning to her home town for the next round of competition. She is first seen assassinating a fellow contestant in a convenience store, then casually asking for bean dip. Her scenes also provide the more reflexive moments in the film – for example, when Dawn complains that she is pregnant and thus needs help to eliminate her competitors, her crew reply that this would violate the 'reality' of her scenes. (The audience is meant to immediately recognise the absurdity of the crew's pretensions to documentary production: having constructed a violent game show premise that has nothing to do with the everyday lives of its contestants, the programme's link to any 'reality' is purely rhetorical.)

Three arguments on hybrids

Each of these films looks to develop a critique of a specific hybrid form, but all articulate familiar critical discourses on hybrid forms as a whole. Dovey identifies and critiques three such positions which have become associated with documentary hybrids, as part of the presentation of his own speculations on their social-political significance (Dovey, 2000: 83–91). His summary provides a more than useful frame through which to consider the rhetorical positions on hybrid forms that are offered by these films.

Two of these arguments appear in incomplete form in *The Truman Show*, *EDtv* and *Series 7*. The first of these is that hybrid forms in some cases offer clear evidence of a democratisation of the television medium, that their prioritising of the voices of everyday people offers a form of 'empowerment' over institutional discourses. Significantly, this is a position regularly offered by the broadcasters themselves. Instances of this empowerment are seen in video diaries, some examples of docu-soaps, and the varieties of reality formats which feature in-depth looks at various public institutions in the course of their duties (police, emergency services, hospitals and so on). Dovey critiques this perspective as an incomplete one in that it does not acknowledge the political and economic structures that challenge and limit the ways in which that voice is transmitted and disseminated. Ouellette (1995), for example, argues that any such efforts to explore the democratic, or even politically subversive, potential of ubiquitous camcorder ownership have been quickly channelled into more passive and reactionary television forms. (Instead of citizens participating in a camcorder surveillance culture which acts as a watchdog on powerful economic and political institutions, they are encouraged to send spectacular footage of freak accidents to television networks, which packages such video as voyeuristic entertainment.)

This relatively positive rhetorical stance towards hybrids is left unexplored by the three films discussed here. None suggests much sense of 'empowerment' for the characters caught within its respective constructions of hybrid programmes. Much of the drama generated within these films in fact comes from the increasingly desperate attempts of the main characters to escape from the corporate

242

surveillance and manipulation that are central to their hybrid programmes. All three films offer various degrees of success in these attempts: the main characters in *Series 7* pathetically fail (all but one is killed), *EDtv* simply provides a fantastical manner of escape as Ed uses his primetime profile to gather embarrassing information on television executives in order to force his release, and Truman dramatically leaves the comforting environs of Seahaven Island to an uncertain and unseen future. Rather than exploring the subversive potential of prioritising the everyday voice of their main characters, all three films effectively reduce a critique of media institutions to their central characters' struggles to regain control over their lives (Bishop, 2000).

Another argument relating to hybrid forms summarised by Dovey, derived from postmodernist theories of the media, is that these programmes in fact constitute the disappearance of any actual reality from television screens. Docusoaps, Reality TV, reality game shows and the like are here viewed as further evidence of the erasure of any distinction between reality and fiction. Drawing in particular upon Baudrillard's notion that such tendencies are obscene, this nightmarish perspective on hybrids has been expressed in early writing on hybrid forms by documentary theorists such as Nichols (1994). One of Nichols' complaints about these types of programmes, for example, has been that they are 'cannibalised' and 'assimilated' into the metadiscourse of television. In stark contrast to the 'call to action' of documentary, anything 'real' within hybrid forms is reduced to the level of spectacle for the instant gratification of the (assumed) passive voyeurism of the television viewer. *Natural Born Killers* attempts to present this argument visually, using a variety of cinematic techniques to suggest the mental states of the main characters (Helms, 1994; Gross, 1995) and to effectively reject any representation of the social-historical world as its reference point.

This is an argument which becomes untenable when examined in detail, a fact which *The Truman Show* effectively demonstrates. Of the three films this draws most explicitly on postmodernist rhetoric, with Truman initially seen to be unable to discern the fictionality of the Seahaven Island studio – for him there is no distinction between image and reality. This is a useful rhetorical position for the film to take in terms of its general thematic concern with developing a critique of modern society's dependence on those fictions which audiences choose to take as realities. When asked why Truman has never discovered his role, Christof replies that '[w]e accept the reality of the world with which we're presented. It's as simple as that'. However, this is a stance which undermines the credibility of Truman as a character – it doesn't seem reasonable that Truman would take 30 years to discover the conspiracy constructed around him, and this failing both detracts from the drama of his eventual escape and limits any wider statements that the film can make about media in relation to reality. (This is also central to the two-dimensional manner in which Truman's audience is portrayed, as discussed below; pp. 245–8.)

Of the three arguments regarding documentary hybrids which are summarised by Dovey, the one which is most frequently articulated by social and political commentators is the 'trash TV' position. Here the response to hybrid forms is to identify them as evidence of both the culmination of increasing trends toward blatant exploitation within commercial television and clear signs of a decline in the collective taste and intelligence of contemporary mass audiences. This argument falls most clearly within the overall trajectory of the cinematic commentaries on television articulated within such key films as *Network*. Television is constructed here as a direct cause of a collapse in social values, or at the very least a reinforcement of a continuing social decline. This 'trash TV' argument draws upon a well-established discourse invariably directed at new popular media forms, with critics and commentators typically viewing such developments as the latest attempt by television broadcasting (and other media) institutions to pursue a narrow commercialist agenda, and as the abandonment of the high standard demanded by a public-service ethic. The same rhetoric is repeated in newspaper editorials, critical columns and journals, and by a variety of political and cultural commentators who express alarm at the 'depths' to which television in particular is seen to have fallen.

All three of *The Truman Show*, *EDtv* and *Series 7* can be seen to clearly articulate such sentiments. In *The Truman Show*, Truman has been exploited since before he was born, chosen to be the subject of a perpetual docu-soap because he was born at the right time, 'on cue' for when the programme began broadcasting. In an extension of the corporate agenda behind docu-soaps, Truman is championed as the first baby legally adopted by a corporation, but despite (or because of) his popularity is also apparently the target of 'Free Truman' campaigns. During a Christof 'interview', for example, we see a brief flashback of an attempt by a parachutist to alert Truman to the fact that he is the prisoner of a global television production.

While Christof offers a relatively complex (but paternalist) face for the corporate agenda behind Truman's imprisonment, the television executives within *EDtv* more explicitly fall within the long tradition of cinema's simplistic characterisations of television personnel. Ed and his family are initially easy prey for the seductions of television celebrity, and when the 24-hour surveillance of the programme's camera begins to tear Ed's family apart the network executives smugly dismiss their pleas for escape from their contract. Instead, the network begins to broaden its surveillance to directly include all members of his family. Ed is forced to fight back using his primetime popularity, asking viewers to call him with embarrassing information on the private lives of television executives that he can use to bargain for his freedom.

Of these three films, *Series 7* provides the most savage portrayal of its hybrid's commercial agenda, with the show prepared to literally sacrifice participants in the pursuit of ratings success. The film's voiceovers reduce these participants to stereotypes, and it engages in regular slow-motion replays of each death, placing these within a self-serving moralistic frame for viewers. The 'players' in the game of elimination are neither volunteers nor prepared for the level of violence that is required for them to survive. In fact their amateur status is the source of much of the drama of the programme itself, with contestants prolonging the game through their inept attempts to dispense with their competitors. They cover the usual range of middle- and lower-class participants 'exploited' by reality game shows – a middle-class teenager with overbearing parents, an elderly nurse, a trailer-park drunk, a loser with a young family and a man dying of testicular cancer who is eventually revealed to be an ex-boyfriend of Dawn's ('Jeff', played by Glenn Fitzgerald). Dawn and Jeff eventually emerge as the last survivors. They attempt to escape from the game by turning their weapons on their camera crews. It is at this point that the film turns into a version of *America's Most Wanted*, with these last two contenders hunted down. The demise of Dawn and the hospitalisation of Jeff become raw material for an obviously heavily fictionalised dramatic reconstruction of their climactic showdown with programme representatives.

Hybrids and their viewers

One of the main failings of the 'trash TV' rhetorical stance on hybrid forms is that it is unable to convincingly explain the nature of their appeal to a wide variety of audiences. The constructions of viewers made by commentators draw upon the assumptions stereotypically made about the motivations and viewing practices associated with other 'suspect' media forms such as comics, soap operas or violent computer games. Familiar phrases such as 'addiction' are used to explain the nature of the engagement of viewers with these texts – with the assumption not only that these texts have no redeeming qualities, but that viewers are unable to comprehend this and are therefore either of low intelligence or incapable of releasing themselves from the seduction of their appeal. Phrases such as 'lowest common denominator' and 'dumbing down' are generally applied to these television texts, as part of a wider critique of the political economy of television production and transmission which also implies a host of negative audiences traits – viewers are effectively viewed as needing to be saved from these forms and redirected back to traditional authoritative, public-service forms such as documentary proper.

The Truman Show, *EDtv* and *Series 7* all illustrate, again, the key dilemma of representing such rhetoric in cinematic form, in that they clearly articulate the pretence that it must be 'other' viewers which must fall into such categories. The critique of hybrids within these films is consequently both limited and ambivalent (just as with the earlier *Network*), as they are faced with the dilemma of whether their representations of hybrid viewers should be broadened to include the very viewers of the films themselves. They largely suggest (with one exception, discussed below) that such hybrid programmes attract only a niche audience, with which no one in the film's audience is encouraged to identify.

In *EDtv*, Ed is selected from the many television viewers who enthusiastically compete to become an instant celebrity. He does not fall within the collection of dysfunctional characters typically associated with television viewers within cinema, but there are nonetheless echoes of the lead characters of *The King of Comedy* and *To Die For* within other viewers in *EDtv*. Viewers are continually seen to interfere in Ed's life, either abusing or cheering him in the street, or coming into the video store where he works, in order to appear on camera. He becomes a media phenomenon when he begins a romance with his brother's girlfriend, Shari (Jenna Elfman), and viewers become 'addicted' to this real-life soap opera for reasons which they cannot articulate (a gay man tells his partner: 'I don't know, it's just...just let me watch!'). Although television executives are constructed by the film as willing to do whatever it takes to make a format successful, there is also the explicit suggestion that such hybrids would not succeed without some sort of impetus from viewers themselves – that 'EDtv' is tapping into something basic, and perhaps unconscious, within human nature. At the end of the film is perhaps the clearest articulation of its perspective on Ed's fans; the producer of the programme sees some lower-class kids waving at their images captured by a closed-circuit television system at a convenience store, and smiles in recognition of the fact that the urge to be on television is so irresistible and universal.

The subtext to *The Truman Show* is the suggestion that it is really the programme's *viewers* who are captives of the show, rather than Truman. The film presents viewers who seem unable to discern the difference between television and reality, who have an insatiable hunger for an obviously constructed 'reality', no matter how readily its construction is acknowledged, but who nevertheless have a short attention span (the same themes developed in a more direct way within *Network*). Outside the barely glimpsed 'Free Truman' segment of the audience, viewers are shown never to have considered the possibility that they are implicated in keeping a man a prisoner for his entire life purely for their own amusement.

The one critical viewer who is seen is Sylvia (Natasha McElhone), a minor character on the show who was attracted to Truman and fired when she attempted to warn him of his fate. She provides the motivation for Truman's escape and watches only for signs of his 'awakening'. She rings Christof during a live talkback interview to denounce the imprisonment of Truman, and their exchange summarises the film's assumed dichotomy between the paternalism of the television network (personified in the fatherly assumptions that Christof has of Truman) and the rejection of the entire premise of the programme by an 'enlightened' few. The complacency of the producers and the programme's main audience towards Truman's fate (they have been watching, and effectively been implicated in, Truman's imprisonment for decades) is nicely expressed by Christof's initial lack of concern when Truman discovers his starring role. Christof believes that Truman will prefer life in this 'cell' to the dangers and emptiness of real life – just as apparently the audience members prefer his fake suburban paradise to their own realities. His underlying arrogance comes to the fore during Truman's escape when in a moment of wrath he appears to be prepared to let Truman die rather than to escape his control. The fact that Christof does not kill Truman is the clearest sign of the film's distinction from the satiric bite of *Network*. Here the production team are seen to have Truman's interests at heart; their manipulation and imprisonment of Truman is viewed as misplaced, rather than malevolent.

Both *The Truman Show* and *EDtv* ultimately offer conservative representations of audiences of hybrid forms. As mentioned above, in each film a critique of media institutions is effectively reduced to the struggle for one person to regain control over his life, while any wider debate over the implication of audiences' engagement with media in general is quietly sidelined. While Truman undergoes the conventional transformation of an archetypal hero (overcoming obstacles and becoming psychologically complete in the process), there is no suggestion that his television audience makes that same transition with him; its participation in his escape is purely vicarious.

The viewers we see most frequently throughout *The Truman Show* are a pair of waitresses at a bar full of apparently regular Truman viewers. Easily falling within the stereotype of soap watchers, both have an obviously deep knowledge of all of the events in Truman's life (one has a 'greatest highlights' tape) and are continually distracted from their jobs by the television screen on the wall behind them. We also see a couple of elderly ladies on a sofa (with a Truman cushion) who appear to have bonded over their shared affection for Truman, a middle-aged man who seems to be perpetually watching from his bathtub (even falling asleep there), and a family of Japanese viewers also using the programme to learn English. The first and last viewers seen in the film are a pair of security guards at a parking garage – stereotypical television viewers, they are overweight and in low-paying jobs. They are initially seen complaining that they don't get to see anything once Truman and his wife go into their bedroom, and they seem to each take a turn going out for food while the other watches. When Truman begins his dramatic escape from Seahaven Island, like all other viewers they are riveted to the screen, and don't even turn from the television to address a customer (instead waving for him to 'leave the keys in the car'). After Truman finally escapes, they pause in satisfaction, then immediately look around for the *TV Guide* so they can see what else is on. Collectively, these viewers exhibit the full range of shallow, reactive and fickle responses to the programme that are envisaged by the 'trash TV' argument.

A much more interesting set of issues is raised by *Series 7*, despite it only including a brief glimpse of the viewers of the programme it constructs. When Dawn and Jeff are on the run they storm into a film theatre, take the audience hostage and discover that their captives are thrilled to be involved with people they recognise as media celebrities. Dawn rings the producers on her cell phone and shouts that they will begin to shoot hostages if they don't get safe passage off the show. The film audience claps in encouragement, at which Dawn turns and yells, 'That means you, arseholes!', and the audience goes quiet. Just as the programme's viewers presumably do not seem to recognise the horrific nature of the premise of the game show, so they also fail to register what the implications might be when the programme invades their own lives. The key difference here is that the film suddenly makes the leap that *Network* only flirts with and *The Truman Show* and *EDtv* cannot even contemplate – it explicitly implicates its own audience in its critique of hybrids, rather than displacing negative assumptions about spectatorship onto an assumed niche of 'other' television viewers.

This is a brief scene, with the film quickly retreating to its mock-documentary satire of hybrid form, and in its representations of viewers also clearly repeats the tradition of representing hybrid viewers as passive, addicted voyeurs that *Truman Show* and *EDtv* similarly draw upon. The real significance of this scene is its reminder of the *potential* to develop a more complex perspective of the social-political significance of hybrids than any of these three films explore. All three films aim to engage their audiences in detailed critiques of documentary hybrids, and all clearly expect their viewers both to grasp the complexity of cultural references that they make and to consider some of the social implications for their fictional extensions of existing hybrid forms. However, by largely avoiding the direct suggestion that we as their audience are collectively implicated in the development of hybrids, these films not only demonstrate the limits of their satire of hybrids; they also point to the value of more recent theoretical work on the wider significance of these forms.

Dovey (2000, 2002) and Corner (2001, 2002) have each provided some of the groundwork for a perspective on documentary hybrids that moves beyond a simple dismissal of hybrid forms as a violation of treasured fundamentals of the documentary genre. Instead of viewing hybrids as signs of an abandonment of any meaningful social and political role that might be played by television as a medium, Dovey and Corner each open the possibility that hybrids might instead be more meaningfully understood as evidence of significant changes within the nature of social and political organisation itself. Dovey has been more detailed in his speculations, using the term 'emotional democracy' (Dovey, 2000: 168) to suggest a society which, among other attributes, increasingly values the emotional resonance of other people's experiences over the knowledge offered by social and political institutions. The erasure of boundaries between the 'public' and the 'private', the acknowledgement of performance and the playful reflexivity that exist to varying degrees within different examples of hybrid programming are all seen as potential signs of such a transformation.

Similarly, Corner's more cautious speculations on the development of a 'post-documentary' culture (2002: 263–6)[5] attempt to position these forms in relation to fundamental changes within the agenda of the documentary genre as a whole.

> Neither postmodern skepticism nor the techniques of digital manipulation present documentary with its biggest future challenge. This will undoubtedly come from the requirement to reorient and refashion itself in an audio-visual culture where the dynamics of diversion and the aesthetics of performance dominate a greatly expanded range of popular images of the real.
>
> (Corner, 2002: 267)

Central to these recent theoretical developments is a recognition that a more complex understanding of the ways in which viewers engage with and understand hybrid forms is a core part of any grounded appreciation of their significance. Films such as *The Truman Show*, *EDtv* and *Series 7: The Contenders* play a distinctive role in relation to such debates. In part, they articulate in popular form the variety of critical and theoretical debates associated with the rapid expansion and proliferation of documentary hybrids. Perhaps more significantly, however, such articulations also clearly express the limitations of many such current debates – by effectively demonstrating their consistent failure to incorporate detailed and convincing explanations of spectatorship into their explanations for hybrids' popularity.

Notes

1   The term 'hybrid form' is increasingly used to suggest the manner in which these texts deliberately play with the lines between fact and fiction genres. These programmes borrow heavily from the assumptions underpinning fly-on-the-wall and other documentary modes, but are presented within entertainment formats derived from genres such as game shows and soap operas.

2   Obviously, the tension between cinema and television as media competing for audiences needs to be seen within the context of their complex institutional and economic connections. Considering the industrial interdependence between the corporate structures of film studios and television networks, it is a moot point whether these two media can in fact be said any longer to be 'competitors' in any concrete sense. Such competition exists largely at the discursive level discussed here.

3   *America's MostWanted* was an early example of a 'hybrid' format.The popularity of such current affairs-derived 'RealityTV' programmes eventually led to the development of more recent hybrids such as docu-soaps, and the reality game shows (or 'game-docs') that *Series 7* satirises.
4   Derosia notes that the pattern of hybrid programmes based on covering law enforcement has been to represent the divide between criminals and law enforcers in ethnic terms, with a largely white police force seen to be holding the line against a black criminal underclass (Derosia, 2002).
5   Corner always presents the term 'post-documentary' with a question mark, as he intends to use the term to promote debate over hybrids, rather than necessarily to identify a definitive break with the genre itself.

References

Anderson, Christopher (1991) 'Hollywood in the Home: TV and the End of the Studio System', in James Naremore and Patrick Brantlinger (eds) *Modernity and Mass Culture*, Bloomington, IN: Indiana University Press.

Barr, Charles (1986) 'Broadcasting and Cinema 2: Screens within Screens', in Charles Barr (ed.) *All Our Yesterdays: 90 Years of British Cinema*, London: British Film Institute.

Bishop, Ronald (2000) 'Good Afternoon, Good Evening, and Good Night: *The Truman Show* as Media Criticism', *Journal of Communication Enquiry* 24(1): 6–18.

Blumler, J. G. (1999) 'Political Communication Systems All Change: A Response to Kees Brants', *European Journal of Communication* 14(2): 241–9.

Brants, K. (1998) 'Who's Afraid of Infotainment?', *European Journal of Communication* 13(3): 315–35.

Bruzzi, Stella (2000) *New Documentary:A Critical Introduction*, London: Routledge.

Corner, John (1996) *The Art of Record: A Critical Introduction to Documentary*, Manchester: Manchester University Press.

Corner, John (2001) 'Documentary in a Post-Documentary Culture? A Note on Forms and their Functions', European Science Foundation 'Changing Media – Changing Europe' programme.Team One (Citizenship and Consumerism) Working Paper No. 1; available at: http://www.lboro.ac.uk/research/changing.media/publications.htm.

Corner, John (2002) 'Performing the Real: Documentary Diversions', *Television and New Media* 3(3): 255–69.

Derosia, Margaret (2002) 'The Court of Last Resort: Making Race, Crime and Nation on *America's MostWanted*', in James Friedman (ed.) *Reality Squared:Televisual Discourse on the Real*, New Brunswick, NJ: Rutgers University Press.

Dovey, Jon (1995) 'Camcorder Cults', *Metro* 104: 26–30.

Dovey, Jon (2000) *Freakshow: First Person Media and FactualTelevision*, London: Pluto Press.

Dovey, Jon (2002) 'Confession and the Unbearable Lightness of Factual', *Media International Australia* 104: 10–18.

Friedman, James (ed.) (2002) *Reality Squared: Televisual Discourse on the Real*, New Brunswick, NJ: Rutgers University Press.

Gross, Larry (1995) 'Exploding Hollywood', *Sight and Sound* 5(3): 8–9.

Harries, Dan (2000) *Film Parody*, London: British Film Institute.

Helms, Michael (1994) '*Natural Born Killers*', *Metro* 100: 14–17.

Kolker, Robert (2000) *A Cinema of Loneliness: Penn, Stone, Kubrick, Scorsese, Spielberg, Altman* (third edition), Oxford: Oxford University Press.

McDonald, William (1999) 'Memo to Hollywood, Re TV: It's Not that Bad', *New York Times*, 28 March: 15–16.

McLoone, Martin and John Hill (eds) (1998) *Big Picture, Small Screen: The Relations Between Film and Television*, Luton: University of Luton Press.

New Line Productions (2002) '15 Minutes'; available at http://www.15minutesmovie.com (accessed November 2002).

Nichols, Bill (1991) *Representing Reality: Issues and Concepts in Documentary*, Bloomington, IN: Indiana University Press.

Nichols, Bill (1994) *Blurred Boundaries: Questions of Meaning in Contemporary Culture*, Bloomington, IN: Indiana University Press.

Ouellette, Laurie (1995) 'Camcorder Do's and Don'ts: Popular Discourses on Amateur Video and Participatory Television', *Velvet Light Trap* 36: 33–44.

Roscoe, Jane and Craig Hight (2001) *Faking It: Mock-documentary and the Subversion of Factuality*, Manchester: Manchester University Press.

Ruoff, Jeffrey (2002) *'An American Family': A Televised Life*, Minneapolis, MN: University of Minnesota Press.

Sanes, Ken (2001) 'The Truman Show'; available at http://www.transparencynow.com/truman.htm (accessed November 2002).

Stokes, Jane (1999) *On Screen Rivals: Cinema and Television in the United States and Britain*, London: Macmillan.

Weinberg, Michael (1995) '*Natural Born Killers*: A Postmodern Analysis'; available at http://nbk.weinberger.us (accessed November 2002).

12

BIG BROTHER

Reconfiguring the 'active' audience of cultural studies?[1]

Estella Tincknell and Parvati Raghuram

The emergence of interactive Reality TV as a major media form during the late twentieth and early twenty-first centuries, with shows such as *Survivor* (2001–2, ITV, UK), *The Club* (2003, ITV, UK) and *Pop Idol* (19TV/FremantleMedia for ITV, 2001–2, UK) featuring a combination of live camera footage, 'ordinary' contestants and audience participation, presents us with interesting questions for cultural studies' idea of the 'active' audience (Livingstone, 1998; Couldry, 2000; Johnson *et al.*, forthcoming). In this chapter we consider one such text, the enormously successful reality game show, *Big Brother* (2000–, UK),[2] and explore the extent to which it challenges, or helps to reconfigure, conceptualisations of the 'active' audience in relation to the television text.[3] We therefore situate the programme within the context of the complex history of cultural studies' attempts to 'think the audience' for popular media. In the first section we outline some aspects of this theoretical and methodological history. In the second we look at the generic elements that contributed to the popularity of *Big Brother*, before moving on to explore the ways in which Reality TV constructs a version of 'the real'. In section four we examine the programme in relation to its surrounding intertextual framework, and in section five we consider its implications for notions of interactivity. Finally, we return to the idea of 'resistance' in relation to this analysis and consider its implications for audience agency.

'Sharing the sofa': cultural studies' conceptualisations of the audience

Popular media texts such as soap operas, news programmes and women's magazines were initially examined by cultural studies researchers throughout the 1980s and early 1990s as sites for the production, organisation and negotiation of ideological discourses around class, gender and power were produced, organised and negotiated (Hobson, 1982; Morley, 1980; Ang, 1985, 1991; Gray, 1992). Such work sought to emphasise (against the Frankfurt School model) that audiences were active agents rather than passive subjects in their enjoyment of popular texts, and that the process of understanding was one of negotiation rather than imposition. This work focused mainly on the audiences for 'mass' commercial culture – precisely because such groups were taken for granted yet relatively under-researched, and because of the discipline's political commitment to the social formation under-stood as the 'working class', 'the masses' or 'ordinary people'. For researchers in cultural studies, then, the audience was conceptualised as a *relation* rather than as a fixed site of consumption, and there was an explicit rejection of behaviourist and empiricist models of audience psychology or media 'effects'.

Although specific researchers like Ien Ang (1985) and David Morley (1980) set out to demonstrate the active agency of audiences by using methods drawn from ethnography, cultural studies often seemed to operate through a contradictory assumption that the ideological constraints of the text were – ultimately – too powerful to resist. Thus, while John Fiske's work, in particular, extended the idea of the active audience through his notion of 'semiotic resistance', the text never-theless remained the primary determinant of meaning (Fiske, 1989a). Indeed, the idea of the active audience remained predicated on the assumption that activity constitutes an intellectual engagement *with* a text, rather than an intervention *in* a text, involving the refusal of dominant meanings and the production of new and oppositional meanings. Such interaction was therefore primarily understood as taking place at the moment of reception, so that any shifts in meaning were produced at an extrinsic level, rather than changing a text's formal constituents. And as long as 'the audience' was conceptualised as being at home sitting on the sofa rather than anywhere else (at least when it came to the consideration of popular television), the location of the production of such texts remained sepa-rated from the location of their reception. However active the audience might have been in their response to and production of meanings about the text, they could not *intervene* in it.

The question of audience agency poses both conceptual and methodological problems. Because audiences are transitory and contingent groupings and are hard to determine and identify, they may pose difficulties for research. While cultural studies has established that audiences are neither passive in their recep-tion of media texts nor homogeneous in their constitution, the question of how and where they are defined remains. Ien Ang (1991) points out, 'audiences' do not exist independently, but are themselves produced by the media industry. Indeed, when researchers 'share the sofa' with a group of fans or a family they are also 'producing the audience' by constructing a 'researchable category'. Since the early 1990s, however, a number of more pressing questions have been raised about the entire concept of the 'active' audience – particularly the potential need to rethink the nature of reception and the degree to which audience interpretation may be understood as a form of resistance (Dahlgren, 1998: 301). In fact, Sonia Livingstone (1998) has argued that the recognition of the limitations of a 'resistant reading' of popular media texts has led to a retreat in cultural studies away from work on popular audiences. However, what we suggest here is that the development of new kinds of 'interactive' media texts makes the idea of the 'active' audience newly interesting, suggesting that such audiences may go beyond simply responding to a text – they may also help to *change* it. The political implications of this shift thus repay careful consideration.

Definitions both of interactive media and of interaction as a process can be generalised and contradictory. As Toscan and Jensen (1998) point out, the term 'interactive television' is used to describe a whole range of services and technologies, not all of which share the same infrastructures or *modus operandi*. 'Interactivity' is also a multiply discursive concept. Toscan and Jensen helpfully differentiate here between interactivity obtained via *hardware* (the technology of television itself) and interactivity derived through *software* (at the level of individual programmes), identifying technological and sociological definitions of the concept. Our interest here, however, lies in the cultural dimensions of interaction, the values, meanings, investments and assumptions that are part and parcel of any interactive engagement with media, and these may be less readily determined by reference to technology or even traditional models of social relations. In particular, the mediation of such relations by television or other communication technologies is central to our argument. Such an analysis is particularly important in the context of *Big Brother*'s own tendency (and that of other reality shows) to draw on popular versions of behaviourist psychology that emphasise individual rather than cultural explanations of the contestants' actions.

The particular success of *Big Brother* throughout the UK, Europe and the USA in the summer of 2000 was, we think, linked both to its deployment of a range of sites of access, including webcams and Internet chat rooms, and to the role of the audience in the show's narrative development. By inviting audiences to participate in the programme and by making that participation central to the 'plot', *Big Brother* marked a new moment of interactive television. For those researching media and culture, this innovation also represents a watershed in the longstanding debates about the precise relationship between audiences and text. In the next section we examine some aspects of the television genres which such interactive television has raided and developed, and the ways in which these have altered the relationship between the programme and its audiences.

Back to basics? *Big Brother*'s success

Big Brother first appeared on British television in the summer of 2000, a year after its first appearance in the Netherlands in August 1999. Despite being screened on a 'minority' channel in the UK, Channel 4, the programme garnered over 6 million viewers (Ritchie, 2000). Shown on six out of seven weekday evenings, including an omnibus edition of weekly highlights, *Big Brother* became the media 'event' of summer 2000: its contestants were turned into minor celebrities and the comings and goings of the house they shared were continuously dissected – and effectively *re*-presented – by other media commentators, the British tabloid press in particular (see also Couldry, 2002).[4] The programme went on to considerable European success, with versions of the show appearing throughout Europe over the next eighteen months, as well as in the USA, Australia and Argentina (for an interesting reading of the Australian version, see Roscoe, 2001).

Such widespread appeal is symptomatic, not simply of the increasing popularity of Reality Television in general, but of the specific appeal of the *Big Brother* format, which artfully combined the 'voyeuristic' aspects of the reality programme with the competitive elements of the game show, producing a text whose apparent 'banality' was mediated by crucial moments of suspense. What seems most significant, however, is that *Big Brother* has become the definitive example of a whole range of programmes which have deployed combinations of the syntactical elements of forced confinement, competitive individualism and emotional conflict as entertainment: *Castaway 2000* (Lion TV for BBC1, 2000–1, UK), *Survivor*, *Pop Idol*, *Fame Academy* (Endemol for BBC1, 2002, UK), *The Salon* (Endemol for C4, 2003, UK). A number of these shows effectively attempted to capitalise on the cultural impact of *Big Brother* – although few matched its success. Perhaps one reason for this crucial difference lay in the character of *Big Brother*'s technology and the connotations it produced: the webcam images offered a convincing sense of immediacy and 'liveness' precisely because they drew on the technological and aesthetic conventions of documentary realism.

A further crucial dimension to the programme was its apparently innovative use of audience interaction. This primarily focused on two nodal points. First, the public were invited to vote to evict from the house one of two inhabitants compulsorily 'volunteered' by fellow inmates every week. Second, regular tasks to be completed by the inhabitants (circus skills, mounting a play, a fashion show) were set by the audience. These elements clearly structured audience participation in the 'text'. *Big Brother* also drew on the three popular contemporary television genres which depend most heavily on audience participation for important aspects of its style and mode of address: the 'reality' show, the television talk show and the game show.[5] All three genres have effectively changed or challenged the relationship between television and its audience in different ways. 'Reality' television programmes (especially those later referred to as 'docusoaps') emerged during the early 1990s, and presented, in one strand, the 'real-life' drama of police work, rescue operations and accidents, and in another, the small-scale conflicts of everyday life. In the UK these programmes frequently also focused on the transient spaces of contemporary consumer culture – airports, shopping centres and hotels. Such shows were marked by their shift away from the documentary tradition of examining the role of macro-economic and social structures in the production of 'reality' (Palmer, 2002), towards an emphasis on personal and domestic relationships and a concern with issues of sexuality and gender identities. This shift has been read by some commentators as marking a 'dumbing down' or 'tabloidisation' of popular television, as Roscoe points out (2001: 474). Yet, while there are undoubtedly 'voyeuristic' aspects to some of these shows, they have also worked to clear discursive space for the exploration and legitimation of new definitions of the personal and the familial, especially as older forms of the family and of kinship are replaced by new models, including same-sex relationships and extended networks based on friendship rather than blood. Certainly, *Big Brother*'s creation of an artificial community in which the participants shared a common culture rather than family ties seemed to draw on these new models. Indeed, this highly contingent community – that is, the members of the *Big Brother* household – was effectively constructed through the relationship the participants had with the television show itself. The implications of this process for the relationship between 'text' and 'audience' are complex, as we explore below (pp. 258–60).

Reality programmes also seemed, at one level, to represent a return to the 'basics' of television and a re-simplification of its aesthetics and its subject matter in an age of increasingly technology-driven and spectacular media. The technologies involved in their production were highly sophisticated but aesthetically diminished, entailing the use of handheld cameras and largely diegetically produced sound, while the narratives focused closely on intense but narrowly defined dilemmas and conflicts.[6] As Arild Fetveit argues,

> the proliferation of reality TV could be understood as an [*sic*] euphoric effort to reclaim what seems to be lost after digitalisation. And what seems to be lost is...a sense of being in contact with the world by way of indexicality. The powerful urge for a sense of contact with the real is inscribed in much of the reality TV footage.
>
> (Fetveit, 1999: 793, see also Hill, 2002)

This emphasis on the expression of apparently direct and unmediated emotions by 'real' people in 'real' time, and on the conflicts of everyday life, marked a significant shift, not only in the nature of television texts themselves, but also in the relationship between text and audience as the 'difference' between the two seemed to narrow.

The discursive strategies involved in *Big Brother* drew precisely on those preoccupations with ideas of reality, closeness to reality and detailed experience which had become familiar from this emergent television genre – strategies which articulate a desire to hold on to something 'real' in the context of increasing social fragmentation. Such programmes offer this through what Fetveit calls 'the audio-visual evidence' of what 'really' happened, because 'the format heavily propagates a belief in visual evidence' (ibid.). So the sense that participants are speaking directly and 'now' to the viewer works to draw the audience in, producing the effect of a more *direct* relationship to the text. The appearance of 'liveness' is crucial to this: the transmission of moment-by-moment footage in what feels like real-time helps to produce the affective discourse that is so important to the power of Reality Television.[7]

In the case of *Big Brother*, 'proof' that it was 'real' lay in these affective dimensions to the kind of technology used, and in the physical spaces it seemed to open up for inspection by the audience: the webcams produced hazy and unfocused images of the private spaces of bedrooms and bathrooms which emphasised the sense of gaining access to the forbidden, while the 'unedited' quality of the programme – however spurious – confirmed the sense of liveness. Where more traditional media texts (such as scripted dramas and documentaries) mobilise highly complex visual conventions that seek to represent reality seamlessly and invisibly, *Big Brother* sought to do the opposite. As Ruth Wrigley, the executive producer of the British version, explained, 'the team did not want to impose their own perspective on the show – they wanted it to be as truthful as possible…they only reported facts without editorial comment' (quoted in Ritchie, 2000: 10). The camera footage was thus represented as 'raw material' from which a range of conclusions could be drawn and a variety of narratives constructed. However, contrary to Wrigley's somewhat disingenuous claim, it is clear that not only is Reality TV as dependent on narrative as other kinds of popular media – the primary difference is that in such shows a narrative is constructed *after* the material has been recorded – but *Big Brother*'s 'story' (the one told by the short evening programmes which had the largest audiences) was also obviously heavily mediated by a combination of editing and voiceover commentary. These helped to produce a 'preferred' version, which often centred on the sexual behaviour of the contestants.

This focus on the sexual, the emotional and the domestic also borrowed elements from the participatory talk shows first popularised in the USA in the 1990s and presented by Oprah Winfrey, Jerry Springer and Ricki Lake. Such shows shifted radically between the beginning and end of the decade so that '[t]opics moved from personal issues connected to a social injustice to interpersonal conflicts which emphasised only the visceral nature of confrontation, emotion and sexual titillation' (Shattuc, 1998: 212). The difference between the audience for talk shows and their performers also became increasingly blurred during this period as the emphasis on interpersonal conflicts extended, and as programmes began to depend almost entirely on audience participation and on 'ordinary people' for their material. *Big Brother* thus combined the agenda of talk television with the style of the docusoap and the format of a game show, and was therefore able to address a wide and potentially diverse television audience. What it also did was to extend those formats, and in so doing it shifted the nature of the relationship between audience and text.

Playing games with reality: *Big Brother* and the 'people show'

Reality TV claims to feature 'ordinary' people doing 'ordinary' things. As a genre, the 'people show' minimises the distance between the audience and the 'actors' through its emphasis on everyday life, so that the viewer is invited to recognise the participants as belonging to her or his own habitus. A viewer sitting at home is not only invited to identify *with* the actors; she or he can *become* one of them by volunteering to tell her story, become a contestant, or by taking part in the show as one of the studio audience. Such programmes thus constantly solicit the audience to 'be the text', through their necessarily extensive and repeated appeals for participants. This widening of the possibilities for participation constitutes a kind of 'democratisation' of television, insofar as the range and diversity of people represented on the screen may be said to have broadened to include a greater number of working-class, lower-middle-class, black or Asian 'characters' and the range of 'legitimate' issues for discussion has shifted. However, the increased visibility of 'ordinary people' on television is underlain by powerful commonsense assumptions about what constitutes the 'real world', in which the 'real' is defined phenomenologically. It is limited to what can be determined through the experiential and is frequently reduced to 'everyday' life. Thus, the book-based knowledge of experts who are invited on to such programmes is often unfavourably contrasted to the authority of ordinary experiential knowledge. This democratising process is further limited, by the agenda and preoccupations of Reality TV's format and by the nature of its incorporation of 'ordinary people'. As with the talk show (Shattuc, 1998), through the emphasis on individualised and personalised conflicts (a model which militates against the effective location of racism or sexism within wider social structures, for example), and through the participants' relative lack of power to control the ways in which they are mediated or presented, Reality TV closes off both what can be defined as 'ordinary' and the ways in which it may be offered to the viewer.

Big Brother also offered the promise of 'real-life' television, and in so doing set up a particular relationship with its audience: the suggestion that these were people 'just like' those watching. It did this partly through its use of real-time as a representational strategy, and partly through the way in which the cameras seemed to record all aspects of life in the house, so that even hitherto private spaces were available for public view, as we have noted. In addition, every encounter between male and female contestants, every touch or look, was represented by the voiceover commentary as pregnant with sexual possibility and tension. As such, this 'intimate' knowledge quickly helped to produce audience familiarity with the participants. Moreover, *Big Brother*'s heightening of conflicts and the intensification of relationships, combined with the participants' ignorance of time passing outside, contributed to a discourse in which the programme seemed 'more than real'. The voiceover commentary was thus used to construct a form of closure at the end of each episode in which the sexual possibilities and heightened conflict of the social relations of the participants were foregrounded. In addition to this televisual meta-narrative of intensive emotional dissection, the participants themselves, with few other distractions or tasks to occupy them, began to explore and reflect on their relations with each other in growing detail as the weeks proceeded, becoming more self-preoccupied (if not always very self-reflexive) as the outer world became more distant from their immediate experience.

However, this self-preoccupation tended to problematise *Big Brother*'s status as Reality TV, or rather pointed to the very contradictory status of the idea that television (as a *re*-presentation) can make such a claim to 'the real'. The house in which the participants lived in the first series was effectively a starkly lit theatrical set dressed with props, one that was especially built and equipped for the show. Moreover, the heightened 'nowness' experienced by the participants, in which everything they did during the duration of the programme acquired a significance that far exceeded its importance in a wider social context, drew attention to its *performative* aspects (see Chapter 5; and also Roscoe, 2001). Perhaps more importantly, although the programme focused upon the social relations between the participants, these were not structured around kinship, friendship, workplace relations or other recognisable social formations in contemporary society. Unlike the hitherto conventional models for such reality-based programmes on British television there was no pre-existing organisation or set of relations, such as those within a university, an airport or the police force, to structure the interactions involved. These relationships were formed in isolation, without access or reference to the outside world, and were intensified to a far greater degree than in 'real life'.

Big Brother also differed from other Reality TV shows at the time in that the participants themselves had no knowledge of or control over the way in which they were represented on the programme, the website and in the newspaper accounts until they were evicted. Their intervention in the production of meanings about the text was thus limited to a contained performance whilst they were in 'the house' (despite attempts by some participants to control their public image), almost as though they were characters in a fictional text. As Tom, one of the participants, remarked on his eviction:

> The outside world is again going to have an influence on my life. It's always unreal when you are not making decisions about your own life. It's a bit like an extended holiday. I'd like to see it through to the end…but it's out of my control now. That's the exciting thing, that it's the viewers, the public, who choose.
>
> (Tom; quoted in Ritchie, 2000; 104)

This meant that the audience always knew more about the events being enacted than any one of the 'characters', just as they would if *Big Brother* really were a fictional drama. However, this changed dramatically as soon as the contestants left the house. By giving interviews and providing material for media profiles and articles, and by authoring various autobiographies and books of personal philosophy, the contestants actively intervened in the production of meanings about themselves and each other. In effect, they generated a whole new range of texts that helped to reframe their experience, recast their roles and redefine *Big Brother* itself.

Intertextuality: dislocating the audience for media texts

The popularity – and cheapness – of 'people shows' meant not only that they became increasingly central to network television during the 1990s and early years of the twenty-first century, but that their success involved significant shifts in definitions of who constitutes the audience and how 'performance' is mediated. As the work (Fiske, 1989b) on the textual relations of fandom and popular media demonstrates, all texts have intertextual dimensions which inform or even supersede the circulation of meanings about them, and the role of audiences in organising or transforming those meanings is central. These issues become particularly interesting when we consider the case of *Big Brother*. The programme was perceived to have been and was represented as a great popular success. Although the viewing figures for the television programme did not, in every case, match those for other popular genres such as soap opera, the specific nature of *Big Brother*'s intertextuality helped to suggest that the audience was both extended and dislocated: it was not confined to the viewers who actually watched the television programme; nor did it depend on their presence at a specific time or place.

While the television show remained the central focus, the *Big Brother* phenomenon far exceeded the confines of television in a number of important ways. In addition to the show, which basically consisted of edited highlights from the day's or week's video footage, structured by the voiceover commentary, *Big*

Brother offered continuous visual access to the house inhabitants via the webcams. The 'official' Internet site offered regular discussion of the programme and provided links to related sites such as those of the fan club, compilations of newspaper articles on the programme and profiles of each of the participants, including speculation on likely winners. The audience could therefore 'tune in' to the website at any time they liked in order to watch what was going on, rather than simply waiting for the edited and structured version offered as a nightly programme. In effect, the use of the Internet changed the status of *Big Brother*: it became a *media* event as well as a television programme. And, in contrast to the way in which other media extend, transform or problematise the meanings offered by, say, a soap opera through their representation of new meanings about actors playing particular roles but do not decentre the television text, the Internet's relationship to *Big Brother* made the question of the 'central' text more uncertain – as Holmes also suggests in Chapter 5 in an analysis of the press coverage in the construction of the participants' celebrity status. Indeed, the multiple technologies available for accessing the programme in addition to its take-up as a story by newspapers and magazines helped to reconfigure the wider textual relations of *Big Brother* in significant ways, with consequent implications for conceptualisations of its audience.

What and where exactly, then, was 'the text' of *Big Brother*? First, rather than being confined to a single television show, the programme itself offered multiple sites for the production of meaning. Second, it was taken up by other media outside the control of the television producers, including independent websites and tabloid newspapers, which became the source for the development of different meanings about the programme. Third, participants who had been voted out of the house – and later those who stayed longest – began to offer their own versions of the story in various memoirs, interviews and exposés. All of these different texts contributed to the wider text that was *Big Brother* while helping to develop different and sometimes *contesting* meanings about it. To look at the inter-textuality of the programme thus offers us a way of revaluing and redefining the 'context' in which it was produced and circulated, and of understanding the importance of the audience to that process. For example, while the television programme was complemented by an 'official', dedicated website, which could be accessed continuously and which offered 'live' unedited images of what was going on in the house, this source also provided links to other 'independent' sites and chat rooms where *Big Brother* was discussed and dissected in ways that were wholly uncontrolled by the programme-makers. The specific set of 'preferred' meanings being offered by the studiedly neutral voiceover commentary and the psychological experts called on by the programme could thus be challenged, subverted and destabilised by the alternative meanings being developed by chat-room discussions. And, in contrast to other unofficial websites dedicated to particular celebrities or films, the extended network of web-based *Big Brother* sites had a potentially much more direct relationship with events in the house itself since the chat-room audience could make decisions about voting based on these conversations.

However, it was the way in which the 'official' text was taken up and recast by the British press in a host of stories about the programme and its participants which extended and developed its intertextual dimensions in more unpredictable ways. An advertisement in *Gay Times*, for example, urged readers to vote for the lesbian contestant, Anna, wholly on the grounds of her sexuality. Other parts of the tabloid press especially began to express preferences for particular contestants in less overtly participatory but no less manipulative ways through their mobilisation of particular discursive strategies. One of the contestants who, in the defining episode of the first series, was discovered to have tried to influence the process of nominating housemates for eviction, was effectively demonised as 'Nasty Nick', and was subjected to the kind of intense coverage usually reserved for 'real' celebrities even after he had been made to leave the house. The intertextual relations between popular television and the British tabloid press thus worked to familiarise the figure of 'Nasty Nick' even to those who had never viewed the programme or accessed the website, whilst also – presumably – helping to secure the audience for following episodes. Moreover, the 'real' Nick, Nick Bateman, was able to capitalise on the circulation of meanings about the 'character' by publishing a novelty guidebook on 'how to be nasty'. Other participants in the programme were similarly taken up during the months after the television show had finished, and were invited to appear on a range of other 'people shows' and reality-based programmes in ways that both extended their celebrity status and helped to recirculate knowledge about *Big Brother*. Such knowledge – about the participants and their behaviour, and about the phenomenon of the programme – and its circulation in particular ways and through particular discursive structures would inevitably influence the possible readings available to the audience as well as altering the boundaries and the form of the text itself. How, then, can we understand the programme's meaning and impact in the context of research into audiences? Is the notion of the active audience changed or problematised by a programme like *Big Brother*? Does the extension of audience participation to include a wide range of sites of access also broaden the possibilities of intervention in media texts in ways that are significant?

Active/interactive audiences

The sheer *availability* of access to *Big Brother* across multiple sites, together with the rearticulation of the show by other media, meant that a precise definition of who and where the audience might be at any given time became difficult to ascertain. These multiple sites also effectively changed the nature of the audience. It is possible, for example, that the audiences for the television programme and those for the website were not the same, or overlapped only in relatively contingent ways. Many viewers of the television programme would not have had access to the sophisticated technology required to view the webcam or even visit the websites, while for others the technological challenge of accessing online material may have been an end in itself, with the television show a much less important source of interest. Alternatively, the two media forms may have reinforced each other, with viewers of the television programme keeping up to date with the latest news by visiting the websites and, indeed, 'creating the news' by posting their opinions. The extraordinary success of the British website, generating between 3 and 3.5 million page views a day during the first series, suggests that the interactive dimension to *Big Brother* was crucial to its success, even amongst those whose participation remained at the level of viewing other people's contributions to the discussion (Ritchie, 2000). Furthermore, the levels of participation available to the audience varied enormously, ranging from simply watching the television programme once a week to joining the *Big Brother* club. This range of possibilities means that to conceptualise the audience for *Big Brother* in singular or homogenising terms is to underestimate the different ways in which mediation is produced and consumed. The audiences for *Big Brother* were not spatially or temporally confined to a particular programme slot; nor were they readily identifiable as a distinct group. Indeed, it is worth remembering that 'the media' itself (if we can use such a reified concept) was also one of the audiences for *Big Brother*, since the newspapers and television shows which monitored the activities in the house, and helped to structure and organise the meanings about it, did so within the same limited terms as members of the public. Denied direct communication with the housemates who remained inside, they had no prior knowledge of how events would turn out, even though they worked hard to influence the final outcome – the winner.

The regular voting procedure, whereby viewers could not only access the show but also could determine its outcome, was presented as the crucial additional interactive element to the programme. In considering the programme's implications for conceptions of the 'active' audience, this is significant. As such, it is important to stress here that, while the actual range of opportunities available to the audience to influence 'the story' was fairly limited (in that it was confined to removing or holding on to one of two nominated contestants), the *idea* of agency was probably central to *Big Brother*'s success. Indeed, this idea of 'agency' was constantly inscribed, constructed and reiterated by the programme presenter, Davina McCall, when addressing the television audience, using phrases such as 'Their fate is in *your* hands', '*You* decide!' or 'This is how you have voted'. Because the contestants themselves had no means of accessing the media, the power of the audience to influence the direction of the programme was further emphasised. Arguably, this helped to blur the distinction between audience and performer even further since the narrative and participatory trajectories converged in the high point of each week's episodes as the 'losers' were announced by 'Big Brother' and asked to leave.

The sense of participation engendered by this process, as well as the heated debates about the contestants on the chat sites and in the tabloids, may thus have increased the feeling of ownership experienced by audiences and led to an intensified *engagement* with the text. It certainly meant that the relationship between the 'active' audience of cultural studies – negotiating or resisting the preferred meanings being offered by a text – and the 'interactive' audience of new media was, for perhaps the first time, visibly articulated. From this perspective, it might be argued that the changed relationship between audience and text that *Big Brother* offered also worked to destabilise assumptions about authorship and authority in media texts: through the casting of votes the audience became – effectively – the 'author' of *Big Brother*. The sense of 'liveness' produced by the combination of the technological and narrative strategies and the direct and apparently transparent effect of voting was probably central to the audience's sense of empowerment as the real 'author' of the programme's outcome.

Importantly for cultural studies, then, the potential expansion and transformation of the audience through these shifts in media access direct us to a reconsideration of the agency involved in the relationship between audiences and texts. That the *Big Brother* audience was not defined by clear social and spatial locations, and that there was very visibly no single audience, was foregrounded by the participatory elements largely facilitated by new technology, and this had clear consequences. Because the 'story' was overtly and almost immediately influenced by audience preferences, the idea that the programme's 'preferred meanings' are driven by institutionally structured ideologies was rendered problematic. However, although the level of participatory authorship in *Big Brother* was arguably both greater than had been hitherto experienced in popular television and a crucial factor in the show's success, the extent to which this constituted the power to determine the meanings produced *in* and *by* the text is debatable. The production company, Bazal Productions, certainly emphasised the importance of audience participation and the production of a 'transparent' text, representing its relationship to the television show in terms of a minimal intervention in the 'truth' of what was shown. However, the company clearly retained editorial control of what was seen and heard on the programme. This is suggested by Ruth Wrigley's comments on the textual and aesthetic shaping of the programme when she described how 'we were planning to put it out late in the evening, whereas it had been on at 8pm…in Holland and Germany. It was a bit too slow. We needed it to be pacier and more sophisticated' (quoted in Ritchie, 2000: 10).

The audience(s) would have operated a process of 'self-selection' around which elements to view since it is unlikely that anyone would have been able to watch a computer or digital television continuously or even manage to catch every edited episode. The audience's agency was thus confirmed through the availability of choices about what and when to watch, but the level of real interactivity was more akin to that of the computer game: 'players' could intervene only at certain points and in limited ways. Unlike computer games, however, the points at which interaction could take place were discursively constituted both through the primary product – the programme – and through other, secondary media representations, such as the web pages and popular press. At the same time, the extent to which the intertextual relations between these various representations of *Big Brother* worked to influence nominating and voting strategies cannot be underestimated.

A resistant audience?

How, then, can we make sense of the possibilities *Big Brother* seemed to open up for a reconsideration of the role of the 'active' audience? Because *Big Brother* operated on and was accessed through multiple sites, it was not a single text in a simple sense, yet nor was it a set of fragmented and different texts. Instead, the combination of textual nodes working in a complex relationship seemed to confirm that there was something called '*Big Brother*' but that it was not confined by or limited to a television programme.

It is tempting to see *Big Brother* as 'proof' of the active agency of the audience, and the programme itself acknowledged and depended on this; but such a model of agency is goal driven and highly specific. As we have suggested, the audience could intervene in the text at the level of production in terms of narrative development, but only, ultimately, in certain limited ways. To 'choose' between one contestant and another was itself a fairly prescribed activity – an option of potential narrative 'paths' pre-selected by the dynamics of the text itself. Yet there are further political implications at work here. As a 'reality' show, and one primarily addressed to a youthful audience, it was imperative for *Big Brother* to find candidates who represented the currently dominant conceptualisation of contemporary Britain as a heterogeneous society. As has become increasingly common in Reality TV texts, this meant having a range of contestants who personified various gender, sexual and ethnic identities. Indeed, in many ways *Big Brother* could be seen to be *managing* social and cultural difference. The confines of the house enabled the programme to offer a space of 'safe multiculturalism', because ethnic variations were presented not as racially conflicting but primarily as consensual. A black participant, Darren, for example, was a figure whose racial difference was mediated by his conformity to the social conventions of contemporary British masculinity. He was – effectively – 'different' enough without being threatening. The inclusion of lesbian Anna also articulated and helped to make visible contemporary shifts in sexual identities. Regional variations were also catered for, with the inclusion of individuals from the major metropolises, where viewers were likely to be concentrated.

On the other hand, the participants were not *that* different. The variations of ethnicity, regionalism, gender and sexuality were largely overcome by the broad similarities of cultural positioning. All the contestants were aged between 20 and 40, in an age group where Western culture assumes regular sexual activity. Not only were they often available to be sexualised and, indeed, produced themselves largely in sexualised terms, their occupation of a relatively narrow cultural habitus was striking. The grounds on which the participants were initially selected thus defined the scope for audience choice, as well as limiting the possibilities for resistant readings.

The idea that the 'active audience' will ultimately be a resistant or radical audience is further problematised by the way in which the selection of favoured participants proceeded. Women who were produced (or produced themselves) as working class, 'stroppy', sexually undesirable, or as heterosexually desiring in unconventional ways (such as Caroline and Nichola in the first UK series) were voted out of the house as the weeks went by. A reading of resistance might, of course, look to the success of Anna, the lesbian runner-up in the first series' curious final battle between conventionalised, heterosexual masculinity and oppositional identities. However, the 'people's choice' turned out to be a young white man, Craig, whose laddish public persona articulated both the anxieties and the continuing certainties of contemporary (and specifically English) masculinity. Similarly, the success of a gay contestant, Brian – the winner of the second UK series – might be interpreted less as a liberating shift in the validation of homosexual identity than as evidence of its successful incorporation into dominant culture (as Chapter 10, on the representation of gay identity in Reality TV, explores). Indeed, a closer reading of Brian's persona suggests that only a performative, camp version of homosexuality sufficiently unthreatening to contemporary heteronormative sexual discourse could be endorsed.

The first winner, Craig, may equally, of course, be read as a 'resistant' figure in this context. His seminal confrontation with the middle-class, public-school-educated 'Nasty Nick' (which exposed Nick's cheating tactics) was in some ways a playing out of class politics, so that Craig's eventual victory could be seen as a validation of working class (that is, northern) authenticity.[8] It is even possible that a vote for Craig might have been interpreted as a form of resistance to the supposed tyranny of 'political correctness' and female cultural power – a lads' mag-style two fingers up to notions of gender equality. In both instances, however, the form of resistance being articulated produced an outcome that reasserted the dominance of white masculinity. From this perspective, the resistant audience is not necessarily a radical one. Equally, as Holmes (forthcoming, 2004) has suggested with respect to the different context of *Pop Idol*, it is also worth noting here that this concept of ascertaining or 'measuring' the 'resistance' of an audience by looking at the outcome of an 'interactive text' is highly complex in itself. This is particularly so given the emphasis we have placed here on the careful construction of the text – its *re*-presentation for audiences – and the extent to which their intervention *in* this sphere is limited.

At the same time, as Livingstone (1998) argues, it is important to see 'the audience' as a concept that works at both a macro and a micro level, and this is probably especially important in the case of a text like *Big Brother* where there can be no single site for the audience and no single determining factor in its production. We therefore propose that *Big Brother* points us back to cultural studies' early emphasis on the idea of audience as a set of *relations with a text*, rather than a fixed and determining social category to which we may or may not belong. It is the indeterminacy of the *Big Brother* audience that is interesting here, as well as the temporal and spatial complexities involved in its production. This focus on the relationship between what may be a range of textual sites and multiply-produced or -located audiences means that audience research must take account of the processes involved in 'becoming' an audience, as well as the meanings produced once the audience has been solicited. It may also mean that the idealisation of the 'active audience' must be tempered by a recognition that discourses become hegemonic because they are often able to incorporate and recuperate resistant elements.

Big Brother changed some of the ways in which 'the audience' could be conceptualised, but it didn't transform the power relations involved in the production of the audience particularly radically; nor did it lead to an outcome that represented a shock to existing social relations. It was certainly interactive – in a limited fashion – but this did not necessarily have a direct relation to the production of an active, resistant response. Nonetheless, the impact of the programme – and the 'text' of *Big Brother* as a whole – was significant both to the important shifts in media produced by the development of new and more complex technologies and to the expectations that audiences may have about their relationship to television.

Notes

1 This chapter is a revised version of our article of the same title (Tincknell and Raghuram, 2002). We would like to thank Sage Publications for giving permission for it to be reprinted in this revised format. We would also like to thank Su Holmes for her valuable comments on the earlier version.

2 This chapter primarily focuses on the first UK series of *Big Brother*, screened in summer 2000.

267

3 See Livingstone (1998) for an overview of research methods in audience studies.
4 At the time of writing (spring, 2003), two further series of *Big Brother* have appeared on British television, in 2001 and 2002. Some aspects of the format were changed in series three, including dividing the house into a 'poor' and a 'rich' section, and this seemed to ensure more consistent audience ratings in contrast to other national versions.
5 It thus extended the concept of reality-based shows such as *The Real World*, which had been broadcast on MTV since the mid-1980s, and which also featured real people sharing a house, incorporated a game-show format and invited viewer participation.
6 This 'return to basics' at the level of technology has also influenced recent film-making approaches which emulate or reference the tradition of the documentary and offer themselves as relatively unmediated texts. See Conrich and Tincknell (2000) for a discussion of this.
7 See Claus-Dieter Rath (1989) for an interesting discussion of 'liveness' in television as 'pure' and 'impure' forms of broadcasting.
8 As a builder, Craig was not strictly speaking a member of the 'working class' in its Marxist sense. However, the shifting nature of class boundaries, together with his Liverpudlian background and 'laddish' persona, meant that he was able to occupy the space of authentic masculinity which has been ascribed to and claimed by working-class cultures.

References

Ang, I. (1985) *Watching Dallas – Soap Opera and the Melodramatic Imagination*, London: Methuen.

Ang, I. (1991) *Desperately Seeking the Audience*, London: Routledge.

Conrich, I. and E. Tincknell (2000) 'Film Purity, the Neo-Bazinian Ideal and Humanism in Dogma 95', *p.o.v.* 10: 171–80.

Couldry, N. (2000) *Inside Culture: Re-imagining the Method of Cultural Studies*, London: Sage.

Couldry, N. (2002) 'Playing for Celebrity: *Big Brother* as Ritual Event', *Television and New Media* 3(3): 283–93.

Dahlgren, P. (1998) 'Critique: Elusive Audiences', in R. Dickinson, R. Harindranath and O. Linne (eds) *Approaches to Audiences*, London: Arnold.

Dauncey, H. (1996) 'French "Reality" Television: More than a Matter of Taste?', *European Journal of Communication* 11(1): 83–106.

Fetveit, A. (1999) 'Reality TV in the Digital Era: A Paradox in Visual Culture?', *Media, Culture and Society* 21(6): 787–804.

Fiske, J. (1989a) *Reading the Popular*, London: Unwin Hyman.

Fiske, J. (1989b) 'Moments of Television: Neither the Text nor the Audience', in E. Seiter, H. Borchers, G. Kreutzner and E. Warth (eds) *Remote Control: Television, Audiences and Cultural Power*, London: Routledge.

Geraghty, C. and D. Lusted (1998) *The Television Studies Book*, London: Arnold.

Gray, A. (1992) *Video Playtime: The Gendering of a Leisure Technology*, London: Routledge.

Hill, A. (2002) 'Big Brother: The Real Audience', *Television and New Media* 3(3): 323–40.

Hobson, D. (1982) *Crossroads: The Drama of a Soap Opera*, London: Methuen.

Holmes, Su (forthcoming, 2004) '"Reality Goes Pop!": Reality TV, Popular Music and Narratives of Stardom in *Pop Idol* (UK)', *Television and New Media*, 5(2), May.

Jensen, J. (1998) 'The Concept of "Interactivity" in "Interactive Television" and "Interactive Media"', in C. Toscan and J. Jensen (eds) *Interactive Television: TV of the Future or the Future of TV*, Aalborg: Aalborg University Press.

Johnson, R., D. Chambers, P. Raghuram and E. Tincknell (forthcoming) *The Practice and Politics of Researching Culture*, London: Sage.

Livingstone, S. (1998) 'Audience Research at the Crossroads: The "Implied Audience" in Media and Cultural Theory', *European Journal of Cultural Studies* 1(2): 193–217.

Morley, D. (1980) *The Nationwide Audience*, London: British Film Institute.

Palmer, Gareth (2002) '*Big Brother*: An Experiment in Governance', *Television and New Media* 3(3): 295–330.

Rath, C. (1989) 'Live Television and Its Audiences: Challenges of Media Reality', in E. Seiter, H. Borchers, G. Kreutzner and E. Warth (eds) *Remote Control: Television, Audiences and Cultural Power*, London: Routledge.

Ritchie, J. (2000) *Big Brother: The Official Unseen Story*, London: Channel 4 Books and Macmillan.

Roscoe, Jane (2001) 'Big Brother Australia: Performing the "Real" Twenty-four-seven', *International Journal of Cultural Studies* 4(4): 473–88.

Shattuc, J. (1998) '"Go Ricki": Politics, Perversion and Pleasure in the 1990s', in C. Geraghty and D. Lusted (eds) *The Television Studies Book*, London: Arnold.

Tincknell, Estella and Parvati Raghuram (2002) '*Big Brother*: Reconfiguring the "Active" Audience of Cultural Studies?', *European Journal of Cultural Studies* 5(2): 199–215.

Toscan, C. and J. Jensen (1998) *Interactive Television: TV of the Future or the Future of TV*, Aalborg: Aalborg University Press.

13

'JUMP IN THE POOL'

The competitive culture of *Survivor* fan networks

Derek Foster

> It's only a television show. We think we are a huge international fan
> force, but there are really only a few thousand of us board fans.[1]

Posted on an Internet forum, this comment from a *Survivor* fan does not simply
demonstrate a direct reference to the fan 'community' constructed around the
programme, but also explicitly acknowledges the political significance – or
otherwise – of its very existence. This chapter investigates elements of the
audience reception of the American version of the Reality TV show *Survivor*
(Mark Burnett Productions for CBS, 2000–, US), and the comment above
raises some of the central issues I aim to address here. I will explore the
programme in terms of its construction of fan cultures, and examine the
implications of this in relation to existing theoretical and critical work on
fandom. The audience activity I consider takes place within the context of
Internet forums, where there are two main arenas for the construction of fan
culture – 'fantasy pools' and 'spoiler sites'. In fantasy pools, viewers can speculate on the outcome of the show and compete with others by earning points
based on correct guesses, while spoiler sites are bulletin boards which share
information and speculation with regard to how the series (and individual
episodes) will end before they are broadcast.

Through online activity, *Survivor* viewers competed with one another just as
the competitors battled against each other in the weekly challenges on screen.
They competed in pools in friendly games of one-upmanship and vied for status in
a loosely organised community of viewers that sought to 'spoil' the surprise of the
show. It is this very sense of competition that, I argue, partially *distinguishes* the
American response to *Survivor* from interaction in other types of fan cultures.
Jenkins argues that a 'strange mixture of fascination and frustration [is] characteristic of fan response' (1988: 95). If this is the case, *Survivor* fans are interesting for
their apparent lack of community and the degree of their dedication and frustration – not just with the show, but with each other. In exploring the construction

270

of this fan culture, it is possible to understand elements of the audience reception which characterise *Survivor*'s brand of Reality TV, while at the same time contributing to our understanding of the relations between the Internet and fandom – and the increasingly important implications of this relationship for conceptualising our relations with media culture.

Survivor first aired in the US on CBS in mid-summer 2000. Broadcast on a weekly basis, the basic premise of the show was that a group of diverse people (divided into two tribes) were stranded in a remote locale and forced to 'survive' through their own wit and resourcefulness. They were deprived of creature comforts but given the chance to win these in reward challenges. The 'castaways' also had to compete against each other in immunity challenges, with the losing tribe voting one of their team off the show each week. In the end, the surviving contestant won $1 million. Viewers at home watched the participants work out, week by week, how to play the game. As they watched the narrative unfold, they too learned how to 'play the game'. In fact, when *Survivor* first aired in the US it drew 15.5 million viewers and its audience grew both throughout the first episode and over the course of the series (Wolf, 2000). Its first season finale drew 51.7 million viewers and become the highest-rated (regularly scheduled) show of 2000 (Wolf and Chandross, 2000). This was especially impressive considering that it aired in a traditionally slow summer period and had only 13 episodes to build an audience (compared to other series which take hundreds of episodes to build to a finale). At the time of writing (summer 2003), the fifth instalment of the series – *Survivor: Thailand* (CBS, 2002, US) – has just finished. While it was not the runaway hit of the original *Survivor*, it still represented the fifth most popular show on American television and attracted 24 million viewers for its final episode (Doyle, 2003: R2).

There are, of course, various degrees of audience involvement with such a programme (and a consequent ambiguity involved in distinguishing a fan from a non-fan). Yet it is worth stressing here that:

> In the business of television, viewers matter more than fans, but the product itself matters more to fans than to other viewers. The distinction between a television viewer and a television fan is an important one. To 'view' television is to engage in a relatively private behavior. To be a 'fan,' however, is to participate in a range of activities that extend beyond the private act of viewing and reflects an enhanced emotional involvement with a television narrative.
>
> (Bielby *et al.*, 1999: 36)

Television and cultural studies have long since conceived of audience engagement with media texts as 'active'; that is, negotiating, and sometimes 'resisting' the meanings offered to them (see Morley, 1989). Particularly since the intervention of work by Jenkins (1988, 1992), conceptualisations of fandom have often been located at the extreme end of this continuum. That is, in reappraising earlier (and stereotypical) conceptions of fans as media dupes, passive consumers or 'nerds', fans are conceived as particular examples of an 'active' audience. Fans, however, are not just an active audience. Their activity is marked by an emotional invest-ment in a text and a sharing of that meaning with other fans. As Jenkins suggests,

> one becomes a fan not by being a regular viewer of a particular program but by translating that viewing into some type of cultural activity, by sharing feelings and thoughts about the program content with friends, by joining a community of other fans who share common interests.
>
> (Jenkins, 1988: 98)

As is now widely recognised, in acknowledging how fans operate from a position of marginality and weakness in relation to the production and circulation of media culture, Jenkins described fans who actively contest the meanings of a text or appropriate it for their own uses as 'poachers' (ibid.). With respect to *Survivor*, given the inability of most viewers to participate directly in the show and interact with its participants, contact with one's fellow viewers offers a social collectivity that constitutes a fan culture.

As indicated, however, there is at best a loosely structured community when it comes to *Survivor* fans. While they discuss the text just as fans of other shows do, the nature of their comments often reveal a competitive subtext that mirrors the content of the show. Clerc, for instance, spoke of an instance when the online fan network for the *X-files* (Ten Thirteen Productions for 20th Century Fox, 1993–2002, US) expressed dissatisfaction with regard to the show's narrative. This prompted the posting of 'impressions to the online groups, countering or supporting each other's interpretations until a loose consensus was reached' (Clerc, 1996: 37). *Survivor* fans, on the other hand, seem to actively *court* frac-tiousness. The resolution they seek is not 'consensus' amongst fans, but the hidden 'secret' as to the resolution of the show itself. To get to this point, however, fans must argue at length amongst themselves and negotiate with the responses of other viewers.

Observing the quantity and quality of online posts dedicated to *Survivor* reveals a decidedly emotional involvement in the text on the part of many viewers. Grossberg identified *sensibility* as that which differentiated fans from other consumers of popular culture and suggested that 'the fan's relation to cultural texts operates in the domain of affect or mood' (Grossberg, 1992: 56–7). The affective sensibility of fans is defined by the level of invigoration produced by particular experiences, as well as by the ways in which such events are made to matter. One question to be asked, then, is whether Reality TV viewers are affected differently than audiences for other programmes.

An 'escape' into the mundane? Conceptualising *Survivor* fandom

To answer this one must distinguish – albeit at a hypothetical level – between different sorts of fans and the different avenues for fan participation. There are viewers who enjoy the show but are not aware of (or interested in) 'underground' appropriations of the text in fan-produced sites and games. There are also members of 'official fandom' (who might tune in to the show religiously and may purchase official merchandise, but who do not 'play' with the text beyond the meanings established by the producers of the show). Then there are those who seek to 'spoil' the text, an engagement which might be seen as akin to the 'guerrilla erotics' of slash literature (see Penley, 1991: 136). There are also those who one might call 'anti-fans', people who derive pleasure not so much from consuming the show itself, but from verbally 'bashing' it. In many cases, however, programme content 'overflows' (Brooker, 2001) from the show to web forums on the Internet.

The concept of media 'overflow' was formulated by Brooker (2001) to conceptualise the ways in which television viewing has changed due to websites offering an immersive, participatory experience which extends the 'text' of the show beyond the time and space in which it is broadcast. Brooker's analysis here points to a number of broader issues which arise from the increasing growth of fandom online – and indeed the wider impact of the Internet on the cultural construction and circulation of fan culture. It is clear that the Internet has opened up a technological and cultural space in which fan activity has proliferated (Baym, 1998; Clerc, 1996; Jenkins, 1998; Pullen, 2000), something which has simultaneously had the effect of 'mainstreaming fandom' (Pullen, 2000: 56). In fact, when explaining the concept of televisual 'overflow' Brooker emphasises how this type of intertextual network is now not simply directed at fans, but increasingly constructed 'as part of the regular "mainstream" viewing experience' (2001: 470). As a result, this media structure has important implications for approaching the nature of fan response, the construction of fan communities and the political significance of audiences' consumption of popular culture. In this respect, Brooker considers Jenkins' (1998) division between 'media convergence' and 'cultural convergence'. 'Media convergence' refers to the role of producers in marketing a text across a number of different media platforms, while 'cultural convergence' refers to the ways in which fans make meaning from this media culture. As this emphasises, there is a dual phenomenon at work in this new media environment given that any 'creative poaching' by fans increasingly takes place within the media web developed by producers. This fosters a form of 'structured interactivity' which keeps the audience interested in the programme and feeds them back to their original franchise (Brooker, 2002: 325). For instance, on the official CBS *Survivor* site one can participate in bulletin boards set up by the show's production team. As Brooker observes, this is fandom conceived less as 'grassroots' fan communities than audiences which 'follow the trail laid out by media producers' (ibid.). It is thus clear, as he points out, that within this greater 'mainstreaming' of fandom it is difficult to distinguish between Jenkins' ideas of 'media' and 'cultural' convergence, which remain somewhat interlinked. Given that, as the viewing figures above (p. 271) indicate, *Survivor* was very much a mainstream television text, this changing media context is a significant factor to consider here. However, as I will suggest, while the duality described above necessarily structures elements of *Survivor* fandom, it is also significant that the majority of opportunities for online participation here tended to be generated *by* fans, rather than by CBS. As a result, people are arguably asked to buy into the competitive experience of the show more often than they are asked to buy 'official' merchandise.

Regardless of which stance one takes, there are important implications for conceptualising the fandom of Reality TV here. Online fandom in programmes such as *Survivor* and *Big Brother* represents further opportunities for televisual content to 'overflow' from its time slot and find incorporation in viewers' everyday experiences – something that is becoming increasingly common in the circulation of television culture. As Brooker describes, 'rather than watching *Buffy*, it now seems, the teenage viewer in particular is now invited to live *Buffy*' (2001: 460). This immersion in the text is arguably different in Reality TV, where – as the term 'Reality TV' suggests – the fan isn't drawn into the simulation of a 'fantastic' world as much as offered the chance to participate in one that is meant to be already familiar. Fans can get to know the characters intimately and immerse themselves in the situations on screen because the characters are meant to be 'one of us', potentially enabling viewers to see themselves on the screen. However, it is important to stress here that this is also perhaps equally applicable to more 'fantastic' texts, and it is not my intention to suggest a dichotomy between 'fantastic' and 'Reality' fandom. A text with a non-contemporaneous setting can equally become applicable to, and enmeshed within, the everyday lives of its fans. However, what I am suggesting here is that – in comparison with Reality TV – this may produce an element of both distantiation and 'escape'.

This apparent realism was crucial to *Survivor*'s popularity. The show was the antithesis of a cult favourite. *Survivor* was not set in the future or in an alternative universe; nor did it contain a strong element of fantasy, situations that 'allow for discussion of real-life issues unconstrained by real-life circumstances' (Penley, 1991: 138). The typical fan relationship between these fictional texts and non-fictional circumstances was one where an individual's desire 'to enter fandom is to escape from the mundane into the marvelous' (Jenkins, 1988: 99). Ironically, Burnett's version of Reality TV offered this very same response. Real-life drama could be seen acted out by *Survivor*'s castaways, marooned in 'unreal' circumstances. However, in this case the marvellous (in the form of *Survivor*'s exotic locales) was merely a narrative hook designed to facilitate interest in the 'mundane'. According to the producers of the show, the perceived 'reality' of its portrayal was in its depiction of interpersonal relations. As Burnett describes: 'The outcomes are real – the setting is not.... *Survivor* is a reflection of life, and its outcome is rather close to workplace politics all over America' (Burnett, 2000). Pools reinforced this as interpersonal networks of friends, co-workers and so forth joined together to battle it out in competition with the goal of eventually emerging as triumphant. By participating in pools, *Survivor* fans didn't insert themselves into the fantastic, exotic locale where *Survivor* castaways were stranded. Instead, they reinforced the reality of their everyday interpersonal politics.

'Outwit, outlast, outplay': approaching spoiler sites

Like any successful drama, the underlying appeal of the show was perhaps the suspense of trying to figure out how it would end. Unlike a 'whodunit', the suspense was based on who would be the last person remaining and win the $1 million. Filmed months in advance, this secret was tightly guarded in order to ensure a blockbuster finale where the suspense would build each week as, one by one, the 16 castaways were narrowed down to one. *Survivor* fever spread, much like the 'Who shot J.R.?' or the 'Who killed Laura Palmer?' collective fascinations that gripped the nation (previously inspired by the TV shows *Dallas* [Lorimar Television for CBS, 1978–91, US] and *Twin Peaks* [Lynch/Frost Productions for ABC, 1990–1, US], respectively). As the senior editor for *TV Guide* On-line said, *Survivor* became 'a huge event, there's no denying that this has captured the interest of the country.... Key to the event is the secrecy, in this day and age it's hard to keep a secret' (Ausiello; quoted in Chandross, 2000). Indeed, CBS went to great lengths to guard the outcome of the show, even spreading false predictions on the Internet. A well-known example of this was an incident where photos of cast members had been modified to make it appear that evidence of the winner was prematurely revealed (see Mr. Showbiz, 2000). As indicated above, online sites that circulate such news are known as 'spoiler sites'.[2] They feature theories proffering true and false leads in an attempt to decipher what happens on the show in advance. In doing so, they generate a pleasure which is in part produced by audiences – distinct from the goal of the show's producers, which is to keep the audience guessing as long as possible. Given that someone is voted off the island on a weekly basis, there is a constant opportunity to deconstruct the metatext of *Survivor*. This means consulting the other *Survivor*-related information that circulates each week in a range of media, and which discusses how the game has changed and how it might develop. The Internet allows this information to be amassed from a range of intertextual sources which – once selected and 'archived' – can be circulated amongst fans so that they can equip themselves as better-informed viewers for each episode.

A linchpin of spoiling an episode is the analysis of video grabs. Network teasers designed to promote the upcoming show to the general audience are an opportunity for dedicated fans to search for the smallest hint that might be imbued with some 'hidden' significance. The 'official' website might be examined for examples of misdirection, and other fans (especially those with past success at predicting cast member 'evictions') are consulted for their insights. The contestants who were most recently ousted have their post-eviction chats analysed for any possible clues about who might be next to join them, while news reports about castaways are examined for significant details such as extreme cases of weight loss (signifying a long stay on the island and hence pointing back to the dynamics of and possible outcome of the game).

Some spoiler sites have declared their ambivalence for the quality of the CBS product by modifying the official slogan of the show. 'Outwit, Outlast, Outplay' became 'Outspoil, Outbump, Outflame', 'Outspoil, Outspoof, Outrageous' at www.survivorblows.com, and 'Outwhine, Outlust, Overact' became the catch-phrase of www.truedorktimes.com/s5. In fact, it would seem that *Survivor* 'fandom' often carved out a place for the fractious and abusive 'bashing' of both fellow fans and the show itself. With respect to popular culture in general, a quick search online reveals a number of anti-fan sites dedicated to disparaging or mocking everything from music industry stars, through professional athletes to sports teams. The example of the 'SurvivorBlows Bashers Board' is part of this trend:

> SurvivorBlows Bashers Board is an equal opportunity offender, and does not discriminate on the basis of gender, color, religion, sexual orienta-tion or any other basis. If you browse our site and find that you have NOT been offended, please send us some e-mail describing the partic-ular group of people we forgot to offend, and we'll see what we can do about it.

These different forums confirm Clerc's suggestion of a fragmentation in online fandom that is an extension of the interlocking circles that describe offline media-fan culture (1996: 43). Thus, spoilers exist alongside 'true' fans. 'Bashers' might, at first glance, seem to be anti-fans. Posters at www.survivorblows.com certainly seem motivated by a dislike of *Survivor* (and some of its viewers) rather than any affection for the show. However, anti-fans are affected by the text just as much as devoted, loving fans, even if this is expressed negatively. After all, as already described, fans direct both fascination and frustration towards their chosen text. As Jenkins explains: 'If the programs did not fascinate fans, they would not be motivated to draw upon them as raw materials for their own cultural productions' (1998: 87). Anti-fans love to hate *Survivor*, only their pleasure is derived from the cultural activity engaged in around the series itself. Those seeking to spoil the ending of the show for others still invest significant amounts of time and energy in decoding the metatext of the show. If this isn't a labour of love it is still 'labour', and this is still generated by some degree of fascination with *Survivor*.

As sites of controversy and conversation, spoiler sites frequently provide an opportunity to declare one's apathy about the show and to critique its production. These may be considered as examples of the 'new (digital) possibilities afforded by technology that allow people to talk back to corporations and challenge their fetishization as an audience that only exist as consumers' (Coombe and Herman, 2001). Yet – reflecting back on the inextricable relationship between 'media' and 'cultural' convergence' (Brooker, 2001) – these sites simultaneously work to feed fans back into the circuit of production and consumption even as they talk back. Indeed, although all of these sites are fan (or 'anti-fan') constructed, CBS clearly benefits from all this narrative speculation. When the producer Mark Burnett was asked, 'What do you think about people online who try to spoil the show's outcome?', he replied: 'I think it's fun! Actually, they help keep the secret better, because so many of these spoilers have different opinions about who wins and what's happening, so it's more confusing. It's a benefit' (Burnett, 2002). His power as a producer, then, is here seen to be enhanced by multiplying the semiotic meanings of the text. Keeping the outcome of the show a secret evidently encourages multiple interpretations of the text, and this works to fuel the narrative speculation and participation clearly central to this type of fan engagement.

However, this cannot solely be conceived as a form of 'structured' interactivity mapped out by media producers (Brooker, 2001: 468). Much like slash writing (where fans take characters and reconstitute them in situations of their own making, often elaborating issues of gender and sexual politics that remained unexplored in the original texts), spoiler sites can also be classified as examples of 'tactical maneuvers of relative powerlessness to resist, negotiate, or transform the system and products of the relatively powerful' (Penley, 1991: 139). Just as slash writers create alternative narratives, so too do authors of scenarios that seek to spoil the outcome of *Survivor*. As Penley suggests, these 'fans do more than "make do", they make' (ibid.: 140). Commentary from the people at www.acmebrain-trust.com demonstrates how spoiler information can be packaged as a distinct and original product. In the beginning of *Survivor: The Amazon*, one castaway, Daniel, was predicted as the next evictee. Based on his uneasy relations with another castaway, a spoiler was created that wittily spun a tale of his fate to the tune of 'Daniel' by Elton John. An excerpt should suffice: 'Daniel is travelling tonight on a boat; I can hear his whiny voice, crying about the vote; Oh and I can see Daniel waving 'buh-bye'; God it looks like Daniel, must be the spoilers in my eyes'.[3] However, it is important to emphasise here that such creative re-narrativisation is not necessarily an example of a 'resistant' response with respect to the programme itself. Furthermore, these fans make their own texts using characters not of their own construction, but borrowed from other media sources. They are also in the minority of those who dedicate such time and energy to enjoying *Survivor*. As Brooker observes, 'we should be careful not to take "fans" – those who produce the artifacts we see online...as equivalent to the less active but far larger group of "viewers"' (2001: 468).

'Bragging rights and the chance to defend [your] title': deconstructing fantasy pools

Some *Survivor* fans use spoiler sites for different purposes, and to support their own performance in another set of online fan-centered texts: *Survivor* fantasy pools. Long an adjunct of sporting events, fantasy pools extend the entertainment value of a product by setting up a friendly competition among fans. Fans set up a fantasy roster of players and, through some pre-established formula, generate points based on their successful speculation about weekly winners and losers. While there might sometimes be financial reward involved, the real currency here is the circulation of bragging rites. The same process takes place in *Survivor* pools. In the more complex of these, a fan compiles his or her own fantasy tribe (just as there are competing tribes on the show). Points accumulate based on the weekly performance of the castaways chosen by the fan. In other versions, fans simply make a number of guesses about who will get voted off, and who will win immunity and reward challenges. Because there is a predetermined number of points to be distributed among all one's guesses, the greater the gamble one takes on one castaway, the greater one's own performance in the pool.

The fantasy pool is a parallel game that the viewer can engage in alongside the one they follow on their television screens.[4] A viewer who wishes to demonstrate his or her inside knowledge or 'instinct' for the game can spend a number of additional hours seeking information that will raise the chance of success in the pool. Because the most dedicated of *Survivor* fans participate in these pools, and because great rewards in the pool come from confidence in an expected outcome, there is a high demand for information about who might be the next castaway to be voted off the show. Hence, the most competitive fans of the show (aping the 'tactical' strategies of the most successful contestants on the programme) consult spoiler sites to get an inside edge on their fellow pool participants. One such game stated its purpose thus: 'The person with the most points at the end of the season wins. "What do they win?", you ask. Bragging rights and the chance to defend their title during *Survivor* 6, that's what! Isn't that grand?'[5]

Fans in pools try to act 'tactically'. This is not to overthrow the power of the *producers* of the primary text, but rather to establish leadership over other viewers. Again, audience activity here parallels the content of the show: *Survivor*'s viewers are deprived of information, whereas on the show characters are deprived of food, shelter and creature comforts. In both cases these conditions generate entertainment for others. As with the spoiler sites, these pools – given their dependence on an accumulated knowledge of the show – also function to feed viewers back to the metatext of the programme itself. Indeed, although not until the beginning of the fifth instalment of *Survivor*, CBS finally featured a fantasy game on its own website for fans to play instead of going elsewhere. This is arguably a clear example of media producers using the possibilities of the Internet effectively to keep fans 'in their own playground' (Brooker, 2001: 459). By encouraging this fan(tasy) activity on the CBS site, the intellectual property holders of the *Survivor* brand attempted to reincorporate fan activity and use it to further advance the commodity value of their product (see Netsurfer Digest, 2000). However, it is important to stress here that not all the fan activity can be reduced to this model. The official CBS *Survivor* website offers far less information than some non-official sites do, and its fantasy game is only one option among countless others available for selection online. CBS, it seems, offers few direct opportunities for viewers to extend the show's pleasures into their everyday lives – at least when compared with the wealth of options constructed by the fans themselves. Fans set up, own and support the vast majority of the sites I've examined and should, therefore, be seen as 'active' – even if these sites are obviously dependent on the narrative text constructed by the producers of the show itself.

National reception: *Survivor* as a microcosm of American values

A show's fundamental meaning must dovetail with the dominant meanings of its audience for it to be compatible with the lives of its viewers. With its competitive framework *Survivor* did just this, and it might be conceived of as a microcosm of American values. As Burnett's earlier reference to *Survivor* displaying a comparable ethos to 'workplace politics all over America' (2000) suggests, it in some ways reflected and reinforced the Horatio Alger theme of the self-made individual whose hard work and self-reliance will invariably triumph in the face of adversity. This belief is built upon the idea that perseverance, combined with a little bit of 'luck', can propel anyone onward and upward and provide hope and promise in the face of hardships. The product of a long-ago past, it has permeated the American consciousness through the success of such figures as Ray Kroc, the founder of McDonalds. The sign on the wall of Hamburger University outlines all that is necessary to achieve success: 'Persistence And Determination Alone Are Omnipotent' (Love, 1986: 112).

This attitude is demonstrated over and over again amongst the most successful of *Survivor* contestants, although here Alger's simple tales of honesty triumphant have been recast for a more alienated and hardened population. Today, characters on Reality television shows are still expected to be able to turn adversity into opportunity. But if 'decency' and 'morality' have to be sacrificed in order to achieve the holy grail of victory (and a $1 million prize), then so be it. Toughness and triumph seem to mean the most in this modern 'dog-eat-dog' environment of Machiavellian power politics (as Gray Cavender, in Chapter 7, about the programme's ultimate undermining of community, concurs). Just as in real life, carefully chosen alliances and strategic friendships could bring success on *Survivor*. The brand of reality depicted on *Survivor* reinforced the widespread notion that self-interest ultimately trumps self-reliance, just as it coincides with the formula for successful television programming: conflict is compelling and conflict sells. As Mark Burnett clarified, '[c]ompelling television comes from seeing rather ordinary people put in uncomfortable situations – social interactions, not in the peril of their lives. The best way to describe the show is social Darwinism' (Burnett, 2000). Clearly, the Western values described above are not exclusive to the US. In fact, this ethos is common to the entire range of competition-based formats of Reality TV, with their emphasis on a ruthless elimination/eviction structure and elevation of the individual 'winner'. However, it would seem that (although it originated in Britain) (Higham, 2001), *Survivor* structured this format in such a way that it struck a particular chord with the American public. My discussion of these national specificities – and the consequent ways in which they shaped the structure of its fan cultures – can be better understood through a tentative comparison with another competitive Reality show, *Big Brother*.

In North America, *Survivor* set the formula for other Reality shows to follow and *Big Brother* (Endemol for CBS, 2000–, US) was the most immediate offspring. The American version of *Big Brother*, however, enjoyed nowhere near the success of *Survivor*, while it is often commented that in Britain the situation was the reverse (Ellis, 2001). The reasons for this are manifold and complex, and the ways in which a text taps into the cultural mores and 'tastes' of a culture constitute a highly complex and often intangible process. However, it is possible to speculate on a range of potential explanations which relate to pragmatic factors (such as the economics of scheduling and audience demographics), as well as broader cultural expectations and tastes concerning televisual entertainment. First, in the US

Survivor came first. Its immediate success created expectations that were difficult for *Big Brother* to live up to:

> [*Big Brother's*] first U.S. episode received a Nielsen rating of 27, scoring well with the all-important demographic group of viewers in the 18–34 age group. But by the end of the first week, the show, which was televised every night, only attained a Nielsen rating of 10.
>
> (Wong, 2001: 491)

Furthermore, airing every weeknight, *Big Brother* did not have what might be described as high production quality in terms of either 'narrative' or 'character development' (although, as I will suggest, from a different perspective this is clearly central to its claim to 'the real'). The outcome of *Survivor* was known to producers before the first episode was broadcast, and character arcs could be built that people recognised as more *conventionally* 'compelling television'. In fact, in terms of comparing this with *Big Brother*, it was later suggested that '[f]or *Big Brother* II, CBS planned to broadcast fewer shows per week and to make the program more in line with other reality TV shows, emphasizing competition between contestants' (ibid.).

There is a third reason relating to the specificity of the American context which may explain the differential reception of these shows – audience demographics. Reality programmes have often catered to a younger audience that has been siphoned off from the networks by more speciality channels (see Hill, 2002). When *Survivor* debuted on CBS in 2000 the median age of its viewers was 42.5, while the average age of CBS's overall viewership was 53 years old (TruthNews.net, 2000). The network was better known for themed fare such as *Diagnosis Murder* (The Fred Silverman Company for CBS, 1993–2001, US) that catered to an older audience. *Survivor*, however, carefully cast a broad range of contestants where age was concerned, potentially allowing both older and young viewers to identify with participants (or 'see themselves') on screen. It also incorporated a strong game-show dynamic (the tightly structured routine of competition), which positioned it as more akin to game shows that viewers were used to seeing on CBS. In comparison, *Big Brother* was more resolutely youth focused. Although its formula for producing dramatic tension was not entirely dissimilar to MTV's *The Real World* (Bunim–Murray Productions for MTV, 1992–, US), this show featured young people on a speciality channel dedicated to younger viewers. As a result, it is possible to suggest that *Big Brother* represented an uncomfortable fit with CBS's demographic, although it may have found greater success on another network that catered to a younger audience.

Perhaps most importantly, though, it seems that *Survivor* succeeded in the US because it followed the conventions of successful American television. Twitchell argues that 'the simulacrum of television is not "real life," but television life' (1992: 203). In other words, the most successful TV shows don't typically try to 'accurately' depict 'real life' and real situations. Instead, audiences are presented with familiar formulae and narratives that they are already used to seeing on television. *Big Brother*, on the other hand, seemed to try and make television more like 'everyday life' (see Roscoe, 2001). As such, it represented more of a disjuncture with other programming on the air at the time. Observing its success elsewhere, it is possible that CBS counted too much on the novelty value of 24-hour surveillance in a house from which participants could not escape. However, while I am not intending to imply a 'passive' viewer here, it is possible to suggest that American audiences have been 'conditioned' for more formulaic drama (which *Survivor* was able to deliver).

In considering these issues of national reception, it is significant that with respect to the UK context Ellis speculates on the relative 'failure' of *Survivor* by pinpointing the very qualities that I have argued made the programme such a success in the US:

> *Survivor* is dead television, *Big Brother* live. We all know that *Survivor*'s events have already taken place and that the game's outcome is being kept from us to maintain the suspense. *Big Brother* offers the different thrill of live television, where no one knows what will happen next, as well as the chance to influence the outcome by voting to evict one of the two house members nominated secretly by their fellows.
>
> (Ellis, 2001: 8)

In conjunction with these different approaches to 'narrative' construction, temporality and audience involvement, Ellis also describes how the slick production values of *Survivor* further detracted from the programme's appeal to 'the real'. On the other hand, it is possible to suggest here that the simulation of 'reality' for *Survivor* was less important than the stimulation of an emotional response from the audience. After all, 'realism need not be of an empirical kind. Stories can be recognized as realistic at an emotional level, rather than at a literal or denotative level' (Morley 1989: 31). The fact that it wasn't 'live', I have argued, also meant that the stories could be made more (traditionally) compelling through *familiar* devices of fictional television. While it might be 'dead' television within the rhetoric of Reality TV's temporal and aesthetic claim to 'the real' (a topic considered by Kavka and West in Chapter 6, on the construction of time in Reality TV), it was still – in dramatic terms – 'good television'.

But this speculation on the differences between the programmes doesn't only foreground elements of reception in national contexts. The formats of these shows – and the ways in which they solicit audience involvement – are also important in elucidating the ways in which online *Survivor* fandom took the form that it did. Unlike the interactivity of *Big Brother*, in which audience participation (through voting) is central to the 'plot' (as Tincknell and Raghuram discuss in Chapter 12), in the American versions of *Survivor* audience interaction was never formally incorporated into the series. Only the castaways decided who stayed on the show and, ultimately, who won.[6] Perhaps, then, fan activity in online pools represents a means for this component of the audience to make the story 'come to life' in a fashion not permitted through a more 'direct' intervention in the text itself. Ellis argues that *Big Brother* viewers are encouraged to immerse themselves in the narrative of the show through 'live' video streams online that are available around the clock (2001: 8). However, it is possible to view online *Survivor* spoiler sites and fan forums as a different outlet for this same audience desire for around-the-clock involvement in the show. These spoiler sites are an outgrowth of a fan base interested in a show whose premise is to keep the secret of its outcome from them. Because of what Ellis terms its 'dead' (rather than 'live') aesthetic, *Survivor* fans who wish to learn more about the intricacies of the game are, for the most part, forced to *create* these themselves. Seen from this perspective, *Survivor* and *Big Brother* are in fact perhaps less different than they are alike. Each set of audiences 'look[s] for a moment of authenticity in relation to selfhood.... The "game" is to find the "truth" in the spectacle/performance environment' (Hill, 2002: 337). Yet, for *Survivor* fans, the 'truth' isn't to be found in supplied video feeds. They must 'search' for it within the relationship between the series itself and its various forms of intertextual 'overflow' (Brooker, 2001) – including of course, the possibility of 'misdirection' by producers. Consequently, online spoiler sites are just the most visible expression of this audience desire.

The competitive community: reflecting on *Survivor* fandom

Fans' desire to engage in close readings of the narrative, to critique characters and to decipher the unfolding plot is also paralleled by the activities of fans of other forms of narrative-based entertainment. With this in mind, it could be suggested that *Survivor* fans relate to the show much as soap opera fans do to theirs. *Survivor's* brand of manufactured realism shares with soap operas a sense of chronological realism – an unfolding of a narrative with characters one can relate to and a story-line that emphasises everyday concerns (see Dyer *et al.*, 1981). Furthermore, the pleasures of prediction and speculation that are crucial to engagement with soaps (see Geraghty, 1991) are also evident in the fan gossip surrounding *Survivor*. However, there is arguably a crucial difference here: soaps' narratives are meant to continue without *end*. Serialised Reality TV, however, features a cliffhanger every week, different from the episodic cliffhangers of soaps in 'the suspense of not knowing how things will work out [works towards]…a resolution, an ending, within *a clear and predetermined time-frame*' (Ellis, 1999: 65; emphasis mine). Casual fans of *Survivor* might behave much like those of soaps: 'If we miss a few episodes, we might ask friends or family to fill us in, much as we would inquire after a friend who had been away somewhere interesting' (Lewis, 1991: 51). Yet online fans who seek to spoil the weekly secret of how the show will end, or those who need to be updated to play along in their weekly fantasy pools, can be seen to behave differently, arguably deriving a different kind of pleasure from their shared gossip. Following this evolving narrative in *Survivor* demands additional commitment as every episode explores and resolves new conflicts which then *significantly* change the direction of the next episode. While soap opera may also be seen to do this, the difference is that these rapid narrative shifts clearly have a determinate effect on the viewer's perception of – and orientation toward – the possibilities of the *final* outcome. However, *Survivor* may of course have this in common with fandom of fictional series which also adopt a 'closed' narrative structure with an ending that is shielded from an interested audience. As Clerc describes (in relation to *The X-Files*): 'With…series that feature continuing story lines, fans do not need to construct the metatext as much as they need to understand it – the producers seem to have some plan in mind and the fans want to decipher it' (Clerc, 1996: 38). This close attention to the detail of narrative conventions of *Survivor* (including the interrogation of producers and their authorial intent) is exactly what spoiling is about. Yet, at the same time, my argument has suggested that there is an attempt here to 'construct' meanings as much as decipher. Indeed, given the nature of their engagement with the programme, bashers and spoilers alike show a low degree of fidelity to the 'original' text.

In fact, what I have described as the often conflictual and competitive nature of this fan culture – or rather the picture of an atomised aggregation of fans – makes sense if one considers that these fans didn't originate in a traditionally 'marginalised' subculture (as with earlier conceptions of sci-fi fans, for instance). Reality fandom is as conflictual as everyday reality because the wellspring of fans' values wasn't the show, but rather the overall fractious and competitive culture itself. This is quite distinct from the aim of other fandoms that seek to escape into a fantastic text. As indicated, to escape into *Survivor* didn't mean an escape to an exotic locale; it meant a reinforcement of the mundane and the everyday interpersonal interactions that were depicted on the show. Speaking of fandom in general, MacDonald argues that 'texts provide a focal point through which fans can identify to which community they belong. They might even adopt ideals, beliefs, and values…that they feel the text valorizes' (1998: 136). Reality TV, however, may mean a reversal of this logic. A show such as *Survivor* was meant to represent 'ordinary' individuals that the audience could relate to (even if it did not place them into an 'ordinary' environment such as *Big Brother*'s pseudo-domestic context). As discussed, executive producer Mark Burnett intended the show as a microcosm of American culture. In this sense, fans didn't necessarily adopt the values of the show as much as the inverse: the show adopted the values of the 'everyday citizen'. Online forums demonstrated the competitive – sometimes antagonistic – relations depicted in the show because these relations are in some ways analogous to everyday relations in the 'real' world.

In fact, a study of *Survivor*'s American viewers in *Psychology Today* provided further support for this idea of a low degree of affinity among the fan culture. It found that there was little evidence of the commonly held notion that Reality TV viewers watch in order to talk with friends and co-workers about the show:

> Although some people may watch because it helps them participate in the next day's office chat, fans and non-fans score almost equally when tested on their sociability.... The attitude that best separated the regular viewers of reality television from everyone else is the desire for status.
>
> (Reiss and Wiltz, 2001: 52)

This supports the idea, outlined above, that gossip is valued less for its communal function than for revealing how one is 'positioned' in relation to other fans. It also reinforces the underlying rationale for participation in spoiler and pool fan sites.

I suggest that the operative term in Reality TV is not 'reality' but '*television*'. Fetveit has in fact argued that:

> Reality TV comes with a unique promise of contact with reality, but at the same time it promises a secure distance. Too much reality is easily dispensed with by a touch on the remote control. It is not reality, it is reality *TV*, reality *show*.
>
> (Fetveit, 1999: 799)

In fact, *Survivor*'s brand of Reality TV was like all other television, the purpose of which is to keep you watching (Twitchell, 1992: 200). Yet I have argued that *Survivor* fan culture provided an avenue for the reinforcement of 'reality' – distinct from the traditionally escapist impulse of earlier forms of fandom – although it is clearly the case that this shift has been a further effect of the wider 'mainstreaming' of fandom and its designation of a much broader range of texts as worthy of fan activity (Pullen, 2000). In this capacity, online *Survivor* fan activity strengthened television's overall function as described by Ellis:

> [M]aterial is not so much processed into a finished product as continually worried over until it is exhausted. Television attempts to define, tries out explanations, creates narratives, talks over, makes intelligible, tries to

marginalize, harnesses speculation, tries to make fit and, very occasionally, anathematises.

(Ellis, 1999: 55)

Just like spoiler activity, television itself is unstable, filled with a multiplicity of
meanings that vary (Fiske, 1992). This doesn't mean that fandom is politically
ineffective, although, as was indicated in the epigraph at the beginning of this
chapter, the potential of this is recognised by one fan – Wezzie – when he states:
'It's only a television show. We think we are a huge international fan force, but
there are really only a few thousand of us board fans.'[7]

This comment confirms Grossberg's belief that 'empowerment is an abstract
possibility.... It is not synonymous with pleasure...nor does it guarantee any
form of resistance' (1992: 64), and this must again be seen within the changing
context of the broader process of 'mainstreaming' fandom which I have acknowledged here. Even when considering the relatively autonomous cultural activity
exhibited by the spoiler 'community', it would seem that, for the majority of
viewers, engagement with the 'show's extra-textual discourse may be confined to
what Jenkins called media convergence' (Brooker, 2001: 469), although I have
also pointed to ways in which it might be seen to exceed this.

It is true to suggest that competition in pools and spoiler sites offers fans the
opportunity to reflect on how they're cultivated as audiences – particularly when
it comes to the issues surrounding the shrouding of the outcome and attempts to
decode representations that are meant to keep them in the dark. This online
activity entails a questioning of the character of the show (as well as the strategies
of engagement used by other viewers), while at the same time it is structured via
the very narrative strategies which address fans as an 'audience'. I have argued
here that *Survivor* fandom is in some ways similar to other types of fan culture,
though distinct in others. If those fans who participate in spoiler sites and fantasy
pools manifest a different sensibility to other fans this is due, in part, to two chief
factors. First, the metatext of information about the show evolved and changed so
rapidly that it demanded an intense relationship with this minutiae. Second,
shaped by the format of the show, fans were encouraged to immerse themselves
in a competitive culture that was closer to mundane experiences than the marvellous. By posting a message on a spoiler site or by competing in a pool, fans
attempted to elevate their status amongst other fans by convincing them of the
accuracy of their readings of the text. The primary idea behind other forms of
'fantasy production' is 'what would reality look like if you were the producer?'
The competitive format of fantasy pools, however, changes this dynamic. Here,
the fantasy is not so much that one can become a television producer for a day but
that one might succeed in the mundane battle over television's meanings – outwit
Survivor's executive producer Mark Burnett and outplay one's fellow fans.

286

Notes

1 http://publ24.ezboard.com/fsurvivorsucksfrm2.showMessage?topicID=153.topic&
index=1529.

2 See: http://www.survivornews.net/snn.php?sid=spoilers for a selection of spoiler
news about the show. For a specific definition of what constitutes a 'spoiler' in one of
these fan forums, see http://pub124.ezboard.com/fsurvivorsucksfrm2.show
Message?topicID=15332.topic.

3 http://www.acmebraintrust.com/index.php?page=197.

4 See, for example, http://www.survivor-challenge.com or http://www.survpool.
com.

5 http://www.surviiivor.com/ – this site also contains other *Survivor*-based games such
as Gold Diiiger (a stock market-style simulation with *Survivor* castaways as currency)
and Loser Biiingo.

6 Perhaps as a response to the disappointing performance of the first series of *Survivor* in
comparison with *Big Brother*, the second UK series of *Survivor* (2002) incorporated an
element of audience interactivity when it came to deciding the final winner. The votes
to decide the final winner (out of two remaining contestants) came primarily from
the judging panel – formed out of previous contestants from the series. However, this
was supplemented by phone votes from the home audience, which represented the
equivalent of one vote from the panel.

7 http://pub124.ezboard.com/fsurvivorsucksfrm2.showMessage?topicID=15313.topic
&index=1529.

References

Baym, Nancy K. (1998) 'Talking About Soaps: Communicative Practices in a Computer-
mediated Fan Culture', in Cheryl Harris and Alison Alexander (eds) *Theorizing Fandom:
Fans, Subculture and Identity*, Cresskill: Hampton Press.

Bielby, Denise D., C. Lee Harrington and William T. Bielby (1999) 'Whose Stories Are
They? Fans' Engagement with Soap Opera Narratives in Three Sites of Fan Activity',
Journal of Broadcasting & Electronic Media 43(1): 35–52.

Brooker, Will (2001) 'Living on *Dawson's Creek*: Teen Viewers, Cultural Convergence, and
Television Overflow', *International Journal of Cultural Studies* 4(4): 456–72.

Brooker, Will (2002) 'Overflow and Audience', in Will Brooker and Deborah Jermyn
(eds) *The Audience Studies Reader*, London: Routledge.

Burnett, Mark, with Martin Dugard (2000) *Survivor*, New York: TVBooks.

Burnett, Mark (2000) 'USA Today Chat with Survivor's Executive Producer'; available at
http://www.usatoday.com/community/chat/0719burnett.htm (accessed 1 December
2002).

Burnett, Mark (2002) 'CBS Chat with Mark Burnett'; available at http://www.cbs.com/
primetime/survivor5/about/mark—chat2.shtml (accessed 1 December 2002).

Chandross, Nancy (2000) 'Survivor Thrives'; available at http://abcnews.go.com/
sections/entertainment/DailyNews/survivor000823.html (accessed 1 March 2003).

Clerc, Susan J. (1996) 'DDEB, GATB, MPPB, and Ratboy: *The X-Files*' Media Fandom,
online and off', in David Lavery, Angela Hague and Marla Cartwright (eds) *Deny All
Knowledge: Reading The X-Files*, Syracuse: Syracuse University Press.

Coombe, Rosemary J. and Andrew Herman (2001) 'Defending Toy Dolls and Maneu-
  vering Toy Soldiers: Trademarks, Consumer Politics, and Corporate Accountability on
  the World Wide Web'; available at http://web.mit.edu/m-i-t/forums/trademark/
  summary.html (accessed October 2002).

Doyle, John (2003) 'New Survivor Separates the Women from the Boys', *Globe and Mail*,
  15 January: R2.

Dyer, Richard, Christine Geraghty, Marion Jordan, Terry Lovell, Richard Paterson and
  John Stewart (1981) *Coronation Street*, London: British Film Institute.

Ellis, John (1999) 'Television as Working Through', in Jostein Gripsrud (ed.) *Television and
  Common Knowledge*, London: Routledge.

Ellis, John (2001) 'Mirror, Mirror', *Sight and Sound* 11(8): 8.

Fetveit, Arild (1999) 'Reality TV in the Digital Era: A Paradox in Visual Culture?', *Media,
  Culture and Society* 21: 787–804.

Fiske, John (1992) 'British Cultural Studies and Television', in Robert C. Allen (ed.) *Channels of Discourse, Reassembled*, Chapel Hill, NC: University of North Carolina Press.

Geraghty, Christine (1991) *Women and Soap Opera: A Study of Primetime Soaps*, Cambridge:
  Polity Press.

Grossberg, Lawrence (1992) 'Is There a Fan in the House? The Affective Sensibility of
  Fandom', in Lisa A. Lewis (ed.) *The Adoring Audience: Fan Culture and Popular Media*,
  London: Routledge.

Higham, Nick (2001) 'The End of Reality TV?', *BBC News*; available at http://
  news.bbc.co.uk/1/hi/entertainment/tv—and—radio/1344160.stm (accessed 1 March
  2003).

Hill, Annette (2002) '*Big Brother:* The Real Audience', *Television & New Media* 3(3):
  323–40.

Himmelstein, Hal (1984) *Television Myth and the American Mind*, New York: Praeger.

Jenkins, Henry (1988) '*Star Trek* Rerun, Reread, Rewritten: Fan Writing as Textual
  Poaching', *Critical Studies in Mass Communication* 5(2): 85–107.

Jenkins, Henry (1998) 'The Poachers and the Stormtroopers: Cultural Convergence in
  the Digital Age', available at http://commons.somewhere.com/rre/1998/ (accessed
  30 June 2002).

Jenkins, Henry (1992) *Textual Poachers*, London: Routledge.

Kilborn, Richard (1994) ' "How Real Can You Get": Recent Developments in "Reality"
  Television', *European Journal of Communication* 9: 421–39.

Lewis, Justin (1991) *The Ideological Octopus*, New York: Routledge.

Love, John F. (1986) *McDonald's: Behind the Arches*, New York: Bantam.

MacDonald, Andrea (1998) 'Uncertain Utopia: Science Fiction Media Fandom and
  Computer Mediated Communication', in Cheryl Harris and Alison Alexander (eds)
  Theorizing Fandom: Fans, Subculture and Identity, Cresskill: Hampton Press.

Modleski, Tania (1990) *Loving with a Vengeance: Mass Produced Fantasies for Women*, New York:
  Routledge.

Morley, David (1989) 'Changing Paradigms in Audience Studies', in Ellen Seiter, Hans
  Borchars, Gabrielle Kreutzner and Eva-Marie Warth (eds) *Remote Control: Television
  Audiences and Cultural Power*, London: Routledge.

Mr. Showbiz (2000) 'X May Mark Sole Survivor'; available at http://abcnews.
go.com/sections/entertainment/DailyNews/survivor000718.html.

Netsurfer Digest (2000) 'Survivor Boosts CBS Web Site Ratings'; available at
http://beteigeuze.epigenomics.net/digest/nsd.06.23.html (accessed 31 March
2003).

Penley, Constance (1991) 'Brownian Motion: Women, Tactics and Technology', in
Constance Penley and Andrew Ross (eds) *Technoculture*, Minneapolis, MN: University
of Minnesota Press.

Pullen, Kirsten (2000) 'I-love-Xena.com: Creating Online Fan Communities', in David
Gauntlett (ed.) *Web.studies: Rewiring Media Studies for the Digital Age*, London: Arnold.

Reiss, Steven and James Wiltz (2001) 'Why America Loves Reality TV', *Psychology Today*
34(5): 52–5.

Roscoe, Jane (2001) '*Big Brother* Australia: Performing the "Real" Twenty-four-seven',
International Journal of Cultural Studies 4(4): 473–88.

TruthNews.net (2000) 'TV Show "Survivor" Teaches Scheming and Betrayal'; available at
http://www.truthnews.net/culture/2000—08—survivor.html (accessed 1 March
2003).

Twitchell, James B. (1992) *Carnival Culture: The Trashing of Taste in America*, New York:
Columbia University Press.

Wolf, Buck (2000) 'Survivor Survives Regis'; available at http://abcnews.go.com/
sections/entertainment/DailyNews/survivor000613.html (accessed 1 March 2003).

Wolf, Buck and Nancy Chandross (2000) 'And the Sole Survivor Is…'; available at
http://abcnews.go.com/sections/entertainment/DailyNews/survivor000824.html
(accessed 1 March 2003).

Wong, James (2001) 'Here's Looking at You: Reality TV, *Big Brother*, and Foucault', *Cana-
dian Journal of Communication* 26(4): 489–501.

AFTERWORD[1]

Framing the new

John Corner

'Reality TV' or 'Reality programming' was, as some of the chapters in this book indicate, a trend few audiences, critics or TV professionals saw coming in the late 1980s. Even in the emerging area of documentary studies, which we might have expected to provide some early warning of generic changes in factual output, there was little indication of what was to happen over the next few years. Indeed, the dominant tendency was growing regret at the displacement of the 'factual' from primetime schedules by fictional and light entertainment formats.

It is significant that the first uses of the phrase appear to come from within the US television industry itself. 'Reality programming', as preceding chapters note, initially describes a new range of surprisingly successful television show formats grounded in actuality footage. It is useful here to see how Nichols' polemical comments on developments in America (Nichols, 1991) compare with Kilborn's synoptic and finally quite worried essay on European tendencies, published the same year (Kilborn, 1994).

The name perhaps only worked at all in the first instance because it carried out its broad definition against various kinds of highly stylised and authorially dense fictional programming then getting the attention, and making the profits, within the US schedules. It is perhaps another case of the appeal of the 'raw' amidst so many inventive as well as traditional varieties of 'cooking'. Such a coinage is hard to see originating in Britain and many other European companies at all, since, whatever the degree of subsequent shift towards popular factual entertainment, the strong television tradition of documentary forms, including observational formats with a mission to please as well as inform, would have worked against so abrupt, bold and perhaps banal a designation. Britain (and, for instance, Germany, Denmark and Holland) had reality television long before 'Reality television', although this did not stop the name being imported to describe some of the newer (and often US-influenced) formats of the early 1990s, such as the BBC's *999*. I remember going through a period of awkward orientation towards the new term, wondering whether I needed it or not to write about some of the programmes (including the dramatisations of *999* and the much earlier *Crimewatch UK* [BBC, 1984], as well as observational series like *Sylvania Waters* [BBC, 1992]) in which I was then interested. As I related these programmes to earlier, sometimes controversial, series like *The Family* (BBC, 1974) or *Police* (BBC, 1982) I began to recognise that one kind of application of the new label, increasingly visible in press coverage, had the effect of displacing a specific national history of factual television. Its sense of a new development was often offered against a background of almost total ignorance about what had gone before. Yet another case of Americanisation, this time of a critical vocabulary and not just of programme formats themselves. It is not surprising, then, that an awkward relationship of 'Reality television' to conventional documentary output, one both distancing ('it's not the same thing at all') and (subversively) close ('it's trying to be documentary and it's rubbish') often characterises the European debate, although some of the previous chapters indicate its presence in US commentary too.

As many of the contributors here document in different ways, since the early 1990s the idea of 'Reality television', always treacherously broad for some broadcasting systems and traditions, has become stretched a little(!) beyond analytic usefulness. Like a number of contributors, I see developments as being divisible into relatively discrete, if overlapping, phases. Across all of them, the relationship between *industrial* and *cultural* factors at work in innovation needs to be addressed, and it is useful that several of the pieces here have attempted to chart their mutual dynamic. It is clear that, in Britain, the greatly increased requirement for more television programmes as channel choice expands, and then the intensified terms of competition, combine to produce an interest in cheap but attractive programming, initially to the side of primetime slots. At the same time, there is what we might call a continuing 'colloquial turn' in the culture and a shift towards greater engagement of the media with everyday terms of living and the varieties of ordinary 'private' experience, both pleasant and traumatic (the rise of the talk show for ordinary rather than celebrity guests is one further indication of this). An expanded desire for 'emotional knowledge' about events – about what it is like to be 'inside' an event, 'inside' an experience – has appeared across a number of factual genres, including news, encouraging new modes of the subjective both in visual style and speech. These background factors, along with others, need to be kept in mind when engaging with the programmes themselves across the short, phased history of 'Reality television'.

What of this history? I offer my points here 'over the top' of the more detailed genealogies offered earlier in the book and in general support of them. First of all, there seems to be the phase of the 'action/incident' programme, drawing extensively on the work of the emergency services and of the police. Within varying formats drawing partly on the intensities of surveillance (the cultural meaning of which develops in significance and ambiguity of value during the

1990s), this phase constructs its viewing offer around short scenes of 'strong' eventuality. So, for instance, there are moments of police raids, car chases, arrests, accidents and physical misadventures and confrontations of all kinds. Such events are either reconstructed dramatically (as notably in Britain with *999*, moving away from the studio anchoring of *Crimewatch UK* to provide sustained location and narrative values) or portrayed by using actuality footage. The organisation of the programmes into separate 'stories', the use of commentary and the precise styling of the dramatic or observational sequences vary considerably.

Following this, we have the development of 'docusoap' formats, in which more relaxed observational styles than those informing first-phase work are combined with some of the pleasures of narrative development and characterisation associated with the British, European and Australian 'soap' tradition, in which ordinary lives are the primary focus. In Britain, popular series like *Hotel* (BBC, 1997) *Airport* (BBC, 1996–) and *Airline* (ITV, 1997–) showed this working engagingly within the terms of occupational and institutional settings. In the process they connected not only with soap, but also, if only partially, with the formats of situation comedy and the talk show. Not surprisingly, given its very different history of popular series drama, mostly involving the lives of the rich, US television does not display this phase of work with any prominence.

Currently, as several chapters explore in detail, there is hectic innovation around combinations of the 'real' with the self-declared and openly performative 'artificial'. Elements at work in both the 'action/incident' formats and the 'docusoap' variants are mixed in a combination with 'game frames', a game-show interest in tests, challenges, prefabricated circumstances and time constraints. Some of these shows have, of course, incorporated elements of the talent contest, now expanded to include intensive 'backstage' and biographical attention, with phenomenal success (*Pop Idol* [ITV, 2001–] is a defining UK example). Playing 'ordinary' and 'celebrity' values off against each other in a way that resonates with broader tendencies – both aspirations and uncertainties – in popular culture, these extend well beyond the studio setting to produce what we can broadly and only provisionally call the 'gamedoc' (the 'doc' suffix perhaps begging too many questions in some applications).

As I write, many of the newer programmes being aired combine elements of all three above phases in different ways. At the same time they relate back, in their practices and their 'look', to the pre-1990 models of observational documentary programming with varying degrees of directness.

Form and function in dispute

'Reality television' had produced a wide range of debate both inside and outside the academy and many of the chapters in this book benefit from reference to the earlier judgements, whether critical or approving. For a while, newspaper commentary on the new trend placed what might be considered finally to be a usefully questioning focus on the whole relationship between television and the real world, however inevitably simplified or even crude the terms of analysis here. Within the television industry, there have been conflicting views of what the new formats meant to the overall health of factual programming and the condition of television more generally. In Britain, this was one further working-over of those points of tension between the public and the popular, between knowledge and entertainment, that have nearly always accompanied new trends in the output of the main channels and which, although prone to exaggeration and absurdity, can also be seen more positively as an indicator of a continuing interest in the medium's social responsibilities and consequences.

One can perhaps find three different kinds of critique being placed against Reality programming. Each of them has its industrial, journalistic and academic variants and each of them can be combined with the others in varying degrees as well as being found as single strands of complaint.

First, there is the charge that Reality programming dupes its audience as to the true status of what is screened in relation to real events. This is the familiar argument about 'staging' and 'trickery', leading to a suggestion that a kind of cognitive fraud is being committed against viewers, without necessarily thereby assuming undue levels of gullibility in audiences, although the relation between duping and gullibility is a sensitive one here, as always. Sustaining this criticism finally involves having to address the evidence from audience frameworks of viewing and perceptions. Although this is a challenging task and the risk of overstating the frequency and scale of 'deceit' is high, there is no shortage of indications that audiences are disappointed and often annoyed when they discover that certain kinds of manipulation have occurred, even if they seem happy enough with, say, the degree of camera-conscious performance in many docusoap scenes. And that the audience is 'media-savvy' and also knows that no programme can show 'the truth' unproblematically is not, I think, by itself an excuse for many of the more fundamental practices of 'management' that some new programmes have employed. Those contributors who have chosen to focus on the audience offer useful data and differing evaluations on this and related points.

Second, there is the charge that the typical content of Reality programming is trivial, the product of kinds of irresponsibility (a slippage of values in ethics, taste and social judgement) among the programme-makers. This irresponsibility is able potentially to transfer itself, at least in part, to audiences, who become implicated by their very engagement and viewing involvement. Here, sensitive contact is made with the long-running arguments about 'taste' and popular culture, signalled fully in the introduction as well as by most of the contributors, who draw on the wide literature of previous dispute in this area. Quite outrageously condescending commentary has sometimes been offered, yet I would not want to see the articulation of doubts about the values of certain kinds of successful entertainment being judged as undemocratic *per se*. A debate about cultural values is democratically essential. Quiet acquiescence in the market construction of 'the popular' is the complementary problem to that of instant, schematic rejection.

Third, there is the charge (chiefly heard from within certain factions in the industry) that such programming works to drive out the more serious work from the schedules, that it upsets the ecology of television (already, it might seem, precarious enough) by affecting budgets and reconfiguring the relationships of value within television production. Here, again, we need more evidence of just how the pattern of serious provision has changed and how the refashioning of approaches in mainstream output has modified the integrity of what is offered. For it is clear from some of the preceding studies that certain restylings have achieved larger audiences with relatively little if any loss of strength in the overall projected seriousness of the theme, whereas elsewhere the degree of concession to 'diversion' has been obvious and compromising.

All three of the charges can be developed, opposed or, indeed, revised and qualified, with different kinds of argument and evidence. There is also a pronounced national dimension to the debate too, one that is easy to forget either in too strong an orientation to the American instance or in too unqualified a commitment to the 'international' perspective. A retrospective glance at some of the turbulence caused within British broadcasting may be helpful here.

Views from within

At the 1997 Sheffield International Documentary Festival, John Willis, then commissioning editor for Channel 4, remarked that documentary was 'surfing on a new wave of success' (reported in Fry, 1997: 20). Not everyone agreed. In its 'Genre Audit', the trade magazine *Broadcast* assessed the manner in which a range of serious documentary formats was being displaced and under-funded as a result of a corporate commitment to 'reality show' series with stronger human interest. In this connection, it noted a marked bias towards programmes that had an observational narrative rather than a structure of inquiry and exposition (ibid.).

Anxieties about the consequence of the new formats grew in the following year as 'docusoaps' – often shadowing the methods of observational documentary but with a different tone and 'look', a more performative 'offer' to camera by participants and an often teasingly coy, nudging voiceover – spread further across the channels. Writing in the *Daily Mail* early in the year, the film-maker Paul Watson (who had made the pioneering series *The Family* in the early 1970s and the ur-docusoap *Sylvania Waters* in 1992) noted:

> I despair of what's happening, for this rash of docu-soaps sums up the
> very worst of programme-making. This is television at its cheapest and

laziest, fobbing off the viewers with something not much better than moving wallpaper.

(Watson, 1998: 9)

He went on:

What saddens me about such stuff is that it's pushing better programmes to the margins. Why pay a fortune to put on original drama, or invest in a serious, investigative documentary, when you can get away with a cheap series simply by pointing a camera at someone wanting self-promotion.

(Watson, 1998: 9)

These criticisms open up some of the complexities of popular television culture at the time. The claim that viewers were being 'fobbed off' fits awkwardly with indications that many viewers were enjoying the new programmes and making them weekly favourites. This tension between critical judgement and audience response (amounting here to a kind of 'false consciousness' diagnosis of audience choice) was to continue as a problem in mounting a popular critique of the new formats. Watson also raises questions both about technical accomplishment ('lazy') and about the integrity of the documentary subject (people who are 'self-promoting') which appear regularly in other critical assessments. It is, nevertheless, his point about the implications for the television economy (and, within this, the economy of documentary production) that articulates what continued to be the core issue – centred upon Gresham's law of culture, heard so often across the 20th century, that the bad was driving out the good.

Broadcast's 1998 'Genre Audit' showed an internal debate that had heated up over the course of the year. Peter Dale, a commissioning editor, lamented the fact that, 'today, documentaries are cherished because they entertain' and urged the need to 'demand from our documentaries the rigour, passion and insatiable curiosity we expect from the highbrow award-winners' (Dale, 1998: 17). Yet in the same edition of the journal, Tim Dams reported that many documentary directors believed that docusoaps had been an unfair target for criticism and that their reviving influence on the genre as a whole had been neglected. He quoted BBC director Chris Terrill's robust views on the new developments:

Terrill admits factual programmes have been taught a lot by the docu-soap. 'If you look at some of the classic documentaries, they are bloody boring', he says. 'We commanded post-watershed graveyard slots. We weren't challenged enough to reach a bigger audience.'

(Dams, 1998: 17)

Dams noted that a 'Trojan horse' view was held by many docusoap directors, with the new formats seen as helping documentary as a whole 'burst into the mainstream' rather than as threatening it. Docusoap, here, was a welcome source of renewal.

This tension between a view of serious documentary as in peril from 'the new' and, conversely, of it being exposed to stimulation and opportunity is to be found elsewhere. Sometimes, rather than dispute, it produces a genuine ambivalence of judgement, both positives and negatives registered in a play-off whose outcome it is thought needs more time to work through. John Willis, writing more recently about the general situation, illustrates this internally rather uncertain approach:

> Our own schedules are full of documentary soaps about airlines or hotels, doctors or vets. As one BBC producer inelegantly told me, 'We're drowning in a tidal wave of vets with arms up cow's bums'. Now to some commentators, this renaissance is a disaster. Documentary soaps are more akin to entertainment and can be intrusive, sometimes dishonest. They're the Big Macs of documentary, bland and rather tasteless, a symbol of the terrible commodification of factual television. And I think that's partly true. But for those of us who've seen years of documentary budgets being cut and documentaries pushed to the edges of the television schedule, it's a pleasure to see so much factual programming, at peak time.
>
> (Willis, 2000: 100)

New programming here offers a 'renaissance' for documentary as a whole; it has reversed the budget cuts rather than caused them. Willis' viewpoint, in order for it to be so warmly inclusive about change, is close to embracing a notion of the genre shorn of its social function. Documentary variety becomes a matter of *taste*. Here, there is a concession to the negative 'Big Mac' view of docusoap put forward by critics (see Dovey, 2000, for a perspective on 'McDox' tendencies), but this is offered in a populist, only half-serious vein (along the lines 'OK, some of it is absolute rubbish but let's not get too po-faced about standards'). As such, it does not impede the positive rhetorical tone of the general assessment. 'Terrible commodification' is really someone else's view, endorsed by Willis only as a 'part truth'.

Academic commentary has reflected some of these industrial tensions, although it has tended to locate them within a more critical sense of television and its current economic and corporate settings than those who work in television would normally choose to employ. The studies gathered here have worked productively with such a broader, critical framing.

Tele-reality in context

When surveying the broad tendencies and their impact on more established forms of factual practice in a webpaper (Corner, 2000), I used the title 'Documentary in a Post-Documentary Culture?' Elements of the paper were revised in a later article (Corner, 2002). The idea, in both versions, was to indicate both the continuation of the documentary project and the quite significantly changed contexts of its production and reception. I mooted the idea of 'post-documentary' for the latter (the title of the webpaper is importantly posed as a question not an assertion) because it seemed to me that there had been a decisive shift away from the old co-ordinates, aesthetic and sociological, which had variously worked to position documentary (sometimes a little precariously) as a specific project of recording the real. There had been a further degree of generic dispersal, a further degree of instability and uncertainty around what have always been blurry borders. In using the term, I also wanted both to keep Reality television articulated to elements of the documentary tradition and yet to signal the transformations, in a manner I described earlier in this afterword.

There was calculated overstatement in my choice of terms (and a certain mischievousness in using 'post' yet again in academic analysis!) but it is clear that some commentators misread the argument as being one about the *end* of documentary not the new, rather paradoxical circumstances of its *continuation* (a section of my paper was subheaded 'The survival of documentary'). This, despite such comments as the following:

> I would not expect the production of serious documentary simply to disappear in these circumstances. My use of the idea of 'post-documentary' is not meant to signal that documentary is now finished…established strands of practice will undoubtedly continue in recognisable form.
>
> (Corner, 2000)

Ib Bondebjerg, in a thoughtful review of the whole area, takes issue with what he finds to be my claim 'that commercial tendencies will kill off the traditional forms of documentary' (Bondebjerg, 2002: 167). But the 'kill-off' idea is simply not mine; nor indeed is the idea that it is simply 'commercial tendencies' that are causing the changes. I am arguing for a shift that is broader and more subtle than this both in audio-visual culture and in the culture of viewing, although undoubtedly the television economy is a part of it. What it brings is essentially a revised set of values to television's 'real' and its 'factual', together with quite pervasive new ways of looking and telling. It thereby radically complicates documentary's established economy, ethics and forms of representation, but it does not, by itself, bring about 'death'.

It is useful to get this established, not simply to clarify my own position, but because the extent to which new developments relate to established forms has been a key point of dispute from the start of commentary on 'Reality TV' (it is centrally there in the debate within the industry, from which I have selectively quoted) and it is likely to continue to be a point of reference. I quite understand Bondebjerg's concern about premature obituaries; these are both inaccurate and, in certain contexts, risk conceding just too much to positions hostile to documentary values.

However, we do seem to have gone beyond the initial phase of shocked and perhaps overexcited response to the new forms of the tele-real, the phase of 'moral panic'. Within the academic debate, certainly, the emergence of more research grounded in studies of the factual television economy, factual production and audiences for different kinds of factual output will improve the quality of arguments, supplying them with evidence and reducing the dependency on speculation.

Just what consequences 'Reality television' will finally be seen to have had for various national television systems and for the generically packaged relationship between television and culture it is still too early to judge. Intriguingly, in a poll for the *Radio Times* (Pile, 2001) viewers placed documentary as top of the 'best programmes' and 'like to watch' lists and 'Reality television' as bottom in both. These figures may reflect as much about self-conscious perceptions of 'correct' taste as about real viewing behaviour (soaps lagged 15 per cent behind documentaries, so the statistics show some conflict with ratings data), but they are interesting and perhaps surprising indicators of the brand duration of the established against the new.

On the lesser issue of consequences for the study of television, at the end of this book one can point with some confidence to the welcome provocation that the 'Reality television' issue has offered to our thinking about genre, narrative, knowledge and pleasure, to the very idea of the 'truth' that a camera can record under *any* circumstances, and to our broader sense of why television continues to be important.

Note

1   At many points, Ib Bondebjerg of Copenhagen University has offered productive criticism and disagreement as well as encouragement in my development of these ideas. I thank him for this. My commentary on the situation within the British television industry here draws on a longer piece that I wrote for the 2002 edition of the Copenhagen University *Film and Media Studies Yearbook* (*Northern Lights*). Again, I thank Ib and also here his colleague Anne Jerslev for their interest. An opportunity to talk the issues through with those who work in Australian and New Zealand television was provided by the 2001 'Visible Evidence' conference in Brisbane and I thank Jane Roscoe for inviting me to participate.

References

Bondebjerg, Ib (2002) 'The Mediation of Everyday Life: Genre, Discourse and Spectacle in Reality TV', in Anne Jerslev (ed.) *Realism and Reality in Film and Media: Northern Lights Film and Media Studies Yearbook*, Copenhagen: Museum Tusculanum Press.

Corner, John (2000) 'Documentary in a Post-Documentary Culture?'; available at http://www.lboro.ac.uk/research/changing.media/John%20Corner%20paper.htm (European Science Foundation working paper).

Corner, John (2002) 'Performing the Real: Documentary Diversions', *Television and New Media* 3(3): 255–69.

Dale, Peter (1998) 'Docs in Danger', *Broadcast*, 23 October: 17.

Dams, Tim (1998) 'Time To Move On', *Broadcast*, 23 October: 16–17.

Dovey, Jon (2000) *Freakshow: First Person Media and Factual Television*, London: Pluto.

Fry, Andy (1997) 'Factual's New Soft Sell', *Broadcast*, 17 October: 20–1.

Kilborn, Richard (1994). 'How Real Can You Get: Recent Developments in Reality Television', *European Journal of Communication*, 9(4): 421–39.

Nichols, Bill (1991) *Blurred Boundaries*, Bloomington and Indianapolis, Ind.: Indiana University Press.

Pile, Stephen (2001) '*Radio Times* View of the Nation Television Survey', *Radio Times*, 1–7 September: 30–4.

Watson, Paul (1998) 'When I Made "The Family", Viewers Were Shocked to See Real People on TV. Today, These Cheap, Pernicious "Fly-on-the-Wall" Shows Just Treat Us Like Fools', *Daily Mail*, 17 February: 9.

Willis, John (2000) 'Breaking the Boundaries', in J. Izod, R. Kilborn and Matthew Hibbard (eds) *From Grierson to the Docusoap*, Luton: Luton University Press.

INDEX